OCCUPATION
AND
RESISTANCE

JOHN LOUIS HONDROS

Occupation and Resistance

THE GREEK AGONY 1941-44

PELLA
PELLA PUBLISHING COMPANY, INC.
NEW YORK, NY 10018
1983

PRINTED IN THE UNITED STATES OF AMERICA
BY
ATHENS PRINTING COMPANY
337 West 36th Street
New York, NY 10018

For
Elias, Vasiliki, Demetrios, and Evanthia

TABLE OF CONTENTS

PREFACE

Although the Second World War ended thirty-seven years ago, two events, one in 1974 and another more recently in August of 1982, dramatize the continuing imprint of the wartime experience on Greek political life. On a cold December night in 1974, David Tongue, the London *Observer* correspondent, held a clandestine interview with two Greek fugitives in the mountains of Crete. One of the fugitives, Georgios Tzombanakis told Tongue, "We laughed when we read about Japanese soldiers surviving in the Philippines for so many years after World War Two. We wished we could have lived like them—without the hunting, the ambushes, the shootings, the betrayals."[1] Tzombanakis had been in hiding, or on the run, since 1949. He had fought in the Albanian war against Italy, which had followed the historic "Ochi" of Ioannis Metaxas to Mussolini's ultimatum of October 28, 1940. Following the Nazi invasion and defeat of Greek and British forces in April 1941, Tzombanakis returned to Crete and with his friend, Spyros Blazakis, took to the mountains to continue the resistance against the Axis along the side of the British officers. After the German withdrawal from Greece in late 1944 and participation in the Greek Civil War which soon followed the liberation, Tzombanakis and Blazakis were among the last of a small Communist band which remained in the mountains rather than face certain reprisal should they return home. To their friends and supporters these two became "eagles," but to the authorities, who hunted and tried to kill them for twenty-five years, they remained outlaws. During these years, some members of the band died from exposure or in clashes with the gendarmerie. Others, more fortunate, escaped abroad. One surrendered after an official guarantee of safe conduct only to be killed, torn apart by two Jeeps.

Like the experience of Tzombanakis and Blazakis the

[1]*Observer*, January 5, 1975, p. 1.

9

second event highlights the bitter legacy of the wartime violence which shook Greece as the Albanian epic of 1940 gave way to the Nazi onslaught, resistance, and civil war. In one of the many ironies of history, the government of Andreas Papandreou, the son of the Greek prime minister Georgios Papandreou, who headed the government which confronted the wartime Resistance during the crisis and insurrection of December 1944, submitted a bill to the Greek parliament on August 25, 1982 which granted official recognition to the wartime Resistance. When the bill appeared for a vote the opposition party, the New Democracy, walked out of the chamber in protest. Although this boycott did not prevent the bill from becoming law, it underscored the residual intensity of the political cleavage which grew out of the war and the continuing bitterness expressed toward the Resistance.

Of all the European anti-fascist resistance movements only participation in the Greek Resistance has been viewed as an onerous stigma until the recently passed laws and obviously still is by a significant number. This peculiar legacy is the consequence of the tendency to equate the wartime resistance of 1941-1944 with the experience of the Civil War of 1946-1949. From this perspective, the Civil War is interpreted as the Greek Communist Party's third attempt, or "third round," in the 1940s to seize power and establish a communist dictatorship. The two earlier "rounds," from this point of view, are October 1943 ("round one") and December 1944 ("round two").

This book challenges that overly deterministic interpretation. To judge the wartime resistance only from this post-civil war perspective is, I think, to obscure our understanding of the wartime era. Relying primarily on captured German wartime documents, on deposit in the National Archives in Washington, D.C., and the declassified British wartime documents available in the Public Records Office in London, this study seeks to contribute a better understanding of the major issues and controversies associated with the goals, policies, achievements, and failures of the Greek Resistance and its impact on Greek politics. Toward this end I have tried to present a balanced narrative of a complex and critical period of modern Greek history which emphasizes the open-endess of these wartime political events. The product of this era was a deep cleavage between the

Greek left and right, which dominated Greek politics until the mid-1970s and continues to affect contemporary events. Of course, I make no claim of being definitive. Since the manuscript went to the publisher, several important new works on this period have been published. I see this book as one contribution to an ongoing effort which will enhance our understanding of this critical era in modern Greek history.

This book began as a Ph.D. dissertation at Vanderbilt University under the direction of Professor Charles F. Delzell, and I wish to express my appreciation for his support and encouragement. I want to thank the Committee on Leaves and the Trustees of the College of Wooster for their generosity of granting a year's leave, which took me to London and Athens in 1974-75, and enabled me to revise and expand the doctoral thesis. Philip Brower and Robert Wolfe of the National Archives provided vital assistance in locating pertinent German documents, and E. G. Boxshall in London was helpful in answering my questions about Special Operations Executive records and gaining permission for me to examine an important document which had not yet been filed in the Public Record Office. I am indebted to my departmental colleagues at Wooster, John Gates and W. A. Hayden Schilling for their criticisms of the manuscript. I owe a special debt to Hagen Fleischer who gave the galleys a close reading and saved me from foolish errors. Needless to add, I alone am responsible for errors which appear in the text.

Further gratitude goes to Jean Shunk for typing the manuscript, but my deepest debt and appreciation goes to my wife, Rena, and our children, Lisa and James.

Wooster, Ohio
October 13, 1982

CHAPTER ONE

HISTORICAL BACKGROUND

On August 4, 1936, the diminutive soldier-politician Ioannis Metaxas executed a *coup d'état*, establishing a dictatorship over Greece. Metaxas used the specter of bolshevism to justify the *coup*, but the reason for the dictatorship lay in Metaxas' and George II's (1922-1924, 1935-1947) disdain and contempt for the Greek political system.[1] The matrix of this system has been described as "clientage, kinship, family factions and alliances . . . characterized and infused with fluidity, pluralism, omnipresent tension and insecurity."[2] Although these words refer to nineteenth century Greek politics, they are an apt characterization of Greek events from 1912 to 1936, particularly of the instability between 1922 and 1936.[3] The tensions produced by this system and compounded by great power interests and involvement could not always contain or neutralize conflict. Often the results were deadlock, breakdown, and the ever present threat of civil war.[4]

The constitutional issue of the monarchy, which had been dormant since 1862, was revived in the second decade of the twentieth century by the conflict between King Constantine I (1913-1917, 1920-1922) and Eleutherios Venizelos over Greece's entry into the First World War. In 1916, Venizelos led a revolution which placed Greece in the camp of the Entente, but the conflict between Constantine's neutralism and Venizelos's interventionism created a national schism between Venizelists and anti-Venizelists.[5] During the period between the two wars, the constitutional issue acted as a facade for the political parties, which continued to group around the patronage of powerful personalities rather than dominating political principles. The parties were concerned with gaining power to enjoy the "sweets of the system" rather than in administering to the needs of the nation. The emphasis on personalities

13

resulted in bitter personal quarrels. Eleutherios Venizelos nearly fought a duel with his one-time lieutenant, Georgios Kaphandaris, and after the abortive republican *coup* of March 1933, an attempt on the life of Venizelos involved the police chief of Athens. Government crises occurred over such questions as which party should have the rights to the coffee concession in the parliament building. Corruption was common, and in 1931 the Minister of Health in the Venizelos government was forced to resign after it was discovered that the quinine dispensed by the government monopoly was worthless powder.[6]

Increased instability came in the wake of the Anatolian debacle in 1922. Since that venture took place under the aegis of King Constantine I, he and his ministers had to bear the blame for its failure. A revolutionary triumvirate, consisting of Colonels Nikolaos Plastiras, Stylianos Gonatas, and Navy Captain Fokas, led a revolution against Constantine, forcing him to abdicate in favor of George II. The rebels organized a Revolutionary Committee which appointed a commission to fix the blame for the defeat. As a result of the "witch hunt," three ex-premiers, two ex-ministers, and the former commander-in-chief of the army were tried by a court-martial, found guilty, and executed as scapegoats. The vengeful action embittered political life and marked the unwanted imposition of the military on the political parties. Royalist officers attempted a *coup d'état* in 1923, but this proved abortive and served only to give the Venizelists the opportunity to abolish the monarchy in January 1924. George II left the country on December 19, 1923, and did not return until November 5, 1935. The removal of the monarchy did not achieve political peace but established the dominance of antagonistic Venizelists who struggled among themselves for control of the state machinery. Between 1924 and 1928 there were eleven *coups* or *pronunciamentos.*[7]

Short-lived stability returned between 1927 and 1933. General Georgios Kondylis[8] swept aside the dictatorship of one-time Venizelist General Theodoros Pangalos[9] on August 22, 1926. Kondylis's move made possible a new republican constitution and the return to political power of Venizelos, who had opposed the method of abolishing the monarchy in 1923-1924, and had been in self-imposed exile since that time. Venizelos made notable progress in the field of foreign affairs and especially in working out a *rapprochement* with Turkey, but he failed to tackle the crucial social and economic issues created by the Asia Minor refugee problem and the Depression.¹⁰ Further, Venizelos alienated the smaller parties and members of his own Liberal Party by brusque and arbitrary treatment, a habit he developed in his old age. As a result of these personal and economic troubles, his government fell on August 18, 1932. As Venizelos's popularity declined, that of the anti-Venizelists grew. In 1933, the conservative and royalist Populist Party formed a government, and the prospects of restoring the monarchy increased. To reverse this trend, General Plastiras attempted a *coup d'état* in 1933. The abortive action received no support from either the military or the nation, but it secured the Populist government of Panagiotes Tsaldaris. The Tsaldaris government, which included the outspoken critics of parliamentarianism Metaxas and General Kondylis, began a purge of the Venizelists from the army and state machinery. The Populists soon divided over what the government should do with the explosive issue of the monarchy and the officers and politicians involved in the *coup*. Metaxas initiated action in the Chamber to impeach Venizelos, but the moderate Tsaldaris blocked the motion by granting an amnesty to the conspirators. The problem of the rebel army officers remained unresolved, however. The republic had a bicameral system and, since the Liberals and republicans controlled the Senate and the Populists dominated the Chamber, the normal political means of resolving the issue proved inadequate. Venizelos advocated reconciliation, but Plastiras acted to settle the issue with a second *coup* in March 1935. Its failure forced Plastiras and Venizelos into exile and marked the long-term ascendancy of the royalists.

General Kondylis, who put down the second Venizelist rising, emerged as the kingmaker of Greek politics. To appease the anti-Venizelist extremists who desired vengeance for the events of 1922, Kondylis tried over 1,000 republican officers and civilians. One active officer and two generals who led republican officer military organizations were condemned to death. Kondylis and the royalist officers wanted to bring back the monarchy, but Tsaldaris refused. The rebuffed Kondylis then forced Tsaldaris to resign and pressured the Chamber to dissolve the Liberal republican dominated Senate and to adopt the Constitution of 1911, returning Greece to a constitutional monarchy. The exiled King George II refused to return, however, until the nation expressed its feeling in a plebiscite scheduled by Kondylis for November 3, 1935. In the meantime,

Kondylis took the title of Regent and completed the purge of all anti-royalists from the civil service, universities, and the courts. To make certain that the Greek people voted correctly, the General "fixed" the plebiscite to return a phenomenal 97 percent of the vote in favor of restoring the monarchy. The King arrived on November 5, 1935, and the Regent resigned to take a cabinet post.[11]

Events following the monarch's return indicated that George II and Venizelos had arranged in Paris to smooth the transition to constitutional monarchy. Soon after his return, the King granted an amnesty to all those involved in the *coup* of March 1935, and from Paris Venizelos publicly called on his supporters not to oppose the monarchy. The important question of reinstatement of the Venizelist republican officers involved in the *coups* and the general exclusion of the Venizelists from the system remained unresolved, however. The controversy over these thorny issues led to the political impasse of April 1936 and the establishment of the Metaxas dictatorship.

The Political Stalemate Of 1936

The King's policy of reconciliation alienated Kondylis, who resigned from the cabinet to head the Athens police. The King remained undeterred and continued his policy. To accent his commitment to constitutional government and to emphasize that he considered himself "King of all the Greeks," he called a conference of all party leaders, including Alexandros Papanastasiou, the prime minister of the government that had abolished the monarchy in 1924. Then he named a nonpolitical government under the generally respected Constantinos Demertzis to conduct the elections set for January 26, 1936. The elections turned out to be the most honest of the interwar period.[12]

The elections took place under a system of proportional representation that allowed seventeen parties to participate. The royalist-oriented parties included the Populists under Tsaldaris, the National Radical Union under Kondylis, Ioannis Theotokis, and Ioannis Rallis, and Metaxas' Party of Free Opinion. The opposition parties included the Liberals under Themos Sophoulis, the Republican Federation headed by Andreas Michalakopoulos, and the Democratic Union, a coalition of smaller parties under Georgios Papandreou, Georgios Kaphandaris, Alexandros Papanastasiou, and Alexandros Mylonas. Of the 1,278,085 votes cast, the republicans won 43.8 percent and 141 seats, while the monarchists captured 47.33 percent and 143 seats. The balance was held by the *Kommounistiko Komma Elladas* (KKE–Greek Communist Party), which held 5.76 percent of the vote and fifteen seats.[13]

The Greek historian Georgios Daphnes viewed these results as the refusal of the Greek electorate to give uncontrolled management of its affairs to either of the two older major parties. Daphnes believed that the electorate desired the moderate Liberals and Populists to join in a coalition government. This solution was possible, he pointed out, since the platforms of these parties did not differ significantly and the situation demanded their cooperation if parliamentary government were to succeed.[14] Political platforms were not the issue, however.

Sophoulis met Tsaldaris on January 28, 1936, and the Populist wanted to cooperate, but the problem of the reinstatement of the rebel officers of the 1935 *coup* prevented agreement. Tsaldaris was checked by Kondylis's refusal to accept the officers, and many of Tsaldaris's deputies threatened to leave his party if he accepted Sophoulis's terms. A second meeting nearly succeeded in reaching an agreement when Tsaldaris agreed to accept all republican officers from the rank of major and below and to indemnify the rebel commanders in place of reinstatement. When the military learned of the compromise, they informed the King that they would not accept this solution. The talks collapsed.[15] Uncertain whether the King would hold to the advice of the military, the monarchist newspaper *Vradini*, on February 2, 1936, appealed to pro-royalist generals to move their troops into the capital to compel the King to reject the rebel officers in the event that he should relent.[16]

Vradini had reason to be concerned about the King's attitude. On February 1, 1936, General Kondylis died, and his party disintegrated. Ioannis Theotokis took all but twelve of the late general's deputies into Tsaldaris's party. This development strengthened the hand of Tsaldaris and increased the possibility of forming a coalition with the Liberals. Theotokis's move balanced the political spectrum. The twelve followers of the late Kondylis, including Ioannis Rallis, who declined to follow Theotokis (and became the second quisling premier during the German occupation), joined seven deputies of

Metaxas to constitute the anti-parliamentary right wing. These nineteen deputies balanced the Popular Front representatives. In the center stood the great majority, emphasizing the electorate's rejection of the two political extremes and the need for a coalition government of moderate Populists and Liberals. In response to the new situation, the King announced on February 7 that only those officers court-martialed after March 1935 had been permanently barred from the army. Those officers who had been expelled, continued the King's announcement, or who had retired at half pay would be allowed to return. The monarch's action would have permitted 150 of the 570 officers involved to return. The gesture, however, failed to appease the Liberals and angered the extreme royalists and militarists.[17] Renewed negotiations collapsed not over the issue of the Venizelist officers but over Tsaldaris's demand for three ministries including the Ministry of the Interior. The Liberals feared that, with control of the army and the security forces, the Populists would permanently exclude the Venizelists from the establishment.[18]

Failing in yet another effort at political compromise with the Populists, Sophoulis embarked on a political maneuver to frighten them into a coalition with him. He hoped to achieve this by using the Popular Front's fifteen deputies as a political club. On the day following the January 26, 1936, elections, the Popular Front announced that it would never support an anti-democratic government but would support the Liberals if they would agree to grant a general amnesty to the communists. Both Populists and Liberals negotiated with the Front, but only Sophoulis succeeded in working out an agreement. The results of these talks were not publicly revealed until March 6, 1936. Alarmed by these contacts with the communists, the followers of the late Kondylis pressed the King to dismiss the caretaker government and establish a dictatorship. Distrustful of these independent-minded officers, the King refused and appointed Metaxas Minister of War on March 5. As Minister of War, Metaxas quickly set about to reorganize the military commands and to eliminate those officers who had been associated with Kondylis. The army was soon a firm and docile supporter of the monarchy.[19]

On the day after Metaxas became Minister of War, the votes of the Popular Front elected Sophoulis President of the Chamber, providing him with the required majority to form a government. Amid rumors of a threatened military *coup*

d'état, Sophoulis was received in audience by the King on
March 7, ostensibly for the purpose of requesting authority to
form a cabinet. Using the Front's deputies as a trump, however,
Sophoulis made an about-face by asking Tsaldaris to join him
in supporting a nonpolitical cabinet. Sophoulis's maneuver
failed. The Populists refused, and the *volte-face* by the Liberal
leader enraged the Popular Front, which immediately published
the details of their discussions with the two parties. Metaxas
capitalized on the affair to discredit the parliamentary process
and to incite public opinion against the "Bolshevik danger." [20]
The King temporarily resolved the crisis by renaming the
elderly Demertzis as a caretaker premier with Metaxas as vice-
premier. The crisis soon reopened on April 13. Demertzis died
suddenly, and the King, without consulting the major political
party leaders, named Metaxas premier.

On April 21, 1936, Sophoulis requested an audience with the
King. During this meeting the King asked the Liberal leader
to support Metaxas until the two major parties could work out
an agreement on a new government. In return for this support,
the King assured Sophoulis that he had no intention of violating
the constitution, and he emphasized that the parliamentary
system faced no danger from the crown. The King went on to
state that he would find some means to resolve the issue of reinstatement of the republican army officers and that he would
investigate and purge the gendarmerie of criminal elements. [21]
The King had no such intention. Three months earlier in a conference with the British minister to Athens, he told Sir Sydney
Waterlow of his distaste for Greek politicians and politics. The
monarch further expressed his decision to give parliamentary
government a chance, but stressed that he was quite prepared
to use unconstitutional means if he deemed them necessary. [22]
The appointment of Metaxas as Minister of War and then
Prime Minister indicated that the King had decided unconstitutional means were indeed necessary, but Sophoulis and the
Chamber accepted the King's pledge as sincere. Sophoulis reopened his negotiations with Tsaldaris, and the Chamber gave
Metaxas a limited vote of confidence which Tsaldaris termed a
vote of tolerance. Metaxas was given authority to govern by
decree subject to approval of a Committee of Forty which was
to be drawn from the leaders of all the political parties except
the Communist Party. Parliament then adjourned until September 30, 1936, but as events determined, it would not meet
again until after the Second World War. [23]

Two factors strengthened Metaxas' control of power and abetted the move toward a dictatorship. Death cleared the field of several important individuals who could have proved strong obstacles to Metaxas' policy. Kondylis had died unexpectedly on February 1, 1936. Venizelos passed away on March 18, followed by Demertzis on April 13, and Tsaldaris on May 16. The second factor lay in the dire social and economic crisis which had served as the background for politics since 1932. The public disorders unleashed by this crisis between May and August 1936 provided Metaxas with the opportunity to exploit the fear of revolution; however, the proposition that Greece was threatened by a communist revolution in the summer of 1936 is unfounded.

During the first week of May tobacco workers throughout all of Greece went on strike for higher wages. On May 8, 1936, 5,000 to 6,000 disgruntled tobacco laborers demonstrated in front of government offices in Salonica. When other laborers joined them, the united strikers decided to hold a twenty-four hour protest strike. The next day 25,000 workers stayed home, and rioting followed police attempts to arrest picketers. The police action immediately spawned a huge protest rally which the authorities finally broke up after killing twelve and injuring 250 persons. On the day of the victims' funeral, 150,000 citizens turned out into the streets of Salonica to express their sympathy. The strike ended on May 11, after the state agreed to a 20-30 percent wage increase. By the end of May, a series of strikes and disturbances in Thrace ended, and the government relaxed all the extraordinary measures that had been used against the strikers. Strike activity renewed in the first week of June, but it quickly faded after a general strike called in Salonica collapsed in the wake of the government's arrest of 260 persons, including thirty-five members of the KKE, two of whom were members of parliament.[24]

The communists tried to exploit the situation, and appealed for a revolutionary offensive against Metaxas' "fascist" policies. These activities included strikes, street fights, and inflammatory propaganda.[25] This rhetoric, however, presented no danger of a communist revolution. Sir Sydney doubted the riots were designed to bring about a leftist revolution.[26] Metaxas must have doubted it too as he rejected a request from the Committee of Forty for an official inquiry. A report from the British Consul-General in Salonica concluded that "real distress among the working classes and not communist activity is the compelling factor in the present wave of labor unrest." [27] The violence broke out after ten days of constant demonstrations which exhausted the police, who overreacted in repressing the violence with greater counterviolence. The British Consul-General concluded that the communist bogey was being exploited by anti-Venizelists for their own political ends. [28]

An analysis of communist publications of the period leads to the conclusion that the KKE had decided on a policy of infiltration rather than revolution. [29] Since the communists had not gained any support in the trade unions, the army, or the Greek peasantry, [30] the KKE lacked a social or institutional power base. Infiltration was the path chosen in 1936. The significance of the communists lay not in their ability to foment a revolution but in their function as a noisy, highly visible group which provided Metaxas with the opportunity to incite public opinion against the "communist danger." [31]

Alarmed by the events of May and June, Sophoulis wrote a letter to Metaxas on June 23, 1936, reminding the prime minister of the crown's commitment to parliamentary democracy. Metaxas responded by assuring Sophoulis that an end to government by decree would take place slowly but certainly. As a result, the Liberal leader did not force the issue and did not provoke a discussion of Metaxas' policies in the Committee of Forty. Sophoulis instead waited to see what Metaxas would do, and he renewed negotiations with the Populists, who were now led by Theotokis, the former Kondylis associate and successor to Populist leadership on the death of Tsaldaris. Theotokis agreed to accept all the Republican rebel officers who had not been court-martialed after the March 1935 *coup*, thus making possible an agreement between the Populists and the Liberals to form a government with a comfortable majority. In a meeting with George II on July 22, 1936, Sophoulis informed the King of this agreement. When the King inquired when the government would take office, Sophoulis replied that this would occur on October 1, 1936, the day parliament reconvened. The King reportedly appeared relieved at the delay, since the postponement gave Metaxas the necessary time to subvert the democratic process. On the evening of the day he spoke with Sophoulis, George II informed Metaxas of the meeting and the Liberal-Populist agreement. The following day, July 23, Metaxas called in three close aides, Colonel Theodoros Skelakakis, Georgios Papademas, and Ioannis Diakos, and informed them that the King had given him authority to implement a *coup d'état* within ten to fifteen days.[32] The excuse for establishing the dictatorship came quickly. After the strikes of May and June the government had agreed to demands for pay increases and the establishment of a minimum wage, but Metaxas coupled these concessions to a decree enforcing compulsory arbitration of labor disputes and government control of trade union funds.[33] The labor unions considered these measures repressive and planned to protest by calling a general strike on August 5. The call for a general strike fitted neatly with the mandate Metaxas received from the King on July 22. Claiming that the strike threatened to end in a Communist revolution, and under the authority of the King, Metaxas suspended the constitution and dissolved parliament on August 4, 1936. The suspected mass proletarian revolution failed to materialize, leading one to question if it had actually existed. Henceforth, there was no immediate challenge to Metaxas' authority.

The establishment of the dictatorship lay not in the threat of communism but in the King's and Metaxas' rejection of parliamentary government and in the disruptive consequence of returning any republican officers to the army. The Sophoulis-Theotokis agreement would have led to changes in the army and would have facilitated an investigation and purge of the gendarmerie, including those officers implicated in the attack on the life of Venizelos in 1935 but still on active service. Metaxas' failure or refusal to move in these directions, as agreed upon as the condition of the Sophoulis-Tsaldaris support for his premiership under the Committee of Forty, caused Sophoulis to withdraw his support for the general and to work out the coalition agreement with Theotokis.[34]

In the days immediately following August 4, the King lamely justified his action by claiming that the coalition between Sophoulis-Theotokis had come too late and by referring to the sinister bolshevik danger. Once again he admitted to Sir Sydney his contempt for politicians and parliamentary government.[35] The King rejected Sir Sydney's suggestion that the *coup* had been premature and defended his decision by drawing the analogy of his acting as a surgeon to administer a direly needed injection to speed the recovery of his patient's health.[36] The suggestion that Sir Sydney or the Foreign Office knew beforehand of the plans for the *coup* and gave their approval is not corroborated by the Foreign Offiice records in the PRO.[37]

The Regime of the Fourth of August

If the King was the prime mover of the dictatorship, Metaxas emerged as the leading figure of the regime. Before the crisis of 1936, Metaxas had been in and out of Greek politics for over a decade, but he had never been a major political figure. His reputation rested on his career as a soldier. As a student at the War College in Berlin, he was known as *"der Kleine Moltke,"* and after serving in the war against the Ottoman Empire in 1897, he became chief of staff during the Balkan Wars of 1912-1913. During the First World War he supported King Constantine, but on strategic grounds he opposed the Anatolian campaign of 1921-1922; nevertheless, he remained a staunch monarchist. He had a deep repugnance of liberal democracy and admired the authoritarianism of imperial Germany. After serving in different cabinet posts in the 1930's, he formed his own political party but never received more than 51,000 votes in any free election. Like Metaxas, the King found Greek democracy unsettling. Foreign Office officials once described the King as having a "Nordic temperament" completely different from his subjects, whom George II once referred to as an "excitable Mediterranean people," too excitable for self-government, as events proved.[38] The King's concern in 1936 was the preservation of the monarchy, and he was generally aloof from public opinion.

The regime has often been called fascist or monarcho-fascist.[39] If fascism is used to describe all noncommunist dictatorships or authoritarian regimes, then the Regime of August Fourth was fascist. This definition, however, is too broad and too simple. The standard typologies of fascism generally associate it with middle class movements which are antidemocratic, anticommunist, and connected to revolutionary action and violence. The role of ideology and a mass party is crucial. Further, new elites emerge to join the traditional elites, and the fascist movement under a charismatic leader aims toward a revolutionary break with the present and the creation of a new man, a new order.[40] Neither Metaxas nor the King headed any mass political movement. The regime that came to power in 1936 was conservative but not revolutionary. Beyond putting an end to the squabbling politicians and securing their own power, neither the King nor Metaxas had a clear political program. After the *coup*, a muddled ideology of sorts was created for the regime by a Greek journalist, Theologos Nikoloudes. Taking his cue from the "Third Reich" and the "Third Rome of Orthodoxy," Nikoloudes invented the idea of "The Third Greek Civilization," or Metaxas as successor to Classical Greece and Byzantium. Aping Mussolini's fasces, the Minoan double ax was adopted as a symbol of the Third Civilization. Metaxas spoke on the spiritual values of God, King, Family, and Country. There were vague racial notions about the "Slavic menace" to the north but no antisemitism. Indeed, on this point, the regime had a better record than the republic which preceded it.[41] The regime never developed a mass party, nor did its ideology go much beyond anticommunism and antiparliamentarianism.[42]

The dictatorship was a product of the political system, and the immediate cause was the political deadlock produced by the 1936 elections, which intensified the schism between Venizelists and royalists. Rather than risk uncertainty with a parliamentary regime, the King decided to dispense with politics and parliament. No social or economic institutions were changed as the royalists consolidated their control. One Greek elite excluded the other more in the style of the royal absolutism of early nineteenth century Greece than of twentieth century fascism. The King created a police state by suspending key articles of the 1911 constitution, which enabled Metaxas to abolish political parties and to suppress all political activity and civil liberties. Metaxas and the King ruled through decree.[43] Dictatorship, of course, was not new to Greece, and, as previous leaders had done, Metaxas packed the state machinery with his own people. Still the regime did differ from the dictatorships of Pangalos and Kondylis.

While Pangalos took some measures in 1926 to improve the conditions of the peasants and workers, he proved to be ineffectual and left no lasting mark on Greek politics. The dictatorship is best remembered for its regulation of the length of women's skirts, which required policemen to carry rulers as a means of enforcing modesty in dress. In 1935, General Kondylis's short term dictatorship was concerned exclusively with the restoration of the monarchy. In contrast to Pangalos and Kondylis, Metaxas created the first modern dictatorship in recent Greek history, and thirty years later it became the model followed by the colonels on April 21, 1967. Metaxas purposely tried to create a corporate state similar to Mussolini's Italy. He instituted a social and economic program that included raising the minimum wage, establishing unemployment insurance and maternity benefits, and reviving a public works project which had been languishing since the late 1920's. The dictator organized all professions, rural cooperatives, and the Chamber of Commerce along corporatist lines, and Robert Ley, the Nazi labor leader, was invited to come and organize state-controlled labor unions. Those seeking employment had to present a "certificate of social acceptability," which was issued by the Minister of the Interior and indicated official approval of the recipient's political ideas. Special commissions investigated and imprisoned individuals considered "dangerous to the public safety," that is, those who spoke out against the regime.[44]

The net gains of the social and economic reforms were inconclusive. Unemployment declined and the balance of trade improved until the war upset the economy in 1940, but these improvements were offset by a higher cost of living and higher taxes.[45] The regime never enforced the benefits designed to help labor. As Metaxas remained the force behind these changes, the Crown, aside from ceremonial functions, receded from participation in national life and moved further away from the people.[46]

In spite of those measures and Metaxas' exhortations about spiritual values, popular support for the regime failed to develop. After being in power for two years and failing to generate widespread support, on March 25, 1938, he launched a movement to create a national party by transforming the *Ellenike Organosis Neoleas* (EON—National Youth Organization) into 200,000 "phalangists." The youth group had been organized in 1936, but it failed to develop until the dictator took personal direction of it late in 1937. At first, membership was voluntary, but when recruiting lagged Metaxas made membership mandatory for all school children. He failed, however, to create a national party. It remained for Mussolini, by his ill-starred invasion of Greece in 1940, to galvanize Greek nationalism behind the Metaxas regime.

Education became a state monopoly geared to instill nationalist support for the regime. The control of curriculum for this purpose went to the absurd extreme of eliminating Pericles's funeral oration from Thucydides's history and excising references to liberty in Shakespearean and Greek tragedies. The whole of Sophocles's *Antigone* was banned, and book burnings of "decadent" authors were organized.[47] Although the system emphasized duty to the state before loyalty to the family, Greeks found subtle ways to resist. The Ministry of Education required the singing of the national anthem at the beginning of each school day, but students sang the word *Eleutheria* (liberty) with such force that the Ministry revoked the order.[48]

Although Metaxas certainly ranks among the great "antis" of the interwar years—he was antiparliament, antimarxist, anticommunist, antilabor, antiplutocratic democracies (Great Britain, France, and the United States) — and although the regime had the external trappings of a fascist state, he never identified himself with the Greek fascists. The Greek Nazi Party was founded in 1931. In 1941, they sent a telegram of congratulations to Hitler after the Greek capitulation. They were incensed at the selection of General Georgios Tsolakoglou to head the collaborationist government. To these fascists, Tsolakoglou and his ministers were mere opportunists who were not true fascists but had come over to the Axis because of German power and success. The Germans were not impressed with this nagging and ordered them to halt their criticism and to support the Axis-sponsored Tsolakoglou regime.[49] Contemporaries of the Metaxas period did not identify the regime with other fascist governments, and Metaxas cited Salazar's Portugal as his model, not Mussolini's Italy or Hitler's Germany.[50] Although Metaxas may have desired Greeks to follow his *Fuehrerprinzip*, he never mastered complete control of the state machinery. The army remained closer to the King, and the British minister believed that George II did not hesitate to use this influence against Metaxas.[51] Rather than being fascist, the Regime of August Fourth is best described as a royal bureaucratic dictatorship, not an uncommon development in central and southeastern Europe between the two world wars.

The regime did not have to be fascist for the Greeks to reject it. The suspension of constitutional government and the ensuing political repression were sufficient to generate widespread revulsion against the King and Metaxas. The dictatorship had to rest on the two pillars of the authority of the throne and the power of the army. This failure to win broad support alarmed the British minister to Athens. Sir Sydney feared the unpopularity of the regime threatened the future of the monarchy. By February 1938, London shared this concern and preferred that the King drop Metaxas, but the Foreign Office saw no way to achieve this end. On his own initiative, in December 1938, Sir Sydney suggested to the King that he use the army to replace Metaxas, but the King refused. London reacted sharply to its minister's action and ordered Sir Sidney to end these unauthorized forays and to be more circumspect in his behavior toward the regime. By the end of 1938, London had concluded that Metaxas was a competent leader and that the status quo served British interests.[52] The British did express to the King their concern about the lack of popular support for the dynasty and of a free press, but the King replied that popular acceptance of the regime was unimportant to him.[53] By the beginning of 1939, Waterlow despaired over the lack of enthusiasm for the monarchy from any segment of Greek society.[54] After the collapse of Greece in 1941, the King carried this aloofness and general disregard for the feeling of his subjects with him into exile.

After the turbulent politics of the post-First World War era, contemporaries expected Metaxas to provide Greece with a much-needed period of internal peace and stability.[55] In the years following the Second World War, supporters of Metaxas argued that in addition to the communist danger, the dictatorship was necessary to curb the excesses of the politicians and to prepare Greece for the coming international struggle. These historians stressed the mildness of the regime in contrast to the totalitarian governments of the era.[56] One must admit that, under Metaxas and the King, Greece was more prepared to meet the Italian attack of 1940 than might otherwise have been the case.[57] However, it stretches the evidence to state that Metaxas or the King foresaw the coming struggle with Italy in 1936 and used this as the cardinal reason for initiating their coup d'état. There is, however, another side to the story which the brief but outstanding success against Italy [58] has forced into the background, that is to say, the long-range impact of the Metaxas regime on Greek politics.

Since the publication of C. M. Woodhouse's Apple of Discord in 1948, it has been common to view the period following the Axis invasion and the collapse of the dictatorship as a clean break with the past, creating a tabula rasa upon which a new form of Greek politics was written. This interpretation overlooks the important political fact that out of the Metaxas years emerged the beginning of an ideological cleavage of Greek politics into a left labeled "communist" and an anticommunist right made up of both prewar Venizelists and anti-Venizelists. The process was accelerated and completed by the Second World War.[59]

At one time or another Metaxas imprisoned and exiled every major political leader, and those whom he allowed to return to Greece had to pledge not to engage in any political activity. In January 1938, former political leaders tried to publish and circulate manifestoes against the regime, but the police arrested them and banished them to Aegean exiles. Of the twelve party leaders arrested, four were former cabinet ministers. One prominent political prisoner, the republican Andreas Mikalakopoulos, became ill while in island exile and died shortly after his return. To complete the paralysis of the opposition, all political organizations were dissolved, and the last significant resistance within Greece occurred in July 1938, when a Venizelist uprising in Crete proved a fiasco. It is too often forgotten that for five years Metaxas destroyed free political life.

To avoid the regime's reaction, the communists went underground, but they too failed to elude the government. The policies of Minister of the Interior Constantine Maniadakes, a strong supporter of Nazi Germany who kept a picture of Adolf Hitler on the wall behind his desk, shook the very foundations of the Greek Communist Party. Yet even those who approve of his police state tactics admit that force alone was inadequate in dealing with communism.[60] In the long run, the conspiratorial Communist Party suffered less than the free democratic organizations, a fact which made it possible for the Greek communists to exploit the political situation after the Axis invasion. The communists were the first to organize a broad-based national resistance to the Axis, opening the way for the emergence of a powerful and organized left in Greek politics by the end of the war.

The communists were not alone in organizing resistance to fascism. Exiled Venizelists opposed to the dictatorship from its inception became active between 1941 and 1943. They viewed their struggle against Metaxas as part of the fight against fascism, and they looked forward to a postwar democratic reconstruction of Greek political life. The wartime resistance, communist and noncommunist, shared the common commitment that the monarchy, which had endorsed the dictatorship, should not return to Greece. Although the regime glittered during the epic struggle against Italy, the monarchy's position was not enhanced by the debacle that followed the German invasion of April 6, 1941.

CHAPTER TWO

THE REGIME BETWEEN GERMANY AND GREAT BRITAIN

Near the end of his life Metaxas recorded in his diary his distress that Mussolini and Hitler had failed to see the affinity of the Regime of August Fourth with the fascist states.[1] This affinity, however, did not interfere with his sense of national dignity, and Greece met the Italian attack with determination. Metaxas had hoped that Greek neutrality would spare his country from the war, but this policy failed because of Mussolini's pique at Hitler's successes, which drove the frantic Duce to invade Greece on October 28, 1940. After the attack, Metaxas, the King, and the Commander of the Greek Army, Alexandros Papagos, believed Hitler would not come to the aide of Mussolini before Greece could defeat the Italians. The Greeks erred. The Albanian conflict could not be limited to an Italo-Greek affair once the Fuehrer had decided on the invasion of Russia. The Nazi need to secure the southeastern flank shattered Greek policy.

The Regime and the Coming of the War

The erosion of Greek neutrality began in April 1939 when Mussolini seized Albania. Although it publicly proclaimed the British guarantee which was issued immediately after Mussolini's action to be a unilateral declaration, Athens privately encouraged and accepted it on April 13. Moreover, as the Italian threat developed in 1940, Greece moved closer to Great Britain. The King, Metaxas, and the army leadership were of one mind in their determination to forcefully meet any Italian aggression, but the Greek leadership was divided over continuing resistance against a Nazi attack.

In the prewar years, Metaxas was aware of Greece's general vulnerability not only to an Italian threat but to other great power influence. Germany and Great Britain possessed the means to disturb Greece's internal affairs. Germany accounted for 43 percent of Greece's exports and 31 percent of her imports. By the eve of war, Germany had replaced Britain as Greece's dominant trading partner. Although Hitler did not include Greece in his expansionist plans, Germany's trade hegemony made Greek internal affairs subject to German economic manipulation.[2] Metaxas initially expressed similar concern that a British blockade could create an economic crisis which in turn could trigger internal disruption of the regime, but in the face of the Italian danger he revised his anxiety about Britain. Metaxas was well aware that a war could lead to an upheaval against his unpopular regime.[3] In the summer of 1940, the British Foreign Office and Special Operations Executive (SOE) expressed similar concerns. They were fearful that a war would sweep away not only Metaxas but the monarchy as well.[4] This concern for the survival of the regime was confirmed after the Italian invasion. Metaxas refused to reinstate Venizelist officers who desired to serve in the battle against Mussolini for fear of the hostile reaction from the Army officer corps.[5] Clearly, neutrality served the domestic and foreign interests of the regime, and in the months following April 1939 Metaxas sought to avoid any provocation of the great powers.

Although Sir Sydney Waterlow had made an effort to move the King to dismiss Metaxas in 1938, and Metaxas was not popular in London, the Foreign Office concluded the regime served Britain's interest. These interests were economic, political, and strategic. London desired a friendly government in Athens that would ensure continued payment to foreign bondholders of the Greek debt and would protect communications with the empire east of Suez. After the Italian conquest of Ethiopia, Britain's concern for the security of the eastern Mediterranean made a friendly government in Greece a strategic imperative. Within this perspective, Metaxas appeared to London as an efficient if unpopular administrator, Papagos as the ablest general in the Balkans, and the King a good friend of Britain.[6] London chose to look the other way regarding the ugly, repressive aspects of the regime and to concentrate on keeping the regime friendly. To secure these ends in the years before the war, London tried unsuccessfully to prevent German

economic penetration and expanding political influence. The
Foreign Office asked British cigarette manufacturers to purchase Greek tobacco and sought to raise private capital for
long-term economic development in order to ease Greece's
bonded indebtedness.[7] Both endeavors failed.

After the outbreak of war in 1939, France pressed Britain
to support the activation of a Balkan or Salonica front, but
London refused to give the plan serious consideration. Fearing
that a military move in the Balkans would precipitate Italy's
entry into the war, British officials successfully put off the
French proposal.[8] During this period, Greece's neutrality
served London well. British communications remained intact,
and Athens encouraged Greek seamen to sail under the British
flag and allowed London to lease sixty Greek ships. In January
of 1940, Athens signed a £500,000 credit agreement with
Britain.

If Britain was pleased with Metaxas' policy, Italy and
Germany were not. Germany expressed deep displeasure with
Greece over the British guarantee and the leasing of the Greek
ships, but in the first ten months of the war Hitler had no
immediate concern for the Balkans. Mussolini, however, had
designs on Yugoslavia and Greece, but until the late summer
of 1940 Hitler had refused to countenance any Italian meddling
in the Balkans. Mussolini's revived interest in the area in
July 1940 coincided with Stalin's renewed activity in the
southeast.

The Nazi-Soviet Pact of August 23, 1939, divided eastern
Europe north of the Danube between Hitler and Stalin. At
that time neither dictator desired to become embroiled in
southeastern Europe. Hitler's economic interests, Rumanian
oil and Balkan ores, had been secured by economic agreements,
and he did not want to give France and Britain any opportunity
to disturb his security in the region. The sudden Soviet ultimatum to Rumania on June 26—demanding not only Bessarabia but also northern Bukovina, which had not been part of
the Nazi-Soviet pact—inflamed the whole area. Taken together
with Soviet activity in Bulgaria and Hungary, and Russia's
reestablishment of relations with Yugoslavia, Hitler concluded
that Stalin intended to move into territory marked for German
control.[9]

Hitler had expected to dominate southeast Europe, but the
region played no part in the Fuehrer's expansionist course.[10]
Until the Soviet leader acted, the Germans were content to

leave the Balkans in peace as long as the desired economic resources continued to flow smoothly into the Reich. The Russian action, however, unsettled Hitler. He was no longer secure with tight economic agreements alone; he was determined to strengthen them through tight political agreements. The Russian move came just after the fall of France and the discovery of the *La Charité* documents (the records of the Supreme Allied War Council which included the French proposals for a Balkan front). This discovery and Stalin's annexation of Bukovina made Hitler even more uneasy about the Balkans.[11] Furthermore, he sensed another threat to Germany's economic interests when the Soviet move precipitated the Hungarian decision to regain Transylvania from Rumania. When war threatened to break out between Hungary and Rumania, Hitler feared that this would lead to expanded Russian intervention.[12] To compound matters even more, Italy began to beg for German help in an offensive against Yugoslavia and Greece.[13] These difficulties in southeast Europe, coupled with the uncertainty of victory over Great Britain (which was now actively wooing the Soviets), served as the background to Hitler's decision on July 31, 1940, to set in motion the operational plan to "smash" Russia and become master of Europe. Until he was ready for that invasion, Hitler did not want to see an explosion in the Danubian-Balkan area,[14] and he set about to secure it bloodlessly through armed diplomacy.

Hitler pressed Hungary, Rumania, and Bulgaria to settle their problems over borders through direct negotiation. Bulgarian-Rumanian discussions yielded southern Dobrudja to Bulgaria without difficulty, but the Rumanians refused to budge in their dispute with Hungary over Transylvania. Hitler intervened by ordering Foreign Minister Joachim von Ribbentrop to settle the issue. Ribbentrop summoned the interested parties to Vienna, and, on August 30, 1940, granted Hungary two-thirds of its claim against Rumania. The award solved one problem for Hitler, but at the expense of further alienation of the Soviets, since the settlement was contrary to the spirit of the Nazi-Soviet Pact. Germany's interests in Rumania were secured, however. On September 6, the Rumanians expelled King Carol, whom they held responsible for their disasters, and replaced him with his son, Michael. Power soon fell to the future dictator, General Antonescu, on September 14. General Antonescu repeated an earlier appeal by King Carol for a

German military mission, and Hitler, who had already made his decision, dispatched the mission on October 12, 1940.[15]

The Italian Invasion of Greece and Germany's Reaction

If Hitler had secured his interests and reestablished a relative peace in the affairs of Rumania, Bulgaria, and Hungary, there remained the problem of Greece and Italy. Since the outbreak of the war, Greece had followed a policy of "practical neutrality," which meant that its neutrality would last until forced into the conflict. Its interests made it lean toward the Allies, however. Greece accepted the British guarantee in April 1939 after Italy seized Albania and began to purchase arms from Britain.[16] Mussolini's interest in the Balkans was both historic and economic. Part of his Fascist mission aimed at completing Italy's unachieved war aims of 1915-1918 along the Dalmatian coast and at gaining the copper and bauxite mines of Yugoslavia. Acquisition of northern Greece formed part of the rounding out of the Italian Empire in the Mediterranean.[17] German and Italian discussions repeatedly made it clear that Yugoslavia and Greece would go to Italy, but the Germans kept putting off final decisions. On July 7, 1940, Hitler met Italian Foreign Minister Galeazzo Ciano and apparently agreed to Italy's plans for Yugoslavia and Greece, but he rejected any immediate action. He feared that Russia might come to the aid of Yugoslavia, and that common interests resulting from any Italian attack might bring the Russians and British together.[18]

Mussolini and Ciano became impatient, and tried persistently to prove that Greece was a British base which threatened to become Italy's "Norway." As early as June 18, 1940, soon after Italy entered the war, Mussolini charged that Suda Bay on Crete was being used to support British warships, even though the Italian consul, whose house overlooked the bay, reported to his government that no British ships had entered the waters.[19] On July 1, Hitler informed the Italians of the nature of the La Charité documents concerning Allied plans for a second front in the Balkans. The documents revealed that the Greek Minister of War had given permission to land Allied troops at Salonica.[20] Other points of friction between Italy and Greece lay in the naval war in the Mediterranean, the Italian possession of the Dodecanese, and the belligerent Italian governor of Rhodes, Count Cesare De Vecchi. Ciano championed a Greek campaign, and he pressed Mussolini to take up the venture in August when he frightened the Italian dictator with fears that peace might break out, thus leaving Italy with no gains. Ciano pushed his program in spite of accurate dispatches from the Italian ambassador in Greece, Emanuele Grazzi, who described the Greek government's correct neutrality and efforts to avoid conflict with Italy, but also its determination to resist if attacked.[21]

On August 9, 1940, the German military attaché to Rome, General Enno von Rintelen, learned that the Italian General Staff had received orders from Mussolini to prepare an attack on Yugoslavia and Greece should the contingency arise. Since Italy's military machine was in no way prepared for the Greek project, General Mario Roatta requested 5,000 motor vehicles from the Third Reich and a military conference with the Nazi *Oberkommando der Wehrmacht* (OKW—German Armed Forces High Command) to work out the plan of attack.[22] Although the Germans had complaints about Greek neutrality, Hitler rejected the Italian request out of hand. Germany charged Greece with selling chrome ore to Britain, delivering war *matériel* to it, and allowing it to use the Greek merchant fleet. The Germans suspected that the 20 mm and 37 mm shells produced from German-imported metal by the Bodosaki plant in Athens and delivered to Turkey were finding their way to Britain. On August 10, Metaxas assured the Germans that no ammunition was being shipped to Britain and that he had taken steps to prevent any possible future deliveries.[23]

These topics continued to be discussed until the Italian invasion, but Germany did not consider them serious enough to justify military action. Hitler wanted peace on his southern flank, and he warned the Italians not to give the British an opportunity to return to the continent and establish their air force in Yugoslavia and Greece. On August 13, the Italians created a border incident in Albania designed to provoke the Greeks, but it failed. Two days later, the Greek cruiser *Helle* was torpedoed by an "unidentified" submarine while at anchor in the Cyclades. Both incidents failed to provoke dictator Metaxas, who was determined to play down the affairs. The day the *Helle* sank, Hitler ordered Rintelen to tell the Italians not to take any action against Yugoslavia or Greece, and that any preparations should end only in a study. He forbade giving the Italians any German information on Yugoslav defenses, and he declared that there would be no military conference.[24] During these incidents Metaxas appealed to the Germans to restrain Italy, and he emphasized how Greek neutrality served Germany's interest. At the same time, he made it quite clear that Greece would resist if Italy attacked. Although the German government refused to allow German newspapers to publish the Greek version of the border incident and gave no assurances to the Metaxas government that it would restrain its ally, the Germans moved quickly to halt the Italians.[25] On the day Rintelen carried Hitler's message to the Italian military, Germany's ambassador to Rome, Hans Georg von Mackensen, relayed another message from Hitler to the Italian government, telling Mussolini of the need to work in concert with Germany against the British Empire and to give up the Yugoslav-Greek venture in favor of this cooperation. By August 19, the Italians gave in and postponed the invasion.[26] Hitler forced Italy to postpone its Balkan plans during the Hungarian-Rumanian crisis which threatened to erupt into open hostilities. After regaining the diplomatic initiative and establishing relative calm in those areas in which Germany was interested, Hitler seemed less inclined to keep a close rein on Mussolini's designs. Mussolini acceded to Hitler's request, but he reinforced his Albanian army with three new divisions, indicating that he still planned to move at his convenience.

Alarmed, the Greeks appealed to Berlin and London. Ribbentrop refused to see the Greek ambassador until he learned that the Greeks had mobilized. Then he met the Greek ambassador to Germany, Alexandros Rizo-Rangabé, at Fuschl on August 26. Rizo-Rangabé requested German intervention to mediate the Italo-Greek dispute, but Ribbentrop refused. He informed the ambassador that Germany considered the Mediterranean to be in the Italian sphere of influence where Germany had no direct interest. The Greek government, continued Ribbentrop, must come to an agreement with Italy on its own.[27] Ribbentrop and the German Foreign Office never deviated from this position between September 1940 and April 1941. Metaxas became convinced that the Axis would move in the Balkans or Russia in the autumn. The Greek dictator was prepared to meet this threat, and he asked London what aid the British could provide for the defense of Greece. While the answer was not reassuring—the British could offer only the fleet and a place at the postwar peace conference—the regime prepared to resist any attack.[28] In August, Hitler wanted peace in the Balkans, and the crisis passed when he met Ciano at Obersalzburg on the twenty-eighth and cancelled any Italian attack. Hitler explained that he wanted peace to keep Russia out and to forestall any Anglo-Russian combination.[29] Then the Fuehrer settled the Hungarian, Rumanian, and Bulgarian differences. This stabilization, however, was short-lived.

On September 11, 1940, in response to a request for a German military mission, several hundred *SS* men arrived in Rumania to help repatriate *Volksdeutsche* from Bessarabia. German experts of all types soon followed them. The German government explained their arrival as a response to a call from Antonescu to reorganize the Rumanian army. By October 8, it became apparent that Germany had occupied Rumania on request.[30] The Germans did not inform Mussolini, who was furious. On October 15, the Duce decided to invade Greece. He first set the date for October 26, but later revised it to October 28.[31]

It has always been believed that the Italian invasion of Greece caught Hitler by total surprise and that Mussolini planned it when Germany was distracted elsewhere on the continent. In fact, the *OKW* received its first information as to the Italian venture on October 22, 1940. On the day before, a colonel on the Italian General Staff had told the chief of the German liaison staff to the Italian Air Force that Italy had set the invasion of Greece for October 25 or 26.[32] By October 24, further reports from German intelligence of Italian intentions against Greece caused the *OKW* to ask Rintelen to speak directly with General Roatta. General Roatta personally denied any such intentions by Italy. This reaction caused *Reichsmarschall* Hermann Goering to observe that Italy was keeping her preparations secret because she had been instructed very late as to German intentions in Rumania. The *Reichsmarschall* recognized the strategic advantage to the Axis if Italy succeeded in gaining control of Greece, but he realized the greater disadvantage if it failed and Britain seized Crete as a base from which to bomb Rumanian oil fields. Colonel General Franz Halder noted in his diary on October 24 that Ciano was busy planning the occupation of Corfu and western Greece.[33] Confirmation of the impending attack came from General Rintelen on October 25, who based his conclusions on a talk with the Italian Chief of Staff, Marshal Pietro Badoglio. On October 26, Field Marshal Wilhelm Keitel tried to reach Badoglio to ensure that the Italian attack included plans for

seizing Crete, which was of great concern to the German Navy
and Air Force.[34] This intelligence regarding the Italian attack
was independent and supplemental to the contents of Mussolini's letter to Hitler received by the Fuehrer at Yvoire on the
evening of October 24.[35]

There is no reason to doubt that Hitler, who had left Germany on October 22 to talk with Pierre Laval and to meet
Generalisimo Franco, was kept posted by the *OKW* on information coming from Italy. Keitel would hardly have tried to
influence Italian strategy on October 26 without Hitler's knowledge or approval. If Hitler had wanted to stop Mussolini again,
he had enough time to veto the Duce's plans, four days at least
and possibly six. Since he had successfully resolved other
Balkan problems, he was evidently prepared to let the Italians
have their lead so long as Crete was included in the attack.
He may even have had reason to expect an Italian success.[36]
At any rate, he was prepared to let them try.

Hitler's reversal of his attitude on an Italian attack on
Greece has been explained by his "peripheral" strategy.[37] The
"peripheral" strategy was developed by General Alfred Jodl as
an alternative to any direct assault on the British Isles. Britain,
according to Jodl, could be defeated by an attack in the Mediterranean. From this perspective, Hitler was prepared, between
September and November 1940, to give Mussolini a free
hand in Greece as it now became a "Mediterranean" rather
than a Balkan country. Hitler rejected any Italian intrusion
into the Balkans, where the Fuehrer continued his diplomatic
approach. Yugoslavia was therefore excluded, but the way
for an Italian attack on Greece was open if the Duce seized the
whole peninsula and Crete rather than simply annexing north-
tern Greece. Hitler expressed his anger at Mussolini after
the attack had failed and threatened not only Germany's Balkan
diplomacy but presented Britain with an opportunity to return
to the continent.[38]

When Hitler met Mussolini in Florence the morning after
the Italian invasion, he revealed no anxiety or displeasure.
By November 2, however, his mood changed as the Italian
failure began to make itself clear. General Franz Halder reported that Hitler was very much annoyed at the Italian
maneuver and not at all interested in helping them out. The
KTB/OKW indicated his reaction to be "negative on all
points." [39] By November 4, the Greeks pushed the Italians out
of Greece, and the full impact of the disaster fell upon Hitler.

Previously, he had received information that British troops had landed on Crete and that the Royal Navy had occupied Suda Bay. On November 5 and 6, erroneous intelligence arrived in Berlin that British aircraft had landed on Lemnos and that British troops had landed at three points on the Gulf of Salonica. Believing that the Rumanian oil fields now came within the range of British bombers, Hitler ordered a German air defense line established in Bulgaria and dispatched 200 men and officers there. The Greek victories and the alleged British threat prompted Hitler to order the German Army High Command to prepare an operation against Greece.[40] On November 14, General Wilhelm Keitel told Marshal Badoglio that Hitler desired the annihilation of Greece because it was becoming a British air and naval base. Hitler repeated this same point to Mussolini on December 31, 1940.[41] In order to force Britain to violate Bulgarian air space by any attack on the oil fields of Rumania, Hitler instructed the Bulgarians to remain neutral.[42] The Fuehrer warned the Greek government not to allow any air attacks on Rumania lest it face the consequences of German retaliation. Metaxas made certain no offensive British action took place which might serve as a provocation to the Germans. About the same time the German military attaché in Rome reported home after an inspection of the Italian front in Albania. This first full report from Rintelen attributed the Italian failures to the commitment of too few troops on too large a front, poor organization, extremely difficult terrain, poor weather conditions, and poor communications with Albania. He did not expect any Italian success in the near future.[43]

The Italian failure coincided with Mussolini's failure in North Africa to push British Empire forces back into Egypt. These setbacks paralleled Hitler's defeat in the Battle of Britain and the encroaching power of the Soviet Union in Bulgaria. Foreign Minister V. M. Molotov had been invited to Germany in October, and he arrived in Berlin on November 12. The Soviets became concerned over German moves in Finland and alarmed over Hitler's occupation of Rumania. They did not accept Hitler's citing of the "English danger" as an adequate explanation. After a stormy discussion of Finland, Molotov switched the talks to the Balkans, which Hitler had not planned to discuss. Hitler reemphasized the British threat, but Molotov reversed the situation by citing Britain's danger to Russia, referring to the Straits as "England's historic gateway for attack on the Soviet Union." Russia's security demanded good

relations with other Black Sea powers, and he proposed a Soviet
guarantee for Bulgaria. The Soviet guarantee, if accepted,
would have wrecked Hitler's plans for southeast Europe. Hitler
evaded answering Molotov's proposal, and the conference
ended in failure.[44]

These pressures served as the background for Fuehrer
Directive No. 18, signed on November 12, the day Molotov
arrived in Berlin. The Directive surveyed Hitler's strategy in
southeast Europe and the Mediterranean. It indicated that if
Britain could not be defeated by a direct attack, Hitler might
achieve the same end indirectly either by a continental strategy
of attacking Russia, thereby securing the East and preventing
any possible British-Soviet cooperation, or by a peripheral
strategy in the Mediterranean. Seizure of Gibraltar and Suez
would lead to the isolation and strangulation of Britain.[45]
Directive No. 18 confirmed earlier orders to prepare for the
occupation of northern Greece from Bulgaria in order to put
the *Luftwaffe* within striking distance of targets in the eastern
Mediterranean which endangered the Rumanian oil fields. Ten
divisions were thought necessary for the operation.[46] The
following day, however, Hitler explained to his military leaders
that he wanted to keep the war in the Balkans limited, and that
only British air attacks on Rumanian oil justified the commitment of German armed forces to Greece.[47] Hitler did not intend
to bail out his ally unless a direct threat to German interests
occurred, and only if it served his general goals. His decision
rested on his awaiting Stalin's formal reply to his talks with
Molotov. There was no need for a German move in the Balkans
until Hitler was certain of Stalin's response. Until that time
he would try to avoid a Balkan campaign, even though on the
day he issued Directive No. 18 Mussolini appealed for a German
attack on Greece through Bulgaria and application of pressure
on Yugoslavia.[48]

When Hitler met Mussolini in Vienna on November 20, he
pointed out the Duce's mistakes. The Italians, for example, had
failed to include Crete in their operation, even though Hitler
had offered a parachute division for this purpose. Consequently,
Britain had seized the island. The Italian invasion had created
deleterious psychological repercussions by making Bulgaria
reluctant to join the Tripartite Pact, by increasing Russia's
concern in the Balkans, and by making Axis relations with
Yugoslavia difficult. Furthermore, the military consequences
of the action had brought the Rumanian oil fields and ports in

both Italy and Albania within striking distance of the British air force. The British bases in Greece, continued Hitler, would be difficult to destroy, while the oil installations in Rumania were now quite vulnerable and if regularly attacked could cause severe problems for the Reich. To eliminate this danger Hitler proposed that Spain be brought into the war as a means of sealing the western Mediterranean from Britain. At the same time he suggested diverting Russia's interests toward the "East." To ensure success in these matters and to avoid the complications of any German move against Greece, Hitler planned to arrange a Turkish-Bulgarian settlement that guaranteed Turkish neutrality, and he proposed to win Yugoslav cooperation in the settlement of the Greek question. If Britain, however, attempted "to consolidate a real position in Thrace," the Fuehrer assured Mussolini that he was prepared to intervene with decisive forces at "any risk." [49] Hitler was prepared to leave Greece alone so long as British strength did not increase and Greece did not provoke the Reich. If either of these eventualities occurred, however, Hitler would strike, and Metaxas understood this point quite well.

German intelligence overestimated the number, strength, and location of British armed forces on the Greek mainland. As the Greek government had been warned that any attack on the Rumanian oil fields would elicit a German response, the Metaxas regime scrupulously avoided any action that might anger Germany. After the Italian attack, Greece requested aid from Great Britain, and Churchill's government dispatched three Blenheim bomber squadrons, one Gladiator fighter squadron, and two antiaircraft batteries. Metaxas refused to allow Britain to establish air fields north of Athens so that there were no bases in Thrace and no troops were landed in the Gulf of Salonica. Metaxas realized that such actions would only provoke the Germans. Moreover, he refused to allow the British bombers to attack either the Rumanian oil fields or the Italian bases in Albania. The British air units were limited to providing aerial support for the Greek army against the Italians, something far short of Churchill's hopes for bombing the oil fields and opening a second front.[50] On November 22, after issuing Directive No. 18 and meeting with Mussolini, General Rintelen sent an accurate estimate of types and number of British forces in Greece, estimated at 3,800 air force personnel.[51] Although the British armed forces in Greece at the end of November 1940 did not threaten Germany, Hitler continued to fear the potential danger they represented. As long as British forces in Greece remained limited, Russia and Turkey would remain quiet, but if the British established themselves in force, Germany feared that "Russian and Turkish action in the Balkans would immediately be very great," Keitel informed Antonescu on November 24.[52] This potential threat of a second front in the Balkans always remained uppermost in the mind of Hitler and the *OKW*, and, in the final analysis, precipitated Hitler's decision for a campaign in Greece that would again expel Britain from the continent.

Even though he had requested British support in expectation of the Italian attack, Metaxas continued to avoid any provocation of Hitler, and Greek officials kept the Germans well informed on Anglo-Greek relations. Caught between Britain, which pressed Athens for an expanded British role in the Balkan conflict, and Germany, which made it clear that any British threat to Rumanian oil would bring immediate Nazi retaliation, the Athens government pursued the chimera of keeping the Italo-Greek conflict isolated. The Greeks were banking on Hitler's desire to keep the Balkans quiet. Indeed, Hitler would not invade Greece until his decision to attack Russia had become final, but once that decision was made in December 1940 Greece was doomed. To reassure Berlin that Greece would not become a British base, the Greek press withheld all polemics against Germany, and the Greek government made certain that German citizens in Greece were not molested. Indeed, the press looked to Germany for mediation of the conflict. On November 4, Rizo-Rangabé called on State Secretary Ernst von Weizsaecker to emphasize the positive feelings for Germany in Greece.[53] A number of informal contacts between the two states followed this meeting with Weizsaecker but to no positive resolution. By the end of December, Metaxas came to realize the muddle of Greece's policy, and he recognized that there was no way out of the struggle because Germany would not allow a local defeat for Italy in the Balkans.[54]

Unknown to the Greeks, the German Army and Navy advised against a Balkan campaign because of the delays and other adverse effects it would have on the forthcoming invasion of Russia scheduled for the spring of 1941. Poor weather conditions and roads (there were only five practical roads across the Balkan mountains and bridges were weak) did not help endear the German military to the notion of a Balkan campaign.[55] They preferred a nonmilitary solution in Greece, a mediated truce. Admiral Wilhelm Canaris, Chief of *Abwehr II* (*Amt Ausland Abwehr Abteilung II*—Armed Forces Foreign Service Intelligence Branch), championed this course. The military leaders, anxious about the operation planned against Russia, warned Hitler of the delay and drain that a Balkan campaign would place on a German move against the Soviets. Admiral Erich Raeder spoke against the plan to the Fuehrer on December 3. At a conference with his military leaders on December 5, when they presented him with the plans for Operation *"Barbarossa,"* Generals Franz Halder and Walther von Brauchitsch voiced their reservations to Hitler. In response, Hitler declared that the German warning to the Greek government that any attacks from Greek soil against German spheres of influence would lead to retaliation had thus far prevented any such incursions. He expected this situation to continue for the next few months. Nevertheless, he considered German intervention against Greece necessary in order "to clarify the situation once and for all." Only if the Greeks ended the war with Italy on their own initiative and compelled the British to leave Greek soil would German intervention become "superfluous," since the hegemony of Europe would not be decided in that area—an ironic comment in light of later developments. Yet Hitler considered the concentration of German troops for such an operation as absolutely essential since, if they were not used against Greece, they would still be ready for the move against Russia.[56]

The day before the Fuehrer's conference with his military leaders, the Greeks launched another offensive that broke the Italian lines and appeared on the verge of capturing the Italian port base of Valona. Mussolini considered asking Hitler to mediate a truce, but Ciano and Dino Alfieri (Italian Ambassador to Germany but then in Rome) talked the panic-stricken Duce into holding on and asking the Germans for assistance. On December 5, Alfieri flew to Berlin for discussions. There he described the Italian situation in Albania as so desperate that Hitler and the *OKW* considered sending two armored divisions to encircle the Greek army in Albania. As conditions were not favorable for a quick, decisive military operation, Hitler allowed informal mediation contacts with the Greeks.[57] On the day of Alfieri's arrival and conference, the Germans approached the Greeks through the Hungarian Minister to Madrid, R. Andorka, who informed the Greek Minister to Spain, Admiral Perikles Argyropoulos, that Athens should approach

Berlin for a mediated settlement favorable to the Greeks.[58] The German military may have been encouraged in their hopes for a mediated settlement by their contact with Nikolaos Plastiras, who was living in exile in Vichy France. Soon after the Italian attack, German agents approached the exiled general in November to ask him if he thought Greece wanted peace and if he would act as a mediator. Plastiras's reply is disputed. A letter allegedly signed by him and published after the war indicated that he gave the German agents a positive response on both counts, and that he tried to contact the Athens government. Plastiras claimed that he did reply that the Greeks wanted peace, but he rejected the claim that he was willing to act as a mediator. Instead, he argued, he suggested that the Germans use a neutral to make the mediation offer. He emphasized that he made it clear to the Germans that Greece would fight if the Nazis attacked.[59] The Athens government did not accept the German offer, and the Italians managed to stabilize their lines to prevent the fall of Valona and Durazzo.

On December 9, 1940, General Archibald Wavell launched his offensive in the western desert of North Africa, causing Mussolini to face one disaster after another for the next six weeks. In response to the deteriorating situation in Greece and North Africa, Hitler dispatched German air units to Sicily to attack British shipping on December 10, and he issued Fuehrer Directive No. 20, Operation *"Marita,"* on December 13. Directive No. 20 planned to foil British efforts to establish, behind the protection of a Balkan front, an air base which would threaten Italy and the Rumanian oil fields.[60] During this same period, Admiral Canaris, on a mission to see Generalissimo Franco, gave to Andorka a German proposal for mediation of the Italo-Greek War with instructions that the Ambassador pass it on to the Greeks. The Hungarian minister delivered the proposal on December 17 to Argyropoulos.[61] Andorka explained that the proposal was official and could be transmitted to the Greek government. According to Argyropoulos, the German offer proposed that Greece hold on to all territory conquered in the war except for a neutral zone between the Italian and Greek armies, this to be occupied by the German Army in order to prevent any breaches of the truce. In return, Greece would tell Britain to leave. Admiral Argyropoulos telegraphed the proposal to Athens with a recommendation to accept in order to avoid later German intervention which would be disastrous for Greece, but he never received any response from the Metaxas government.[62] Metaxas was reconciled to carrying on the struggle even though he realized Greece's efforts were in vain.[63]

Shortly before Christmas Eve, 1940 (probably just after the Greek government received the report from Argyropoulos), Alexis Kyrou, who headed a section of the Greek Foreign Ministry, contacted Major Clemm von Hohenberg, the German military attaché in Athens. Major Hohenberg was a friend of Admiral Canaris and an early member of the *Abwehr*. Kyrou took the military attaché to his home for a discussion with other Greek officials. These official Greek government representatives explained Greece's predicament to Hohenberg and expressed the hope that Germany might help resolve it.[64] The Italian invasion, according to the Major's account of the meeting, had forced Greece into the war against her will, and Greece wanted to keep the war limited against Italy. For these reasons, explained the Greek officials, Metaxas had repeatedly rejected British offers of support. Greece received only air support and *matériel* from Britain, nothing more. Both of these items, they added, had been insufficient in quantity. Metaxas realized that if the war did not end soon, Germany would intervene to save the prestige of her ally. Britain would then move into Greece, making it the center of the struggle. Metaxas wanted to spare his country this devastation and suffering. The Greek ambassador to Germany, Rizo-Rangabé, had repeatedly tried to get Germany to intervene, but the German Foreign Ministry rejected his efforts. Metaxas realized that the German military leaders remembered the First World War and wanted to see a friendly Balkan front in the present conflict. Since the Greek government no longer trusted the German Foreign Ministry, the Greek representative pledged Major Hohenberg to absolute secrecy in regard to the chief of his mission in Greece, Ambassador Viktor Erbach-Schoenberg, and Kyrou asked the Major to carry a message directly to Admiral Canaris. The Greek government offered an armistice on the basis of the status quo, and, in return for a German guarantee, the Metaxas government would resist every attempt by Britain to land troops on the Greek mainland. Major Hohenberg did as Kyrou asked, but received orders from his superiors to halt his forays into diplomacy and to confine his reporting to military affairs.[65]

Parallel to the Hohenberg-Kyrou contacts, an alleged offer from the Germans arrived in Athens through Professor Boehringer, the German cultural attaché. Boehringer told Maniadakes, Metaxas' Police Chief, that the Fuehrer and Foreign Minister had commissioned him to sound out the Greeks on German intervention on the same terms explained to Admiral Argyropoulos. The Greek government exhaustively debated these proposals, and Metaxas decided to request the German government to resubmit them through official channels. No official response came from Berlin,[66] but the German Minister to Athens, Prince Erbach, called on Metaxas on December 20, a rare occasion since the dictator no longer received chiefs of missions. Erbach's instructions have not been found. A record of the meeting indicated that no mention was made of German mediation, but Metaxas used the occasion to once again emphasize that Germany had no reason to fear a British military initiative from Greece. Greece would continue her correct relations with Germany.[67] Shortly after the meeting, Metaxas realized that Hitler would not allow an Italian defeat and that Germany would invade.[68]

Was Hitler's December offer of a mediated peace genuine? The evidence suggests it was not. Preparations for the invasion of Russia had been under way since the summer of 1940. The development of the "peripheral" strategy was haltingly improvised after the Italian setback in Albania. On November 26, 1940, Hitler received official confirmation from Stalin that the Soviet dictator would not be deflected from the Balkans, and the invasion of Russia would soon be confirmed. The suggestion that the Athens government approach the Germans for a mediated truce was conveyed to the Greeks on December 5, the day Hitler received the plans for *"Barbarossa."* On December 8, Hitler learned that Spain would not join the Axis in the war, and the "peripheral" strategy was scrapped. Greece once again became a "Balkan" country.[69] Parallel to these developments, Wavell's offensive had the Italians in full retreat across North Africa, increasing the British danger to the south. Hitler signed the directive for the invasion of Greece on December 13 and for Russia on December 18. The terms of the Nazi mediated truce were not conveyed to the Greeks until December 17, after Hitler had signed the directive for *"Marita."*

Metaxas and the King were correct in interpreting the German initiative as an attempt to divide the Greeks and the British in order to relieve the pressure on the Italians. For their part, the Greeks were not eager for mediation. The King and Papagos did not expect a German attack, and they still had hopes of defeating the Italians before Germany could intervene.[70] On January 7, 1941, Hitler reiterated his earlier position on Greece and Britain to the Bulgarian Minister President Boris Filov, saying that he had learned his lesson from the First World War, and that he would prevent the British from establishing a second front at Salonica.[71]

One week later Bulgaria agreed to join the Tripartite Pact in return for gaining territory in Thrace between the Strymon and Maritsa rivers and part of Macedonia.[72] At the time Bulgaria agreed to join the Axis, Athens called on London to send a military mission to Greece to discuss the extent of British military support for the country's defense. On January 13, Air Chief Marshal Longmore and General Wavell flew to Athens to confer with Metaxas, who was dying and would be dead within three weeks, and the Commander-in-Chief of the Greek Army, General Alexandros Papagos. The British were convinced that the German army would strike south from Rumania and drive into Greece. The Greeks told them that a minimum of nine British divisions were needed to meet the German attack, but the situation in North Africa, though favorable to Britain, did not allow London to offer the Greeks more than a few engineers, aircraft, antiaircraft guns, and tanks. Metaxas declined the offer as too small to be useful but large enough to provoke a German attack. The talks were inconclusive as Britain remained concerned about Egypt and North Africa.[73] The weakness of the British offer and the failure of the Greek offensive of January to be decisive against the Italians, in conjunction with the increasing danger of a German invasion, prompted a renewed Greek approach to Berlin. The evidence is inconclusive as to whether this new approach was officially sanctioned by the Athens government. It is clear, however, that after Metaxas' death on January 29 the Greek resolve against Hitler weakened and cracked.

The Greek military attaché to Turkey, Colonel Apokoritis, arranged to meet with the German military attaché and Ambassador Franz von Papen on January 16, 1941, just after Longmore and Wavell left Greece. The colonel categorically denied any presence of British ground troops on the Greek mainland and emphasized that they existed at only one base on Crete. The British aid, he continued, consisted only of *matériel*, along with naval and air support, and fell short of what was promised. Greece continued to refuse the offer of British ground troops as it could never be extensive and would only call in Germany. The colonel reemphasized the local character of the war with Italy and stressed that Greece sought only to achieve security against any further Italian threat. He placed the Elbasan area as the limit of the Greek advance into Albania. Control of this area guaranteed Greek security since no more than ten divisions could be concentrated beyond that line. The Greek officer emphasized Greek concern over the German build-up in Rumania, which indicated a drive against Greece.[74]

Two days later, January 18, the Athens government handed a formal note to the British minister stating that the aid available from Britain was not adequate to resist a German attack. Metaxas requested that British troops not land in Greece until the Germans crossed the Danube. The note concluded with a reaffirmation of Greece's determination to resist to the end.[75] On February 7, however, the British Military Mission reported that Papagos still believed Greece could wrap up the Albanian war before the Germans attacked. Papagos based his optimism on his February offensive against Tepelini, and he pressed the British mission to supply trucks, planes, and ammunition in large quantities to give the Greeks the margin of victory.[76] The Greek offensive failed, and the lines between the two armies did not change.[77] This failure brought about a change of mood in the Greek commander and other Greek generals.

In an attempt to strengthen the battle against the Axis after the death of Metaxas, the King suggested the formation of a government of national unity that would include leading Venizelists, an action the British had desired since 1940. The Army, however, vetoed the proposal.[78] Indeed, one group of officers went even further. According to the Bishop of Ioannina, a group of officers allied with him considered a *coup d'état* immediately following the death of Metaxas with the goal of negotiating a peace with the Axis. On behalf of these officers, the Bishop traveled to Athens on February 5, 1941, to persuade the new Prime Minister, Alexandros Koryzis, and the King to end the war. They rejected his appeal. Similar suggestions from generals Drakos, Kosmas, and Papadopoulos led to their dismissals.[79] In the same period, Papagos wavered and suggested that British troops not land in Greece until the Germans had entered the country.[80]

In the north, Hitler did not hesitate. He set the date for crossing the Danube into Bulgaria for February 15, with the expectation that the Bulgarian-Greek frontier would be crossed on the first of April.[81] Defenses against aerial attacks on the Rumanian oil fields were established, as British strikes were expected as soon as the invasion began. The Bulgarian army would not mobilize until German troops entered the country.[82]

The Capitulation

While preparations for *"Marita"* were completed, Hitler turned his attention to Yugoslavia. The only rail line through Bulgaria into Greece ran within twenty kilometers of the Yugoslav border. If *"Marita"* was to succeed without a hitch, Yugoslav neutrality was imperative. Yugoslav representatives met Hitler at Obersalzburg on February 17, and he pressed them to join the Tripartite Pact by offering them the Greek port of Salonica. They deferred all decisions to the Regent, Prince Paul, and made it clear that they were not interested in Salonica but in the creation of a Yugoslav-Bulgarian-Turkish bloc that could prevent any foreign landing in the Balkans and could mediate the Greek-Italian conflict.[83] Although he referred them to Rome on this question, Hitler knew their quest was futile as he had worked out the Bulgarian-Turkish pact on that very day, and Bulgaria had already committed itself to the Tripartite Pact.

On February 11, the London government decided that the successes in North Africa enabled them to offer substantial aid to Greece, and Churchill dispatched Foreign Secretary Anthony Eden and General Sir John Dill to Athens for discussions with the Greek government. Eden and Dill arrived in Athens on February 22 amidst rumors that Greece wanted to make peace with the Axis. Eden was treated to a little ceremony by Koryzis to reassure the British that the government was determined to resist to the end. The British believed the occasion was staged by the King to overcome the rumors.[84] The Eden mission resulted in the still controversial decision of the two governments to defend the Aliakhmon line (Mt. Olympus-Veria-Edessa-Kajmakcalan), which meant withdrawing Greek armies and sacrificing Albania and Salonica to the enemy.[85] Eden then traveled to Turkey to try winning Turkish support and returned to Athens on March 2. There he found the Greeks defeatist and less cooperative.[86] On March 1, Bulgaria publicly adhered to the Axis, and German troops crossed into the country. To Eden's surprise Papagos had not only not begun the withdrawal of Greek forces to the Aliakhmon line, but he had no intention of doing so. Papagos based his decision on his view of the original agreement that the Greek army would not fall back to Aliakhmon until Yugoslavia indicated it would not join with Greece and Britain against Germany. Since he had not received any information from Britain on this point, the Greek commander had not withdrawn the Greek troops.[87] The crisis was resolved by the King's intervention, which brought Papagos around to accepting the Aliakhmon line and resisting Germany.[88] The first British troops sailed from Alexandria on March 4, and took their positions between March 16 and 19.

To the very last, the German military leaders remained hopeful that the Balkan campaign could be avoided.[89] As events moved toward a climax, and without informing their ally, another unofficial appeal for a negotiated settlement went out to the Germans from Athens on March 10. Colonel Petinis, Chief of Staff of the Army of Northern Greece, made the following proposal to the German Consul at Salonica: if the Germans replaced the Italians and guaranteed that negotiations of the Albanian-Greek frontier would be concluded without the Italians, Greece would halt hostilities on the Albanian front, and the Greek Army would see to it that British Empire forces left Greece. Colonel Petinis emphasized that Britain occupied Crete without the approval of the Greek government, and that Greece still limited British forces to south of the Aliakhmon River. He ended by saying that if Germany attacked through Bulgaria, Greece would fight to the last.[90]

The day Colonel Petinis contacted the German Consul, Major Hohenberg began a series of conversations with Georgios Merkoures, a former Greek cabinet member, who told the major that Minister Council President Koryzis asked him to approach the Germans on the possibility of Greek-German discussions to settle the Albanian situation without a conflict. According to Merkoures, the Minister President desired nothing more than "an early peace in Albania which would preserve Greek honor and make possible the withdrawal of the English from the continent." Greece wanted to avoid conflict with Germany, but, said Merkoures, it believed that Germany was determined to resolve the issue by force in consideration of her ally. This determination had forced Greece to seek aid from Britain.[91]

Ribbentrop responded that "The Greeks are mistaken if

they think they can pass on to us the responsibility of taking the initiative in ending the conflict.... [The Greek government] seems to harbor illusions regarding the price which it would have to pay for such termination." The Foreign Minister ordered Hohenberg to halt his discussions with Merkoures and not to resume them without Ribbentrop's personal approval.[92] On March 6, the former Venizelist and dictator, Pangalos, approached Erbach, saying that he was representing influential persons. Pangalos proposed to carry out a *coup* and establish a pro-Axis government if the Germans would work out a peace in Albania on the basis of the status quo. One week later, the Greek Permanent Undersecretary for Foreign Affairs, Nikolaos Mavroudis, contacted Erbach to inquire if a German invasion could be avoided. Following the Mavroudis-Erbach meeting, the Greek army made another approach to the Germans, and on March 15 Mavroudis reiterated to Major Hohenberg that Greece wished nothing more than an honorable peace in Albania that would allow the British to withdraw from the continent.[93] On March 18, the Greeks made a final and official approach to the German government. Greek Ambassador Rizo-Rangabé called on State Secretary Weizsaecker to deliver a message from his government. During the discussion Weizsaecker stated that "Greece had made her decisive error by accepting the British guarantee.... Two things were certain: Greece was at war with our ally and had drawn units of the British armed forces into her country. But it was intolerable to us to have the English on the continent." [94] When Rizo-Rangabé indicated Greece would send the British home if the Albanian war could be ended, he received no positive response from Weizsaecker. After this rebuff, the ambassador went to Admiral Canaris and gave him the note with the request that he deliver it to Hitler. The Admiral gave it to Keitel, who refused to pass it on to Hitler but gave it to Ribbentrop, who refused even to read it much less give it to the Fuehrer. The note summarized Greek policy toward Germany since October 1940 and emphasized the measures Greece had taken to keep British aid limited to defensive action against Italy, not allowing British bombers to attack the Rumanian oil fields or British troops to land until after German troops crossed into Bulgaria. The note ended with an appeal to Germany not to "stab us in the back at the moment we are defending ourselves in a very unequal struggle." [95]

Hitler had decided in December 1940 to crush all British

forces in Greece at any cost. After the December and January successes in North Africa, Hitler feared a "second Salonica," and he was determined to deal Britain a second Dunkirk.[96] The invasion of Russia would never be secure as long as Britain had a foothold in the Balkans. On March 17, 1941, Hitler issued new orders for *"Marita"*: the operation would proceed until every British soldier was expelled from the Greek mainland and the Peloponnese.[97] On March 24, Ambassador Erbach received instructions to hold no further discussions with the Greek government.[98] After much delay, Yugoslavia joined the Tripartite Pact on the following day, and the Germans waited for the first signs of good weather to launch *"Marita."* The Belgrade *coup d'état* forced Hitler on March 27 to improvise his plans to include Yugoslavia in the attack.

The Italian invasion united the Greek nation into one great dynamic effort, and the Regime of August Fourth must be given its due regard for its part. The same cannot be said of the manner in which the regime met the Nazi attack. In this case the nation proved to be ahead of the government. Field Marshal Wilhelm von List's Twelfth Army launched the invasion on April 6, 1941, Easter Sunday for Orthodox Christians. Immediately, the Athenians staged a huge anti-Axis demonstration in front of the German legation, but the poor preparation and the weakness of the combined Anglo-Greek forces could not stop the Germans, who struck south from Bulgaria at four points.[99] The largest of these forces moved south along the Strymon valley and within a few days occupied Salonica, and on April 9 the isolated Greek West Macedonian Army surrendered. Three days later Belgrade fell, and the West Macedonian Army began to move toward the Aliakhmon line. The Greek generals had not been enthusiastic supporters of the plan to resist Germany. The Greek army in Albania did not respond as readily to the Anglo-Greek plan, and German panzers moving toward Ioannina threatened to cut it off. The Commander of the Epirus Army, General Ioannis Pitsikas, reflecting the general sentiment of the field commanders, wanted an armistice before the Greeks were driven from Albania, but the King refused and told him it was essential to retreat and to hold out as long as possible.[100] Pitsikas obeyed, but, in the face of the hopelessness of the situation, continued to press for an armistice. The British force attacked at Olympus, but on April 14 withdrew to Thermopylae.

The King began to think of fleeing, and the government

panicked. In contrast, the Greek public was remarkably calm, and the rank-and-file of the armed forces maintained good order.[101] By April 12, the government-controlled press was encouraging defeatism. On April 16, the Minister of War, Georgios Papademas, ordered the army home for two months leave and announced to the press that he was leaving Greece. The Minister of Finance ordered all government officials to receive four months salary and to go home. On April 17, anti-Axis posters were removed from the streets of Athens, and the Minister of the Interior released political prisoners. All of these individuals acted without authority.[102] At the same time, a personal emissary from General Pitsikas arrived in Athens to demand an immediate armistice. This was too much for the Greek Prime Minister, who committed suicide on April 18. Fearful of a total collapse, the British pressed the King to end the defeatist attitude by appointing a military cabinet of national unity to continue the war until the British troops could evacuate. Papagos was reluctant, but the King rallied and committed Greece to fight on.[103] Unaware of his offer to Erbach, the British suggested General Pangalos head the military cabinet, but the King preferred the Venizelist General Alexandros Mazarakis. Mazarakis, however, refused to join the government unless the King dismissed Maniadakes. The King either refused or was unable to dismiss him and called on Emmanouil Tsouderos to form a government. On that day, April 20, General Georgios Tsolakoglou mutinied and signed an armistice with the commander of the SS "Adolf Hitler" Division in Epirus. With the full approval of the Greek government, the British Empire contingent began its evacuation on April 21. General Alfred Jodl flew to Larissa to sign the Greek capitulation on April 22, but the Italian representative had not been authorized to sign, and a third surrender to pacify Mussolini was arranged for April 23.[104] The King fled to Crete on that same day. The Germans entered Athens four days later.

The steadfast loyalty of the King to Britain was long remembered by Churchill and the Foreign Office, and they were doggedly committed to returning him to his throne at the end of the war. The capitulation and debacle that ended the Regime of August Fourth, however, reopened criticism of the monarchy. The American minister, Lincoln MacVeagh, reported to Washington that the Greeks would not forget the monarch's role in the dictatorship and his flight, and he warned that the people and the politicians may not allow the King to return at Greece's liberation. MacVeagh noted that the monarchy's chances of returning depended on its future behavior, and that those interested in Greek politics should be mindful of the Greeks' desire for a republic.[105]

Without any changes in the structure of the Metaxas regime, the Germans installed General Tsolakoglou as the first quisling premier. The Axis occupation had begun.

CHAPTER THREE

THE GERMAN OCCUPATION

The German invasion had been motivated by the strategic necessity to secure Hitler's southern flank in his planned attack against Russia. This military emphasis remained the first principle of the occupation throughout the war, and every other consideration remained secondary. The force of this policy ruined the Greek economy and splintered its political structure. Officially, the Germans gave the defense and administration of the country to the Italians, but in practice the Germans remained the primary power. Limiting themselves to the areas around Athens and Salonica and a few islands in the Aegean, including the larger part of Crete, the German authorities were not to interfere with the Italian and Bulgarian zones of occupation. In practice this became impossible, and both the Italians and Bulgarians, as well as the Greeks, were forced to comply to Germany's needs, which took precedence almost from the very hour of the Greek capitulation. The consequences for Greece were catastrophic, but out of this chaos grew the resistance.

Structure of the Administration

Following Greece's defeat, the Axis powers divided the country into three zones of occupation. The Reich absorbed the key economic and strategic areas of Athens-Piraeus, Salonica and its hinterland between the Aliakhmon and Strymon rivers, and the Aegean islands of Crete, Cythera, Anticythera, Melos, Lemnos, Mytilene, Chios, and Skyros. The Bulgarians annexed a section stretching from the Strymon river in eastern Macedonia through all of Thrace to a buffer zone, reserved by the Germans, on the Turkish border. The remainder went to the

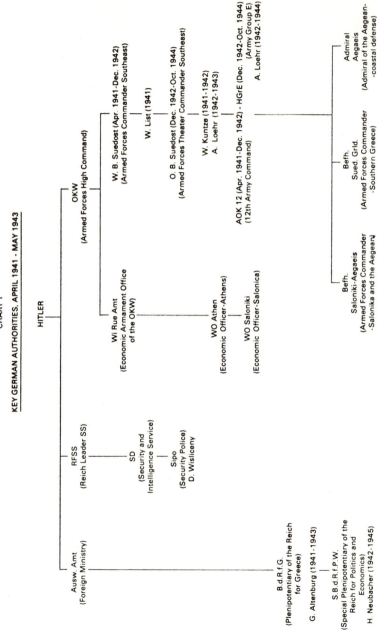

CHART 1

KEY GERMAN AUTHORITIES, APRIL 1941 - MAY 1943

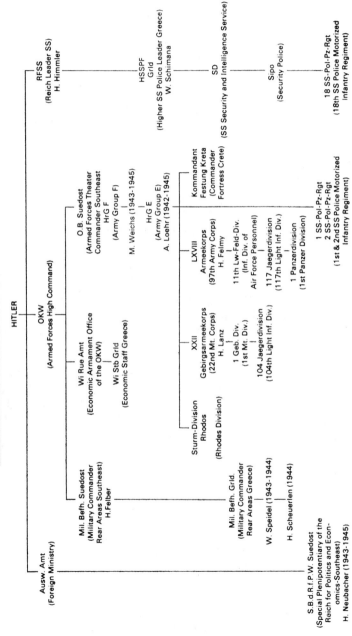

CHART II

KEY GERMAN AUTHORITIES FOLLOWING REORGANIZATION JUNE-AUGUST 1943

HITLER

OKW
(Armed Forces High Command)

Ausw. Amt
(Foreign Ministry)

Mil. Befh. Suedost
(Military Commander
Rear Areas Southeast)
H.Felber

Wi Rue Amt
(Economic Armament Office
of the OKW)

Wi Stb Grld
(Economic Staff Greece)

O.B. Suedost
(Armed Forces Theater
Commander Southeast)
HrG F
(Army Group F)
M. Weichs (1943-1945)

HrG E
(Army Group E)
A. Loehr (1942-1945)

RFSS
(Reich Leader SS)
H. Himmler

HSSPF
Grld
(Higher SS Police Leader Greece)
W. Schimana

SD
(SS Security and Intelligence Service)

Sipo
(Security Police)

18 SS-Pol-Pz-Rgt
(18th SS Police Motorized
Infantry Regiment)

Sturm-Division
Rhodos
(Rhodes Division)

Mil. Befh. Grld.
(Military Commander
Rear Areas Greece)
W. Speidel (1943-1944)
H. Scheuerlen (1944)

XXII
Gebirgsarmeekorps
(22nd Mt. Corps)
H. Lanz
1 Geb. Div.
(1st Mt. Div.)
104 Jaegerdivision
(104th Light Inf. Div.)

LXVIII
Armeekorps
(97th Army Corps)
H. Felmy
11th Lw-Feld-Div.
(Inf. Div. of
Air Force Personnel)
117 Jaegerdivision
(117th Light Inf. Div.)
1 Panzerdivision
(1st Panzer Division)

Kommandant
Festung Kreta
(Commander
Fortress Crete)

1 SS-Pol-Pz-Rgt
2 SS-Pol-Pz-Rgt
(1st & 2nd SS Police Motorized
Infantry Regiment)

S.B.d.R.f.P.W. Suedost
(Special Plenipotentiary of the
Reich for Politics and Econ-
omics-Southeast)
H. Neubacher (1943-1945)

Italians until their withdrawal from the war on September 9, 1943, when they were replaced by the Reich. Italy controlled the Ionian Islands, and the provinces of Ioannina, Thesprotia, and Prenza became part of their satellite state of Albania. The German occupied zones, along with old Serbia, formed the territorial command known as the *Suedost* (Southeast), under the *Wehrmachtbefehlshaber Suedost* (*W. B. Suedost* – Armed Forces Commander Southeast), headquartered first at Kifissia near Athens, then at Salonica. The Armed Forces Commander Southeast until October 1941 was the commander of the invasion army, Field Marshal Wilhelm von List, who was then replaced by General of the Engineers Walther Kuntze. In August 1942, Lieutenant General of the Air Force Alexander Loehr replaced Kuntze and remained the highest ranking officer in Greece until the German retreat in October 1944. As a result of Fuehrer Directive No. 47 of December 28, 1942, the *W. B. Suedost* was transformed into the *Oberbefehlshaber Suedost* (*O. B. Suedost* – Commander-in-Chief Southeast) and the *Armeeoberkommando 12* (*AOK 12* – 12th Army Command) was transformed into the army group, *Heeresgruppe E* (*HGrE*–Army Group E). Lt. General Loehr was in command during most of the occupation. The primary task of the *W. B. Suedost*, and later *HGrE*, was to build a base of defense and to supervise the military administration of the German zones.[1] To fulfill these tasks, the *Befehlshaber Saloniki-Aegaeis* (*Befh. Sal.-Aeg.*– Commander Salonica-Aegean), the *Befehlshaber Sued-Griechenland* (*Befh. Sued-Grld.*– Commander Southern Greece), and the *Admiral Suedost* (Admiral Southeast) were subordinated to *W. B. Suedost* (later *HGrE*).[2]

Paralleling this military organization, Hitler appointed *Gesandter* Guenther Altenburg as *Bevollmaechtigter des Reiches fuer Griechenland* (*B.d.R.f.G.*– Plenipotentiary of the Reich for Greece) to handle relations with the Greek quisling government and political affairs in general. In nearly all cases, however, the *W. B. Suedost* overruled the Plenipotentiary. As conflicts between these two administrations increased and the economy deteriorated, Hitler appointed a special personal envoy on October 12, 1942, in hope of clearing up the confusion. Dr. Hermann Neubacher, *Sonderbevollmaechtigter des Reiches fuer Politik und Wirtschaft* (Special Plenipotentiary of the Reich for Politics and Economics), superseded Altenburg, but the latter's office was not consolidated with Neubacher's until

November 1943. From the beginning of the occupation, there existed a duality of authority which was further complicated by the reorganization of the whole southeast after the Italian surrender on September 9, 1943.

In expectation of Italy's collapse, the whole southeast was reorganized on August 15, 1943. The *Oberbefehlshaber Suedost* was shifted to Belgrade under Field Marshal Maximilian von Weichs, who also served as commander of a new army group, *HGrF*. Loehr remained commander of *HGrE*. While Weichs and Loehr commanded all tactical operations, the rear areas were placed under the *Militaerbefehlshaber Suedost* (*Mil. Befh. Suedost*—Military Commander Southeast). The branch of this military government in Greece was the *Mil. Befh. Griechenland* (*Mil. Befh. Grld.*—Military Commander Greece), Lt. General Wilhelm Speidel, who held the post until June 1, 1944, when he was replaced by Brigadier General Hans Scheuerlen.[3]

The purpose of the *Mil. Befh. Grld.* was not only to fight the partisans and defend against an Allied landing, but, more importantly, to supervise the Greek government and civil service, secure supplies for the German armed forces, and manage economic material vital to the German war effort.[4] Much of this work had been done by the *Befh. Saloniki-Aegaeis* and *Sued-Grld.* before the reorganization. In pursuing its administrative supervision, Speidel's office received its orders from *Mil. Befh. Suedost*, General Hans Felber, but in any tactical operations he followed the orders of *HGrE*. The Military Commander Greece had four staffs to carry out its work, the *Kommandostab* (Command Staff), *Militaerverwaltungsstab* (*Mil. Verw.*— Military Administration), the *Wehrmachtwirtschaftsstab* (*Wi. Stb. Grld.*—Economic Staff), and the *Hoehe-SS-Polizeifuehrer* (*HSSPF* — Higher SS Police Leader). The *HSSPF* proved to be an independent force, however. *HSSPF* Walther Schimana received his orders directly from *Reichsfuehrer SS* Heinrich Himmler, and he commanded nearly ten times the number of troops under the *Mil. Befh. Grld.* All of the Greek police forces also came under his control. The Military Commander Greece exercised his power through the *Oberfeldkommandantur Saloniki* and nine other regional military governors in Larissa, Lamia, Messolonghi, Chalkis, Ioannina, Athens, Corinth, Crete, and Rhodes. These local commanders were to cooperate with the *HSSPF* in keeping order. Since the Military Commander Greece had only one security battalion to enforce its orders, it became more of a clearing house for orders to the rear areas. It competed with Special Plenipotentiary Neubacher in political and economic affairs. The Military Commander worked closely with the quisling governments, and his control over Greek civilians included violations of listening to foreign broadcasts, illegal possession of firearms, possession of short-wave radios, strikes, anti-German propaganda, membership in outlawed organizations, and sabotage against the German and Greek authorities. Reprisal orders against civilians for anti-German and anti-quisling government acts came from the Military Commander, but others—*HGrE*, *HSSPF*, and Neubacher — also had executive authority to order reprisals. Although technically responsible for peace and security in the rear areas, the shifting nature of the war made it impossible to distinguish between the rear and theaters of war, making the armed forces commanders the supreme authorities. In May 1944, the Peloponnese was declared a theater of war, confusing lines of authority and delaying the making of decisions between the Military Commander and the International Red Cross for supplying the civilian population.[5]

Overlapping the work of the Military Commander were the offices of Plenipotentiary Altenburg and Special Plenipotentiary Neubacher, whose functions were combined in November 1943. Altenburg was responsible for the political, economic, and cultural interests of the Reich with the quisling government until the resumption of full diplomatic relations. He was to be supported by the *Wehrmacht,* and they were to concur on measures for the country as far as the military situation permitted. This led to some confusion. Altenburg and the Foreign Ministry were responsible for propaganda in Greece, but the actual distribution lay in the hands of the *Wehrmacht* propaganda staff. It took one year before this confusion could be cleared up in favor of the military so that the official news agent in Greece, *Deutsche Nachrichten in Griechenland,* could be made public at the same time the Greek newspapers hit the streets.[6] The arrival of Dr. Neubacher on October 15, 1942, with a special charge to restore the faith of the Greeks in the Axis powers by arresting the political and economic deterioration, restricted the military government. Neubacher eventually became responsible for the appointment and dismissal of Greek civil servants, the supply of the civilian population, regulation of wages and prices, regulation of the transportation system, export and import of produce, and management of Greek finances. The *Mil. Befh. Grld.* was concerned with the same problems, and the duplication caused a great deal of friction.[7] In September 1943, a commission made up of two members of Neubacher's staff, two from the *Mil. Befh.* command staff, and one from the *Wehrmachtindendant*, was established to bring unity to the military government, but it failed to resolve the problems.[8] The confusion that emerged is explained in a report by Colonel Klaus Lambert, chief of the *HGrE* economic staff. In execution of his duties, Lambert received orders from the *Mil. Befh. Grld.*, the *Wehrwirtschaftsstab Suedost*, the *Mil. Befh. Suedost*, and *HGrE*. In Greece, economic matters came under the concern of six agencies : Lambert, Neubacher, Speidel, Loehr, the economic staff of the regional military government in Salonica, and the *Wehrmachtindendant*. Lambert claimed it was impossible to make a quick decision on critical problems since no one had clear knowledge of where responsible authority lay and most of the time was spent on working out mutual agreements among the six agencies.[9]

Underneath these various German organizations lay the Greek government, and, until September 1943, the Italians had to be brought in on most of the details of administration. The phrase coined by Alexander Dallin to characterize the administration of German Eastern Occupied Territories aptly describes the administration of Greece, "authoritarian anarchy." [10] Amid this anarchy one power emerged as the dominating force, the Armed Forces Commander. For most of the war the commander was Alexander Loehr, who was *W. B. Suedost* from August 1942-July 1943, and was chief of *HGrE* from January 1943 to October 1944. He became supreme by virtue of the strategic role of Greece, which placed more men under his control and gave him greater authority over all other agencies. The only agent that challenged his authority was *HSSPF* Schimana, who sought after January 1944 to gain control of all anti-partisan operations. This bid led to a sharp but unresolved conflict between Schimana and *HGrE*.[11]

The Economic Catastrophe

In the other occupied countries of Western Europe the Germans followed a pattern of rational exploitation of economic resources when it served their interests. In France, Belgium, the Netherlands, Denmark, and Norway, the German authorities spared the existing economic productive capacity, continued the monetary mechanism, and worked to prevent or control inflation. If the policy of "rational exploitation" offered only minor benefits, however, the Reich resorted to plundering and indifference. Greece and the Ukraine are prime examples of the latter.[12]

Germany had two major economic interests in Greece, foodstuffs and ores. There was only one important munitions factory, the Bodosaki Works near Athens, but since its materials had to be imported, primarily from Germany, its machine tools were dismantled and shipped there, and the buildings were converted into repair shops for the *Luftwaffe*.[13] What happened to the Bodosaki Works happened generally to the Greek economy. Between May 1, 1941, and October 15, 1942, the Reich absorbed nearly every useful economic item and gave little or nothing in return. It became impossible to restore order to the economy after that time. This policy of expropriation was conducted by the *Wehrmachtwirtschaftsstab Suedost* with its two offices in Athens and Salonica (*Wehrwirtschaftsoffizier Athen* and *Wehrwirtschaftsoffizier Saloniki—WO Athen* and *WO Saloniki* respectively). In the general reorganization of August 1943, the two offices were combined to make the *Wehrwirtschaftsstab Griechenland (Wi. Stb. Grld.)*. These economic staffs were under the direct control of *Wehrwirtschafts und Ruestungsamt* of the *OKW (OKW/Wi Rue Amt* — Military, Economic and Armament Officer of the Armed Forces High Command). In Greece, the *WO Athen* and *WO Saloniki* seized and secured the management of all economic materials important to armament and supply of German troops. It was supposed to cooperate with Plenipotentiary Altenburg in this task, but the two offices soon came into conflict.[14]

The entire tobacco crop was seized and purchased at a price fixed at the 1939 level, and dispatched to Germany. On May 21, 1941, what remained of the Greek merchant marine was purchased at 50 percent of its value. Greek business firms were purchased at 60 percent of their value. Leases on ores were purchased at prices fixed by the *WO Athen* and by German metallurgical corporations. These purchases were cleared by a society of German firms known as *DEGRIGES (Deutsch-Griechische Warenausgleich-Gesellschaft)*.[15] All stocks of olive oil, olives, raisins, and figs were seized to either feed the occupation troops or for shipment to Axis troops in North

Africa. The textile industry lost 305 tons of silk cocoons and 5,200 tons of wool before September 1941, crippling one of Greece's most important industries and leaving thousands unemployed. Between May 1 and September 30, 1941, 45,700,000 *Reichsmarks* worth of goods had been exported to Germany, and by the end of the year the total had reached 150,000,000.[16] All these purchases had been made in occupation currency, *Reichkreditkassenscheinen* (RKK), arbitrarily set at a ratio of 1:50 drachmas (drs.). Portable valuables were taken from individuals and homes, and all motor transport was commandeered, making it difficult for the cities to be supplied by normal means.[17]

The Economic Staff viewed the potential of Greece's mineral ores with particular interest: chrome, bauxite, manganese, molybdenum, and nickel were vital in making alloys for munitions. By proper development, they hoped to export enough ore to cover 30 percent of Germany's need for chrome, 15 percent for nickel, and 25 percent for bauxite. The mines were leased by German companies, but the *WO Athen* and *WO Saloniki* (later *Wi. Stb. Grld.*) managed the mines by recruiting labor and securing their wages and food supply.[18] The Germans were quick to secure these ores before the Italians had an opportunity to appropriate them, a fact which explains why the Reich included in its zone the hinterland of Salonica with its important chrome mines. The Italians were left only the lignite and nickel mines. The lignite was needed to supply Athens with fuel.

The early expectations of the *WO Athen* failed to materialize, however. In 1942, the "best" year of the occupation, 62,000 tons of chrome ore came from the mines at Domokos and Tsangli, compared to a total production of 32,000 tons for 1938. Most of this chrome was shipped to Germany. Production dropped drastically in 1943, and only 33,000 tons went to Germany. In 1944, only 31,600 tons made it to the Reich. The main cause of this decline was partisan attacks on the mines and railways. Only 91,000 tons of bauxite were shipped to Germany for the whole period of the occupation as partisans destroyed the mines in March 1943. In 1938, Greece had produced 180,000 tons of bauxite. Only 71,000 tons of nickel went to Germany between 1941 and 1944, and the nickel mines were destroyed in April 1944. The 1938 production of nickel had been 52,370 tons.[19]

The cost of supporting the occupation forces destroyed the financial structure of Greece. Before the war tobacco, olive oil, dried figs, and raisins had been Greece's principal exports. The Axis confiscated these stocks. The merchant marine, which played an important role in bringing revenues into the country, no longer existed. The war closed off cash remittances from Greeks living abroad. These losses made it impossible to pay for the cost of the occupation, which in 1941 amounted to four times the anticipated revenues of the Greek government for the twelve month period after October 1941.[20] Even without incurring the occupation costs, the Greek economy would have had trouble in meeting its commitments. The war of 1940-41 caused a deficit of 4,563,000,000 drachmas for 1940 and 7,516,000,000 drachmas for 1941. The Axis policy of acquisition and false purchasing accelerated the deterioration of the economy and threw it into chaos. Deprived of tax sources and other regular revenues to pay the cost of the occupation, calculated to be 40 percent of the national income for 1941 alone, the quisling governments resorted to printing more drachmas. In 1942, the occupation costs reached 90 percent of the national income. This process began a spiral of inflation that reached fantastic levels before the liberation in October 1944.[21]

Conflict over the costs of the occupation emerged between the Plenipotentiary of the Reich Altenburg and the armed forces almost immediately after the end of hostilities, and the dispute was continued by Altenburg's successor, Dr. Neubacher. The *Wehrmacht* viewed its task as strictly military, and it reported to the *OKW* on July 1, 1941, that it had followed its directives of "non-interference" in political affairs, which were delegated to Altenburg.[22] The *OKW* did not consider its economic exploitation and excessive occupation costs as related to political problems, and it never did concede such a connection until the economic catastrophe pointedly threatened their military position. On the other hand, Altenburg, who worked with the Greek government, became acutely aware of the real condition of Greece and the danger this presented to German interests. His attempts to remedy the situation were in vain, however, as were those of Special Plenipotentiary Neubacher. Neither Altenburg nor Neubacher could move the *OKW* to reduce the occupation costs, or make them see the fundamental role that economic and political stability played in assuring internal order and security.

On September 25, 1941, Altenburg dispatched a clear analysis of the financial problem to the *OKW*. He requested a reduction in the occupation costs to prevent the collapse of the Greek economy. In concluding his report, he appealed to the military interests of the *OKW* by pointing out that the ruination of the Greek economy would be detrimental to the *Wehrmacht's* use of Greece and would lead to the loss of ores and olive oil which were much needed in Germany.[23] He demonstrated how the occupation costs and the issue of the *RKK* and Italian occupation lire forced the amount of drachmas in circulation to increase from 24 billion in July 1941 to 30.7 billion in September 1941, with the *RKK* rising from 6 million to 100 million for the same period.

The *OKW's* reply became the standard response of the occupation period. The *OKW*, Keitel answered, was concerned about the inflation in all the occupied countries, but the occupation costs had to be paid, and the printing of drachmas was unavoidable. He advised the Greeks to combat their inflation in the way the Germans did, through price and wage controls.[24]

As the occupation costs rose, the government presses moved to meet the new demand, causing prices to rise as the flow of drachmas increased. This in turn forced occupation costs up, causing a new cycle. By this process, the amount of drachmas in circulation rocketed to astronomical figures as the course of the war increased the *Wehrmacht's* demands on Greece. In July 1941, the amount of drachmas in circulation reached 24 billion; December 1941, 49 billion; December 1942, 306 billion; June 1943, 550 billion; and December 1943, 3.1 trillion. In the last month of the German occupation, October 1944, the *Wehrmacht's* demands grew to 50 billion drachmas daily! The government presses turned out four to five hundred billion drachmas each day! The resulting inflation was catastrophic.[25]

Only for one period did the Germans temporarily check the rampant inflation. On October 15, 1942, Hitler appointed Dr. Hermann Neubacher, the former Nazi mayor of Vienna and an expert on the Balkans, as Special Plenipotentiary for Greece.[26] Neubacher had full authority to deal with all economic and financial matters, and even the military were ordered to cooperate fully with him. On October 19, 1942, Neubacher ordered the complete halt of the export of foodstuffs from Greece and restricted purchases of the Axis armed forces. The rampant inflation is revealed in Table I. To reduce the occupation costs, Neubacher began a series of negotiations to arrange for the *Wehrmacht* to import its building materials from Germany. To improve the housing situation, he requested that the armed forces, especially the officers, move out of their

TABLE I
DATES AND COST IN DRACHMAS

Item per oka*	10/1/40	9/1/42	10/1/43	1/1/44	4/1/44	9/1/44
Bread	10	7,000	13,000	34,000	460,000	34,000,000
Cheese	60	44,000	120,000	600,000	6,000,000	1,160,000,000
Olive oil	50	30,000	80,000	200,000	2,800,000	400,000,000
Olives	26	7,000	22,000	80,000	1,200,000	400,000,000
Shoes (pr.)	450	300,000	800,000	–	–	2,204,000,000

* 2.82 lbs.

requisitioned living quarters in order to free dwellings for the civilian population. The Special Plenipotentiary realized that these measures alone were inadequate, and he knew the situation would improve only if he could secure adequate food supplies for the population. Help in this area came from the International Red Cross mission, whose goods began to flow into Greece at a steady rate in October 1942. Neubacher was able to bring in limited amounts of dried vegetables, potatoes, and sugar from Germany and southeastern Europe.[27]

The total amount of foodstuffs imported by Germany into Greece for the whole period of the occupation was as follows: 1941-42, 56,000 tons of grain; 1942-43, 20,000 tons of wheat, 30,000 tons of dried vegetables, 12,000 tons of sugar, 20,000 tons of potatoes; and 1943-44, 23,000 tons of dried vegetables and 5,000 tons of sugar.

Through these measures, Neubacher hoped to restore the confidence of the Greeks in the Axis authorities and bring about stability in the economy. Neubacher's action, plus the International Red Cross food, secured a 50 percent drop in prices of food, which had reached levels 600 to 800 percent higher than the prewar level. The gold pound, which stood at a ratio of 1:375 drachmas before the war, had reached a ratio of 1:600,000 drachmas, dropped slightly and held steady for about five months. The Germans also credited the Allied victory in North Africa as a stabilizing force by raising hopes among the Greeks of an early return of the Allies to Greece. The *Wehrmacht*, however, exempted itself from Neubacher's controls and, by separate negotiations, reserved the right to set the occupation costs as it saw fit. It never agreed to import adequate building materials from Germany, which was one of the larger items of the costs, and it did not free the dwellings as requested by Neubacher. The victories of the Allies in North Africa caused a threat to the Balkans, and a build-up of military forces there in 1943 forced occupation costs to rise even higher.[28] Unable to prevent the military from increasing the occupation costs, Neubacher attempted a scheme to reduce and control the inflation by turning the black market into a free market. In May 1943, he began a policy of selling gold at the rate of four million *Reichsmarks* per month on the Athens bourse, which until then had technically been illegal, as a means of curbing the speculation and stabilizing the drachma. The scheme had limited success. The gold pound dropped from a ratio of 1:540,000 drachmas to 1:340,000 drachmas between May and July 1943. The military build-up which Hitler initiated during the same period, however, raised costs at a faster rate than before. Even the scheme for selling gold could never cover these costs for more than two-thirds of the amount needed at any one time. The gold resources of Neubacher declined so rapidly that only two million gold *Reichsmarks* were available after January 1944, and the scheme was reduced in May of that year. While the occupation costs pushed up the cost of living, wages and salaries fell by over 1,000 percent.[29] By September 1944, the ratio of the gold pound to drachmas was 1:8,100,000. Putting an end to this chaos became the great burden of Great Britain at the liberation, and eventually it required massive United States aid.

The Famine

Before the Second World War, even in the most productive years, Greece had to import between 400,000 and 500,000 tons of grain annually. It would not be self-sufficient in grains until the early 1960's. The Axis occupation shut off the normal means of securing this vital balance. The situation worsened with the poor harvest of 1941, which produced less than half the normal average. The Axis acquisition of food stocks intensified the crisis, and the division of the country into three zones of occupation complicated supplying the civilian population. Though the Bulgarian zone of eastern Macedonia and Thrace held only 11 percent of Greece's population, it produced 40 percent of Greece's domestic wheat, 60 percent of its rye,

60 percent of its eggs, 50 percent of its legumes, and 80 percent of its butter. Before the war, the balance of foodstuffs for internal needs was imported from Canada, Australia, and the United States. Shortly before the German invasion, the Greek government had ordered and paid for 47,000 tons of grain from Australia to cover the country's needs through the summer of 1941. At the time of the capitulation, the ships carrying the grain reached Suez, but they did not proceed any further. The failure of this wheat to reach Greece created an immediate food crisis.

Before the end of April 1941, the German military and political authorities knew the situation was critical. The Bulgarians, in a reign of terror to "Bulgarize" the Greek population in their zone, suppressed Greek schools and confiscated Greek property. In Kavalla, seven hundred shops were expropriated. The Bulgarians imprisoned Greeks, and even forced many of them to change their names. The Bulgarian occupation provoked a rebellion in Drama on September 28, 1941. In retaliation, the Bulgarians executed thousands of people, and over 25,000 Greeks fled toward the German zone around Salonica.[30] Well aware of the Bulgarian action, the Germans did not expect them to deliver any grain to the Reich's zones, which were heavily populated urban areas. The population of the Athens-Piraeus area nearly doubled its prewar figure as a consequence of people fleeing the war zones. The *Wehrmacht* Economic Officer in Athens estimated that Greece would need 500,000 tons of grain for the twelve-month period from July 1941 to July 1942, but provided no clue to solving the problem. The Germans did not believe that Great Britain would lift the blockade and allow the grain at Suez to pass on to Piraeus, and the propaganda section of the *Wehrmacht* began at an early date to blame Britain for the crisis and the famine to come. The newly installed government of General Tsolakoglou hoped the loss of the previously ordered wheat could be made up from Germany, Rumania, and southern Russia. If these sources could not be secured, recorded the Economic Officer in Athens, famine, which had already begun to appear by the first of July, would become widespread.[31]

On May 7, 1941, when only a twenty-four-day supply of grain stocks remained, Altenburg informed the Foreign Ministry and the *OKW* that a famine would develop if the food gap was not closed, and he requested orders for dealing with the situation. In Berlin, discussions were held among representatives of the High Command of the Army (*OKH*), the Reich Ministry for Agriculture, the Reich Bank, and the Reich Ministry of Economics. The reply to Altenburg of May 15, 1941, flatly ordered him to reject any request for grain from Germany and informed him that deliveries from Russia were not feasible.[32] Under no circumstances, the reply continued, was the area under the Italians to be supplied by Germany. The Reich accepted responsibility only for its zones, which contained the largest concentration of population and were the least able to feed themselves. Later, on October 9, 1941, Hitler would assign to the Italians full responsibility for feeding all of Greece.

As part of their acquisitions of May and June, the Germans "bought" the British-owned Kopais Corporation, a land company which had developed the Kopais area near Athens through scientific agriculture and irrigation. The Germans planned to use it as a model colonial school for Balkan agriculture and to have it feed the population of Athens. Both expectations failed. The 1941 yield in the Kopais was half its normal production since, in the face of forced requisitions, the peasants secured their own needs first and held up the export of goods from the area. Although Greek police covered the whole region, only 30 percent of anticipated deliveries to the authorities were collected in face of the passive resistance.[33]

Altenburg tried to ameliorate the food crisis by requesting 10,000 tons of grain for July and August, but the Reich Ministry of Agriculture refused. Only after reports from Altenburg and the *Wehrmacht* in Greece indicated that the economic crisis threatened Germany's military interests did the Reich Ministry for Food release for shipment to Greece 10,000 tons of grain consigned to Germany from the Banat. The Italians were asked to send another 10,000 tons. Negotiations got underway to raise 40,000 tons to cover the need for October to December 1941 from among Italy, Germany, Hungary, Rumania, Bulgaria, and Turkey. The same group was to try to raise another 90,000 tons for the first half of 1942. Bulgaria announced, however, that it would not spare any grain for Greece. Germany lost interest in the project after it learned that Britain was negotiating with Turkey to allow some food to go to Greece. The Germans told Altenburg that the Greeks could not expect any more grain from Germany after the last segment of its 10,000 tons reached Athens on September 12, 1941. The Reich Ministry emphasized in its report to Altenburg that since Belgium, Norway, and Holland were more important than Greece to the military economy, they would come first in any consideration for food deliveries.[34] Thus, Italy became responsible for feeding the Greeks.[35] Berlin remained unimpressed by Altenburg's dispatches describing the effects of the occupation costs on the financial structure, or the fact that Greece was one of the poorest European nations, with a large war debt and growing inflation.[36]

By the first week of October 1941, the famine that had been predicted in May became acute. All grain stocks in Greece were empty. The normal bread ration of 200 grams per capita per day fell to 96 grams. The plan to bring in 40,000 tons of grain failed to materialize, and the bread ration dropped further during November and December.[37]

When Mussolini learned that Hitler had made Italy responsible for feeding the Greeks, he told Ciano, with some justification, "The Germans have taken from the Greeks even their shoelaces, and now they pretend to place the blame for the economic situation on our shoulders." Then he added that he would accept the responsibility if Germany would "clear out" and leave Greece to the Italians.[38] The Italians tried to pressure the Bulgarians, who occupied the most productive regions of Greece, to send 100,000 tons of grain, but the Bulgarians refused. Pressure from Germany also failed to move the Bulgarians.[39] The Bulgarians, however, did join the Ella-Turk society along with Yugoslavia, Rumania, and Turkey. In the winter of 1941-42, these nations made critical deliveries of dried vegetables, rice, and sugar totaling 3,450 tons.[40]

After learning of Bulgaria's refusal, the Italians dispatched 800 tons of grain, and the Germans released a second 10,000 tons. Unfortunately, the ship carrying half of the German shipment was sunk by the British off the coast of Greece. Altenburg requested another 10,000 tons on November 11, 1941, which was available in the Banat, but the military failed to release the necessary transportation to take it to Athens. By November 15, 1941, only a three-week supply, rated on a 92 gram ration per day, remained.[41]

The famine hit Athens and Salonica hard in the winter of 1941 and 1942. It did not relent until the last quarter of 1942, as the International Red Cross began significant deliveries of food relief in October 1942. In 1939, bread consumption per capita for 7.3 million Greeks stood at 179 kilograms. In 1941, with 6.4 million Greeks in the German and Italian zones, the figure declined to 100 kilograms, and in 1942 it fell to 40 kilograms. The severe famine from January to March 1942 accounts for the sharp drop for that year. *Wehrmacht* officials recorded a death rate of 300 per day in Athens for December 1941. The figures of the International Red Cross (IRC) explain the situation graphically presented in Table II.[42] Table III is a comparative listing of the number of deaths for all of Greece for 1940, 1941, and 1942.

TABLE II

NUMBER OF DEATHS BASED ON INTERNATIONAL
RED CROSS FIGURES

Region	Sept.-Nov. 1941	Dec.-Jan. 1941-42	March-May 1942	June-July 1942
Athens and Surrounding Localities	8,896	20,244	13,620	8,849
Central Greece and Euboea	696	1,789	1,700	1,145
Peloponnese	1,461	2,956	2,410	2,402
Thessaly	534	1,347	1,504	1,236
Macedonia	1,195	2,771	2,246	2,399
Epirus	189	313	286	275
Crete	382	458	354	333
Islands	1,373	3,640	2,788	1,487

TABLE III

COMPARATIVE LISTING OF THE NUMBER OF DEATHS FOR ALL
OF GREECE FOR 1940, 1941, AND 1942

Month	1940	1941-1942
September	1,907	3,196
October	2,052	4,268
November	2,473	7,262
December	3,372	11,207
January		11,715
February		10,957
March		10,586
April		7,962
May		6,091

These figures point out that the areas which suffered the most were Athens and the islands (Mytilene in particular among the latter), while the rural regions, Epirus and Central Greece, were the least affected. On the mainland, in order to protect their own areas, the Axis prohibited the export of food from their respective zones, which made it difficult to move the small surplus in the rural areas to urban centers. The lack of transport held up even the meager supplies available for the islands. The average caloric intake of a laborer before the war ranged between 2,500-3,000 calories per day. In the winter of 1941-1942, it dropped to 875, and it rarely rose above 1,300 for the period after October 1942.[43]

The Germans did not try to respond seriously to this crisis until the fall of 1942. The impact of this failure on Germany's position in Greece was recorded by Altenburg in a dispatch to his superiors on January 14, 1943. The Plenipotentiary reported, with some exaggeration, that ninety-five percent of the Greeks supported Germany soon after the capitulation and would have provided strong support in Germany's struggle against communism if there had been an enlightened German occupation policy. Instead, concluded Altenburg, by January 1943, ninety percent of the population opposed Germany, in large part because of the exploitation of the country by the Axis.[44] This exploitation was to be a significant factor in explaining the rise of the Greek resistance movement. Altenburg exaggerated the pro-German feeling of the Greek people, but he accurately summed up the attitude of the leadership of the nation at that time. Soon after the invasion of Russia, General Georgios Bakos, who was Minister of Defense in the quisling government, a former friend of Metaxas, and a hero on the Albanian front, wanted to raise a Greek Legion to fight on the Russian front.[45]

Food and medical supplies came from neutral countries via Turkey, with encouragement from Britain. The Turks provided enough supplies to keep the soup kitchens of Athens and Piraeus in operation for the winter of 1941-42, feeding about 150,000 persons daily. The famine, however, was too great to be solved by these token measures, and the Turks soon had difficulty in feeding their own population. For this reason, Turkey had to cut off its supply of grain to Greece in January 1942. The plight of the Greeks in the winter of 1941-42, however, elicited an international response to feed the civilian population. The International Red Cross established a Greek mission in the late summer of 1942, and a High Committee, made up of representatives from the Swiss, Greek, German, and Italian Red Cross, and the Turkish Red Crescent, supervised the distribution of medical supplies and a limited quantity of foodstuffs through its Action Committee, made up of Swiss and Greek representatives.

The United States government, very concerned over the situation created by the famine, which German propaganda blamed on the British blockade, asked the British government to confirm or deny the German charges on December 3, 1941.[46] While waiting for the British to reply, Washington received a series of desperate pleas from the Greek government-in-exile that the United States take action to relieve the famine. In response, Washington requested the Turkish government to explore the means of increasing the supply of food to Greece. After waiting for one month without any response from London, the American ambassador, Frederick Winant, received instructions to "please expedite" a reply on January 5, 1942. The British reply from Foreign Secretary Anthony Eden finally came on January 13, 1942: [47]

> I can ... give you the facts as regards the Axis propaganda story that we are preventing the dispatch to Greece of wheat bought by the Greek Government. There were at the time of the occupation of Greece several cargoes of wheat and flour afloat which had been purchased by the Greek Government. ... The situation was fully discussed at all stages with Greek authorities ... and it was agreed that His Majesty's Government should take over the cargoes of cereals owned by the Greek Government at the free on board price paid by them. It was also agreed that should any of the cargoes be required for the purposes of the Greek Government in unoccupied territory or for the Greek forces, they could be released for that purpose. At no time was any objection raised to this arrangement by any Greek authority. ... The cargoes in question have of course long been disposed of by the Middle East Supply Center.
>
> As the Greek authorities acted throughout of their own free will in the arrangements made as regards these cargoes we have so far thought it best not to broadcast the full facts of the case in answer to the

Axis stories since we do not wish to cause any possible embarrassment to the Greek Government. It is, however, obvious that Allied shipping could not proceed to enemy occupied ports and the arrangements agreed upon between ourselves and the Greek Government were clearly necessary and reasonable.

Considering Germany's record of wholesale requisitioning during the summer of 1941, the British fear of letting this grain pass on to Greece appeared justified, but why did it take Britain so long to answer the American request? London objected to any direct shipment of any goods to Greece, but it was willing to let neutrals ship goods to Greece on a small scale through Turkey. Britain's main concern remained strategic; the Axis, not Britain, were responsible for feeding the populations in territories they occupied, and the blockade would not be lifted to aid any occupied country. By the end of January, however, realization of the full horror and extent of the famine in Greece induced the government in London to ship 8,000 tons of grain through the blockade and to try to remove 2,000 children to Turkey. London soon realized that 8,000 tons were inadequate, and the plan for removal of the children failed to materialize.[48]

On February 22, 1942, Britain informed the United States that it was willing to lift the blockade and initiate a major relief scheme for Greece. Concerned over the precedent of lifting the blockade for an occupied country, London insisted that Sweden appear as the originator of the action, and that Sweden be the controlling power over organization and distribution of the relief food. The United States joined the British on March 2 in asking the Swedish government to undertake the relief program. The Swedish Foreign Minister, Erik Boheman, and Prince Karl, chief of the Swedish Red Cross, contacted the Axis on March 19. The Allied proposal, or the "Swedish plan," had four essential points: (1) safe conduct for ships engaged in carrying foodstuffs to and from Greece; (2) a neutral commission to direct the distribution of the relief goods; (3) foodstuffs originating in Greece to be reserved exclusively for Greeks, and, if the Axis consumed any of them, to be replaced by imports from Germany or Italy; and (4) the commission's right to verify by free, direct inspection that the conditions were being observed.[49]

The Italians responded favorably on April 7. On April 27, this was followed by an even more favorable reply from

Germany. A quick settlement for immediate implementation of the relief program did not occur, however. Differences between Britain and the Axis over the composition of the relief commission took over three months to resolve. The London government distrusted the IRC, and it insisted that Sweden be responsible for the execution of the relief program. The Rome government, on the other hand, desired the program to be under the supervision of an expanded IRC High Commission which would include the Swedish representatives with the Greek, Turkish, German, Italian, and Swiss already on the committee. The Swedish minister, Boheman, worked out a compromise which was finally accepted by all parties. Pressured by the United States and world opinion, Britain accepted Boheman's plan to establish an Action Committee made up of Swedish and Greek members exclusively, and to make the Action Committee solely responsible for organizing and distributing the relief supplies. This committee eventually regulated the allocation of grain inside Greece and issued new ration cards to the civilian population. The original IRC High Committee acted as a liaison between the Action Committee and the Axis and the Allies. The High Committee's role with the Axis was vital, as the relief commission depended on the Axis, and later Germany, to provide 74 vehicles for the transportation of goods.[50]

The relief mission of the International Red Cross supplied Greece at the rate of 15,000 tons of grain and 3,000 tons of dried vegetables per month for the period of the occupation and the first five months of the liberation. The cost was originally assumed by the Greek government-in-exile and the private Greek War Relief organization. Since they were unable to continue with this burden, the United States accepted the responsibility after January 1, 1943. The relief commission prevented a repetition of the catastrophe of the winter of 1941-42 on a larger scale during the winters of 1942-43 and 1943-44. Estimates in the summer of 1942 anticipated one million deaths if relief did not come from the outside before winter set in.

The Axis, well aware of the critical situation, realized that outside help was imperative to prevent political and military collapse as well as economic chaos. The amount of the bread ration acted as a political barometer. Even the slightest delay, eight months after relief goods began arriving in Greece, caused a drop of thirty grams in the daily bread ration of Athens. As the ration rose and fell, political agitation against the Axis followed inversely.[51] Under these conditions, the Axis powers were anxious to cooperate with the relief mission, and they did not hinder the flow of relief. The German Foreign Office and Neubacher played a vital role in assuring cooperation with the mission in spite of contrary orders from Berlin during the last months of the occupation.[52] The German military always suspected that the IRC acted as an agent of Allied espionage but admitted that the political benefits of the relief far outweighed its risks.[53]

Labor

As a small, poor European nation, Greece did not offer Germany any significant prospects in rich sources of skilled labor. Nevertheless, as the German economy geared for total mobilization in 1942, even Greece's meager supply became important to the Germans. Inside Greece, the *Wi. Rue. Amt.* struggled to recruit labor to increase the production of chrome, bauxite, and nickel. The *Wehrmacht* needed labor for building defenses and maintaining airfields and roads. The recruitment of labor for export to Germany operated through the German Foreign Ministry office in Greece in cooperation with Dr. Fritz Todt, Minister of Armaments and Munitions and the Reich Ministry of Labor. The economic staffs of the *Wehrmacht* filled the needs inside Greece.

The German authorities looked upon these labor requirements as beneficial to Greece by helping to solve the great unemployment problem produced by the war and German methods of requisitioning. In the summer of 1941, the city of Salonica (with a population of 250,000) had over 30,000 unemployed and thousands more underemployed. The textile industry of the city operated on a two-day work week for lack of materials to feed its machines. For those who did work, prices soon outstripped wages. The Germans realized this situation could produce severe political problems for the occupation forces, and they were as interested in a solution to that situation as they were in meeting labor quotas for German industry.[54] The authorities expected to raise 30,000 laborers for export to Germany in 1942. The war, famine, unemployment, and the absence of strong organized resistance to the program made 1942 the best year for labor recruitment in Greece, but the number fell far below the anticipated total.

The 1942 recruitment was carried out on a voluntary basis, and netted 11,977 laborers, twenty percent of whom were women. The 1942 program was unique in two ways. It was the highest total for any year of the occupation, and it was the last large voluntary program.[55] The number of volunteer laborers indicated that even with the attractiveness that Germany offered to the suffering Greeks in the first three-quarters of 1942 (high wages and return trips to Greece), the Greeks preferred to stay at home. Whatever pro-German sympathies the population may have had before April 1941 vanished during the winter of 1941-42. As the tide turned against Germany in the winter of 1942-43, any attractiveness that jobs in Germany may have had decreased, and strong resistance to all kinds of recruitment emerged. These two factors, and particularly the second, made it impossible for the authorities to fulfill either quotas for Germany or for occupied Greece.

When the voluntary program failed, the authorities ended it on November 1, 1942, and resorted to forced recruitment. On February 1, 1943, *Oberbefehlshaber Suedost* Loehr ordered all men between the ages of 16 and 45 to register for labor service. All of those registered who did not have jobs vital to the *Wehrmacht* were liable for service in Greece. Those who failed to comply with the order faced punishments of heavy fines, imprisonment, or forced labor.[56] The order was necessitated by the changing military situation, which was once again making Greece and the Balkans figure prominently in the strategy of both sides. The chief need for labor in Greece lay in construction, repair, and mining.

In November 1942, recruitment of miners ran into difficulty as partisans attacked bauxite and chrome mines, forcing the miners to flee, while fear of further attacks deterred their return.[57] The order of February 1, 1943, mobilizing civilian labor, spawned a series of successful demonstrations and strikes in Athens and Piraeus which manifested the growing power of the Greek resistance. The strikes forced occupation authorities to grant retroactive wage hikes and to suspend the collection of laborers until June. To repair the rail lines, the Germans had to import over 300 laborers from Croatia.[58] The authorities raised only 2,653 laborers for Germany in 1943 and only 2,029 for the first half of 1944. By November 1943, even forced labor could not meet the *Wehrmacht's* needs for occupied Greece. The German army relieved the situation by turning to forced, unpaid Italian labor.[59] Not more than 15,000

Greeks were dispatched to Germany during the occupation, two-thirds of whom were sent in 1942. In occupied Greece, close to 166,000 laborers were coerced into service by a combination of high salaries, extra food rations, and compulsory methods. Over 90,000 of these were forced into service after January 1943. After September 1943, only compulsory methods could fill the *Wehrmacht's* quota, and, by June 1944, even forcible methods failed.[60]

The Collaborationist Governments

Guided by General Georgios Tsolakoglou, who had capitulated to the Germans on April 21, 1941, the Metaxas generals who did not follow the King into exile formed the first collaborationist government of the occupation on April 28, 1941. Not one of the members of this generals' cabinet had any particular political talents for governing in normal times, much less so under the crises of the Axis occupation. General Tsolakoglou headed the government as Minister President. The security police came under General Nikolaos Markou. Markou had failed to distinguish himself in the war against Italy. His chief political talents lay in his friendship with the late dictator Metaxas and in the fact that he headed the Greek mission to Germany in 1938 to purchase arms for the Greek army. General Georgios Bakos, who had distinguished himself in the Italian war, became Minister of Defense. Lesser known officers filled all the other positions except two. The portfolio of Minister of Economics took some time to fill. Professor Doctor Logothetopoulos, the second quisling premier, headed the Ministry of Welfare.[61]

The lackluster political quality of the cabinet appealed to German Foreign Minister Ribbentrop, who was responsible for political problems in Greece. In a cable to Altenburg, he declared that Germany did not want "energetic personalities" in power for the simple reason that they might cause trouble for the Reich. As long as Tsolakoglou "kept the Greek machinery working," continued Ribbentrop, Germany preferred to leave things as they were.[62] In theory, the Italians were responsible for building the Greek goverment, but, as in so many other areas, the Germans held the decisive power. Altenburg's task was to keep the Italians in check if they pushed for vigorous Greek leadership. The main function of the Greek "machinery" was to aid the Axis in the political and economic ruin of Greece. Another major interest of the occupation authorities lay in the Greek police forces. As the Germans were short on security forces, they considered Greek cooperation in this area indispensable. As the war progressed and the resistance developed, the Greek government and its forces became an essential part of counterinsurgency warfare. As the resistance heightened in the winter of 1942-43, the Germans searched hard for energetic figures to firm up the Greek government and to join in the fight against "bolshevism," which they equated with all forms of resistance.

Three different points of view motivated the collaborators. The Greek Nazis accounted for the first but least significant group of collaborators. The Greek Fascist Party had been founded in 1931 by Ioannis Giannaris. It remained a small group with less than 50,000 supporters, but it had some prominent Greeks in its leadership: Spyros Betsaris, an Epirot politician; Pericles Kacdas, a former minister to Germany and Governor General of Thrace during the Metaxas regime; and Franz Potares, a Vice Admiral, constituted the leadership of the party along with Giannaris. In a telegram to Hitler soon after the capitulation, they apologized for Greece having been seduced by "Anglo-Jewish propaganda" to resist Germany in the war.[63] Giannaris's group had rivals, and the Greek Fascists, like the other parties, suffered from disunity. There was a small group in Salonica known as the *Ethnike Enosis Ellados* (EEE–National Union of Greece), and other groups headed by Georgios Merkoures, a former politician, General Bakos, and Dr. Spyros Sterodemas. In the summer of 1941 most of the splinter groups except the EEE merged to form the *Ethniko-Sosialistike Patriotike Organosis* (ESPO–National Socialist Political Organization). Dr. Sterodemas became chief of the new party.

Stereodemas turned to fascism after a scandal over tolls charged by prostitutes, whom the doctor had supervised as a member of Metaxas' medical board, forced him to resign. Stereodemas linked Nazism to the laws of Lycurgus and Plato's philosophy. Since Lycurgus and Plato were Greek, their descendants in the twentieth century could become great by reapplying these old principles. The movement failed to generate popular support. On September 22, 1942, Kostas Perrikos, a young anti-Nazi, entered the office of ESPO, and blew it up. Sterodemas, who was inside the building, was among the people killed. The following month, EEE experienced a similar attack.[64] The Germans encouraged the fascist movements as potential allies in their struggle against communism, but they found other collaborators more efficient and useful. In a prison interview after the war, Tsolakoglou justified his actions, saying that it was better to have had a Greek government acting as a buffer between the *OKW* and the population.[65] Tsolakoglou, however, failed to fulfill his role. On the crucial issue of the occupation costs, he failed to support his own finance minister, Soteris Gotzamanes, in a showdown with the Germans in November 1942. In the light of the winter of 1941-42, Tsolakoglou's statement is incomprehensible. The Germans dropped him in November 1942, replacing him with Dr. Constantinos Logothetopoulos.

Logothetopoulos, who had been a gynecologist at the University of Athens and was Vice Premier in the first quisling government, became premier as a compromise candidate. The Italians had wanted Gotzamanes while the Germans had proposed Ioannis Rallis. The Germans believed Rallis would do the better job in rallying nationalist support against communism, that is to say, the resistance. In view of the adverse course of the war in the Mediterranean, German officials in Greece now felt compelled to search for "energtic leaders" who could galvanize "nationalist," anticommunist support for the occupation powers.[66] In the winter of 1942-43, former royalist and republican officers and politicians became alarmed over the growing influence of "bolshevism" in the resistance and prepared to join the Axis in combating the dominant resistance organization, *Ethniko Apeleutherotiko Metopo/Ellenikos Laikos Apeleutherotikos Stratos* (EAM/ELAS–National Liberation Front/Greek Popular Liberation Army). This fight against communism enlisted a large following, and it became the *raison d'être* for the majority of the collaborators.

The Logothetopoulos cabinet included most of the members of the former government (Generals Bakos, Markou, Moutousis, and Tavoulares for example), but it was no more successful than the government it replaced. The Germans tolerated it until April 6, 1943. Then, as part of a general tightening up of the defenses in the southeast, they replaced Logothetopoulos with Ioannis Rallis. Rallis, who had been a deputy leader to Metaxas, had a long-standing reputation as an anticommunist. The third quisling Premier did not disappoint the Germans, who, even if they were not impressed with his administrative skill and were skeptical of his political contacts with Greek exiled politicians, praised him at the end of the occupation as the "courageous and hard fighter against communism." [67] Rallis organized the Security Battalions to counter EAM/ ELAS, and he defended his actions after the war by claiming that King George II's amnesty for all political prisoners in 1941 excluded the communists.[68] Rallis dropped most of the generals of the previous governments and replaced them with civilians. Anastassios Tavoulares moved up to the Ministry of the Interior. Hector Tsironikos headed the Ministry of Finance, while Nicholas Louvares took over the Ministry of Education. Constantinos Pournaras became Minister of Justice.[69]

Ironically, Rallis did not originate the idea of forming Greek units to battle the "communists." This plan came from General Pangalos and his entourage of right-wing antiroyalists. Pangalos had been playing the role of a gray eminence in Greek politics since 1942. He was responsible for getting Tavoulares and Louvares named to the Rallis government, and he had his protégé, Colonel Leonidis Dertilis, named commander of the newly recruited battalions. Pangalos never doubted an eventual Allied victory, but he and his followers feared that Great Britain would thereafter impose George II on Greece. To foil this British maneuver, Pangalos needed a base of strength inside Greece. This he planned to build by arming units made up of republican anticommunists. He expected the plan to satisfy the Germans, while at the same time providing him with the means to seize power when the Germans retreated. With the anticommunist republicans in control, the King would be prevented from returning.[70] Toward this end, he had a conference with the German police authorities in March 1943, but the Germans distrusted Pangalos and turned to Rallis.[71]

Rallis revised Pangalos's proposal by using fanatical royalist officers instead of republicans, and, according to PRO documents, he pressured other reluctant officers to join by threatening them with loss of their benefits.[72] In a postwar interview with Byford-Jones, a former commander of one of the battalions revealed the ultra-royalism of these units. When asked by Byford-Jones what the best solution to Greece's problems in 1945 would be, the former commander shot back, the return of King George.[73] Rallis's contacts with royalists stemmed from his past political connections. The very existence of these contacts with army officers and politicians in exile, as well as with men like General Constantinos Venderes and Papagos, who remained in Greece but eschewed political activity, caused the Germans to mistrust Rallis at first, but he soon overcame this handicap by his vigorous anticommunism.[74]

The term "Security Battalions" covered a range of collaborationist units under the command of *HSSPF* Walther Schimana. Thirteen different types of units were armed by the *Wehrmacht*. They totaled 16,625 officers and men by the summer of 1944. The Germans and the quisling government referred to its best units as Evzone Battalions, recalling the elite units of the Greek army. The Germans formed five of these units of about 1,000 men each, and they totaled 532 officers, 656 noncommissioned officers, and 4,536 rank and file. These Evzone units were concentrated in the Peloponnese at Sparta, Pyrgos, Kalamata, Tripolis, and Patras, but sometimes they shifted to Athens and its surrounding area for anti-partisan operations. They were armed with Italian weapons, and they never lacked a supply of recruits, particularly from the Peloponnese. In the winter of 1943-44, the Germans authorized four more Evzone battalions, which operated in central and southeastern Greece (Evrytania, Thessaly, Boeotia, Euboea, and Attica), while ten smaller irregular units served the Germans in Macedonia. Supporting these units were assassination squads that received lists of "communists" from the Germans and the Security Battalions. They operated in small teams and wore plain clothes. When acting as a unit, they wore green armbands. These were first organized in March 1944, and within one month they had murdered fifty EAM/ELAS supporters in the Volos area.[75] The first regular units that were formed in Macedonia proved ineffective against ELAS and were disarmed. The Germans found greater reliability in anti-KKE irregular bands. The four Greek units in central and southeastern Greece received support from two battalions of Italian volunteers who had chosen to join the Reich after the surrender of Italy on September 9, 1943. These Greek and Italian battalions were used in anti-partisan operations quite extensively after January 1944 as well as in regular police work. Their duties included carrying out reprisals against the civilian population for anti-German actions of the resistance. They proved extremely useful in holding down German *SS* and *Wehrmacht* casualties. For the period September 1, 1943 to September 1, 1944, *HSSPF* Schimana recorded casualties as shown in Table IV.

TABLE IV
HSSPF CASUALTY FIGURES

	Dead	Wounded	Missing
German (SS)	69	130	170
Italian	23	24	130
Greek (Security Battalions)	637	910	586

For the same period Schimana counted 3,308 dead, 1,750 captured, and 3,258 arrests on the side of the Greek resistance. The number of dead among the resistance does not differentiate between those killed in action and those shot as hostages.[76]

Colonel Dionysios Papadongonas, who commanded the Security Battalions in the Peloponnese, received a special commendation of gratitude from Hitler and Himmler for his services to the Reich.[77] The colonel turned to the Germans after he failed in an attempt to form a right-wing resistance group of former officers of royalist sympathies in the summer of 1943—ELAS dissolved it in August of that year.[78] The colonel's efforts to take to the mountains appeared as a belated effort on the part of royalists to organize resistance, which until then they had disavowed.[79]

The Security Battalions played an important role in covering the retreat of the *Wehrmacht* from the Peloponnese in September 1944. Fierce battles took place between ELAS and the Battalions, which chose to stay behind in an unsuccessful attempt to prevent EAM/ELAS from taking the towns of the Peloponnese. The Germans regretted that they were unable to supply them effectively with weapons and munitions after they had withdrawn to the north.[80] EAM/ELAS vengeance was particularly brutal at the battle of Pyrgos. The Evzone Battalions' field commander, *SS Standartenfuehrer* (Colonel) Hermann Franz, recently praised them as enthusiastic and brave soldiers who were all too ready to die for their cause.[81] The quisling units in Macedonia served a similar purpose in covering the German retreat from Greece in October 1944.[82]

The success of the Security Battalions failed to be matched in raising regular police forces. The occupation authorities found it much easier to find Greeks willing to fight "communist" partisans than to do routine police work. Attempts to draft

persons for police duty failed, and the Germans attributed it
to EAM/ELAS propaganda.[83] One might conclude, however,
that the fight against communism had more appeal than just
working for the Germans.

After the autumn of 1942, the anticommunist crusade
against EAM/ELAS replaced the anti-British theme of German propaganda. Until then, Great Britain was the butt of
most of the propaganda. It was held responsible for forcing
Greece into the war and then abandoning its ally, causing the
famine, and holding only the prospect of further exploitation
of the country. Black marketeers became "anglophiles." Following the German defeats at El Alamein and Stalingrad,
the German and quisling propaganda line shifted. While Germany was presented as being responsible for the improvement
in food provisioning, capitalizing on the work of the relief
mission of the IRC, bolshevism was identified as the great
threat not only for Greece but all of Europe. The propaganda
pictured Britain supporting "bolshevik hordes" in Soviet Russia's bid to seize Central Europe. It stressed that partisans
were bandits and plunderers in the pay of Great Britain, and
that support for the resistance expanded communism. The
propaganda theme after January 1943 became "Balkan solidarity" under German leadership to smash bolshevism.[84]

The Greek government newspapers followed this theme, and
they incessantly proclaimed that an Allied victory would
produce a victory for communism by spreading "pan-Slavism"
to the Aegean. The Greek government propaganda organs emphasized that EAM/ELAS was a tool of international communism and that it had used patriotism and nationalism to gain
the support of the Greek people. The newspapers appealed to
those who had been attracted to EAM/ELAS to renounce communism and to join the Rallis government in combating it.[85]
This anticommunism accounted for the majority of those who
actively supported the occupying powers after January 1943.
Its roots went back to the Metaxas dictatorship, which used
the fear of communism to justify itself. The Rallis government
and right-wing antiroyalists like Pangalos hoped to use anticommunism as the means to restore their version of the prewar
social and political order. Rallis outflanked Pangalos in the
formation of the Security Battalions, and even Pangalos's
protégé, Colonel Dertilis (who was made titular commander of
these units by Rallis in a move to outwit Pangalos), was arrested and jailed in May 1944, along with Pangalos and his

friend, General Gonatas. This action effectively neutralized the right-wing antiroyalists for the remainder of the war and cleared the way for Rallis's success. As a result, the Greek government-in-exile and the Rallis regime ended up working for the same goal: the defeat or neutralization of EAM/ELAS—which both labeled as a communist conspiracy—and the restoration of the monarchy. At the time of the liberation and the crisis of December 1944, the Greek government of Georgios Papandreou would find itself dependent on the police and security forces created by Rallis. The anticommunism of Rallis was equally matched by both royalist and republican politicians in exile, and it became, in the words of Komnenos Pyromaglou, a *"Doureios Ippos"* (Trojan Horse),[86] whereby the old politicians restored the old political game which culminated in the triumph of the right-wing of Greek politics.

Operation "Achse"

Hitler predicated his invasion of Greece in 1941 on strategic necessity. After the Greek defeat, the region's importance lessened, and the twelve divisions were shifted to other theaters. Then, as the British recovered the initiative in North Africa and the United States landed in French North Africa, the strategic role of Greece and the Balkans came into play once again in the winter of 1942. Hitler ordered the *OKW* to report on the consequences of an Axis defeat in North Africa. On November 15, 1942, the *OKW* reported that the Axis could expect an Allied invasion of southeastern Europe via the Dodecanese, Crete, and the Peloponnese, supported by popular risings. The Allied threat and the growing weakness of the Italians made it imperative for the Reich to secure and pacify the Balkans.[87] On December 28, 1942, Hitler issued Directive No. 47, which outlined a program for strengthening German armed forces in the Balkans. The German *AOK 12* became *Heeresgruppe E*, and its commander, Lt. General Loehr, became the supreme commander for the entire southeast. The directive ordered Crete, the Peloponnese, and the Dodecanese transformed into fortresses and directed the German armed forces to join the Italian army in anti-partisan operations.

The *OKW* did not expect the Allies to land in strength and force a breakthrough into the Danubian basin in the early months of 1943, but it expected small landings in the Peloponnese as a first step toward a second front, and it feared landings in the Aegean would be inevitable, creating the possibility of a breakthrough. In response to those possibilities, the *OKW* ordered four divisions to prepare for transport to Greece on February 12, 1943.[88] The motorized *11 Lw-Feld-Div.* (11th Air Force Infantry Division) arrived first, followed in late spring by the *117 Jaegerdivision* (117th Light Infantry Division). These two divisions formed the *LXVIII Armeekorps* (68th Army Corps) under Lt. Gen. Helmuth Felmy. Two Italian divisions were included in his command, and he was made responsible for the defense of the Peloponnese. By June 22, 1943, the *1 Gebirgsdivision* (1st Mountain Division) and the *104 Jaegerdivision* (104th Light Infantry Division) took up positions in western Greece, forming in August the *XXII Armeekorps* (22nd Army Corps) under Lt. Gen. Hubert Lanz.[89]

The *OKW* ordered these divisions and others that followed to secure supply lines and coastal defenses as their main function. Unable to repel a large invasion, they planned to hold until more units could be fed into the area. On July 4, 1943, two *SS Polizei-Panzer-Grenadier Regiments* (SS Police Panzer Grenadier Regiments) began to move into Greece to bolster the defense of the Salonica-Athens rail line, and by the middle of August the *SS Polizei Rgt. 18* joined the other SS units for antipartisan operations in Central Greece.[90]

In March 1942, German armed forces totaled 75,000 men in Greece. By October 1943, the number exceeded 275,000 (173,000 army, 13,700 *SS*, 58,000 air force, 29,000 navy, and 18,000 Italian volunteers).[91] In August 1943, the Germans requested more troops from the Bulgarians to defend northern Greece, and the Bulgarians dispatched one more division to *HGrE*, bringing the total number of Bulgarians under *HGrE* to 54,695. This build-up of German forces resulted from a decision of Hitler, who overruled the *OKW* on the defense of the southeast. Generals Alfred Jodl and Walter Warlimont expected the Allied invasion to strike at either Sardinia or Sicily, then at southern Italy and across the Adriatic into the Balkans. They wanted to withdraw from the eastern Mediterranean to a line from Salonica to the Adriatic. Hitler, however, believed the main Allied thrust would be in the Balkans, and he insisted on reinforcing not only Greece down to the Peloponnese but in controlling all of the eastern Mediterranean. Hitler had always had a strong sense of importance about the Balkans, and this instinct was reinforced by the British secret plan, operation "Mincemeat," which allowed false plans to fall into German hands indicating that Greece and not Sicily would be the main thrust of the Allied invasion.[92] On May 19, 1943, Hitler told the *OKW* that the Balkans were more of a threat than an Italian collapse, and he emphasized that even if the worst occurred, the Italian peninsula could be closed off somehow. He believed it to be of decisive importance for Germany to hold the Balkans with its oil, copper, bauxite, chrome, and above all security, so that there would not be a complete loss there if the situation in Italy collapsed.[93]

How real was the Allied threat to the Balkans? Writing after the war, General Warlimont, who headed the planning staff of the *OKW*, claimed Hitler's strategy put much more strain on the German war potential than the military situation warranted. Hitler's fears, however, had some justification. Churchill, by the late summer of 1943, showed loss of interest in "Overlord" and remained keen on developing a Balkan front after the successful invasion of Sicily. As late as October 1943, the British Chiefs of Staff still hoped to develop the strategic possibilities in the Balkans. Only the stalemate in Italy soured their hopes.[94] "Overlord," however, won out, and Allied efforts in the Balkans were limited to small operations.

The worst did happen in Italy. Relations between the two major Axis powers steadily deteriorated after the Axis defeats in North Africa, and they reached their lowest point of the war on May 19, 1943. The failures in Africa had spread defeatism in the higher ranks of the Italian military, the government, and the general population. This defeatism and a long-standing conflict of interests in the Balkans resulted in a military crisis between the two Axis nations in the last weeks of May 1943.

Hitler feared "high treason" was rampant in the Italian High Command, and he charged that the Italian policy of arming Montenegrin "nationalists" actually armed communist bands and had thus allowed Tito and his partisans to escape Operation "*Weiss*."[95] The charges of "high treason" reached into Greece. In April 1943, the *Abwehr* accused General Carlo Geloso, the commander of the Italian XI Army headquartered in Athens, of being implicated in an allegedly British-sponsored espionage ring in Greece. Rome dismissed Geloso on May 3, and replaced him with General Vecchiarelli. A large number of Italian staff officers were sacked, and twenty-eight Italian women employees of the *Wehrmacht* headquarters in

Athens were expelled from Greece. According to the *Abwehr*, Geloso's "Jewish" mistress, with the aid of British Intelligence, established a call girl service at Geloso's villa to gain information for the Allies from Italian officers serving in the Italian command or as liaisons with the German army.[96]

Forced to contemplate the defense of Italy and the Balkans without the Italians, Hitler ordered, on May 20, 1943, plans *"Alaric,"* for taking over Italy, and *"Konstantine,"* for the German takeover of the Balkans.

Even after the Allied blow fell on Sicily rather than on the Peloponnese, Hitler held fast to the conviction that the Allies would still try a landing in Greece. He appointed Field Marshal Erwin Rommel as commander of the southeast to plan the defense against an Allied attack coming from the Dodecanese across Thrace and into Rumania. Rommel arrived in Salonica on July 25, 1943, only six hours before General Badoglio's *coup d'état* against Mussolini. The news of the events in Rome reached him as he was meeting with the staff of *HGrE*, and he left immediately for Germany.[97] *"Alaric"* and *"Konstantine"* were cancelled and replaced by a single plan for the German takeover in Italy and the Balkans, operation *"Achse."* As preparation for the eventual execution of the plan in Greece, the Italian XI Army was placed under the command of *Oberbefehlshaber Suedost* Loehr, and the Italian VIII Army was placed under the command of Lt. General Felmy of the *LXVIII AK*. The German command ordered the Italian divisions "Forlì" and "Pinerolo" to positions in central Greece where they could easily be disarmed on short notice.[98]

The whole structure of the German chain of command in the southeast underwent reorganization on July 31, 1943. Hitler's Directive No. 48 moved the *O. B. Suedost* to Belgrade and gave it a new commander, Field Marshal Maximilian von Weichs. Weichs commanded *HGrF*, eighteen divisions scattered over the Balkans. Loehr was reduced to a subordinate position under Weichs, but his forces were still known as *HGrE*. Weichs began to make plans for placing German units into strategic defensive positions and initiating a series of anti-partisan operations which were designed to open up the supply lines in the Balkans and to retake some Aegean islands recently lost to the Allies. In support of these plans, *SS Pol-Pz-Gr-Rgts.* 1 and 2 moved into Greece on September 1, 1943, establishing their headquarters at Larissa and Lamia, respectively.[99] On September 7, 1943, as a consequence of Hitler's Mediterranean strategy, Germany had nearly doubled her strength in the Balkans. The number of German divisions rose from 10 to 18, and Bulgaria added two more divisions. In Greece, the number of German units increased from two divisions, one regiment, and one brigade to six divisions, three regiments, and one brigade.[100]

As a means of gaining time to negotiate with the Allies, Badoglio told the Germans that the war was being continued, but Hitler remained unconvinced. Sicily fell to the Allies on August 17, and the Italian mainland was invaded on September 3. Badoglio had begun negotiating with the Allies on August 15, but the resulting confusion forced the Allies to announce the surrender on the night of September 8, 1943.[101] Twenty minutes after he learned of the Allied broadcast, General Vecchiarelli informed *HGrE* of the news, accompanying it with a note explaining that Italian armed forces would not take any hostile action against German forces even if the Allies attempted a landing. This neutrality would continue, wrote the Italian commander, as long as German armed forces committed no hostile act against the Italians. As soon as *HGrE* learned of the Italian surrender, it ordered its units to prepare to execute *"Achse,"* and Loehr issued an ultimatum to Vecchiarelli at 7:25 p.m. to either close ranks with the Germans or surrender all weapons to the *Wehrmacht*. Vecchiarelli was given one hour to reply, but he successfully evaded the ultimatum by denying he had received any official confirmation of the surrender from Rome and claiming that his communications system in Greece had broken down, making it impossible to relay orders to his units. He emphasized to the German commander that he would hand over his heavy weapons at once, but he wanted to lead his army home in a battle-ready condition.[102] The Germans refused to believe him and feared possible defection of certain units to the partisans. These fears were for the most part unfounded. As soon as Vecchiarelli received official word from Rome, he cooperated with *HGrE*, and by September 12, 1943, 250,000 Italians had been disarmed.

All did not go as well on the islands of Corfu and Cephalonia, which were occupied by the "Acqui" Division under General Gandin, and there were some defections among the "Pinerolo" Division in central Greece. Gandin refused to comply with the German orders to disarm which came from Lt. General Lanz of the XXII Mountain Corps. Gandin complained that the terms of disarmament were ambiguous. He requested Lanz to provide clarification of the term "disarmament" and to make explicit the German plans for embarking his troops to Italy. He told Lanz that his men needed their weapons for self-protection against partisans and hostile populations on their return home should they be forced to march overland through the Balkans, but it appeared that the deeper reason for his refusal to comply lay in his troops' fear that the Germans intended either to make them prisoners or, worse, to force them to fight the partisans on the Greek mainland. To ensure that this would not happen, Gandin requested that his men be allowed to keep their sidearms, but Loehr refused.[103] On September 14, 1943, Gandin's fears became a reality. On that day, Hitler ordered that all Italian units which refused to disarm would have their officers shot and their non-commissioned officers and men deported to the eastern front for forced labor.[104] Negotiations between Lanz and Gandin continued until September 17, when the last ultimatum was refused. Lanz's *1 Geb. Division* launched its attack, and within five days the "Acqui" was destroyed and Gandin made prisoner. Four thousand Italians died in the battle; one battalion was totally annihilated. Gandin and his officers were shot in accordance with Hitler's orders. The remainder were made prisoners and shipped to Russia. On Corfu, six hundred Italians died resisting the Germans, and 10,000 were made prisoners.[105]

Of the 265,000 Italians whom the Germans disarmed, 170,000 returned to Italy almost immediately. Of those who remained, 29,000 served as *Hilfswilliger* (*Hiwis*—labor troops) or in the two Italian battalions of *Kampfwilliger* (*Kawis*—security guard troops). Another 15,000 were held as prisoners of war, while some 50,000 others were eventually allowed to return home.[106]

The Destruction of the Greek Jews

The Jewish settlement in Greece reached back into ancient times, but it did not contain large numbers until the fifteenth century when Spanish and Portuguese Jews fleeing the persecution of the Inquisition settled in Salonica. In the seventeenth century, the Sephardic community was joined by Jews from central Europe, and finally in the eighteenth century a number of Italian Jews settled in Greece. They concentrated in Salonica, which offered them more opportunities. By 1900, some

80,000 Jews, predominantly Sephardic, lived in Salonica, making up nearly one-half of the city's population. The Jews of Salonica were prominent in the business and professional classes, and in the nineteenth century Jewish concerns had established the first water, gas, and electric companies. In the early decades of the twentieth century, they imported 26 percent of Salonica's industrial goods.[107] The Salonica community had been the only Spanish Jewish settlement of the Ottoman period to prosper and expand since the founding of the modern Greek state. During the twentieth century, however, the community began to decline. Poverty and a certain amount of antisemitism, which became greater after 1923-24, forced them to emigrate. Still, over 4,000 Jews served in the Greek Army during the Italo-Greek war.[108] By 1941, the city's Jewish population dropped to 49,000 out of a total population of 260,000.[109] Another 13,000 resided in the Italian zone of occupation, and 5,000 to 6,000 in Bulgarian-occupied Thrace.[110]

The first anti-Jewish measures of the occupation began on April 11, 1941, when all Jewish publications were suspended, and the antisemitic *Nea Evropi* (*New Europe*) began publication. The Germans arrested the fifteen-member Jewish council, and, on May 15, 1941, they reorganized the Greek Nazi EEE which Metaxas had banned. General Tsolakoglou's public announcement that there was no Jewish problem in Greece, however, reassured the Greek Jews, but that reassurance was short-lived.[111]

The famine of 1941-42 caused 10,000 Jews to starve to death and spread spotted typhus fever among them. The "final solution" began with the destruction of Salonica's Jewish cultural life, archives, libraries, and liturgical scrolls. On July 13, 1942, the *Befh. Saloniki-Aegaeis*, Lt. General von Krenzki, ordered all males between 18 and 45 years of age to register for forced labor, and 2,000 young men were dispatched to other parts of Greece, where most died from starvation and sickness. The introduction of forced labor in the German zone of Salonica caused many of the Salonica Jews to try to emigrate to the Italian zones. The Germans sought to check this movement, but the Italians refused to cooperate.[112]

The expropriation and requisitioning of Jewish property began in January 1943. On February 6, 1943, *SS Hauptsturmfuehrer*, Colonel Dieter Wisliceny issued the orders for the destruction of the Salonica Jews. He was supported in this work by *Kriegsverwaltungsrat* Dr. Max Merten, who represented the

Befh. Saloniki-Aegaeis. Chief Rabbi Koretz, whom the Jews had chosen as their representative, was made responsible for the civilians of the ghetto. The orders of February 6 forced all but foreign Jews to be marked and their stores identified as Jewish; all but those possessing foreign passports had to move into the ghetto.[113] The first deportations began on February 13, 1943. Following the instructions of Merten, Rabbi Koretz assured the ghetto that it had nothing to fear, and that one section, Baron de Hirsch, would have to be emptied because "communists" threatened the occupation army. This part of the ghetto would supposedly be moved to Poland where its members would find new jobs waiting for them. A few weeks later the Germans struck again. This time they deported the Jews living in the ghetto district known as Aghia Paraskevi. Baron de Hirsch and Aghia Paraskevi contained lower class Jews, but in April and May 1943 the middle class Jews were deported. By August 19, 1943, some 46,000 Jews of Salonica had been deported to Auschwitz with a minimum of difficulty. Rabbi Koretz died in Bergen-Belsen.[114]

The Italian Consul General Castrucci caused the Germans some difficulty by protecting 329 Jews who claimed Italian citizenship, whom he subsequently smuggled out to the Italian zone on Italian troop ships. General Geloso allowed Jews to emigrate from Salonica to the Italian zones. The Spanish *chargé d'affaires* in Athens made efforts to protect 600 Spanish Salonica Jews, but the refusal of the Spanish government to allow them to immigrate to Spain doomed them to Belsen. Some 365 survived and reached Spain at the end of the war.[115] The quisling Premiers, Logothetopoulos and Rallis, protested the deportations but failed to achieve any positive results. Logothetopoulos, supported by Archbishop Damaskinos, suggested that Greek Jews be interned on an island occupied by the Italians and that they be maintained by Jewish assets (communal funds). The Greek Governor of Macedonia, Simeonides, however, wanted this Jewish property for Greek refugees expelled from the Bulgarian zone. Rallis, who succeeded to the Premiership in April 1943, and Rabbi Koretz repeated the petition for island internment, but they were refused. All Jewish property and cash, valued at about $11,000,000, went to Governor General Simeonides for disposal among Greek refugees.[116]

The Italians refused to cooperate in the final solution, and the Jews in the Italian zone were protected until Italy dropped

out of the war and Germany extended its control over the
former Italian zone. The final solution in this area came under
the direction of *HSSPF* Schimana, who ordered the Jews of
Athens to register on October 3, 1943. Schimana expected 8,000
to register, but there were only 3,500 Jews in the city. To punish
the Jews for failing to register, the *Mil. Befh. Grld.* confiscated
their property and turned it over to the Greek government.
Since other Jews were spread out over the mainland, plans had
to be made for their rapid collection. In a series of raids between March 23 and 25, 5,400 Jews were seized and deported.[117]
According to Molho, the seizures in Athens, the Peloponnese,
and the Volos-Trikkala-Larissa area were less than 50 percent
successful.[118] In April 1944, Rabbi Elia Barsilai of Athens joined
the resistance, and between 1,000-2,000 Jews sought safety in
Free Greece. A BLO estimated that EAM/ELAS saved 500
Jews in Thessaly.[119]

The deportations from the islands came under the authority
of Lt. General Loehr. About 2,000 Jews lived on Corfu, 300 on
Zakinthos, 300 on Crete, and 2,200 on the island of Rhodes. The
cooperation of Loehr and the *Wehrmacht* commanders on
Corfu, Crete, and Rhodes facilitated the deportations in the
summer of 1944, but the commander at Zakinthos, an Austrian,
successfully delayed the arrival of *SS* officers and implementation of the order, thereby allowing the island's 300 Jews to
escape to Italy.[120]

Of Greece's 73,000 Jews, the Germans deported more than
60,000. Fewer than 10,000 survived.[121] According to Molho and
Nehama, the close cooperation of Koretz, the debilitation of
the 1941-42 famine, the difficulty of hiding, the terror spread
by the Nazis, and the lack of the Jewish community's contact
with Greeks and the centers of resistance, accounted for the
ease with which the Salonica Jews were annihilated.[122] In other
parts of Greece where factors differed from Salonica, the
Germans were not so successful. The "final solution" was delayed in these areas until the Italian collapse. By that time,
the resistance had grown considerably and the Jews living
outside of Salonica became more aware of what fate awaited
them. The cooperation of Koretz found no parallel in the
actions of the Athenian Jewish leader Rabbi Barsilai. There,
less than half of the city's 3,825 Jews were deported. In the
Volos-Lamia-Trikkala area, one of the strongest areas of EAM/
ELAS, only 450 of 2,727 were deported.[123] In Ioannina, on the
other hand, the action of *Wehrmacht* units and of German and

Greek police was so rapid that 90 percent of the area's Jews, 1,725, were collected and moved out. All their furnishings and food were handed over to Greek officers for distribution to the Greek population to combat hostile propaganda by the local EAM organization. From EDES, which was the dominant resistance organization in Epirus, a German *GFP* dispatch reported that one could hear only full approval of the action.[124]

Hitler's new order brought suffering and death to Greece. There was no single response as individuals struggled to survive as best they could. Yet the catastrophic consequence of the occupation was a common experience shared by a wide spectrum of the population, wide enough to create a rich environment for the development of the Greek resistance to Nazism. The sentiment produced by the devastating situation was well expressed by the words of the nineteenth century poet and patriot, Rigas Pheraios, when he wrote "Better one hour of freedom than forty years of slavery and prison." This was not simply a romantic slogan but an existential reality.

CHAPTER FOUR

THE ORIGINS AND GROWTH OF
THE RESISTANCE

There is a long tradition of guerrilla war in the Balkans, and before the Second World War the *andartiko*, or partisan war, had a respected place in Greek history. Irregular warfare had been successfully employed in the War of Independence, the liberation of Crete from Ottoman rule, and in the struggle for Macedonia in the early decades of the twentieth century. In 1941, the Greek government made no preparations for any form of continued resistance after the April capitulation, but resistance to Axis rule began immediately after the defeat of the regular army. These acts were carried out by isolated individuals and small groups guided by their own consciences and political beliefs. The majority of these individuals remain anonymous, but their actions are recorded in the German records of the occupation. Later, their spontaneous activity was replaced by the organized resistance of Napoleon Zervas's *Ethnikos Demokratikos Ellenikos Synthesmos* (EDES—National Republican Greek League), *Ethnike Kai Koinonike Apeleutherosi* (EKKA—National and Social Liberation), and the *Ethniko Apeleutherotiko Metopo* (EAM—National Liberation Front) and *Ellenikos Laikos Apeleutherotikos Stratos* (ELAS—Greek Popular Liberation Army) dominated by the Communist Party. In the early weeks and months of the occupation, the King's government ignored Greece, and while the prewar political world, including the communists, remained hesitant and in disarray, the antifascist resistance began.

The Spontaneous Resistance

The popular reaction to British prisoners of war brought into Athens on May 10, 1941, revealed the first evidence of spontaneous popular resistance. Their arrival stirred an enthusiastic demonstration for them. As two truckloads of British Imperial troops crossed Constitution Square under German guard, Athenians along the way broke into applause. The Germans, thinking the reception was for them, acknowledged the response, but they soon became indignant and embarrassed when the crowd's laughter indicated otherwise. As the trucks proceeded, the Greeks showered them with flowers, candy, and cigarettes—the latter being no mean sacrifice in 1941. Paralleling this public reaction, individual citizens continued to aid British stragglers to escape although the action carried the death penalty if discovered by the Germans.[1]

On May 29, 1941, the Germans charged that "atrocities" had been committed against them, and the following day saboteurs destroyed two Bulgarian ships laden with explosives at anchor in Piraeus harbor. One of these ships was destroyed by a Venizelist who had been supplied explosives by Britain's Special Operations Executive before British troops evacuated Greece on April 29, 1941.[2] During the same two days, the *Befehlshaber Saloniki-Aegaeis* uncovered a Greek-British anti-Axis propaganda unit, and the Salonica *Geheime Feldpolizei* (GFP—Secret Field Police) reported anti-Axis handbills being spread among Salonica's unemployed and dismissed civil servants.[3] During the night of May 30, 1941, Manolis Glezos and Apostolos Santas stole the Nazi swastika from atop the Acropolis. Greeks throughout the country heralded it as the most spectacular act of resistance until that point. One day later, in Salonica, a munitions dump exploded, killing one Greek and wounding three German soldiers and three other Greeks.[4]

For allowing the theft of the swastika and for tolerating public demonstrations of sympathy toward British prisoners of war, the Germans forced the dismissal of the police officers in districts I and III of Athens. Newly endowed by the Germans with two chairs in German language and literature, the University of Athens opened its doors for the first time since the end of hostilities. Students showed their appreciation for the new chairs by making speeches and carrying out demonstrations against the Axis and the newly installed quisling government.[5] The University closed the next day until the fall term, but another demonstration in November would close it again. Anti-Axis and anti-quisling government actions caused the Greek government to establish special courts to prosecute these "anti-national" offenses. On June 3, 1941, sixty

Athenians received one to three months island exile from these new courts.[6]

Tension between the occupation authorities and the civilian population continued to grow during June, aggravated by the increasingly apparent food crisis. Petty theft and burglary increased radically, mostly in foodstuffs. *Abwehr* reports on plans for a *putsch* by the throngs of unemployed in Salonica, who were being organized, according to the Germans, by "communists" agitating against the Axis, forced the *Befh. Saloniki-Aegaeis* to request another group of *GFP* and the authority to execute reprisals.[7] The increasing agitation and isolated acts of sabotage moved the quisling government to establish the first concentration camps to detain persons arrested by them and the Axis.[8] On July 5, 1941, the first guerrillas made their appearance near the village of Kozani. According to German records, a group of released Greek soldiers fired on a small detachment of Germans. The *Wehrmacht* unit returned the fire and repulsed the guerrillas. In the ensuing pursuit of the *andartes* (guerrillas), the Germans discovered a small cache of arms and burned down two small villages in reprisal.[9]

During the first week of August 1941, saboteurs damaged the telephone system on Lemnos and cut and stole 500 meters of telephone cable on the island of Chios. On the night of August 24, three Greeks were shot down in a street battle with German police in Salonica. They were carrying explosives disguised as cans of olive oil. On the night of August 31, some individual or group tried unsuccessfully to destroy the offices of the EEE, the Greek Nazi faction revived to persecute the Jews of Salonica. In the same period, three Athenians were executed for possessing arms. The German authorities condemned to death three more Greeks in Florina for possessing arms, and the victims' homes were burned. House searches by the *Wehrmacht* in the area around Florina uncovered 4,000 rounds of ammunition, 120 land mines, and 30 kilograms of dynamite. Three more Greeks died and more homes destroyed in reprisal for these discoveries. An incident on Mytilene resulted in another execution. The German occupation of the Kopais led to the passive resistance of the peasants as the Germans attempted to confiscate its produce. As was mentioned before, however, the confiscations yielded only thirty percent of anticipated requisitions.[10]

By September 7, 1941, more armed bands appeared in northern Greece. On that date a large band of 120 *andartes* successfully attacked a Greek gendarmerie post in Nigrita (50 miles northeast of Salonica) and seized control of the village. Then they proceeded to break into food stocks, and distributed them to the local population. As they left the village, the *andartes* relieved the police post of all its money.[11] The *Befh. Saloniki-Aegaeis* recorded six other partisan attacks on villages in northern Greece, and two attempts to blow the rail lines from Salonica to Serres and one act of sabotage on the Salonica-Belgrade line. All of these acts occurred between September 12 and 15. Another ambush by *andartes* on a small German unit traveling along the Salonica-Serres road resulted in the first German casualties of the occupation as two German soldiers were killed in the incident. The month of September 1941 saw the intensification of attacks on Axis lines of communication and the circulation of anti-Axis handbills. After examining these clandestine materials, the *Befh. Saloniki-Aegaeis* concluded that the sources originated from a combination of communist, nationalist, and British sympathizers.[12]

Bulgarian repression in its occupation zone resulted in an armed popular revolt in Drama and Kavalla, a revolt which the Germans concluded was inspired by "Bolsheviks."[13] In Crete, there was no hiatus between the conduct of regular warfare and the beginning of the resistance. After the island fell on June 22, 1941, thousands of Greek and British Empire troops refused to surrender. They continued the struggle against the invader with the aid of the local population. In this running irregular struggle between July and September 9, 1941, 327 Cretans (civilians and regular army) lost their lives and another 194 were captured. The Germans described them as *Freischaerler* (guerrillas), and the pejorative "bandits" (*Banditen*) did not come into use until September 1941.[14]

Dominique Eudes, André Kédros, and a publication sponsored by the Greek political party, United Democratic Left (EDA),[15] have tried to establish that members of the KKE who escaped from Metaxas' detention camps and scattered across Greece during the confusion of the capitulation voluntarily began the Greek resistance in Macedonia, Thessaly, Epirus, Athens, and the Peloponnese. Citing KKE publications, they argue that those communists were responsible for the agitation in Salonica, Drama, and Kavalla and for founding the first *andarte* bands in September 1941 near the town of Kilkis, which carried out their first raids between September 13 and 22.

The German records do not fully sustain these accounts.

The authors claim a KKE band carried out the July 5 attack near Kozani, but the EDA publication does not cite the Nigrita incident. It is not possible to confirm in time, place, and number, Kédros's account of *andarte* activity during October (which witnessed the peak of guerrilla activity during 1941) except in one instance. His claim regarding the attack on the Salonica-Lahana (Salonica-Serres) road is confirmed by the records of the *Befh. Saloniki-Aegaeis.*[16]

Kédros, who cites the recollections of two members of the KKE and later of ELAS, Abraham and Kostas Yakoutsides, claimed that the *Befh. Saloniki-Aegaeis* ordered the destruction of the villages of Kleisto, Kidonia, and Ambelophito and the execution of 96 males on October 25, 1941, in reprisal for the death of two German soldiers. The records of the *Wehrmachtbefehlshaber Suedost* show that on October 18, 1941, the villages of Kato-Kerzilion and Ano-Kerzilion on the Strymon estuary were destroyed and 202 men executed for supporting the Nigrita guerrillas.[17] On October 24, 142 hostages were shot and a village near Ptolemais destroyed, which was over 100 air miles from the area of the Yakoutsides brothers. Neither of these two incidents is mentioned by Kédros. The action reported by Kédros is recorded in the German records on October 26, 1941, as "three villages northeast of Salonica burned to the ground and 67 hostages shot in reprisal." The three villages were Ambelophito, Kleisto, and Kidonia.[18] During the same period, October 18-25, the locomotive repair shops in Salonica were destroyed by sabotage.[19] Kédros does not mention this incident. During October 1941, the Germans executed 488 hostages and seized 164 others for *andarte* raids or acts of sabotage.

Although the KKE was active by September and October in organizing the resistance, the German records reveal that they were not alone. They had been preceded by isolated individuals and groups who intended to continue the fight against the Axis in the spirit of the Italo-Greek war. The Germans were correct when they concluded that the resistance came from an amalgam of sources.

After October 1941, sabotage acts against the Axis decreased sharply, and the few *andarte* bands which existed ceased to operate. The German authorities carried out only two reprisal executions during November. In December, a primitive attempt to sabotage the Athens-Salonica rail line failed, and twelve hostages were shot for the attempted assassination of a

Greek Nazi. While anti-Axis propaganda increased in circulation, only two acts of sabotage occurred during the period from January to February 1942. Greek security forces sufficed to keep order, preempting the use of Axis troops until April 1942. The *andarte* bands that operated during the summer and fall became inactive either through Axis reprisals or the onslaught of the winter and famine, or probably from a combination of the two. The spring of 1942 witnessed the emergence of new bands that were fundamentally different from the previous ones. Rather than seeking out the Axis, these new *andartes* sought food, and, according to the German authorities, lacked the political nature of the 1941 groups,[20] but the armed resistance that reemerged in 1942 gradually evolved from these early bands. The 1941 *andartes* were of mixed origins, individuals who refused to give up the struggle against the Axis after the humiliating capitulation, but the weather, the enemy, and their own primitive support organizations forced them into inactivity during the winter.

Compared to events in Yugoslavia during the summer and fall of 1941,[21] these Greek acts of resistance, along with the destruction of fuel dumps in Piraeus on October 5 and the continued pilfering of German Army food stocks first reported in August, neither appear significant nor are descriptive of anything like a resistance movement. Yet no high ranking officer of the Greek army remained in the mountains to organize a resistance as did Yugoslavia's Draza Mihailović, nor did the Greek government establish a guerrilla command as the Yugoslav government did in April 1940. Under Tito's leadership, the Yugoslav Communist Party had a national network, and it had established military committees throughout the country. No similar organization existed in Greece, and resources to support a large resistance army were lacking. The resistance between April and December 1941 proved primitive and ineffective against the power of the Axis, who did not regard it as threatening or dangerous. Nonetheless, these acts represented a spirit, a sentiment, and a will to resist actively, before any group formally organized to fight the Axis occupation. They indicated that there were individuals and groups of individuals who refused to give up the antifascist struggle. In spite of the April 1941 panic of the government and King, the nation once again remained remarkably calm and proved to be ahead of its leaders. The issue in Greece was who would exploit and develop this willingness to resist.

The Organized Resistance

The Germans and Italians naively expected to establish social and political stability through the government of General Tsolakoglou and the two quisling governments which followed, but they failed. The most effective internal political, social, and economic force emerged in the form of an antimonarchist resistance which seized the initiative in Greek affairs by the early months of 1943. Two factors explain the Communist domination of the resistance. First, the King and the prewar politicians defaulted. Second, the Foreign Office and SOE could not agree on a common policy toward the resistance and exiled government.

The King's failure to plan any form of political or military resistance before leaving Athens and the inability of his exile government to pursue actively organizing occupied Greece proved to be a critical factor in Greek wartime politics. The King and his government intended to await the end of the war and then return. In the first year of the exile, the Tsouderos government concentrated on consolidating its power against Venizelist and antimonarchist exiles rather than establishing and controlling any resistance movement in occupied Greece.[22] The commander of the Greek forces on Crete, General Christos Kitsos, returned to Athens to transmit George II's wish that royalist officers remain out of politics and that they take care to see that younger officers do the same.[23] In response to this call, the royalist officers later formed the Military Hierarchy, whose central function was to preserve the army officer corps so that it could play a role in the postwar era as supporters of the monarchy and a government backed by Great Britain. According to the Hierarchy's records, good discipline along these lines was maintained until General Papagos was arrested and dispatched to Germany on July 26, 1943.[24] Brigadier E. C. W. Myers, the first chief of the British Military Mission (BMM) to Greece, was well justified in his conclusion that the majority of the influential royalist officers had been ordered to have nothing to do with the resistance and to remain in Athens while awaiting the return of the King.[25] Archbishop Damaskinos complained that the exile government neglected its supporters inside Greece for the first years of the occupation, and that, by the time it came to realize what had happened, it had been outflanked by the formation of a formidable antimonarchist resistance.[26] Not all of the officers acceded to the King's request, however. A number followed the monarch into exile and served in reorganized Greek armed forces attached to British units in the Middle East. Another segment served in the Security Battalions raised by the Rallis government in 1943. Still a few others joined, or would try to join, the resistance in 1943, but the majority abided by the King's request.

Early efforts of the exiled Greek government to coordinate subversive and intelligence gathering activities in occupied Greece proved feeble and halfhearted. In September 1941, the Minister of State in Cairo, Sir Miles Lampson, loaned the services of Mr. E. Graham Sebastian to the Tsouderos government. Sebastian had been Consul General in Athens before the war and, following the Anglo-Greek withdrawal from Greece, was attached to Sir Miles Lampson's staff in Cairo as an advisor on Greek affairs. Sebastian quickly became the center of controversy between the Tsouderos government and the Foreign Office on one side, and Cairo officials on the other. He worked with the Anglo-Greek Committee which was formed in September to establish contact with occupied Greece. Sebastian's main contacts in Greece and in Egypt were Venizelists, which the Tsouderos government found alarming and threatening. As a means to bolster support for the monarchy, Sebastian shocked the King and Tsouderos in September 1941 by recommending that the Greek exile government issue a statement announcing the King's intention at liberation to restore liberty and constitutional government. Sebastian further recommended that the exile government be broadened by inviting from Greece Panagiotes Kanellopoulos and Alexandros Mylonas–two men recognized for their opposition to Metaxas and for their commitment to the parliamentary process–to join the King's government. Sebastian also recommended that the King and his government move to Cairo. Tsouderos and the King categorically rejected these suggestions.[27] In December 1941, the Tsouderos government allied with the Foreign Office to remove Mr. Sebastian from Cairo for being too dependent upon and supportive of Venizelists and antimonarchists. They succeeded in March 1942. For his candor and honest reporting of the situation in Greece, Mr. Sebastian was transferred to Scandinavian affairs.[28] The bureaucratic infighting and search for "politically reliable" agents distracted talent, time, and energy from the task of building contacts in occupied Greece. Further delays stemmed from the British need for military security which mandated that the Greek government not be admitted into full confidence regarding military and subversive plans in Greece. The Greek government was not fully informed of SOE plans, and it was not told of the mission to destroy the Gorgopotamos viaduct until after the British parachute team had landed in Greece on the night of September 28, 1942.

The Greek official working with Sebastian was Constantinos Tsellos, who had been a secretary to Kanellopoulos. SOE's and Tsellos's contact in late 1941 and early 1942 was the Venizelist Evripides Bakirtzis, whose code name was "Prometheus I." Due to his leftist political sentiments, Bakirtzis was known as the "Red colonel," but the prewar British minister in Athens had a high regard for the Greek officer, who had received Britain's Distinguished Service Order in the First World War. Bakirtzis actively sought contacts to raise a resistance force, but his activities became exposed and he had to leave Greece in 1942. He was replaced by Major Charalambos Koutsogianno-poulos as "Prometheus II," but the latter's efforts also proved abortive. In August 1942, Major Ioannis Tsigantes arrived in Athens as Cairo's third emissary. He participated in the republican *coup* of 1935, but in 1940 he declared his support for the King. Since London and Cairo suspected that EAM was communist-inspired, Tsigantes was to utilize contacts made through the Anglo-Greek Committee to organize those forces not opposed to the King's return.[29] These contacts were allegedly associated with Kanellopoulos and what proved to be a small organization known as the "Six Colonels" or "Theros." Although SOE believed seventy-two resistance groups existed in Greece by October 1942,[30] nearly all proved to be as illusory as the "Six Colonels" and none of them were large, viable, or sympathetic to the King. The antimonarchist climate allegedly forced Tsigantes to move further right than he may have desired in building a pro-exile government organization. In December 1942, he contacted Christos Zalokostas, a wealthy monarchist, who in 1943 organized a conservative and anti-EAM/ELAS organization known as *Ethnike Drasis* (ED–National Action). Before Tsigantes could consolidate his ties to Zalokostas, Italian police bullets on January 14 put an end to the Major's life and mission.[31] The alleged "Six Colonels" remained the Tsouderos government's only hope for a politically compatible resistance organization, but in February 1943 Major C. M. Woodhouse's mission to Athens proved that the "Six Colonels" was not an effective organization. Following the death of Tsigantes, the Greek exile government would not have another reliable mission inside Greece until the autumn of 1943.[32] By then, the antimonarchist resistance was the dominant force in occupied Greece.

The leaders of the political parties dissolved by Metaxas in the prewar years proved no more disposed toward resistance than the King's officers and his government. The politicians of the center and left, according to Stephanos Saraphes, blamed the King, Metaxas, and Papagos for the defeat of Greece, and they all agreed that a republic should be established after the liberation. None, however, were willing to go to the barricades to ensure a republican victory. Sophoulis, the leader of the Liberal Party, told Saraphes that any attempt to form a resistance was premature and would only lead to arrests and reprisals. Saraphes's account is confirmed by Kanellopoulos, who wrote that the political and military leaders in Athens were totally passive to the idea of going to the mountains or organizing in the cities.[33] The inertia of the Greek political world and the King's instructions to his officer corps helped explain the failure of the Tsouderos government to establish some form of organization inside of Greece. Another factor in this failure were the Greek and British officials in Cairo, who constantly viewed the resistance as a military instrument. There is no evidence that the Cairo officials recognized the need for a political dimension to the resistance, the need to organize and politicize the nation. It was far simpler and less troublesome, it seemed in the early years, to think in terms of military sabotage rather than political organizing. This separation of the military from the political aspects of the resistance confounded official Greek and British policy throughout the war. The KKE, however, seized immediately on the potential gain of building a political resistance prior to any armed resistance. Although Britain did succeed in creating EDES and EKKA, they were useful only as military units, and they proved to be weak political reeds. Even so, EDES and EKKA also began as republican forces.

After 1936, the republican opposition to Metaxas centered in Paris around the exiled Plastiras.[34] Among the supporters of Plastiras were Sophocles Venizelos and Komnenos Pyromaglou, a former instructor attached to the University of Athens. For his republican sentiments and political agitation, Metaxas assigned him a "residence" on the island of Sikinos.

In December 1938, he obtained a release and went to Paris to join the Plastiras circle. The defeat of Greece and the occupation provided this group with the opportunity to advance their cause of republicanism by founding a resistance movement. Their principal aim was to liberate Greece and to allow the Greek electorate to decide the fate of the King in a free plebiscite.

Seeking to fulfill Plastiras's mandate, Pyromaglou sought the support of Athenian political leaders in founding a unified political resistance in Athens and an independent armed resistance in the mountains under the command of GHQ ME. Plastiras's old cronies offered verbal encouragement but little else, while others refused even that much. Pyromaglou also spoke with representatives of EAM, but they were not interested in a decentralized resistance. Faced with these circumstances, Pyromaglou joined EDES in October and later emerged as the chief political officer of that organization.

Zervas, who had been in contact with SOE, agreed to recognize Plastiras as head of his movement and accepted a political platform based on republicanism and social justice. But even though he received 24,000 gold sovereigns from British agents to raise a guerrilla band, Zervas delayed. He did not leave Athens for his native Epirus until late June 1942 when SOE threatened to expose him to the Axis.[35] Gonatas did not join EDES, but he encouraged two colonels, Charalambos Papathanasopoulos and Apostolos Papageorgiou, to associate with EDES. Later Tavoulares and Voulpiotis joined. These latter four members of the Athenian EDES played a double game and eventually worked for the Axis. Zervas officially denounced them in February 1944.

The program announced by EDES had five major points:

1. The establishment of a social democratic regime at the end of the war;

2. The denunciation of the treason of George II and his dictatorial court, and demands for the punishment of all those who participated in the Regime of August Fourth;

3. A purge of all anti-democratic elements from the state, and dissolution of the police and gendarmerie;

4. Establishment of political and social equality to prevent any one group from exploiting another; and

5. Insistence that these goals of EDES be subject to approval by the nation in a free election.

Unfortunately, EDES failed to carry through this political program effectively. Paying little attention to it, Zervas put his trust in military force and his own personality. Under the pretext of necessity, he transformed EDES into an authoritarian clientage organization designed to fit his personal political aspirations, which changed with shifting wartime politics. Zervas failed to pay close attention to the creation of a broad political base to support his armed *andartes*. To keep his movement viable, he relied on British funds and arms, and even on an "understanding" with the Germans.[36] After the war, Pyromaglou summed up Zervas's shortcomings:

> During the whole course of our endeavors we wavered between a superficial democratism and a superficial nationalism, without ever evolving a stable national political policy which could be used to arouse enthusiasm and militancy. We always met the stubborn resistance of General Zervas and of those about him.... The centralization of power which General Zervas insisted on maintaining because of circumstances of the struggle proved to be unwarranted and injurious. Nothing was heard but the slogan "Faith in the leader. All for the leader. All from the leader." [37]

Even so, by the end of 1942 he had a well-armed band of 100 men which played a key role in the Gorgopotamos operation. One of his most energetic supporters in the area was Stelios Houtas, a medical doctor turned *andarte*. Houtas's band dominated the area known as the Valtos in Aetolia, south of the Acheloos River. Houtas gave his band the name *Ethnike Organosis Ellenon Andarton* (EOEA – National Organization of Greek Guerrillas). Later in 1943, when the Athenian branch of EDES became tainted with collaboration, Zervas tried to adopt the appellation EOEA, but EDES remained its popular name.

Zervas's "cult of personality" referred to by Pyromaglou accounted for the major weakness of EDES and its failure to become a nationwide movement. In 1941, SOE officials saw Zervas as something of a disreputable character for his past political escapades. As a Venizelist in 1916, he became an A.D.C. to General Ioannou, a competent but somewhat flamboyant officer. The general's style must have impressed the younger officer, and, whatever Zervas's shortcomings were, lack of style was not one of them. In 1922, he supported Plastiras and was awarded the rank of Lieutenant Colonel, but in 1925 he joined Pangalos and along with his friend and associate, Colonel Dertilis, commanded Pangalos's 5,000 man personal guard. This action earned him the enmity of General Kondylis, who dismissed Zervas from the army in 1926. For the next decade, Zervas was involved in a number of *coup* attempts and political intrigues until Metaxas imprisoned him. He was released from jail in 1941, and he soon reestablished contacts with his friends and "Prometheus." [38] In spite of this history, or perhaps because of it, Zervas was acceptable to SOE and the Foreign Office, but he did not create an effective resistance organization. As late as the summer of 1944, the Foreign Office received reports from its special agent in the field, Colonel David Wallace, that EDES was organized along feudal lines and that Zervas did not have full control of his units. Wallace thought the semi-independent bands associated with Zervas were better than the formal units under his direct control. EDES had failed to develop a press and propaganda network comparable to EAM/ELAS.[39] An Athenian lawyer who had interviewed a number of officers who had tried to join Zervas reported to British authorities in Cairo that Zervas insisted on all officers taking a strong oath of allegiance to him. Officers who were competent but not sufficiently loyal and faithful to Zervas were sent to isolated commands in Corfu and Cephallonia, while the personally loyal, even if incompetent, officers got the promotions and good commands. Zervas's personal and clientage approach, which was not uncommon in Greek affairs, weakened the effectiveness of EDES as subordinates would not follow orders which were not in their interests.[40] These views are confirmed by BLO Captain R. L. Bathgate's report on his tour of Zervas's territory in 1943.[41]

In spite of these shortcomings and in spite of his description of Zervas as pontifical and theatrical, Wallace recognized Zervas as a leader and one whose politics suited Britain's political needs. Zervas was London's loyal client, who, in Wallace's view, was not only Britain's creation but "an instrument in our hand." [42] The instrument proved politically defective. Zervas and EDES were eclipsed by EAM/ELAS, which organized the only nationwide resistance by first building a firm political and economic infrastructure.

The KKE emerged in the 1920's from the Greek socialist movement that began in the decade of the 1870's. During that decade, the first trade unions were organized on the commercial and manufacturing island of Skyros. As the number of laborers increased in Piraeus, Athens, and Volos, individuals better acquainted with international socialism joined the labor movement. Plato Drakoules, a lawyer, founded the first socialist newspaper in 1885 and in 1908 he founded the League of the Working Classes of Greece. Within a year the League evolved into the Greek Socialist Party. The fundamental platform of the new party was social reform at home and peace in foreign affairs through Greece's cooperation with her Balkan neighbors. Like other Greek political parties, it suffered from factionalism. Disputes among its syndicalists, anarchists, utopian socialists, and Marxists, and the smallness of the Greek proletariat, combined with intense Greek nationalism, nullified its political effectiveness. Nationalism and Venizelos's social reforms stole away the Greek workers, who supported the Balkan Wars despite the strictures of their leaders.[43]

Between the end of the Balkan Wars and the termination of the First World War, the socialist movement split into three streams. The Right supported a strong nationalism. The Center remained anti-nationalist, but it would not accept the stringent class war advocated by the Left. The Left gradually shifted into the camp of the Bolsheviks after 1917. During October 1918, Alexandros Benarogias, who had founded a Jewish socialist federation in Salonica, led a movement which formed the *Genike Synomospondia ton Ellinon Ergaton* (GSEE — General Confederation of Greek Laborers), which represented 64,000 workers and contained the entire spectrum of socialist thought. The GSEE remained more a labor organization than a political one, however.

On November 17, 1918, another group of socialists met in Piraeus and organized the *Sosialistikon Ergatikon Komma Ellados* (SEKE–Socialist Labor Party of Greece). The SEKE hoped to unite all socialists under the banner of the Third International, but division over affiliation with the Comintern and the problem of reconciling Greek national interest with Moscow delayed its affiliation until September 21, 1920. Not until 1924 did it adopt the name Communist Party of Greece (KKE). Its official newspaper was *Rizospastes* (Radical), a socialist publication founded in 1917 which gradually shifted to the extreme left. Plagued by internal factionalism over Greek national claims and the interests of international communism, along with more important social and economic conditions which did not provide raw material for the party, the KKE remained on the periphery of Greek politics until the 1932 elections when the party won five percent of the vote. During the constitutional crisis of 1936, a popular front movement under the direction of Nikolaos Zachariades, who followed Moscow faithfully, elected fifteen delegates to parliament, thereby obtaining the deciding voice in the ensuing political stalemate. The front consisted of the KKE and its labor union under Georgios Siantos, the GSEE under Ioannis Kalomiris, the Agrarian Party (AKE), the Socialist Party (SKE), and an independent labor union under Laskaris. Outside of the KKE, Kalomiris and Laskaris were the more influential members of the front.[44] After Metaxas seized power, his Minister of the Interior, Constantinos Maniadakes, waged an effective campaign against the KKE that penetrated and disrupted the party.

The Axis invasion and occupation found the Greek Communist Party in chaos. On the eve of the attack, the phoney KKE established by Maniadakes still functioned and published a spurious *Rizospastes*. Key members of the party's central committee and 2,000 other members were in Metaxas' jails. Among these were Zachariades and the future wartime leader Siantos. The remaining members of the "old" KKE were scattered throughout Athens, Thrace, Macedonia, Thessaly, and Epirus.[45] From his prison cell in 1940 and 1941, Zachariades took three different positions on the war. On October 31, 1940, he issued an open letter, approved by Maniadakes, calling for support of the struggle against Mussolini, which the KKE denounced as a forgery. A second letter of November repudiated the first and called on the Soviet Union to mediate an Italo-Greek peace based on the status of the states before October 28. A third letter of January 15, 1941, but not published until July 1942, explained that the first letter was authentic and that Zachariades supported the war until the Italians were driven out of Greece. After that point, the war had moved from one of "national liberation" to an "imperialist war" that no longer served Greek interests.[46] These ideological contradictions characterized the disarray in the KKE which lasted until July 1, 1941. Then, elements of the KKE met in Athens and elected a new Central Committee that reorganized and redirected the Party. Andreas Tsipas was made First Secretary of the Party, and Andreas Tzimas became secretary of the party organization in Athens. The desperate economic situation and the weakness of the Party made it impossible to respond in full to Stalin's July 3 radio appeal for the Communist parties in Europe to launch a partisan war against Nazism, but the decisions of this plenum set the course of the KKE for the wartime period. After the usual references to the "imperialist war," and charging the "monarchofascist" George II with the responsibility for the enslavement of Greece, the plenum decided that the surest way to help defend the Soviet Union and to promote the KKE to power was to form a single antifascist national front. This front would organize the resistance against the Axis occupation and would attempt to form a government made up of all the prewar political parties.[47]

On July 16, the KKE renewed the 1936 popular front with the GSEE in creating the *Ergatiko Ethniko Apeleutherotiko Metopo* (EEAM — Workers' National Liberation Front). On August 1, the first of a new series of *Rizospastes* appeared and appealed for a common front against the occupation. The KKE efforts to rally the prewar political world were not successful, and only the leaders of the small, left-of-center parties responded. On September 28, 1941, the KKE was joined by the SKE, the AKE, and Elias Tsirimokos's ELD (Union for Popular Democracy), and they formed the *Ethniko Apeleutherotiko Metopo* (EAM). The proclaimed goal of EAM was the liberation of the nation and the establishment of its total independence; the formation of a provisional government after the liberation which would provide for the election of a constitutional assembly based on popular sovereignty; and the affirmation of the right of the nation to decide its form of government and of EAM to halt any reactionary attempt to impose a government contrary to the will of the people.[48] EAM's first handbill appeared on October 10 and set the tone of EAM propaganda for the wartime period by appealing to Greek patriotism. The handbill called on Athenians to greet each other with the words, *"Tsarouchi–EAM."* *"Tsarouchi"* referred to the rustic shoe associated with the rebels of 1821, the equivalent of "V" for victory. Later in the month, an appeal was made for Greeks individually to assemble on October 28, the first aniversary of the *"Ochi"* to Mussolini, at the Tomb of the Unknown Soldier in Athens to commemorate the lives of those who had fallen in the struggle against the Axis. The appeals had a simple and direct message. The "altar" of the nation was, and would forever remain, liberty and honor, and it called upon Greeks to remember the war dead by participating in a "communion" service at the tomb. This appeal, couched in religious terms, remained EAM's basic approach toward arousing Greek patriotism to resist the occupation. When EAM began to spread to the countryside it consciously sought to identify the antifascist resistance with the struggle against the Ottomans. EAM referred to itself as the new *Philike Hetairia,* and in turn called the old *Philike Hetairia* the "EAM of 1821."[49]

Although small bands of guerrillas had emerged spontaneously in the mountains of Macedonia and Crete in 1941, the KKE and EAM were more concerned with organizational problems than with armed resistance. The tempo of activity did not increase to a sustained point until Siantos, with whom the fundamental wartime policy of KKE/EAM is associated, took over the leadership of the KKE in November 1941. Siantos was born in Karditsa in 1890. He became a tobacco laborer at the age of 13, and, following the Balkan Wars, he worked to organize a tobacco laborers' union. He then served for a few years in the Greek army. In 1920 he left the army, and joined the Socialist Labor Party in 1924. There he sided with the faction that joined the Comintern, and, in 1925, he became a member of the KKE's political bureau. In the 1930's he served in the Greek Parliament, but party squabbles caused his eclipse by Zachariades in 1931. After a visit to the U.S.S.R., he returned to Greece in 1934 and was active in organizing the Greek Popular Front. After the Metaxas seizure of power, he was interned on an island, but he escaped to return to KKE activities and was rearrested in 1939. In September 1941, he escaped the Axis authorities and rejoined the Party, and by November he had established a dominant position within it. In January 1942, he became Secretary General of the Central Committee, a position he held until May 1945, when Zachariades returned to Greece from a Nazi concentration camp. He died in 1947 before he was made a scapegoat for the KKE failure in 1944-45 and denounced by the 1950 KKE leadership as a traitor and a British agent.

Under Siantos, the KKE pursued the popular front strategy as the best means to gain political legitimacy for EAM/ELAS—and hence the KKE—which would then open the door to political power in the postwar era. This line determined that the KKE cooperate with the bourgeois parties and Great Britain during the war to gain legitimacy for the *de facto* power achieved by EAM/ELAS. Siantos in fact continued the line established in July, and there does not seem to have been any sharp division within the party over this policy. In the early months of the occupation, the KKE recognized it was a minority party that lacked support among the general population. Success could be achieved only by dropping references to the proletarian revolution and by appealing to Greek nationalism while capitalizing on the popular reaction to the occupation and the Metaxas dictatorship. After the dissolution of the Comintern in 1943, the KKE publicly announced that it intended to follow parliamentary methods in achieving political power. As the war years passed, it became clear that a segment of the Party did not fully subscribe to this line, but the defeat and occupation provided the KKE with an opportunity it never had before, and it made formidable progress toward its goal.

It is clear from the German records of the occupation, that in reaching for that goal the KKE gave first priority to political organization in the urban areas and moved cautiously and hesitantly toward the formation of an armed partisan army. This emphasis, and the defeat of EAM/ELAS in December 1944, provoked the bitter controversy and schism within the Greek Communist Party in the postwar period. Svetozar Vukmanovic ("Tempo"), who served as Tito's wartime liaison to EAM/ELAS, claimed that the failure to raise a mass peasant army resulted in the defeat of 1944-45.[50] Recently, this theme has received an expanded treatment in Dominique Eudes's study.[51] His book is an attack on the policy of Siantos and a defense of Aris Velouchiotis, the ELAS *kapetanios* (*andarte* chief) who vigorously pushed for a full scale partisan war along Tito's model. The conflict within the KKE and EAM is presented in the simplistic terms as one between narrow "Stalinists" stuck to a Leninist model of urban proletarian revolution and advocates of the *andartiko*, principally Tzimas and Aris.[52] According to Eudes, Siantos, supported by the Moscow-trained Ioannis Ioannides, preferred to achieve postwar power by first gaining control of the major urban centers and then joining a government of national unity where the KKE would control the armed forces and the police and security forces.[53]

There were less differences within the Party than Eudes would have his readers believe, and these differences were not patently ideological. After escaping from Haidari prison, Demetrios Partsalides, who rejoined the KKE Central Committee in March 1944, argued that there were no differences or conflicts within the Party over an urban versus a mountain based *andartiko*. He insisted that the KKE did not oppose guerrilla war, but that the Party recognized and agreed that a broad political base had to be established before a partisan war could be launched.[54] Conditions in Greece and the KKE in 1941-42 seem to confirm his view. Siantos was not opposed to partisan war, and soon after his return to the KKE leadership in November the first definite steps toward building an armed resistance were taken. On December 28, 1941, *Rizospastes* called for the establishment of a new phase of the resistance, modeled after the armed struggle in Macedonia and Crete. Siantos was sympathetic to Tzimas's advocacy of partisan warfare, and this support within the KKE led to the dispatch of KKE agents in the winter of 1941-42 to the mountains to investigate the possibilities of an *andartiko*.

In February 1942, the KKE agreed to organize guerrilla warfare in Roumeli, and Tzimas was given the responsibility for this task. On April 10, the first guerrilla bands were officially approved, and, on May 22, Aris Velouchiotis formed the first ELAS band of fifteen members. Aris was limited to Roumeli, and he was told not to execute any actions which would bring reprisals on the local population and hinder the organization of EAM. Further, in 1942 and even early 1943 ELAS made contacts with German commanders to reassure them that ELAS attacks were directed only against the Italians and their Greek puppets.[55]

The conflict that developed within the KKE/EAM/ELAS was not between "Stalinists" and "progressives" over the issue of the *andartiko*, but over the question of how the partisan arm was to be used in EAM/ELAS's search for legitimacy. Clearly the urban centers, especially Athens and Salonica, received first priority, and the policy adopted under Siantos precluded extensive violence that would alienate Greeks and Great Britain. The difficulties of the Siantos policy came with the refusal of the prewar political world to join EAM. This negative response proved decisive in two ways.

The refusal of the politicians to join, and hence to legitimize, EAM left the KKE/EAM/ELAS leadership at odds on the best means to overcome this veto. Their inability to resolve it proved fatal to the KKE.[56] On the other hand, the default of the noncommunist political leaders left the field open to EAM/ELAS to build a national resistance organization that threatened to make the prewar political world superfluous if EAM/

ELAS could legitimize its *de facto* power. In the face of this threat, and lacking any means of local power, the Greek political leaders turned to Great Britain and ultimately to the King's exile government to restore them to power. The seeds of civil war already began to sprout in the last half of 1941.

EAM's cautious policy of concentrating on political organization and relief work and selecting actions that would build popular support succeeded. On March 25, 1942, the traditional date for the celebration of Greece's liberation from the Ottoman Empire, EAM/ELAS subtly transformed a public ceremony commemorating 1821 into a call to arms against the new conqueror. On April 12, 1942, EAM revealed its growing power by calling the first strike in occupied Europe. The strike was a limited success and revealed EAM's caution in organizing the resistance. On April 12, the Athens-Piraeus Greek government postal, telephone, and telegraph workers went on strike for higher wages. As the strike continued for over a week, their counterparts in Salonica joined them on April 21. The Greek employees of the *Wehrmacht* were not called upon to strike. The strike ended after the quisling government agreed to the demands. The Germans, noting the economic basis of the strike and that it made no political demands, did not consider it directed against the Axis but against the quisling government.[57] Not until 1943 did EAM openly strike against the Axis for political purposes. The successs of the strike revealed how effectively EAM gradually exploited the conditions created by the famine and inflation to establish itself as the leading resistance organization.

The development of the guerrilla war did not move as rapidly as the other forms of resistance, but by the fall of 1942, before the arrival of SOE's "Harling" (E.C.W. Myers's) mission of September 28, 1942, indigenous guerrilla bands with firm support institutions had become permanent. Zervas finally left Athens in late June and became active in Epirus by September, when Aris made his first attack on the Axis. By the end of October, ELAS had 500 *andartes* scattered across Central Greece. Throughout October and November 1942, before the Anglo-Greek destruction of the Gorgopotamos bridge, Greek *andarte* bands, ranging in size from twenty to 100 men each, attacked police stations, sabotaged communication lines, and broke open food stores for distribution to the local population.[58] These small scale actions were carried out by EDES and ELAS. By the end of 1942, a small band appeared in the Peloponnese near Kalamata, and bands also formed in Thessaly, Macedonia, and Thrace. Generally, these guerrillas were poorly armed and too weak for direct confrontations with large Axis units.[59] The generally low level of these attacks confirmed the view of Brigadier E. C. W. Myers, the commander of the British mission which parachuted into Greece to destroy the Gorgopotamos viaduct, that Aris had orders to avoid any large actions and that ELAS was limited to sabotage, derailing trains, and gaining booty.[60] After he had obtained Zervas's agreement to join the attack against Gorgopotamos, Myers managed to convince Aris to break his orders from Athens and to support the operation.

The destruction of the Gorgopotamos railroad bridge on November 25, 1942, marked the first major military achievement of the resistance and demonstrated that an indigenous resistance could be useful to the overall war strategy only if it was directed by an outside coordinating agent. In this case, the military goal was to support General Bernard Montgomery's offensive at El Alamein by interdicting the flow of supplies to Axis troops. The problem in Greece was that the military goals of the Allies did not always fit the political goals of the resistance, but in this case the military goal was a spectacular success. The destruction of twenty meters of the span cut the flow of German war supplies to North Africa for over four weeks, and the flow of war *matériel* out of Greece to other parts of Europe was reduced by 40 percent (from 7,641 to 4,458 tons).[61] It also forced a fifty percent cut in the flow of electricity to Athens by slowing the normal transport of fuel into the city.[62] For the resistance movement, it provided a tremendous moral and psychological turning point. The following year witnessed a general expansion of the resistance.

The Growth of the Resistance

The Axis reversals in North Africa and at Stalingrad, coupled with the internal political and economic crisis in Greece, increased the Greeks' expectations of an Allied victory and, along with the Gorgopotamos operation, spurred the growth of the resistance movement. Fearing the possibility of an Allied invasion of the southeast, the Germans began to bolster their defenses in the Balkans. When the German authorities attempted on February 1, 1943, to mobilize Greeks for forced labor service, they precipitated a series of anti-Axis strikes. At first, EAM masked these strikes as economic in purpose and directed not against the Germans but against the quisling government. Within a few months, however, the strikes openly revealed their political character and were directed specifically against the German authorities, whom the Greeks held responsible for the wretched condition of Greece.

The first strike of 1943 came on February 12 when the Athens and Piraeus communications workers carried out a sit-down strike for two hours as a protest against spiraling prices and low wages. They repeated the action the following day. Then on February 16 and 17, an EAM-sponsored strike halted the operations of Athenian and Piraeus banks. The strikers, however, were careful not to hinder the business affecting the occupation authorities. The caution of the strikers was revealed again on February 19. The administrators and operators of the Athens-Piraeus water works walked off the job, but they returned after the quisling Greek government increased their salaries by fifty percent. During the strike, the flow of water to the Axis remained uninterrupted.[63]

The success of these "economic" strikes encouraged EAM to become bolder. By the end of February, political demonstrations emerged. EAM called for a general strike, but it failed. Over 3,000 Greek government employees, however, responded to the call and demonstrated against Europe's "new order." In the ensuing attempt by Greek police to break up the demonstrators, two Greek policemen were wounded by shots fired from the crowd and three demonstrators were killed by police bullets. The government workers received strong support from students.[64]

More significant strikes followed during the first week of March 1943. The German authorities recognized these demonstrations and strikes for what they were—political protests against German occupation. On March 4, EAM organized a strike which called out sixty-five percent of the quisling government's employees and nearly all students. The strikers and demonstrators protested the German order for civilian mobilization of Greeks for German labor service. The next day, March 5, 1,600 of the *Wehrmacht's* 2,500 Greek laborers in Piraeus did not appear for work. They returned only after the Germans announced through mobile loudspeakers that strikers would be treated as saboteurs. This action created a demonstration in which two Greek policemen were killed by a rock barrage. The arrest of thirty-five of the striker-demonstrators forced the men back to work. During the same day in Athens, a mass demonstration against the Axis and quislings destroyed the worker card files in the Ministry of Labor, but five demonstrators were killed and seventy-five wounded. Even the quisling press joined in the Athens demonstration.[65]

The German reprisals in the form of shooting hostages and demonstrators reduced the size of the anti-Axis protests but did not stop them. Early on the morning of March 25, 1943, Greek Independence Day, 300 marchers carried the blue and white flag of Greece through the streets of Athens. Over 3,000 others joined them in two more demonstrations. Three of the marchers were killed and twenty-five wounded by Axis police in breaking up the marches.[66]

The strikes provided the background and impetus for the further expansion of EAM. During the period of intense anti-Axis agitation, EAM announced the formation of a youth organization, *Ethnike Panelladeke Organose Neolaias* (EPON—National Panhellenic Youth Organization), and a counterterror group known as *Organosi Politikes Laikes Amynas* (OPLA—Organization of Political Popular Defense).[67] Three more strikes followed in May, but no more large demonstrations occurred. The immediate results of these strikes and demonstrations proved successful for the resistance. The German authorities suspended their attempt to round up laborers for forced service in occupied Greece. When the effort was resumed in June 1943, it proved unsuccessful. The *Wehrmacht* could fill its labor needs only by forcing Italian internees to work without any compensation after September 9, 1943.[68] The quisling government and the Axis powers granted retroactive wage increases, but the pay hikes were only temporarily effective in the face of the spiraling inflation and deteriorating economy.

Paralleling these developments in Athens-Piraeus, the *andarte* movement expanded rapidly during the first half of 1943. In this period, EDES grew from 500 to 4,000 guerrillas, while ELAS expanded from about the same number to a force of well over 12,000 men. British support enabled Georgios Kartalis and Major Demetrios Psarros of EKKA to field 1,000 guerrillas in the Parnassos Mountains in April 1943.[69]

These figures indicated clearly that EAM/ELAS focused on political organization and agitation rather than on creating a "people's army" on the model of Tito's partisans. If this is the reason EAM/ELAS failed to achieve power in 1944-45, as Svetozar Vukmanovic claimed, it also explained EAM/ELAS's domination of the Greek resistance movement. By superior organization and by concentrating on political organization, the KKE successfully established a broad national base for EAM/ELAS and maintained its control of the resistance.

In each village, four separate sections of EAM were organized. One division took care of relief, while EPON organized the young people for recreation and action programs. Another section served as logistical support for ELAS, the *Epimeleteia tou Andarte* (ETA—Commissariat of the Guerrillas). The key division, however, was the local EAM central committee. The secretary of the local committee was called the *Ipefthinos* ("the responsible one"), and he acted as the chief executive authority in the village and carried out the orders of his superiors. The KKE maintained its control over EAM through this office, which usually fell to a KKE member. The *Ipefthinoi* of a collection of villages elected a district EAM committee, which in turn elected a district *Ipefthinos*. These latter elected a prefecture level of EAM, which then elected the regional (e.g., Thessaly, Epirus, or the Peloponnese) committee. Each of these regional committees of EAM had one representative on the national EAM Central Committee located in Athens. Large cities like Athens and Salonica were represented independently of the regional committees. These cities were organized in neighborhood units. In this way twenty-five elected officials constituted the national central committee of EAM,[70] representing the various divisions of EAM/ELAS (EPON, ETA, EA, EEAM, and ELAS) and other noncommunist political parties and the KKE.

Siantos represented the KKE and served as EAM's national secretary. Tzimas, another member of the KKE and ELAS's political officer, represented ELAS. The two prominent noncommunist members of EAM/ELAS were the social democrats of the Union for Popular Democracy (ELD), Professor Alexandros Svolos and Elias Tsirimokos. Demetrios Stratis represented the Socialist Party, and Demetrios Asimakes represented the United Socialist Party. The radical Constantinos Gavrielides served as the Agrarian Party's delegate. These were the major and important noncommunist members of EAM, who, with the exception of the ELD of Svolos and Tsirimokos, had all participated in the 1936 KKE-sponsored popular front. Only in this sense did EAM represent continuation of the popular front of the Metaxas era. It did not include republican leaders who had opposed Metaxas but had opted either to remain passive or to join other resistance organizations. Other KKE figures who would later play important roles in Cairo (August 1943) and in Lebanon (May 1944) were Petros Roussos and Miltiades Porphyrogenis.

The KKE's control of EAM/ELAS was played down and not generally known inside Greece until the spring of 1943. As late as March 23 the SOE reported to London that, although the KKE dominated EAM/ELAS, the rank and file were not communist and could be shifted away from the KKE to SKE, which SOE erroneously believed to be the larger organization.[71] The actual number of Communists in EAM/ELAS is in dispute. Those who argued that the actual power of the KKE was limited, claiming that the Communists made up an insignificant total of the overall membership, have found support in the German records. They claimed that only ten percent of EAM/ELAS were members of the KKE and argued on this basis that EAM/ELAS would not have threatened Greece with a Communist takeover if a more enlightened Allied policy had tried to isolate them by forming a government of national unity which included the resistance.[72]

The figure of ten percent came from the London *Times* at the time of the Lebanon Conference. The German records afford a means of testing this estimate. *Geheime Feldpolizei* (GFP) reports and *Wehrmacht Ic* (Intelligence branch of the German Army) analyses provide a more accurate gauge of the problem. The *GFP* and *Ic* reports sometimes included captured resistance documents. A September 9, 1943, *GFP* report on EAM/ELAS in the Peloponnese listed fifty-two names and thirty-four occupations of the region's EAM/ELAS. According to this report, the EAM/ELAS leadership in the area included seven teachers, six students, six self-employed individuals (merchants or shopkeepers), five lawyers, four skilled laborers, two former Greek Army officers, two medical doctors, two civil servants, two police officials, and one bookseller. The *GFP* claimed that only twelve of the fifty-two were members of the KKE, a low estimate when one remembers that the Germans labeled as a communist anyone who opposed them.[73] This analysis indicates that approximately twenty-five percent of the leadership in the Peloponnese was communist.

A document of the KKE captured in west central Greece

(Acarnania-Aetolia) indicated that the actual strength of the KKE in the rank and file in rural areas was very low. The captured document, undated but picked up by the Germans in November 1943, is a report of the district KKE for Acarnania-Aetolia on party organization in the area of Nafpaktos, a town on the Gulf of Patras with a population of about 4,200 in 1943. The KKE claimed 196 members for not only the town but the whole countryside surrounding the village. Not all of the 196 were "reliable," nor did they have a full grasp of the meaning of communism.[74] Furthermore, according to the document, the EAM of the district operated independently of the KKE, though the ELAS military commander was an old KKE member.

These figures reaffirm the broad national and social basis of EAM/ELAS as emphasized by L. S. Stavrianos, who listed sixteen generals, thirty-four colonels, and 1,500 commissioned officers of the prewar Greek army in ELAS. There were also six Orthodox bishops, many labor leaders, thirty professors from the University of Athens, and two members of the Academy of Athens in EAM/ELAS.[75] They also indicate that though the percentage of KKE members in EAM/ELAS was higher in the leadership positions it was not anywhere close to a majority. Actual support for the KKE in rural Greece during the war probably varied between ten and twenty percent. One important exception to the EAM/ELAS in the Peloponnese is that no clergymen were listed. As an institution, the Church did not officially support the resistance, but individual churchmen did.

A noncommunist source inside of Greece in 1943 reported that EAM/ELAS was strongest among civil servants, white collar workers, merchants, shopkeepers and professionals in the urban areas and among wealthy peasants in the countryside.[76] Artisans who were members were judged to be above average in number of years of education. Leadership positions went to professional classes and merchants who were motivated by patriotism.[77] EAM/ELAS was indeed a bourgeois movement that brought a new administration to Greece.

When Aris began to organize ELAS in the autumn of 1942, he also began the reconstruction of local government on a popular basis. Upon entering a village to appeal for *andarte* recruits, Aris would ask if villagers were satisfied with their local leadership. If not, they elected a new one. Gradually, by these methods, EAM/ELAS developed a system of local government for all of what became known as Free Greece.[78] Each village elected a seven-man council which directed the affairs of the locality through various subcommittees and under the watchful eyes of the local *Ipefthinos*. A law code drawn up by twenty-two lawyers from Phthiotis-Phokis, Evrytania, and Athens in August 1943 became the basis for a "people's courts" system for all EAM/ELAS-controlled territory in December 1943. The final act of the EAM/ELAS political system came on March 10, 1944, when it created a national government inside occupied Greece, the *Politike Epitrope Ethnikes Apeleutherosis* (PEEA—Political Committee of National Liberation). The PEEA acted as a provisional government and initiated the election of a national council of 250 representatives of Free Greece and Occupied Greece. EAM/ELAS effectively maintained control over the whole system by supervising the local and national elections. The PEEA acted as EAM/ELAS's wedge to pressure the Greek government-in-exile and the Allies into recognizing the significance of the resistance, and into forming a government of national unity. It also served to systematize and control the administration of Free Greece.[79]

The popularity of EAM/ELAS is difficult to judge because the events following the outbreak of civil war have tended to prejudge the view of the period before October 1943. Even after October, in areas like Macedonia and Western Thrace, where food supplies were good and rivals to EAM/ELAS nonexistent, the population was supportive and EAM/ELAS rule beneficent. In areas where *andarte* growth exceeded local resources and requisitions were required, popularity dropped as mules, food, and blankets were confiscated. Reprisals had an impact, but the key to popularity rested on the fairness and efficiency of the local *Ipefthinos*. The greatest blow to EAM/ELAS's reputation was the outbreak of civil war in October 1943, yet even in the Peloponnese, where EAM/ELAS was weak, some villages continued to demand arms from Britain for ELAS to use against the Nazis in spite of the civil war.[80]

The ultimate test of public acceptance was manifested in the general expansion of the resistance in 1943, particularly of EAM/ELAS. Even C. M. Woodhouse recognized the general success of EAM/ELAS efficiency in organizing and administering Mountain Greece.[81] By March 1943, the Siantos policy had succeeded in creating a national resistance from the small beginnings of 1941. EAM/ELAS had not yet achieved the political legitimacy it desired, but it had become valuable—and even essential—to British sabotage efforts throughout Greece. Without the support of EAM/ELAS, British agents would have been limited to the small area of Epirus under Zervas's control and of little or no value to Allied military strategy.[82] The EAM/ELAS dominance, however, created tensions within the resistance and between Cairo and Mountain Greece. In the early months of 1943, the general success of the resistance moved the *andartiko* into a troubled period.

CHAPTER FIVE

THE ANDARTIKO

The year 1943 proved critical for the resistance and Greek wartime politics. The growth of the resistance in the Balkans during 1941-1942 generated rising expectations among the British military chiefs regarding the role of these guerrillas for Allied strategy, but the resistance posed difficult problems for Allied political goals. The fulfillment of the military potential was never realized. Political differences within the Balkan states prevented the complete exploitation of the resistance, especially the Greek *andartiko*. Indeed, by March 1943, London viewed the Greek resistance as a political liability. The responsibility for these developments lay with London and the leadership of EAM/ELAS. The inability of the Foreign Office, SOE, and the Chiefs of Staff (COS) to agree on an integrated political and military policy toward the resistance and the exiled Greek government was a central factor in creating a political impasse by the summer of 1943. The other reason for the dead end was the leadership of EAM/ELAS, which failed to resolve its internal differences and implement a policy consistent with cooperation with Britain and the noncommunist Greek political world. Having emerged as the most powerful clandestine organization in occupied Greece but having failed to achieve political legitimacy—hence security— the leaders of EAM/ELAS in 1943-1944 vacillated between cooperating and making war on their rivals. Still, the military achievements of the Greek resistance were significant, and its political impact was volcanic.

Britain and the Greek Exile Government

The issue that dominated Greek wartime politics was the problem of the monarchy. After the capitulation in 1941,

George II fled to Crete, and then to Cairo and London. The majority of his government followed him into exile, and there was no evidence that the King planned to use this opportunity to break with the past. Indeed, all evidence indicated the contrary. George II's aloofness and disregard for Greek public opinion remained unchanged. The majority of the King's ministers were holdovers from the Metaxas era, among whom the most undesirable were Constantinos Maniadakes, Aristides Demetratos, Theologos Nikoloudes, and Admiral Alexandros Sakellariou.[1] Nikoloudes was Metaxas's chief ideologist, while Maniadakes earned the epithet of the "Greek Himmler." As Minister of Labor under the dictator, Demetrates eliminated the Greek trade unions. Maniadakes discreetly dropped out of the government in June 1941. Demetratos remained until February 9, 1942, but some other members and high ranking officials remained until March 1943.

The monarch's unpopularity was no mystery to British officials in Cairo. On November 9, 1941, Sir Miles Lampson, Minister of State in Cairo, presented a clear analysis of the problem to the Foreign Office. He pointed out that the monarchy was not popular in Greece and could return only through the use of force.[2] Greek Minister-President Tsouderos held the same view, but a number of Greek government officials expected Britain to restore the King even if it required bayonets.[3] The Greeks assumed that Britain was obligated to the King for his steadfast support of it during the crisis of April-May 1941. Indeed, Tsouderos expected Britain to silence critics of the exile government in Egypt, which had a large Greek community that included prominent Venizelists. Britain reluctantly acceded to one request by deporting six Venizelists from Egypt, but it later regretted the action. The six had excellent pro-British records, and one of them, Byron Karapanagiotis, became a cabinet minister in March 1943. In an attempt to finalize this British support, Tsouderos offered London a treaty that would guarantee British bases in Greece in the postwar era in return for adding Northern Epirus and the Dodecanese to the Greek state. London, however, did not intend to sign any treaty with Greece on postwar political ties.[4]

Fearing that Britain would end the war with an unwanted King on its hands, Lampson called for a drastic reversal of British and Greek policy on the monarchy. He believed that the King's chances would be improved if the latter restored the constitution of 1911, purged his cabinet and armed

forces of Metaxist elements, and opened the government to
Venizelists. The Minister of State went so far as to recommend
that Britain drop the King if he did not agree to these changes.[5]
Attributing Lampson's report to Venizelist influences ema-
nating out of Cairo and to a lack of objectivity, Foreign Secretary Eden rejected the suggestions out of hand.[6] Lampson's
analysis was not out of line with other more detached
observers. On June 9, 1941, American ambassador Lincoln
MacVeagh wrote to Washington that, although the population
appeared united in hatred of the occupation powers and con-
temptuous of the quisling regime, the Greeks had not forgotten
the debacle of 1941. The flight of the monarch at that time had
cost him considerable prestige, and the ambassador concluded
that a demand for a plebiscite on the monarchy might well
follow the Allied victory.[7] On November 28, 1941, the Tsouderos
government received similar information from contacts inside
Greece.[8] Eden's rejection of Lampson's recommendations set
the pattern of Foreign Office policy toward the monarchy for
the remainder of the war. Senior officials of the Foreign Office
and the British Prime Minister were so committed to the
restoration of the King that evidence to the contrary did not
penetrate their consciousness until forced by extreme circumstances. This commitment stemmed not only from the King's
loyalty, but was rooted in a curiously nineteenth century pater-
nalistic notion that a liberal constitutional monarchy was best
suited for "the peculiar demagogic Greek temperament [which]
is not ideal for democracy in its most advanced forms."[9]
Whether the Metaxas regime fitted the definition of a liberal
constitutional monarchy or a lower form of democracy was
not made clear.

The apathy of the King's government toward organizing
measures to alleviate famine conditions until they had reached
critical proportions in November-December 1941 further
damaged the King's prestige and future irreparably.[10] The
failure to place himself at the head of a resistance movement
to liberate his country added to his unpopularity and proved
to be a fundamental political blunder. A report by Henry
Hopkinson in Cairo on January 6, 1942, reiterated the points
made by Lampson, but his recommendations were reinforced
by fresh reports on the deepening anti-royalist sentiment in
occupied Greece. Edward Warner of the Southern Department
(and later political advisor on Greek affairs to the Minister of
State-Cairo) rejected Hopkinson's report as a mixture of

"hysteria, sense, and local Greek politics." [11] Hopkinson's position was strengthened by the arrival in Cairo of Soteris Zannas. Zannas brought a letter signed by the prewar political leaders declaring that, with few exceptions, there was no support for the King in occupied Greece. Led by Stylianos Gonatas, the signers included Georgios Papandreou, Themistocles Sophoulis, Georgios Kaphandaris, and Alexandros Mylonas, who were identified as Venizelists (Liberals), and Ioannis Theotokis, Demetrios Maximos, Peter Rallis, and Pericles Rallis, who were royalists. The letter expressed the fear that, although the political leaders did not expect Britain to force the King's return, George II would use the Greek armed forces in the Middle East to effect his restoration. [12]

Sir Orme Sargent dismissed the letter as the work of the "old gang of Greek politicians" who were now emerging from forced retirement. Warner minuted, "[Gonatas] is, of course, an out and out Republican, and I do not suppose that either the King or Tsouderos would attach any value whatsoever to the information which the letter contains." [13] Tsouderos, of course, did not. To the Greek Minister-President, these politicians did not count; therefore, there was no solidarity behind the letter. [14] Tsouderos rejected by a curious argument any notion that his government or the King were linked to Metaxas. According to the Greek premier, the Regime of August Fourth was a "personal dictatorship," and the death of Metaxas ended the dictatorship. Hence the constitution of 1911 was in force. At the liberation of Greece, his government and the King would return and hand power over to an all-party government that would conduct free elections for a Constituent Assembly under the monarch. [15]

The Foreign Office agreed with Tsouderos that the "old gang" of prewar politicians would not receive any support except insofar as they cooperated with the King and his government. Since Greece would be desperate for relief at the time of liberation, the Foreign Office believed that the Greeks would be won over to the King by the political use of food. From this political perspective, the Foreign Office believed adequate grain supplies at the time of liberation were of "cardinal" importance. [16] By doling out relief, Britain expected to win political support for the King and British policy. The only direct response to the Gonatas letter was a demand from Tsouderos that Britain inform the Greek leader that London would work against any effort by him to organize a *coup* to prevent the return of the King and his government. London refused, but the Foreign Office did not press for any changes in the Greek government.[17] Following this incident, the constitutional issue remained dormant until the end of 1942. The lull was deceptive.

Gonatas and the other signers of the letter lacked any political power, but the letter accurately reflected the anti-monarchist sentiment which developed in occupied Greece and in the Middle East during 1942-1943. In April 1942, Pana-giotis Kanellopoulos arrived in Cairo and joined the Tsouderos government as Minister of War and Vice-President of the Council.[18] As Minister of War, Kanellopoulos quickly impressed British officials with his energy and efficiency in organizing and deploying the first Greek fighting unit into the front line in North Africa.[19] The success that pleased Britain alarmed the Greek premier, and the tension between the two men de-veloped into a crisis. In an effort to resolve these differences, Kanellopoulos was called to London in November for a con-ference with Tsouderos and British officials. Tsouderos believed Kanellopoulos was too closely associated with the "Red Col-onel" Bakirtzis and too often advocated Venizelists for ap-pointments in the government and the armed services. When Kanellopoulos requested a Greek passport for Plastiras, the alarmed Tsouderos called on Britain to curtail the young minis-ter's power, but London refused. Then he appealed to Kanel-lopoulos to stay away from the "dissension bulls," Plastiras and his cronies,[20] and the conference ended without resolving differences between the two Greeks.

While in London, Tsouderos and Kanellopoulos agreed on the general principle of broadening the political base of the government and reforming the armed forces, but they did not agree on specific personnel changes. When he returned to Cairo, Kanellopoulos set about to remove ultra-right-wing officers from the armed forces and to reinstate former Venize-lists who had been retired after the abortive 1935 *coup*. Tsouderos considered these officers to be too "far left" and too long absent from duty. A stalemate developed when Tsouderos resisted the changes and refused to broaden his government.[21] By March 4, 1943, Tsouderos became convinced that Kanel-lopoulos was seeking to replace him as head of the Greek exile government.[22] The growing political conflict between the two Greek leaders was overtaken by the events of the mutiny of the Greek armed forces in the Middle East on March 8.

By the beginning of March 1943, the Greek armed forces in exile totaled 18,000 troops, but approximately one-third of these were former officers. There were two brigades, the 1st and 2nd; the Sacred Company, which was a raiding parachute unit made up of 315 officers; and an armored car regiment. For an officer corps that had been politically active since 1909, the high percentage of officers did not help lessen the political problems in the armed forces. Some younger, junior officers but mostly rank and file soldiers formed the leftist *Apeleutherotike Stratiotike Organosis* (ASO, Army Organization for Liberation), which soon identified with EAM. The more conservative senior officers established the *Ethnike Apeleutherotike Stratiotike Demokratike Organosis* (EASDO, National Military Democratic Liberation Organization), which reflected the traditional sentiments of the Venizelists but considered open renunciation of the monarchy as impractical. In December 1942, the ASO exposed a royalist plan to purge antimonarchists from the armed forces. Tsouderos arrested the monarchist plotters, but the suspicions and conflicts within the units were not ended.[23] By February 11, 1943, more attacks on the Tsouderos government and right-wing officers appeared in subversive leaflets distributed among the troops, and British officers expected more serious trouble to occur. The anticipated crisis came on March 8. The immediate trigger for the revolt developed from the unfounded rumor that Kanellopoulos intended to remove a popular republican officer, Colonel Hadjistaris, who had been called to Cairo on March 8 for a meeting with the Minister of War.

The root of the problem lay in the long-standing Venizelist-Monarchist conflict that predated the Metaxas regime but had been intensified by the dictator's refusal to reinstate senior Venizelist officers after 1940. This division was aggravated by a pervasive feeling among the troops that they were being held back from combat to be used later to restore the King. They perceived the proposed merger of the two brigades under an allegedly right-wing commander, General Zygouris (whom Kanellopoulos had brought out of Greece) to be the first step in this direction. The mutiny occurred because each side was convinced that the other was recruiting men from Greece to overcome the other. A prime target of the mutineers was the royalist Greek Chief of Staff, General Maraveas, who was suspected of recruiting monarchists from Greece. British investigators of the mutiny suspected a nonpolitical but personal factor in the revolt. They believed that Colonel Katsotas, the commander of the 1st Brigade who had distinguished himself at El Alamein, feared that the proposed merger would lessen his status, and he may have encouraged the idea of a "fascist plot." Although appalled by the depth of the politicization of the armed forces, the British investigators found few if any genuine communists or fascists. They did find twelve rather extreme monarchist officers, but none were actually pro-Axis. The mutiny succeeded because of the overwhelming sympathy among the troops for republican ideals and goals.[24]

The rebels demanded a more aggressive war effort on the part of the Greek government, a liberalization of the government, and a declaration from the King that he would not return to Greece before a plebiscite, but the mutiny achieved only minor political changes. For his moderation in trying to steer a middle course between the monarchists and the anti-monarchists, Kanellopoulos alienated both sides and was forced to resign.[25] Except for the Minister of Finance, Kyriakos Varvaresos, whom Britain insisted on keeping in the cabinet, all other Metaxist ministers resigned, and three Liberals joined the government. Georgios Roussos became Vice-Premier and Minister of Marine, and Byron Karapanagiotes took over the ministries of War and the Air Force. Emmanuel Sophoulis, the great nephew of the leader of the Liberal Party, became Minister of Public Welfare. Instead of seeking to understand the basis of the discontent, the King, Tsouderos, and the officials of the Foreign Office did not reappraise their policy but remained sanguine over the prospects of the King's restoration. Shortly after the outbreak of the mutiny, Dixon minuted that, as soon as the Greek politicians become aware of the firmness of British support for the King and Tsouderos, they would tumble over themselves to line up with the King and would forget the demand for a plebiscite.[26] Indeed, British and Greek officials sought scapegoats for the political crisis. The King and Tsouderos found one in Kanellopoulos, while the Foreign Office held Zannas and Bakirtzis responsible for the trouble.[27] Although Tsouderos was asked to contact moderate political leaders in Greece who might join the government, there was no basic change in British policy toward the King.

The Foreign Office planned to "sell the King and the Tsouderos Government" to the Greek people by persuading them that the King intended to rule as a democratic, constitutional monarch. Toward this end, the King declared on March 24 that, after his return to Greece, he would base his future on the will of the people, and London assured a skeptical Washington that they did not intend to use force in aiding the King's return.[28]

Foy Kohler of the U.S. Department of State's Near Eastern desk differed with the British analysis. In a paper prepared for Cordell Hull, the American diplomat emphasized that the British policy of "selling the monarchy" would only stir up the situation and cause dissension, not unity, among the Greeks. Quite correctly, Kohler pointed out that the temper of Greek politics in 1943 did not indicate that the monarchy offered the best means to political stability. The return of the King under an Allied army would violate the Atlantic Charter, as EAM/ELAS had emphasized to Myers. Since the major military and political organizations in occupied Greece opposed the return of the monarchy, Kohler concluded that the King's return before a plebiscite would only create strife.[29] He was absolutely correct.

Kohler recommended that the United States take the position that the King should not return before free elections under the Allies had taken place. He wanted the King to make this quite explicit in a public declaration. Kohler warned that, although the Greeks now looked to the United States for support, they would turn to the Soviet Union if Washington failed them. Since the temper of Greek armed forces in the Middle East coincided with the republican attitude of the majority of Greeks in occupied Greece, Kohler approved the King's March 24 declaration as a step in the right direction, but implied that it was not enough to allay the issue of the monarchy.[30]

Although the new cabinet satisfied the Greek army and Great Britain, the ASO remained unreconciled. In the new Greek cabinet, the liberal members began almost at once to agitate for further democratization,[31] which in the following months created tension between the liberals and Tsouderos. In order to hold the government together, Ambassador Leeper became deeply involved in the day-to-day operation of the exile government. Even so, by early July, Leeper became convinced that Tsouderos had lost control of the government, and the ambassador obtained the King's permission to replace the Greek premier. Since London did not want to give public expression to this deep involvement in Greek affairs, the Foreign Office refused to allow the change.[32] While the political crisis in the Middle East intensified during the first six months of 1943, a parallel crisis developed between Britain and the resistance in occupied Greece.

Britain and the Greek Resistance

By the end of 1942, Britain won American support for the invasion of Sicily as a prelude to the cross-Channel invasion of northern Europe. In January 1943, at the Casablanca conference, the British military chiefs put great emphasis on the military potential of the Balkan resistance armies if they could be coordinated with Allied strategy and landings, but the Americans were not disposed toward expanding the Mediterranean war.[33] The Americans feared that an extended war in the eastern Mediterranean would develop at the expense of the proposed cross-Channel invasion ("Overlord"). The British strategists were not opposed to "Overlord." Rather, they expected the operations in the Balkans to draw German forces out of France, and they set about in earnest in the spring of 1943 to expand the Balkan resistance.[34] General George C. Marshall differed. He viewed the Mediterranean as a "suction pump" that would not support but drain the resources scheduled for "Overlord." The American position was so adamant that the British military chiefs convinced Churchill not to broach the subject with President Roosevelt at the Washington conference of May 1943 ("Trident"). The British feared that raising the topic of Allied landings in the Balkans would reopen the debate and jeopardize the decision to strike at Sicily (Operation "Husky"). Still, the British continued to expand their support for the Balkan guerrillas.

Until the conferences at Quebec (August 1943) and Teheran (November 1943), Churchill and General Henry M. Wilson put great emphasis on an eastern Mediterranean strategy that would follow a Rhodes-Athens-Salonica axis and would ultimately link up with Tito's partisans and the Chetniks of Yugoslavia. In October 1943, SOE estimated Balkan guerrilla strength at 230,000, linked to Cairo through eighty British Military Missions in the field.[35] Even following the failure of British troops to recapture the Dodecanese in November 1943, the growing stalemate in Italy, and the decisive agreement at Teheran for "Overlord," Churchill continued to hope to establish small Allied bridgeheads across the Adriatic on the Dalmatian and Albanian coasts to harass the Germans in conjunction with Balkan guerrilla armies. Until late 1943, Churchill continued to expect major achievements in the Balkans. As he phrased it in July of that year, "Great prizes lie in the Balkan direction."[36] Orders toward this effect were given to Brigadier Myers in late 1942.

The original orders to Myers called for the evacuation of the "Harling" mission after the destruction of the Gorgopotamos bridge, but British strategy forced a change in this plan. Rather, Myers was ordered to remain in Greece and raise a nonpolitical resistance. In February 1943, he received specific orders to prepare for a full attack on Axis communications not before June and to raise a popular revolt in support of an Allied landing not before August.[37] These orders proved exceedingly difficult to execute, but despite his political tangles with the Foreign Office and EAM/ELAS, Myers succeeded.

In the SOE briefing before the "Harling" mission left the Middle East, no mention was made of the KKE or EAM, yet the existence and political orientation of EAM was known to SOE and to the Foreign Office.[38] Immediately upon his arrival in Greece, Myers encountered political problems, and, in a series of telegrams during January and February, he reported a clear account of the situation in the country. Myers's analysis was augmented by Major C. M. Woodhouse's report on his ten-day visit to Athens between February 14 and 24. Woodhouse confirmed the weakness of the "Six Colonels" and the importance of the KKE within EAM. As for the colonels, Woodhouse reported that the two whom he met were not interested in the "pinpricks" of Zervas and Aris. SOE relayed key portions of these field reports to the Foreign Office on March 6.[39] Myers explained that EAM/ELAS controlled four-fifths of the guerrillas in Thessaly, the Pindos mountains, and Roumeli, and that ELAS had contributed 100 *andartes* to Zervas's sixty for the Gorgopotamos operation.[40] Each Greek village under EAM/ELAS had a wireless, and the organization distributed accurate daily news summaries on the progress of the war. Since the Communists were a key element in EAM/ELAS, which was steadily growing throughout Greece, Myers predicted the possibility of civil war between Zervas and EAM/ELAS.[41] Further, he reported that EAM/ELAS looked upon the Atlantic Charter as the basis of their demand for a plebiscite on the monarchy before the King returned to Greece, but feared that Great Britain intended to return the monarch at all cost.

The central figure of ELAS until March 1943 was Athanasios Klaras, better known as Aris Velouchiotis. Aris was born
in Lamia, where his father was a lawyer. He served in the
Greek army in 1925 but received no training as an officer. In
1929 he joined the KKE, and during the next decade he was
active as the party's youth leader and strike agitator. For
these activities, he was arrested by the Metaxas police. In
the summer of 1939 he signed a declaration of error and
repentance and was released. It is not clear whether Aris
signed the declaration on orders from Zachariades as a means
of returning to KKE clandestine activity, or if he signed of
his own volition. Regardless, the affair impugned his reputation with the old line KKE leadership,[42] but he recouped this
loss by assisting Andreas Tzimas to establish the KKE's clandestine press in the summer of 1941. The two had met previously in the Gardos Island concentration camp, and in 1941
became enthusiastic advocates of a full *andartiko*. In the following years, Tzimas demonstrated party discipline and re-
straint which Aris proved unable to emulate. Aris returned
to his native Roumeli in early 1942 to organize the first ELAS
andartes from the small loose bands of the region. His cover
name, Velouchiotis, came from the highest mountain peak of
the area, Timfristos, known locally as "Velouchi."

During the resistance, he succeeded in becoming a
charismatic and able guerrilla chieftain, a hero to his followers [43] and a brutal criminal to his opponents. For numerous
acts of violence against his rivals, Woodhouse suggested to his
superiors that the Allies hold Aris accountable for his crimes
at the end of the war.[44] Both reputations were well deserved.
To a young cadet who was among the first to follow Aris into
the mountains and who remained his associate until 1945,
Velouchiotis was a great *andarte* leader flawed by a pervasive
and pernicious distrust of others. Demetrios Demetriou
("Nikephoros") claimed that Aris was furious about the
arrival of the British Military Mission and that he never
wanted to cooperate with it. Rather, he planned the assasina-
tion of Zervas soon after the Gorgopotamos, but the leader of
EDES escaped before Aris could strike.[45] This abortive move
apparently came after the EAM/ELAS and EDES clash over
the defection of Major Kostorizos and twenty-five other
ELASites to Zervas on December 13, 1942.

Brigadier Myers soon discovered that Aris acted independently from Athens,[46] a tendency that later turned the guerrilla

chief into a political liability for the KKE and EAM/ELAS. Aris's dissolution of EKKA and the murder of Colonel Psarros by an ELAS subordinate on the eve of the Lebanon Conference in May 1944 proved to be one of the most politically damaging of these independent actions. Velouchiotis's final act of defiance came in 1945 when he refused to accept the Varkiza agreement, which was signed by the Communist leadership to end the hostilities between EAM/ELAS and Britain following the December 1944 crisis. Soon after this break with the KKE, Greek security forces captured and executed Aris near Trikkala. The *andarte* chieftain's severed head was paraded in the town square.

If Aris opposed the arrival of the British Military Mission, the response of the EAM/ELAS leadership was hesitant and uncertain. Cooperation between the two did not come easily and eventually collapsed by the end of 1943. Myers was not sent to Greece to expand the resistance as a conspiracy against EAM/ELAS. The British Chiefs of Staff were prepared to arm any guerrilla group willing to cooperate with British military authorities. Myers's task was to locate and organize partisans regardless of their political persuasion, but the new bands that emerged in January and February with the aid of the British mission were seen by EAM/ELAS and Aris as a challenge to ELAS. Aris began to disarm them almost at once.

In February 1943 Stephanos Saraphes, a republican officer who had participated in the abortive Plastiras *coup* of 1935, contacted Myers in Zervas's territory. Saraphes was associated with Major Georgios Kostopoulos, a prewar officer of socialist bent and founder of a small band of guerrillas of uncertain quality in 1942, and with a group of fellow republican officers who had founded in Athens the *Agon-Anorthosis-Anechartesia* (AAA–Struggle-Restoration-Independence). Saraphes proposed to unify and expand all existing guerrilla bands into a federation of "National Bands," which would fight the Axis and provide the means of preventing the return of the Greek monarch at liberation. Myers seized upon the idea of non-political "National Bands" as a means to obviate resistance politics and achieve his military goals. Cairo agreed,[47] but politics could not be separated from the *andartiko*.

Until the last months of 1942, Kostopoulos cooperated with ELAS, but tensions developed between the two guerrilla bands over control of supporting villages and the ideological issue of communism. ELAS disbanded the rival *andartes*, but in January 1943 Kostopoulos rallied a new, smaller band of adventurers, gendarmes, and patriots in the area of Trikkala. Saraphes and Myers hoped to raise 2,000 "National Bands" type guerrillas supported by Britain. Within a few weeks of these developments, fifty ELAS *andartes* in Thessaly defected and joined Kostopoulos.[49] This defection along with the Kostorizos affair made it clear to Aris and EAM/ELAS that Myers and AAA threatened the viability of ELAS and competed with EAM/ELAS for support villages. On February 18, 1943, ELAS accused Kostopoulos of informing on EAM/ELAS to the Italians. The charge provoked Kostopoulos to attack ELAS stores. At the end of the month, presumably after Aris's return from a visit to Athens, ELAS counterattacked and dispersed the AAA guerrillas. Kostopoulos was captured, and ELAS seized Saraphes as he was making his way into the mountains to join Kostopoulos. A subordinate of Kostopoulos escaped and rallied the dispersed guerrillas. He struck back at ELAS, but the attack failed and he fled to Zervas. When ELAS demanded his return, Zervas denied any knowledge of the guerrilla's presence in EDES territory.[50] The experience convinced Saraphes of the futility of any resistance outside of EAM/ELAS, and he left AAA to become the military commander of ELAS. During this conflict in Thessaly, ELAS disarmed other bands near Katerini, Agrinion, and Levadia.[51] Since Aris was in Athens during the final weeks of February, these incidents cannot be attributed solely to him. More than likely, EAM/ELAS was genuinely confused on what line to take regarding the arrival of the British Military Mission and the prospects of an enlarged *andartiko*.

In the midst of these events and at the urging of the BMM, Zervas made a political *volte face*. On March 9, Zervas turned his back on republicanism and telegraphed to Cairo his full support of the King of the Hellenes and the monarch's return to Greece. Zervas went further than the BMM had encouraged by denouncing EAM/ELAS as a communist front organization bent on seizing power by force. In London, Colonel Charles Hambro, the executive head of SOE, called on Sir Orme Sargent to deliver the good news of the telegram to the Foreign Office and to impress upon it that the message proved that SOE was not supporting only anti-monarchists in Greece.[52] In view of Zervas's commitment to the King, it is difficult to accept Myers's judgment of March 10 that EDES was wholeheartedly supporting the idea of National Bands "free of all politics." [53] Indeed, the Zervas telegram was deeply political, but it did not lead to unity among the resistance organizations. According to Komnenos Pyromaglou, Zervas's political officer, the telegram was nearly sufficient to cause the dissolution of the predominantly republican EDES.[54]

EAM/ELAS responded to Zervas on April 9. They denied the charges against them and listed a number of countercharges against EDES and Britain. They alleged that Britain unduly favored Zervas with supplies at the expense of EAM/ELAS, which was in fact correct. Between January and May 1943, Zervas received 59,774 lbs. of supplies to EAM/ELAS's 34,672 lbs.[55] EAM/ELAS complained that by using the term "National Bands," which was easily confused with EDES (National Republican Greek League) the British Broadcasting Corporation (BBC) gave unfair credit to Zervas for the Gorgopotamos and for the derailing of trains in Macedonia and Thessaly. The complaints were not unreasonable. EAM/ELAS was the most active resistance in Macedonia and Thessaly, and ELAS did contribute 100 *andartes* to the direct assault on the Gorgopotamos.[56]

Alarmed by the political developments in the Middle East during the early months of 1943 and the growing realization of the strength of EAM/ELAS, the Foreign Office in mid-March set about to block the development of the anti-monarchist resistance. Since January, senior officers of the Foreign Office had been convinced that SOE achievements were inadequate compared to the large sums expended and that SOE subsidized chiefly communist organizations.[57] Although pleased, the Zervas telegram of March 9 was not enough to remove these suspicions. On March 13, the Foreign Office demanded that all support to EAM/ELAS be halted and that Britain support only Zervas and monarchical bands.[58]

The military chiefs and SOE reacted quickly to counter the Foreign Office demand. Churchill's miltary advisor, Lord Ismay, pointed out the need of the resistance to support "Husky" (Sicily) and "Overlord" (France).[59] The founder of SOE and head of all operations, General Colin Gubbins, delivered to Sargent a more complete defense of SOE policy. Gubbins made it clear that the Chiefs of Staff had impressed upon SOE the importance of resistance and sabotage in Greece from any source. He emphasized that the British Liaison Officers had orders to bring the guerrillas under British

military operational control but had to take the guerrillas as
they were and not as the Foreign Office desired them to
be. Gubbins effectively argued that a break with EAM/
ELAS would lead to greater difficulties and would remove the
only lever of control over the resistance, the flow of supplies.[60]
Churchill resolved the debate by ordering limited aid to EAM/
ELAS but full support for any other groups willing to fight the
Axis under British command.[61] In the making of British policy
toward the resistance, the potential value of the guerrillas gave
the military a slight edge over the Foreign Office in March and
for the remainder of 1943. The documents in the PRO do not
make clear how this limited support for EAM/ELAS was made
operational, but the "National Bands" agreement sought by
Brigadier Myers in the following months limited the number
of resistance bands raised and limited the size of the bands
supported by Britain. In October 1943, EAM/ELAS charged
that Britain had limited ELAS to 25,000 guerrillas.

Although set back by the decision to continue support to
EAM/ELAS, the Foreign Office succeeded in winning support
for a policy to sever the communist "head" from the noncommunist "body" of EAM/ELAS.[62] This policy, however, flew in
the face of Myers's experience of January-March. Force 133,
which was responsible for all British clandestine activities in
the Balkans and Near East, was ordered to try and wean the
rank and file of EAM/ELAS away from the KKE and to shift
their allegiance to the noncommunist and "nonpolitical" National Bands, which would function under direct British military command. While continuing its limited support to EAM/
ELAS, SOE ordered the BMM to raise new guerrilla bands
that ignored politics and wished only to fight the Axis. While
working toward this end, the British Liaison Officers were to
prevent clashes between the bands. If ELAS attacked any of
the other bands, British support was to stop until the hostilities
ended and the non-ELAS band was fully restored.[63] With the
exception of cutting off supplies to recalcitrant ELAS units,
this policy was a replay of Myers's earlier policy which had
failed during January-March. The new policy failed again
between March and June. EAM/ELAS was too well organized
to be split and too strong to be affected by threats of reduced
supplies, yet the policy might have succeeded.

SOE believed that the policy could succeed if political concessions had been adopted. Unencumbered by any sentimental
and political attachments to the Greek King, SOE was far more

attuned to the political realities of Greek politics than the Foreign Office was. As early as the autumn of 1942, SOE suggested that Plastiras be spirited out of France and into Greece to lead the resistance and to neutralize the communists. Well aware of the need for a concession on the part of the King, if the policy against EAM/ELAS was to succeed, SOE asked in March that the King publicly declare his intention not to return before a plebiscite, and it revived the notion of sending in Plastiras to rally the allegiance of the noncommunists. The Foreign Office was horrified at the idea of sending to Greece the leader of the 1922 revolt against Constantinos I and an avowed republican of uncertain British sympathies. Plastiras may not have been the answer to the Greek political tangle, but once again the Foreign Office refused any political concessions toward the resistance. The War Cabinet's decision of March stood unchanged.

By the middle of May, the Foreign Office recognized that the policy of attempting to break off the communist element from EAM/ELAS and organizing a "nonpolitical" resistance under SOE had failed.[64] Rather than make any political concessions to the resistance, Tsouderos, Ambassador Leeper, and even Lord Glenconner of SOE (Cairo) advocated a final showdown with EAM/ELAS by threatening to brand the organization as traitorous if they did not respond to British pressure. On the more restrained recommendation of Dixon, British policy remained unchanged and continued to appeal to EAM/ELAS's sense of patriotism to cooperate with Britain and to leave rival guerrillas unmolested. Failing this, Dixon suggested that Britain should cut off supplies to any deviant ELAS units.[65] To smooth relations between the resistance and British and Greek officials, Dixon suggested that the King and Tsouderos bring guerrilla representatives to Cairo for discussions. This suggestion was originally proposed by Tzimas to Woodhouse and relayed by Woodhouse to Cairo. After learning of the request, Leeper adopted the idea on March 17.[66] In making this proposal, Dixon had not mellowed toward EAM/ELAS. Rather, he feared the negative political consequences for Britain if charges against EAM/ELAS reopened the question of Britain's ties to the King and the Metaxas dictatorship.[67] Myers was ordered to continue to organize guerrillas wherever he found them and not to be too careful if ELAS *andartes* ignored ELAS directives.[68]

Neither Britain nor EAM/ELAS perceived one another as

each desired. SOE remained convinced that it had not shown any preference for Zervas, which was not the case, and that EAM/ELAS was "self-seeking." Zervas, on the other hand, remained "nonpolitical" and unselfish. To the British Military Mission and SOE, the canvassing of EDES guerrillas by British Liaison Officers in EAM/ELAS territories was not threatening to EAM/ELAS. British officials naively assumed that the raising of rival guerrilla bands had no political consequences, but a BLO in Thessaly on April 30 reported to Cairo the grave view EAM/ELAS took of British efforts to raise EDES bands in EAM/ELAS areas.[69] In spite of EAM/ELAS complaints, the BBC continued to refer to resistance activities in Thessaly and Macedonia, which were clearly EAM/ELAS areas, as carried out by "National Bands." [70] Since EAM/ELAS was not ignorant of the fact that Zervas received a larger share of British supplies, and in the face of other anti-EAM/ELAS activities, their conclusion that Britain planned to raise a rival resistance to divide and replace them was not unreasonable but fair.

On their side, EAM/ELAS were either too slow or too confused to understand the injury done to their cause by the attacks on rival bands and the failure to cooperate readily with the British mission. The violence done to rival bands confirmed in the minds of British and exile Greek officials the belief that EAM/ELAS was determined to seize power rather than fight the Axis. A policy that welcomed British cooperation would have won prestige for EAM/ELAS in the eyes of the BMM and would have enhanced the position of the Chiefs of Staff who wanted to expand the Balkan resistance. There is evidence that the leadership of the KKE and EAM/ELAS was becoming aware of the negative impact of ELAS violence against rival partisans. Certainly a shift in favor of cooperation did take place after Tzimas arrived in the mountains in March to reorganize and expand ELAS. Behind Tzimas came a wave of new men to the mountains from the towns. Demetriou referred to them as "priest-like ideologues" whose orientation was quite different from the original *andartes*.[71] Until then, the *andartiko* was dominated by semi-independent forces under leaders like Aris in Roumeli and Kostas Karageorgios in Thessaly. Partsalides characterized these *andartiko* chieftains as emotional and quick to follow their instincts, implying that they did not accept party discipline easily.[72]

In May Tzimas established the ELAS General Headquarters (ELAS GHQ) headed by a *troika* designed to control Aris. Saraphes became the chief military officer, and Tzimas was the chief political officer representing the KKE and EAM central committees. Aris was made a *kapetanios*. The new arrangement led to the most cooperative period of the war between Britain and the resistance, but before examining this period of the National Bands Agreement, it is necessary to gain a larger picture of the general development of the resistance.

EKKA and the Other Resistance Organizations

EKKA (National and Social Liberation) was formed by the collaboration of Colonel Bakirtzis, Georgios Kartalis, Colonel Demetrios Psarros, and British agents. Kartalis was a graduate of the London School of Economics and a former associate of the politician Georgios Kaphandaris. The war and the occupation, however, created a new political consciousness in Kartalis, and he shifted to the left in his political ideas. Psarros was a highly respected former Venizelist officer. Both Psarros and Kartalis refused to join EAM/ELAS because of the role played by the KKE and rejected EDES on account of Zervas's dictatorial tendencies.[73] According to Pyromaglou, Bakirtzis joined EKKA after EAM/ELAS refused him a high post in ELAS. While Psarros and Bakirtzis concentrated on organizing a guerrilla force around the nucleus of veterans from Psarros's former regiment, Kartalis served as the chief political officer and played a key role at the Cairo conference in August 1943 and the Lebanon conference of May 1944. The organization's political platform appeared in the first edition of its clandestine newspaper, *Apeleutherose* (Liberation), on April 17, 1943. The program called for the establishment at the end of the war of a *Laocratoumene Democratia* (Popular Democracy) that would break the power of big banks and large economic institutions. The largest property holders would lose their holdings, and all indirect taxes would be abolished. Civil liberties and equal educational opportunities were guaranteed to all citizens. The platform emphasized that the program of social reform would be established only through popular sovereignty as expressed through universal suffrage.[74] Like EDES and EAM/ELAS, EKKA bore a republican character.

Since EKKA emerged late and failed to develop into a cohesive unit, it did not win wide popular support. Throughout its tenuous existence, EKKA depended on EAM/ELAS controlled villages in the area of Mt. Parnassos and British supply drops for survival. According to Major Gordon Creed, the BLO attached to Psarros, the Greek colonel was of undoubted courage and commitment to the anti-Axis struggle, but his senior officers never developed strong ties of loyalty to their commander, and Psarros never established firm discipline over his band. An elderly colonel made off with 500 gold sovereigns and disappeared for the remainder of the war. One of Psarros's subordinates, Major Kapitsonis, became a leading personality who commanded wider allegiance than Psarros. Captain Euthemios Dedouses, a royalist who suffered severe mental and emotional strain for two years as an Italian prisoner of war, became one of Kapitsonis's devoted followers. The prison experience, according to Major Creed, left Dedouses unstable. Whether this condition was or was not responsible is not clear, but Dedouses provoked a number of incidents with EAM/ELAS. Another leading officer, Major Langouranis, joined ELAS in April 1944.

In May 1943, Aris surrounded Psarros and 400 guerrillas and gave them the choice of joining ELAS or disbanding. One week later, the ELAS *kapetanios* dissolved an EKKA band near Agrinion. He told British officers that he was acting on verbal orders from Athens. When Tzimas learned of the incident, he disavowed Aris's action and insisted that the ELAS guerrilla had acted without authority. Myers remained uncertain if Tzimas was correct, but he interpreted the decision to restore EKKA as an expression of a willingness on the part of Tzimas and EAM/ELAS to cooperate with the BMM.[75] Yet, a second dissolution and restoration took place in June. At its peak in 1944, EKKA fielded 1,000 guerrillas, but it never expanded beyond the region of Mt. Parnassos. Major Waterhouse, Leeper's second secretary, concluded that EKKA had been a fragile organization that thinly covered deep personal conflicts.[76] Since EKKA was unable to overcome internal weaknesses and tensions, ELAS easily dissolved the organization in 1944. Kartalis, however, continued to play a key role in Greek wartime politics.

In 1941, a former Venizelist deputy, Angelos Agapitos, and a group of army officers formed *Yperaspistai Boreiou Ellados* (YBE—Defenders of Northern Greece). To avoid Axis capture in the winter of 1941-1942, Agapitos fled from Salonica but lost contact with the Middle East. For a while YBE drifted toward the political right and eventually became defunct.[77] Out of the remnants of YBE, SOE officers in the summer of 1943 assisted two Greek army officers, Major Georgios Goulgoutzis and Major Demetrios Sarris, to form the *Panellenios Apeleutherotike Organosis* (PAO—Pan-Hellenic Liberation Organization). Although PAO included a number of influential persons, SOE's Colonel N. G. L. Hammond reported that EAM leadership was more determined, and PAO could not halt the shift toward EAM/ELAS in northern Greece. PAO became a well-funded organization, and it began publishing a clandestine newspaper, *Ethnike Phone* (National Voice), on June 1, 1943. Gradually, it became an ultra-royalist, urban based group devoted primarily to collecting intelligence for Cairo and conducting Allied propaganda in the area of Salonica. On orders from the Greek exiled government, PAO agents moved only at night, and efforts to link PAO to EDES failed over Zervas's demands for total authority. The passive stance of PAO alienated twenty-five younger officers who went over to EAM/ELAS in July 1943.[78] D. S. Laskey of the Foreign Office's Southern Department hoped to expand PAO into a major organization, but it remained a small and ineffective resistance group which played no important sabotage role.[79]

As reflected in their cautious orders to PAO, the Greek exile government efforts to organize any resistance remained faint, but the growth of EAM/ELAS in 1943 stirred the lethargy of the political world in Athens. While a large number of officers rallied to Rallis in security battalions, other extreme, wealthy rightists rallied around Panagiotes Siphneos, Spyros Markezinis, and Christos Zalokostas, who founded *Ethnike Drasis* (ED—National Action). The leaders of ED had been linked at times to Colonel Tsigantes and General Papagos, but no concrete resistance emerged from these associations. ED believed SOE to be too leftist and distrusted Zervas. They founded six small bands in the Peloponnese between March and August 1943, but only one of these groups survived ELAS attacks in March-April.[80] Closely associated with ED was Colonel Georgios Grivas and X ("Chi"). Grivas concentrated his efforts in the wealthy districts of Athens and expanded X to between 2,000 and 3,000 armed men in 1944. He recruited his men and arms from officers who were retained on the active list under the Rallis government. Other groups like "Theros" and Roumelia-Avlon-Nisi (RAN) were essentially small one-man operations. RAN was made up of former Venizelist army officers turned monarchists. One of their leaders, Colonel Constantinos Venderes, left Greece in 1944 and became the Chief of the Army. In November 1943, these groups formed an umbrella organization called *Panellenios Apeleutherotikos Syndesmos* (PAS–National Liberation League). Although these extremist right-wing groups desired support from Cairo, they received neither funds nor arms from SOE,[81] and they lacked the popular support to become anything more than sectarian organizations.

If hesitation and false starts marked the efforts of the noncommunist resistance on the mainland, the story on Crete was dramatically different. There, the spontaneous resistance gained momentum under local leadership and demonstrated what happened when the traditional political leadership took the initiative in leading the resistance—it neutralized the communists. On the western end of the island at Rethymnos, Colonel Tziphakis organized the town against all rival groups and succeeded in asserting his leadership until 1944. In Chania and Heraklion, no single group emerged to organize these areas. Resistance centered on the local villages and hereditary *andarte* leaders. To the south *Kapetan* Petrakogeorgis held sway, while Kostas Xylouris ruled the Mt. Ida area. Manolis and Yiannis Bandouvas controlled the remaining areas. In November 1943, Manolis Bandouvas led an attack that annihilated a German company and liquidated a number of German informants. This attack brought on savage German reprisals against prominent Cretans and forced Manolis Bandouvas to flee to the Middle East. On the eastern end of the island, Miltiades Porphyrogennis and General Emmanouil Mandakas led the resistance for EAM/ELAS, but as they were unable to extend their power they moved to the mainland in 1944. Gradually, the *Ethnike Organosis Kritis* (EOK–National Organization of Crete), which was founded in 1942 and was strongly supported by Britain, brought the various resistance groups under its control and neutralized the communists under the leadership of the conservative Emmanouil Papadogiannis.[82] Similarly, on Chios, the communists were neutralized by the formation of a unified resistance under noncommunist leadership.[83] On the mainland, however, the default of the political world and the timidity of the exile government cleared the way for EAM/ELAS. Only EDES and, for a short while, EKKA were alternatives to EAM/ ELAS, but they were totally dependent on the external support of Great Britain.

ELAS

Between March and June 1943, EDES expanded to a force of 4,000, while ELAS, building on a larger territorial and political support base, developed an armed body of 12,000 *andartes*. EDES continued to expand gradually until the outbreak of civil war in October 1943. By December, this struggle along with German attacks so weakened EDES by defections and losses—an estimated 3,000 to 4,000 guerrillas dropped out and went home or joined ELAS[84]—that Colonel Woodhouse suggested to his superiors that EDES be disbanded, but SOE refused.[85] With extensive British support, EDES recovered during 1944 but never achieved the efficiency of ELAS.[86] Zervas ended the war with about 7,000 active guerrillas out of a total force of 12,000.[87] By the beginning of January 1944, the Germans correctly identified six ELAS divisions with an estimated strength of 7,000 actives and 24,000 reserves.

The company served as the basic ELAS unit, and at full strength stood at 200 men, including static reserves. The Germans estimated that the actual number of active, mobile ELAS *andartes* averaged fifty per company. Three companies formed a battalion, and three battalions made a regiment. A division consisted of three regiments, and at full strength totaled 5,050, only one-fourth to one-third of whom were active. At the divisional and regional command, the *troika* command, analogous to the ELAS GHQ, prevailed. Below the divisional level, units had only a military commander and a *kapetanios*. By the end of the occupation the Germans identified eight divisions, including the names of the commanding officers, at a strength of 45,000.

The German estimates compared favorably with British estimates. On May 3, 1944, the operations commander of Force 133, Brigadier K. V. Barker-Benfield, concluded that ELAS strength stood at 26,000.[88] ELAS continued to expand during the summer of 1944 and ended the occupation period with an estimated 50,000 *andartes*.[89] Following the December 1944 fighting, the British command in Athens estimated ELAS strength at 41,250.[90] Brigadier Barker-Benfield estimated the total membership of EAM/ELAS at 200,000 in 1944,[91] which was below the estimate of L. S. Stavrianos of between 500,000 to 2,000,000.[92] The German records provided no estimates or figures for EAM, except to report that, by June 1943, 90 percent of the population opposed the Axis and verged on insurrection. If Allied strategy had demanded a popular uprising in July and August, which was one of Myers's contingencies for which he was to prepare, the Greek resistance could have provided it.

The expansion of ELAS took place under limited British support, and PRO records suggest that ELAS could have been much larger. The MO5c Post-Mortem Report stated, "Full support of EAM/ELAS in the summer of 1943 would have probably served the immediate military object ... but there was considerable risk. It would not have served our longer term military objects (OVERLORD) at all well." [93] Since a fire in 1946 destroyed some SOE records, complete figures are no longer available for an exact accounting of British support of the Greek resistance. According to E. G. Boxshall, the official in charge of SOE archives, the amount of support totalled:

2,230,000 pounds sterling (1942-Nov. 1944) ;[a]

1,523 tons of supplies dropped in 1,006 sorties;

4,000 tons of supplies infiltrated by sea (80 percent of these were food, clothing, and medical supplies for relief) ;

5,523 total tonnage of supplies.[b]

---

[a] Since SOE estimated that one gold sovereign was worth two pounds sterling, the total number of sovereigns imported into Greece by SOE was 1,115,000. Woodhouse cited a figure of 1.3 million.[94]

[b] Letter to the author from E. G. Boxshall, March 21, 1975.

Although the recently opened PRO records offer only fragmentary evidence on this point, they give some indication of how this sum was distributed among the resistance and other groups.

Organizations	Number of Sovereigns Received	Chronological Period
Zervas	24,000[a]	1942
	18,000[b]	Oct. 1, 1943-mid-Jan. 1944
	168,000[c]	Jan. 1-Dec. 27, 1944
EAM/ELAS	—	1942
	937[d]	Oct. 1, 1943-mid-Jan. 1944
	8,800[e]	Feb. 1944
	24,000[f]	June 1944
EKKA	3,600[g]	Oct. 1, 1943-mid-Jan. 1944
	1,900[h]	Feb. 1944
Italian POW Relief	5,500[i]	June 1944

[a] Woodhouse, *The Struggle for Greece*, p. 104.

[b] PRO FO371/4369 R2767/9/19, Leeper to FO, Feb. 20, 1944.

[c] PRO WO204/8833, Brigadier Barker-Benfield's Report on Zervas, Dec. 27, 1944.

[d] PRO FO371/43679 R2767/9/19, Leeper to FO, Feb. 20, 1944.

[e] *Ibid.*

[f] PRO FO371/43688 R9842/9/19, Leeper to FO, June 22, 1944. Leeper cites 20,000 sovereigns as a *monthly rate* for relief and 4,000 per month for *andarte* relief. This monthly rate of 24,000 could not have begun before March 1944. The 4,000 figure probably refers to the British policy of compensating families who had either lost a member in the resistance or had property destroyed by German reprisals. The policy aimed to maintain popular support for the resistance by ameliorating the suffering of the civilians. See FO371/37204 R7356/9/19, Pearson to Dixon, Aug. 10, 1943.

[g] PRO FO371/43679 R27667/9/19, Leeper to FO, Feb. 20, 1944.

[h] *Ibid.*

[i] PRO FO371/43688 R9842/9/19, Leeper to FO, June 22, 1944. Leeper referred to this figure as a *monthly rate*, which was probably consistent for the last year of the occupation. If this assumption is correct, the total for Italian relief in 1944 would be an estimated 66,000 gold sovereigns.

If the *monthly figure* for EAM/ELAS cited in Leeper's dispatch of June 22, 1944, is assumed to be the same rate for the period March through October 1944, the total for that period would be 192,000 sovereigns. If the February figure of 8,800 is added, the total sum for 1944 would be projected to approximately 200,800 sovereigns. Considering the March 1943 decision to limit support of EAM/ELAS and to expand non-EAM/

ELAS guerrillas, it is unlikely that Zervas received less in 1943 than in 1944. These projected figures would be:

Organization	Amount	Period
Zervas	24,000	1942[a]
	168,000	1943[b]
	168,000	1944
	360,000[c]	
EAM/ELAS	—	1942[d]
	216,937	1943[e]
	200,800	1944[f]
	417,737	
EKKA	8,400	1943[g]
	5,700	1944[h]
	14,100	
Italian POW Relief	55,000	1943-1944[i]
TOTAL	846,837	1942-1944

[a] This includes only the initial amount given to Zervas to organize a resistance band, and therefore may be an exaggerated underestimate of the total he received in 1942.

[b] A projected figure based on the known amount of 1944, 168,000.

[c] A projected estimate.

[d] There are no records showing that EAM/ELAS received any funds in 1942 from SOE.

[e] A projected figure based on the estimated rate of 24,000 per month between January and September 1943, which of course may be an overestimate.

[f] A projected figure based on the 24,000 monthly rate cited for June 1944.

[g] A projected figure based on an estimated monthly rate of 1,200, which is the average monthly rate based on the established figure for October 1943 to mid-January 1944 (3,600). The figure is a low estimate as it does not try to estimate the amount initially given to EKKA to form a guerrilla band.

[h] A projected amount for the period January through April 1944 based on the monthly rate of 1,900 cited by Leeper for February 1944.

[i] A ten-month projected amount based on the monthly rate of 5,500 cited by Leeper for June 1944, which may be an underestimate as it omits 1943.

Since Zervas was limited to the area of Epirus, the 360,000 sovereigns for EDES becomes even more significant compared to EAM/ELAS, which was a national organization. Further, EAM/ELAS, EDES, and EKKA were not the only groups to receive funds. SOE sovereigns went to independent agents like "Apollo," or Ioannis Peltekis, a wealthy Athenian lawyer who financed innumerable sabotage attacks against the Axis between 1942 and 1944. Peltekis funneled Zervas 24,000 sovereigns in 1942. It is not clear how many sovereigns "Apollo" received between 1942 and 1944; he must have received large sums. "Yvonne" was another independent agent engaged in sabotage, but of whom nothing is known except that he or she existed. In 1944, Colonel Speliotopoulos replaced "Apollo" as SOE's prime contact, and he too must have received considerable sums as Britain prepared for the liberation of Greece. How much he received remains unknown. What is clear is that it is unlikely EAM/ELAS received between three-quarter and one million gold sovereigns as suggested by Woodhouse.[95] Rather, a liberal estimate would conclude EAM/ELAS received about 40 percent, EDES or Zervas 30 percent, and the other resistance organizations and independent agents the remaining 30 percent.

In the area of arms supplies, EAM/ELAS did less well. Woodhouse has suggested that the amount was under 1,000 tons, and in this case he may be correct, but the figure may still be a little inflated.[96] During 1943, before the outbreak of the civil war, EAM/ELAS and the BMM reached their peak of cooperation and efficiency in guerrilla war. According to Michael Howard, Britain delivered a total of 898 tons of supplies to the Greek resistance in 1943. The largest amount, 629 tons,[97] was delivered between July and September. The PRO records reveal the following figures, all in tons: [98]

	January-May 1943	October 1943-mid-January 1944
EDES	29.7 (59,774 lbs.)	88 (74 arms; 14 food/clothing/medical)
EAM/ELAS	17.0 (34,072 lbs.)	56 (22 arms; 34 food/clothing/medical)
EKKA	—	16 (14 arms; 2 food/clothing/medical)

If the 629 tons for July to September is divided equally between EDES and EAM/ELAS, which is unlikely as some of these supplies went to EKKA, EAM/ELAS's total share of supplies for 1943 is only 387.5 tons (17+314.5+56=387.5). Since this figure includes clothes, food, and medical supplies, the figure for the arms would be considerably less. After January 1944, EAM/ELAS no longer served Allied strategic interests and probably received fewer arms in 1944 than in 1943. Rather than 1,000 tons of arms for EAM/ELAS, the figure may well have been 500 tons or less, which would conform to the low estimates suggested in Communist accounts.[99] According to Eudes, total Allied deliveries of arms to ELAS amounted to 3,000 rifles, 300 Sten guns, 30 heavy machine guns, 100 machine rifles (Bren guns), and 10 mortars.[100] By contrast, the PRO documents show that, in 1944 alone, Zervas received the following weapons: 5,000 light machine guns, 7.5 million rounds of light arms ammunition, 140 81mm (three-inch) mortars, and 16,000 mortar bombs.[101] The conclusion is unmistakable: EAM/ELAS gathered most of their weapons from the enemy, especially from the Italians who surrendered in September 1943, and expanded under their own power.

Resistance supplies came from taxes levied in kind on local villages, from goods purchased by the gold sovereigns, which were paid to each *andarte* at a rate of one per each month of service, and the supplies provided by SOE. While EDES allowed each of its members to keep their sovereigns, EAM/ELAS put its allotment into a general fund for common expenditures. This system strengthened EAM/ELAS domination over Free Greece by allowing them to control the flow of gold to individuals or areas that might prove troublesome. ETA distributed 75 percent of the taxes in kind to ELAS, while another 20 percent was returned to the local central committee for local use. The remaining 5 percent went for general relief.[102] This last 25 percent provided EAM/ELAS with another significant means of molding public opinion in support of the resistance.

In the winter of 1941-1942, newspapers appeared as mimeographed sheets, but in the spring of 1943 printed issues with illustrations became common. These served to inform the public on the progress of the war and provided each organization the means to conduct political propaganda. Clandestine publications of EAM/ELAS listed Greeks who worked for the Axis and threatened reprisals unless they either ceased or joined the resistance. Prominent names of individuals connected to the Axis were condemned in clandestine courts and death sen-

tences were published. Executions were carried out by the
EAM/ELAS assassination squads, OPLA.[103]

OPLA's operatives were usually recruited from youths between the ages of eighteen and twenty-two. These agents
operated in villages, towns, and cities, often shooting down or
handgrenading their victims in the streets. By June 1944,
according to the German authorities, five to ten persons died
each day from the hands of such terrorists.[104] Prime targets
were quisling government officials. In the first six months of
1944, OPLA agents assassinated the quisling Minister of Labor,
the prefect of Euboea, and the sub-prefect of Patras; they
kidnapped the prefects of Chalkidike, Cephalonia, Lamia, and
Macedonia. By July 1944, 2,000 teachers had fled Athens in
fear of their lives, and the government could not fill eight
of Greece's forty-one prefectures for the same reason.[105] Local
collaborators, or those believed to be collaborators, suffered
from similar attacks. Individuals were tried by EAM/ELAS
courts-martial for "anti-national" acts and active collaboration. This provided a clear means for eliminating EAM/ELAS
rivals. Wives of alleged collaborators were also condemned to
death.[106]

The National Bands Agreement, June-August 1943

The expansion of the resistance led to competition between
EAM/ELAS and other resistance bands for control of villages
and recruits, and the open hostilities of March carried over into
April and May. The Italians reported that clashes between
EAM/ELAS and other bands involving 100 to 150 casualties
continued into the late spring of 1943. Captured guerrilla
documents revealed that individual commanders were ar-
ranging local truces even after all organizations had committed
themselves to cooperating with the BMM in the National Bands
Agreement of July 1943. These differences, along with the
personal and political ambitions of the resistance leaders,
prevented any genuine unification of the Greek guerrilla bands.
British policy was also a factor. Yet in the period between
June 17 and the first week of July, the resistance did
cooperate for the successful execution of Operation "Animals,"
designed to deflect Axis attention away from Italy and toward
Greece as the expected target of an Allied landing.

On May 18, Myers reported to Cairo that EAM/ELAS had

agreed to full cooperation with Britain, but only as an Allied force of the United Nations. That is, EAM/ELAS intended to cooperate with General Wilson as Commander-in-Chief but insisted on retaining their sovereignty and freedom of action.[107] And although EAM/ELAS did not actually sign the agreement until July 4, the organization cooperated fully from June 22 through the month of July. Even the Foreign Office recognized Myers's achievement, and on July 16 conveyed its appreciation to Myers for his success.[108]

The National Bands Agreement established a Joint General Headquarters (JGHQ) for the resistance and allowed the British Military Mission under Brigadier Myers to coordinate a series of guerrilla actions that were designed to draw German troops into Greece and away from Italy. The JGHQ was established at Pertouli, high in the Pindos Mountains. The joint command facilitated the execution of "Animals" and served to strengthen the administration of Free Greece. A major EAM/ELAS concession was to allow the BMM to raise bands in hitherto exclusive ELAS areas. The agreement limited the number of new bands raised and offered a bonus of fifty additional *andartes* for EAM/ELAS if the new *andartes* tolerated older, non-ELAS guerrillas. Since EDES believed that it could raise more bands than ELAS, Zervas at first opposed the agreement but then relented and signed.[109] The three major resistance organizations were represented, and they set prices for the hiring of animals and purchasing of food supplies. This reduced the friction between EDES and EAM/ELAS. Tax levies in kind were patterned after EAM/ELAS's system. Further reduction in friction resulted from the establishment of joint garrisons in areas where EDES and EAM/ELAS operated. The JGHQ adopted and began to implement for all of Free Greece the provisional code for local self-government and popular justice which EAM/ELAS had already established in central Greece. In the summer of 1943, elections were carried out for committees on administration, popular courts, security, forestry, ecclesiastical affairs, and relief.[110] Unfortunately, the cooperation did not survive the political storms of the summer of 1943 and the civil war of the ensuing winter. The JGHQ disintegrated in October 1943.

But before the problem of the civil war may be considered, it is necessary to complete the story of the events surrounding the success of "Animals" and the continued expansion of the resistance. By June 1943, the resistance had grown so strong that the Axis feared a popular revolt. Armed clashes between Italians and *andartes* intensified during the months of April and May as EAM/ELAS expanded throughout all of Greece. Between April 16 and May 4, 1943, 117 *andartes* died in battles with the Italians, who arrested 885 Greek suspects.[111] By May 15, 1943, ELAS launched its first attacks against the Axis in the Peloponnese. During the first week of June, 123 guerrillas died in clashes around Trikkala, and on June 19 another 143 fell in battles near Karditsa.[112] Between June 22 and July 12, resistance activity reached its peak. ELAS and the BMM cut the key Larissa-Salonica rail line in many places and interdicted the roads south to Athens. EDES destroyed a series of small bridges, successfully cutting the main German supply road through Metsovon pass. EDES and ELAS engaged battalion-size enemy forces for the first time and conducted sabotage against Axis lines of communication throughout Greece.

ELAS refused as too dangerous, however, the BMM proposal to destroy the Asopos viaduct. They also feared Axis reprisals would harm the popularity of the *andartes*.[113] ELAS preferred to destroy the Tournovo tunnel as an Italian train passed through it. The destruction of the tunnel was successful, but the EAM/ELAS claim that 500 Italians died was incorrect. Ninety-two Italians were killed and over 200 wounded, but sixty Greek hostages, who had been placed in a lead car as a deterrent by the Axis, died with the Italians.[114] A British sabotage team tackled the Asopos on their own, and Captain Don Stott played the key role in the destruction of the viaduct.

Operation "Animals" and the National Bands Agreement proved that EAM/ELAS, under the leadership of Tzimas, could cooperate with the BMM. The guerrilla activity reinforced Hitler's conviction that the Balkans were the target of the forthcoming invasion. The OKW ordered the *104 Jaegerdivision* and the elite *1 Gebirgsdivision*, which had been removed from the eastern front and already assigned to duty in Greece, to enter the country immediately on June 19, 1943.[115] Resistance in the cities increased and paralleled the developments in the mountains. An unsuccessful Greek attempt to blow up an Italian ship in port at Piraeus resulted in the reprisal of nine hostages being shot on June 17, 1943. The incident prompted EAM/ELAS to call for a general strike on June 25, an action which proved to be one of the most impressive anti-Axis demonstrations of the occupation. The strike even pulled 1,200 Athenian policemen away from their jobs for one week. They returned only after the Rallis government dismissed 395 of the strikers.[116] Huge columns of protesters had to be dispersed by police and troop gunfire. The German *Befh. Sued-Grld.* concluded that only those Greeks who were making money by supplying the Axis (about 10 percent) remained friendly to the occupying powers. The remainder were overwhelmingly hostile. The Rallis government, which had been able to keep order in Athens as late as April, could no longer survive without massive German support.[117]

German Counter-Resistance Measures

From the beginning to the end of the occupation, the primary function of *Wehrmacht* units in Greece was to resist any Allied landing and to maintain open roads of communication and supply leading into Greece. Until July 1943, the Italians held responsibility for the internal security of the area, including anti-guerrilla operations. German authorities took action only in cases of specific sabotage in their zones of occupation. *HGrE* took command of guarding supply points, supply routes, the more important roads and bridges, supply trains and dumps, and the regulation of movement along roads after Hitler issued Directive No. 48 on July 26, 1943. This directive also ordered *HGrE* to plan a series of large-scale anti-guerrilla operations to begin in the fall of 1943.

The reorganization of the Southeast Command in July placed the security for the rear areas under regular army units, the *SS*, and Greek *Freiwillige* (Volunteer) troops. Particularly useful in this task were the *Geheime Feldpolizei*, which were attached to the German divisions and organized nets of informers and interrogated prisoners. The *HSSPF* directed all police forces, including the *Freiwillige* units. These troops and police were affiliated but not actually attached to the German armed forces. Technically, the *Mil. Befh. Grld.* held the responsibility for the security of rear areas, but in reality he was superseded by the armed forces commander, in this case Lt. Gen. Loehr.

Complete pacification of rear areas required more troops than were available to occupy every village and hamlet. Because of this shortage, the Germans concentrated on occupying key strategic positions along their interior lines of communication and supply. The remainder of the countryside was left to the guerrillas, except for an occasional foray. During the first year and one-half of the occupation, the Greek resistance posed no threat to the invader. Nevertheless, the German policy of dealing with armed bands and acts of sabotage was established on the eastern front during this time. On September 20, 1941, the *OKW* issued orders for the suppression of insurgency in occupied Europe. The order assumed that all insurgents were directed by Moscow and that only severe retaliation could halt the spread of resistance. Between 50 and 100 hostages were to be shot in reprisal for any attack on or death of a German soldier. The *Mil. Befh.* was to carry out the shootings.[118] A modified version of this order served as the standard for dealing with insurgency in Greece. The ratio was fifty executions for every German death and ten for every German wounded. The standard did not remain constant, however.

Until December 1943, the Germans shot first and asked questions later. As this indiscriminate policy of reprisals did not slow down the growth of the resistance movements throughout the Balkans, pressure within the Southeast Command led to a new policy which, at the end of December, ordered that reprisals be held up for forty-eight hours while efforts were made to find those actually guilty of acts of sabotage. The *Sicherheitsdienst* (SD) and the *Abwehr* collected hostages on the basis of who was a true communist or generally uncooperative with the occupation authorities, and they sought to avoid arresting "nationalists." In this more selective way they hoped to avoid alienating the whole population, in particular those who might collaborate. What followed, however, proved rather indiscriminating.[119]

During the summer of 1943, *HGrE* implemented the pattern of defense developed in rear areas on the Russian front. Short on manpower, the Germans established a series of *Stuetzpunkte* (Strong Points) along vital lines of communications and at strategic military locations. They became small forts containing a squad or a platoon but at times a company, depending on the importance of the point. These troops were armed with automatic weapons, mortars, and anti-tank guns. The approaches to the strong point were heavily mined and covered with obstacles and barbed wire. Armored cars maintained communications between them, and heavily armed units were held ready for action in reserve at key points. Although the *Stuetzpunkte* were about six miles apart, they failed to establish German control of the country. Instead, they became prime targets for the resistance, which often reduced them to beleaguered outposts.[120]

The most effective anti-guerrilla force was the *Jagdkommando* (Ranger Detachment), which consisted of the young and inexperienced combined with combat-wise veterans. They were usually platoon or company strength. The *Jagdkommando* engaged the guerrillas and then called in reserves. While they were effective, they were too small and too few to master the situation.[121] "Combing" operations were conducted by battalion strength forces which moved along a road with skirmish lines thrown out about ten kilometers on each side. These actions cleared the road only temporarily, and they had no effect on guerrilla organization. The first German unit formed along these lines for anti-partisan warfare went into action in March 1943. The force was a combination of German troops and Greek Evzones, which operated in northern Greece. Large-scale operations, however, did not take place until September and October 1943.

At that time, the Germans launched a series of *Grossunternehmungen* (Large Operations). These regiment-size operations attempted unsuccessfully to encircle and destroy large concentrations of guerrillas. They usually required one or two weeks to complete. Insufficient forces, the poor mobility of the German units, and difficult terrain combined with the guerrillas' early warning system in every Greek village to defeat these operations. The operations did kill the partisans they intercepted, but huge gaps in the intended circle allowed most to escape. In December 1943, the commander of the *LXVIII* AK concluded that the efforts were futile. If they were to succeed, he continued, the *LXVIII* AK would require one more mountain division, which was not forthcoming. Smaller-sized operations proved partially successful, but these depended too much on surprise and excellent intelligence, neither of which was easily attainable. When the *Jagdkommando* did achieve this result, they were usually too small to take on large units of *andartes*. In regard to civilian control, continued the commander, only when German troops established security by armed guards could the population be influenced against the guerrillas. Where there were no troops, the *andartes* prevailed and exerted their power. The only method to demonstrate

German power to the civilian population and to deter their support for the guerrillas lay in extensive reprisals.[122]

Lt. General Hans Felmy, favorably impressed by the Greek *Freiwilligen-Verbaende* under his command, encouraged *HGrE* to increase their number as a means of supplementing German manpower. *HGrE* was also impressed by them, and Loehr authorized the formation of two more battalions. A summary report on the operations of the fall and winter of 1943 by the command of the *LXVIII* AK recommended that anti-guerrilla actions be limited to small operations (not larger than company-size units) and that *Grossunternehmungen* be used only when extensive reprisals were ordered ("... *wenn umfangreiche Suehnemassnahmen erforderlich sind*"). The report recommended air attacks on partisan centers that were inaccessible by land.[123]

These recommendations were not followed completely in 1944. Larger operations were carried out in January (Operation *"Amsel"*) and in March and April (Operations *"Condor,"* *"Reiher,"* *"Ingel,"* and *"Geier"*). The situation remained unchanged, however. The Germans concluded that these operations "had no meaningful success" as they in no way disturbed the resistance's organization.[124]

For their part, the resistance avoided any pitched battles with the Germans. They retreated into the mountains, leaving behind rear guards to attack isolated German detachments. In this classic guerrilla fashion the resistance avoided the superior firepower of the enemy.[125]

The large operations carried out by the more experienced and better-trained mountain troops of the *XXII Geb. AK* did not destroy resistance organization but did inflict a higher rate of casualties on the guerrillas. This fact stood out in the results of operations *"Panther"* (October 1943), *"Gemsbock"* (June 1944), and *"Steinadler"* (July 1944). Aided by *SS* units and Greek *Freiwilligen-Verbaende*, the *XXII Geb. AK.* under Lt. Gen. Lanz inflicted, on EAM/ELAS territory, casualties of 1,400 (*"Panther"*), 2,500 (*"Gemsbock"*), and 1,426 (*"Steinadler"*). These figures included dead and captured, and they made no distinction between *andartes* and civilians shot as hostages.[126] Attrition alone, however, failed to disrupt EAM/ELAS. When the Germans and Greeks returned to their bases, the *andartes* reestablished their control over the countryside.

Since the attempt to destroy the guerrillas by armed sweeps through the countryside failed, and since the Germans lacked the troops to effectively occupy the whole country, they resorted to the only weapon left, terror—terror directed against the civilian population as a means of discouraging the resistance. This indiscriminate savagery only intensified Greek hatred for the Germans. Authority for execution rested originally with the *Mil. Befh.*, but in Greece the conflicting chain of command gave this power to a number of officials. The *HSSPF*, the *Sonderbevollmaechtigter*, and the *Mil. Befh.* had this authority, and after July 8, 1943, each divisional commander could order reprisals. By virtue of their size, the *HSSPF* and *Wehrmacht* carried out most of the executions. They were assisted by the Greek Security Battalions.

Reprisals varied in intensity. On June 29, 1943, twenty-five "Communist" suspects were shot in reprisal for an attack on a German noncommissioned officer near Naousa. One week later, in retaliation for railroad sabotage near Lithochoron, four villages were destroyed and fifty hostages shot. The ratio of hostages to be shot for losses suffered by the occupation authorities varied. The assassination of a German police captain on December 13, 1943, near Cumic resulted in the execution of fifty hostages taken from the town. Thirty were executed for the killing of a Greek policeman and a series of *andarte* attacks on January 1, 1944. On the other hand, only ten hostages died on January 21, 1944, for the OPLA assassination of a Greek executive. Two hundred hostages died in reprisal for the ambush death of General Krech and his escort on March 28, 1944. One hundred of these were shot by Greek Security Battalion troops. The very next day in Salonica, sixty hostages were massacred for an *andarte* attack on a truck convoy of *Ordnungspolizei* (German uniformed police). This pace continued until the end of the occupation: ten executed for an attack on a train; thirty dead for the murder of four Greek *Freiwilligen;* fifty shot for a partisan attack; and twenty executed for cable sabotage. For the death of an *SS* officer on August 7, 1944, 600 hostages were arrested and dispatched to Haidari prison near Athens. Another 568 were seized after a gun battle in the streets of Athens between EAM/ELAS and Greek Security Battalions.[127]

Savage and brutal as these actions were, the anti-partisan operations surpassed them. By its nature guerrilla warfare made it difficult to distinguish between civilians and *andartes*. German troops had orders to shoot all individuals carrying weapons, those who supported *andartes* in battle even though they may not be armed, and, finally, anyone who did not halt on order.[128] Field reports on guerrillas killed did not always distinguish between those killed in combat and those shot as hostages; neither did they always distinguish between real *andartes* and civilians. On two occasions the *LXVIII AK* did make these distinctions. In December 1943, at the close of the series of *Grossunternehmungen* begun in October, the *LXVIII AK* burned twenty-eight villages and shot 918 Greeks; 839 of these were shot as hostages. It destroyed the town of Kalavrita and shot the entire male population (696) for aiding the *andartes*.[129] In anti-partisan operations in May, the *LXVIII AK* killed 1,149 Greeks, 671 of them being shot as hostages.[130] In the first week of June 1944, the *SS* destroyed the village of Distomon and shot 296 villagers who had allegedly supported local partisans in a sharp fight against the *SS*.

Complete figures of the numbers executed in reprisal or killed as *andartes* are unavailable. Incomplete German records for the period March 1943 to October 1944 account for 21,255 Greeks killed and another 20,000 seized and imprisoned.[131] The reprisals did not slow the growth of the resistance, but only intensified the struggle and alienated the population. The reprisals and anti-guerrilla operations of November 1943 did have their effect on EDES. General Headquarters Middle East issued general orders to the BMM to relax their operations. According to Col. Woodhouse, the British ordered EDES to suspend operations in view of the terrible toll the Germans had inflicted in Epirus during October and November 1943. EAM/ELAS, however, did not relent. During the same period, the Germans encouraged civilian commissions to go into the mountains to plead with the *andartes* not to attack the Germans since the villages and villagers would suffer reprisals. The response of the *andartes* was to exhort whole villages to move into the mountains.

Dr. Neubacher and Minister-President Rallis opposed these savage measures, and they tried to gain control of the reprisal policy. Both men complained that the reprisals ruined their efforts to build a united political and military front against EAM/ELAS, which they equated with communism. Rallis pointed out the stupidity of the destruction of Kalavrita by reminding the Germans that it was the scene of a Turkish massacre during the War of Independence and that the Greeks would recognize the parallel of the two actions. He added that it made his work difficult if not impossible. Neubacher's efforts to bring over to the Germans and quisling government anti-EAM/ELAS individuals who vacillated between resistance and collaboration collapsed in the face of the military's brutal and unsophisticated reprisal policy.[132] In May 1944, Neubacher demanded courts-martial for those responsible for atrocities committed in the destruction of yet another town, Klissoura, but the military refused. They refused even to report to Neubacher (whom Hitler had charged with coordinating an anticommunist policy for the Balkans) and to the *Mil. Befh. Grld.* the nature and extent of reprisals.[133]

From the beginning of the occupation, the *OKW, HGrE,* and their subordinate officers recognized that the basic problem in Greece was political and economic, and by raising the specter of bolshevism in the resistance they managed to gain some benefit from anti-KKE royalists and anti-KKE republicans who aided in building the Security Battalions. The pressing military situation and the blinded vision of the *Wehrmacht* made it impossible to reap the full rewards of the situation. Short on manpower, the *Wehrmacht* took the shortest and what appeared to them easier way out, the terror of armed violence.

The Resistance Balance Sheet

The effectiveness of the Greek resistance has long been questioned. In the immediate years following the liberation and at the beginning of a renewed Civil War, there were a number of authors who tried to discredit the role of the resistance. Some went so far as to state that the resistance was of little or no value to the Allied war effort.[134] In 1949, C. M. Woodhouse did not go to this extreme, but his book, *The Apple of Discord,* which soon became the most authoritative publication on the subject for two decades, deprecated the military value of EAM/ELAS if not EDES. According to Woodhouse, EAM/ELAS was not a fighting national resistance but an ideological party raised primarily against Greeks rather than the Axis.[135] While praising the military value of EDES, he argued that ELAS built an army corps which was useless against the Germans but perfect for establishing martial law in the mountains. Woodhouse preferred to organize small sabotage units operating under direct BLO control to carry out specific battle assignments.[136] The commander of the Allied Military Mission to Greece (after Brigadier Myers left the country) concluded that the resistance was a "running sore" rather than a "vital wound." [137] In 1972, John O. Iatrides reiterated the conclusion that the resistance was of little military value. [138] In his recent publication, *The Struggle for Greece*, Woodhouse modified his earlier harsh judgment, [139] but the overall view remained negative.

Writers more favorable to the resistance, on the other hand, were mixed in their appraisals of the resistance. The extreme defenders of the resistance claimed that it held down over 300,000 Axis troops, annihilated between 19,000 and 22,000 of them, and effectively disrupted Axis lines of communication. [140] A more realistic judgment came from an SOE director, Bickam Sweet-Escott. He defended the role of the resistance and emphasized the key role that the Greek guerrillas played in deceiving the Axis on the invasion of Sicily. He further pointed out the potential value the Balkan resistance would have had if the Allies had accepted Churchill's wishes for landings in the Balkans. [141] Churchill justified his policy of supporting the Greek resistance by arguing that it succeeded in diverting two German divisions into Greece during the invasion of Sicily. [142]

Based on an analysis of German and British wartime documents, the Greek resistance failed to measure up to the achievements claimed by its most ardent defenders, but neither was the *andartiko* as useless as claimed by its critics. Hitler's Mediterranean strategy and obsession with the Balkans led to the German military build-up in Greece during 1943. Hitler took the threat of an Allied landing in conjunction with a partisan revolt as a real possibility as early as 1942. [143] As noted in Chapter Three, the decision to reinforce the Balkans and to create an operational reserve of four divisions in Greece was made between October 1942 and February 1943. The Gorgopotamos operation played an important role in this decision as it revealed the potential threat of the resistance tied to Allied strategy. [144] The *11 Lw-Feld-Div.* arrived in January 1943, followed by the *117 Jaeger-Div.* in May. As the crisis in the Mediterranean deepened, the *OKW* on May 19 added to the operational reserve. German planners expected to have the *1 Geb. Div.*, the *118 Jaeger-Div.*, the *194 Jaeger-Div.*, and the *1 Panzer-Div.* deployed in Greece by mid-June. At the same time, the *OKW* reinforced the German units on Lemnos and Rhodes. [145] All of these units were ordered to prepare for deployment before the intensified *andartiko* of May to July, but "Animals" did cause the immediate deployment of two German divisions in June.

Even after the heavy bombardment of Sicily began on July 3, 1943, Hitler continued to expect the major Allied blow to fall on the Balkans. This connection and his doubts of the determination of the Italians to remain in the war caused the Fuehrer to order additional reinforcements into Greece. The resistance played a critical role in this case. Hitler's concern for the lone rail link in the Balkans, the Athens-Salonica-Belgrade line, pressed him to order into Greece two *SS-Pol-Pz-Gren-Rgts.* and a *SS-Polizei Rgt.*, which were trained for anti-partisan warfare and securing lines of communication. The build-up continued until October, when German troops in Greece reached 273,000. In addition to the Germans, there were 54,965 Bulgarians and 18,000 Italian *Hiwis* and *Kawis*. The total force numbered 346,665.[146] In November 1943, British military intelligence estimated that the Greek resistance was holding down three German divisions, but by early January they concluded that Hitler's fear of invasion and not the resistance accounted for the five divisions in Greece.[147]

The Germans perceived the resistance to be the chief threat to Axis lines of communication.[148] As in the case of the other resistance movements of occupied Europe, the Greek resistance did not permanently halt the flow of goods and men but only delayed and hindered their movement. Similarly, the resistance effectively severed the German east-west link along the Larissa-Trikkala-Metsovon-Ioannina road, but they could not hold Metsovon Pass. As elsewhere in Nazi Europe, German operations like *"Panther"* in October 1943 reopened blocked communications. Had the guerrilla attacks then been combined with an invading Allied army, as anticipated both by Hitler and championed by the British military chiefs, the achievements of the *andartiko* would have been far different. The British military post-mortem on the resistance recognized that a larger, more effective resistance could have been raised if a political compromise had been worked out with EAM/ELAS, but British political considerations ruled out that possibility. Since the resistance would not help "Overlord," the British post-mortem concluded that the resistance had been a mistake.[149] Yet the impact of the Gorgopotamos operation on Hitler's thinking, and the effectiveness of "Animals" for the invasion of Sicily, were noteworthy achievements in sabotage and deception. Indeed, "Animals" was a model military operation of high results and low costs.

Further, for the period March 1, 1943, to October 15, 1944, the resistance took 2,369 German lives, wounded another 4,204, and accounted for another 1,810 missing. Total German casualties were 8,383 for that eighteen-month period. Over 65 percent of these casualties occurred between June and October 1944.[150] The chronology of these attacks is important because critics of EAM/ELAS charged that ELAS did not fight the Germans. Following the severe counter-guerrilla operations of October 1943, British headquarters in Cairo ordered a general relaxation of resistance activities to hold down German reprisals, but BLO "Tom" Barnes used the order to halt all EDES attacks. Pressed by the war with EAM/ELAS, EDES remained inactive against the Germans until the night of July 5, 1944, but even this attack was broken off, and full hostilities against the Germans were not resumed until late August. ELAS, however, continued its actions without a break throughout 1944. By May 1944, SOE reported that ELAS was carrying out the "lion's share" of sabotage acts.[151] The losses inflicted on German army units—1,125 dead, 1,809 wounded, and 435 missing—between January and July 1944 were delivered by EAM/ELAS.[152] If Fitzroy Maclean echoed Foreign Office policy in the Balkans in his judgment that his mission to Yugoslavia was to find out who was killing the most Germans and to suggest by which means Britain could help to kill more, then Britain was supporting the wrong organization in Greece. Between January and August 1944, as for most of the war period, ELAS was the active anti-Nazi resistance in Greece.

The cost of the resistance was paid for by the civilian population. From March 1, 1943, to October 15, 1944, the peak period of the resistance, the German records show 21,255 Greeks killed and 20,000 arrested during anti-guerrilla operations and 1,700 villages destroyed. These figures do not include selective shootings of hostages for isolated anti-Axis sabotage.[153] In this regard, between January and August 1944, the records of the *Mil. Befh. Grld.* show 1,918 hostages shot in reprisal actions in addition to those killed in anti-partisan operations. If Saraphes is correct when he claimed that ELAS lost 4,500 dead and 6,000 wounded for the entire period of the resistance, and if EDES's losses were drastically smaller as it was inactive for the first eight months of 1944, the civilian noncombatants bore the brunt of Nazi fury. The population was caught between the Germans, who stupidly believed ruthless, brutal force could achieve security for them, and the resistance.

Regardless of the military achievement, the political and psychological significance of the resistance proved to be the fundamental fact of the war years. Faced with the economic and political disaster of 1941-1942, and the increasing brutality of the occupation in the following two years, the resistance, particularly EAM/ELAS, provided the nation not only with hopes and goals but the means and organization to participate in the achievement of those aims. The nation responded *en masse* to the struggle against fascism and for the reconstruction of Greek politics. The liberation of Greece and the building of a new society based on the principle of national self-determination, as Komnenos Pyromaglou has reminded us, was the importance of the resistance, and not its military achievements.[154]

Although the suffering and agony were terrible to endure, the Greek resistance originated and developed indigenously out of the wartime situation—and its own resources—and it would have existed without Allied support. British strategy and involvement accounted for the development and survival of noncommunist guerrilla organizations, otherwise EAM/ELAS would have emerged as the only resistance movement in Greece. The British involvement and the program of the resistance put the *andartiko* on a collision course with the Greek exile government. The dominance of the KKE as the only nation-wide resistance alarmed British and exiled Greek officials. If British interests were to prevail and the King to return to Greece, the resistance had to be neutralized. The clash between the politics of the resistance and the politics of Britain and the King's government came in August 1943.

The Cairo Conference

In July, the King's government belatedly dispatched royalist officers to the mountains literally to take command of the resistance.[155] EAM/ELAS rejected them, and most of them turned to EDES. After that fiasco, the King relied on his clandestine newspapers to promote his cause.[156] Since EAM/ELAS had preempted efforts to form another national resistance, and since the KKE played a key role in EAM/ELAS, the problem remained of how to negate the influence of the Communists.

The previous anti-EAM/ELAS policy failed. There remained the possibility of forestalling internal war by forming a real government of national unity, but the opposition of the King—supported by Great Britain—prevented it.

As late as March 1943, the leader of the Liberal Party, Sophoulis, and other political leaders continued to oppose the return of the King, but negotiations initiated by Tsouderos in May and June and the growing awareness of the strength of EAM/ELAS reversed the anti-monarchists. Sophoulis reported that they were prepared to explore ways of cooperation, and they agreed to allow three moderate liberals selected by Tsouderos to join the government. Leeper's political advisor, Edward Warner, interpreted Sophoulis's positive reaction to the Tsouderos initiative as a recognition on the part of the "old gang" of the Communist danger of EAM/ELAS and that Britain and the Tsouderos government provided them with the only means of their return to political power.[157] The "old gang" was not quite ready to "tumble" toward the King and Britain, but they were beginning to warm up to it.

Perhaps encouraged by Sophoulis's message, the King announced on July 4 that within six months after his return there would be free elections. As a gesture of unity, the King's announcement did not please everyone. Greek armed forces that listened to the speech in the Middle East reportedly hissed the statement about the King's return.[158] The Liberals were not convinced either. They sent Georgios Exendares to Cairo to press for political concessions from the King, and EAM/ELAS quickly pointed out the major flaw in the King's message. During the six-month period between the liberation and the elections, the monarchists would arrest the members of EAM/ELAS to ensure a royalist victory. They told Myers that they would not lay down their arms until a plebiscite could be held.[159]

In its April 24 *aide-mémoire* to the State Department, the British Foreign Office indicated that it planned to broaden the Greek government to include representatives of the resistance. Although they did approach the moderate, traditional political leaders, the British authorities made no effort to sound out the resistance. Brigadier Myers had informed Cairo as early as February of the desire of the resistance leaders to go to Cairo for high-level talks on the political future of Greece, but the Foreign Office did not respond until May. Events continued to drift during the summer of 1943. The National Bands Agreement failed to stop the sporadic clashes with EAM/ELAS,

which resulted from baiting on both sides.[160] The various
British Liaison Officers mediated these conflicts in accordance
with the National Bands Agreement. Full-scale civil war was
averted for the simple reason that neither side desired it. As
long as the problem of the postwar government remained unsettled, the prospects for all-out civil war loomed larger and
larger.

In an effort to resolve this fundamental problem, Myers
arranged in July to bring an *andarte* delegation to Cairo for
talks with British and Greek officials. Myers and the guerrilla delegation, which consisted of Pyromaglou (EDES),
Kartalis (EKKA), Elias Tsirimokos, Petros Roussos, Andreas Tzimas, and Constantinos Despotopoulos (EAM/
ELAS), arrived in Cairo on August 10. Tzimas, Roussos, and
Despotopoulos were members of the KKE. The *andartes's*
arrival coincided with the arrival of Exendares. Myers was
accompanied by Major David Wallace. Since the Foreign Office
distrusted SOE, Wallace was sent to Greece in early July to
gather political intelligence on the situation in Greece and to
report directly to Leeper. Fearing that EAM/ELAS might
establish a shadow government linked to Tito and Albania in
some form of a Balkan bloc, London wanted to know the extent
of cooperation between EAM/ELAS and Tito, what links existed between EAM/ELAS and the "old gang," the strength of
anti-EAM/ELAS organizations, and whether the rank and
file of EAM/ELAS shared their leadership's views.[161] Although
his reports were inadvertently delayed by SOE, they did not
differ in substance from those of Myers and Woodhouse.

The events of the *andarte* mission to Cairo were recently
examined in light of the PRO documents by Brigadier Myers
and Richard Clogg.[162] All that is required here is a summary
of the key points of the conference. Myers intended the conference to discuss military matters; how the guerrilla armies
could become part of the Greek armed forces and liaison established between the two groups. The *andarte* delegation made
it clear that their principle aim was to discuss the future
conduct of the war in Greece with the military authorities
and the problem of the monarchy with political officials. Although he publicly supported the *andarte* delegation on the
issue of the monarchy, Pyromaglou privately reported to
British officials that he did not think the issue of the King
was primary. Rather, he insisted the real issue was the balance
of forces inside Greece. Pyromaglou complained to Leeper that

Myers had forced Zervas to join the joint guerrilla command. These points were not lost on his British hosts. Yet the central concern of the communist and noncommunist resistance, as well as of the traditional politicians, had been the question of the monarch's return. The chief aim of the EAM/ELAS delegates was the creation of a government of national unity and an agreement that the King would not return before a plebiscite decided his future.[163] Independent of *andartes* Exendares arrived and supported the demands of the resistance. At the first meeting, the *andartes* immediately raised the issue of the monarchy and demanded that the King accept a plebiscite before he returned to Greece. Ambassador Leeper, who had looked forward to the meeting as a means of resolving political differences among the involved parties, was not put off by the *andartes's* demand. Since the guerrillas did not reject the King as head of state but limited their demand to a plebiscite before he returned, Leeper remained optimistic. The British ambassador even suggested to his superiors that Britain review her policy toward the King and consider the formation of a coalition government as the only means of achieving unity and ending problems in the Greek armed forces.[164]

Since some members of the Greek cabinet initially agreed with the resistance delegation, the *andartes's* demand created an immediate crisis in the Greek exile government. Georgios Roussos threatened to resign if the King and Tsouderos did not accept the delegation's demands. Tsouderos, like Leeper, was initially inclined to compromise, and he advised the King to reconsider his decision to return before any elections.[165]

Uncertain as to what if any accommodation should be made to the *andarte* delegation, Leeper asked the Foreign Office for guidance. While he waited, he learned from Major Wallace the depth of anti-monarchist sentiment in Greece and the strength of EAM/ELAS. In London, Eden was unhappy to learn that Leeper and Tsouderos were considering a compromise, and he rejected it as unfair to the King. Sargent told Leeper to "check the tendency in Cairo to sell out to the EAM delegation." London became convinced that any opening of the Greek government to the resistance would topple Tsouderos, weaken the chances of the King's restoration, and strengthen EAM/ELAS.[166] In Cairo, Myers, Lord Glenconner (Chief of SOE Cairo), and Field Marshal Wilson favored the demands of the delegation as a means of avoiding civil war and as necessary for achieving effective military support for Allied strategy.

In an interview with the King on August 11, Myers told the monarch point blank that his return would foment civil conflict.[167] This support for the guerrillas angered the Foreign Office. Sargent and Leeper concluded that SOE was responsible for the political crisis.[168]

After being told by London to halt any move toward compromise with the *andartes* and learning that SOE had not deciphered Wallace's telegrams from Greece,[169] Leeper made a quick about-face. He savagely and bitterly attacked Myers and SOE as responsible for the political fiasco. The ambassador even went so far as to claim that the guerrilla mission had been thrown upon him as a complete surprise. London initially agreed with Leeper, but after researching their records and being informed by SOE London that on four occasions between January and March SOE had sent four telegrams to the Foreign Office on the desire of the guerrillas to come to Cairo, the Foreign Office dropped this line of attack. Leeper conveniently forgot that on July 21, 1943, he had cabled London stating that he was looking forward to the meeting with Myers and the guerrilla delegation.[170] In spite of this refusal to compromise, the *andartes* continued to press their political demands.

While the guerrilla delegation waited for the Allies to respond to their demands, Pyromaglou and Kartalis discussed in private the future course of Greek politics. Each was well aware of the danger that the KKE presented in EAM/ELAS, but they realized that it was not so extensive that it could not be limited and controlled. They believed that the formation of a national unity government located outside of Greece would be the best way to neutralize the KKE and simultaneously fulfill the aspirations of the hundreds of thousands who participated in the resistance. The chief obstacle to the formation of a unity government was the King. They had hoped the Allies would support the resistance, but the Cairo conference was a rude shock for them. Leeper decided the guerrillas should return to Greece, and on August 22 Wilson ordered them to leave. At the last moment, the guerrillas refused to board the plane for their return trip to Greece and appealed to Tsouderos to continue the talks. The Greek premier agreed. At this point the resistance leaders dropped their demand for a plebiscite and asked only to join the exile cabinet, forming a government of national unity. The Foreign Office again refused any compromise. Leeper was put out by the refusal of his "guests" to behave like "guests" and leave when their "host" wished for them to leave.[171] Churchill too was incensed, and on August 30 he agreed that the guerrillas should be sent back to Greece where he wrongly believed they could do little harm. Since the persistent demands of the *andartes* alarmed the Greek government officials, who began to see the resistance as a rival for political power rather than as a lever against the King, they concurred in the decision to send the guerrillas back to the Greek mountains.[172]

D. S. Laskey correctly interpreted the EAM/ELAS demand for participation in the Greek government as a bid for political legitimacy which would strengthen EAM/ELAS's position in Greece, but he misjudged this demand as a sign of weakness.[173] Before coming to Cairo, EAM/ELAS intensified efforts to get Sophoulis and other prewar politicians to join in a national front government that would hold a plebiscite and elect a constituent assembly, but the Liberal leader refused. Indeed, he relayed EAM/ELAS's letters to British officials in Cairo.[174] These letters no doubt encouraged the Foreign Office to harden its attitude toward EAM/ELAS and reject any political settlement with the resistance. In mid-September, the *andarte* delegation returned to Greece.

The American State Department was not as optimistic as British officials were that a hard line with the resistance was the correct road to follow. American officials feared that the policy of no compromise would lead directly to civil war and necessitate direct Allied intervention, which Washington did not want. The Americans were correct. The failure of the Cairo conference marked the major turning point in the development of Greek wartime politics. The outbreak of civil war in October 1943 and the gradual elimination of the political moderates among the resistance was the first direct result of this failure. Further, the inability to negotiate a government of national unity at Cairo assured the necessity of British military intervention in Greek affairs after the liberation in 1944. While in Cairo, Kartalis observed that the refusal of Britain and the King to recognize the politics of the resistance marked the erosion of the political unity of the resistance. It was this unity, he remarked to Pyromaglou, that presented the best chances for the peaceful evolution of Greek politics.[175] His observations proved prophetic. After Cairo, the divisions within EDES and EKKA sharpened between republicans and those supporting the exile government. Zervas decided to side with Britain at all costs.[176] The failure of the conference fell on the heels of the Germans' and Rallis's anticommunist barrage, which opened up in the fall of 1943 and led many members of EDES to join the quislings. Divisions within EKKA reduced it to a shadow force by March 1944. The traditional parties began to move closer to the exile government and look for British support. As for EAM/ELAS, the failure of the conference convinced it of British hostility and that there was no place for it in Greek politics. Since EAM/ELAS cooperation for "Animals" produced no political advantage, the KKE prepared to strengthen ELAS and to use EAM to establish a provisional government inside Greece and, if necessary, to resort to force to prevent Britain from imposing the monarchy on Greece. With the wisdom of hindsight after the disastrous December insurrection, even the conservative monarchist Panagiotes Pipineles concluded that there should have been a political settlement at Cairo as a means of displacing the communists.[77] The failure of the Cairo conference may be ascribed to the Foreign Office's inflexible policy toward both the King and the resistance. When concessions and changes did come in 1944 at Lebanon, they were too little and too late. The polarization of Greek politics into communist and anticommunist was nearly complete.

CHAPTER SIX

CIVIL WAR AND THE ZERVAS-GERMAN CONNECTION

The political stalemate produced by the failure of the Cairo Conference in August 1943 led to civil war. Convinced that Britain was weakening EAM/ELAS at the expense of its rivals in order to ensure the return of the monarchy, the EAM/ELAS leadership set about to consolidate their power in occupied Greece by neutralizing or eliminating rival organizations. Their prime target was Zervas. Until the winter of 1943, Britain had no intention of dissolving EAM/ELAS. Even after the civil war began in October, the British military authorities prevailed in their desire to maintain the Greek resistance and ELAS. Still there was enough anti-EAM/ELAS activity on the part of EDES and Britain to fuel the suspicions of EAM/ELAS. The attack on Zervas pushed the guerrilla leader into developing a special relationship with the German forces in Epirus.

The first response to the failure of the *andarte* mission came before their return from Cairo. During the second week of September, ELAS representatives at the JGHQ began to limit the functioning of the joint guerrilla command.[1] On September 20, the KKE opened a press attack on Zervas with a charge that the Athenian EDES was collaborating with the quisling government and the Germans—a charge that proved to be valid. While publicly attacking Zervas and EDES, EAM/ELAS made a private appeal to EDES and EKKA to agree in issuing a joint declaration against the return of the monarchy, but EDES and EKKA refused.[2] Stymied by this refusal, EAM/ELAS perceived an alarming trend in Thessaly. Since the signing of the National Bands Agreement in July, EDES had been successfully recruiting in previously exclusive EAM/ELAS areas. The British Military Mission and EDES

171

had convinced many ELASites in Thessaly, including an ELAS division commander, of the need to dissolve all units and to reorganize them into a new resistance.[3] Following closely on this development, the Rallis government in the last week of September publicized a letter, allegedly signed by a British officer, which claimed that British and Greek exile officials approved of the organization of the Security Battalions. Although Woodhouse, who had replaced Myers as chief of the BMM, requested an immediate denial via the BBC, the Foreign Office delayed its response for two weeks. This period of silence gave credibility to the Rallis ploy, and by the time the denial was issued, violence had already begun.[4]

Tensions continued to escalate. On October 2, EDES publications appealed to the noncommunist members of EAM/ELAS to repudiate the KKE leadership which EDES claimed was planning to attack and destroy Zervas.[5] The next day EAM/ELAS gained control of between 2,000 and 4,000 Italian small arms. The new-found arms emboldened ELAS against EDES, and, on October 5, ELAS commanders disarmed EDES guerrillas in Thessaly. Tzimas, however, quickly cancelled this action, which indicated confusion within the KKE leadership over what course to follow in face of the rapidly developing crisis.

Another indication of Britain's anti-EAM/ELAS policy was London's decision to limit ELAS to 25,000 armed men. It is not clear when EAM/ELAS learned of this decision, but they lodged a protest with General Henry Maitland Wilson on October 9 and requested that the message be passed on to Washington and Moscow.[6] The decision to limit the size of ELAS was made in March 1943.[7] Throughout 1943, the BMM had raised guerrilla bands and encouraged them to act independently of the ELAS HQ.

Of further concern to EAM/ELAS was their knowledge of British contacts with anti-EAM/ELAS circles in Athens. The extent of their knowledge of the details of these negotiations remains uncertain, but EAM/ELAS did know of the efforts to build an anti-EAM/ELAS front in Athens around the figure of Archbishop Damaskinos. On September 13, 1943, British Captain Frank Macaskie met Colonel Angelos Evert, the chief of the Athens police and an associate of the Archbishop. The churchman, who had given refuge to Macaskie, arranged the meeting to discuss his proposal for uniting the anticommunist elements into a counterbloc to EAM/ELAS. The nucleus of this bloc was to be Damaskinos, Evert, and an organization referred to only as EDEM, which included Evert and a number of prominent Venizelist generals. EDEM was to serve as the political leadership, while something known as EDAM was to act as the military arm. The Archbishop proposed that the Greek government-in-exile recognize him and Evert as the legitimate representatives of the government in occupied Greece as a sort of regency council. Macaskie was to act as liaison with Cairo, and in return for intelligence supplied by Evert, he would facilitate the arming of 3,000 men under the police chief's command. These forces would serve as the basis of an expanded resistance force to be raised in the mountains around Athens and commanded by Greek officers sent over from the Middle East. If the Germans did not leave Greece, as was generally but erroneously expected in the fall of 1943, the Archbishop proposed to go to the mountains and lead a national rising against the Germans at the appropriate time. Following the liberation, Damaskinos proposed that his council organize the first general elections and supervise a plebiscite on the monarchy. This bold plan of action was well received in London, and Foreign Office officials were enthusiastic about the possibility of forming an anti-EAM/ELAS bloc around Damaskinos. Laskey, however, pointed out that the proposal, if adopted, would ensure conditions for an intensified civil war. He noted that EDEM and ED, which was also mentioned in the proposal, were singled out by EAM/ELAS as having contacts with the Germans, which was true to a certain extent. The proposal was rejected, but Damaskinos and the idea of a regency council gained currency in the minds of British authorities.[8]

Although EAM/ELAS did not publicly link Britain to the individuals and organizations which they charged with collaboration, EAM/ELAS, shortly after the outbreak of hostilities, protested to Cairo that British agents were working with EDES representatives, Damaskinos, and the Germans to build an anti-EAM/ELAS front. The resistance identified the EDES representatives as Tavoulares, Voulpiotis, Colonel Charlambos Papathanasopoulos, and Colonel Apostolos Papageorgios. Tavoulares raised funds from Athenian businessmen and worked with the Germans to arm EDES units in the Peloponnese. Voulpiotis served as a political advisor to German civilian authorities, and he cooperated with Evert, EDEM, and ED. The British considered Voulpiotis a double agent, but his recruiting on behalf of the security battalions made him a collaborator in the eyes of EAM/ELAS.[9] As part of the agreement which ended the civil war in February 1944, Zervas denounced Tavoulares, Voulpiotis, and the Athenian EDES as collaborators.

Macaskie's negotiations were continued by New Zealand Captain Don Stott, who had played a key role in the destruction of the Asopos bridge the previous June. The date of his arrival in Athens is unknown, but on November 4, 1943, he signed an agreement with a group of extreme anticommunists which included a member of the Rallis government. The signers were Colonel Papathanasopoulos (EDES), Colonel Elias Diamesis (EDEM, later Director of General Security for Rallis), Colonel Georgios Grivas (X), Colonel Antonopoulos (ED), Colonel Constantinos Venderes (RAN), and Major Demetrios Syrantakis (Ministry of National Defense–Rallis government). The details of these negotiations were known to EAM/ELAS, but the chronology of Stott's contacts cannot be established from currently available PRO documents. Stott had not been authorized to sign any agreements. After learning of Stott's activities following his return to Cairo in early December and fearing the nasty political repercussions inside Greece and from the Soviet Union, SOE and the Foreign Office repudiated the agreement.[10] The crucial point, however, was that EAM/ELAS was aware of efforts by British agents, whether authorized or not, to build a counter-organization to EAM/ELAS.

These activities were also known to SOE's "Apollo," Ioannis Peltekis. On the eve of the outbreak of violence, he reported to Cairo his assessment of the situation and his recommendation for preventing a civil war. The report noted that the increased intransigence and offensive behavior of EAM/ELAS was a prelude to a seizure of power. On the other hand, EDES in Athens was in close cooperation with the quislings and Germans, and imitating EAM/ELAS in collecting arms for a civil war. As a last effort to avoid conflict and to neutralize the KKE, Peltekis recommended that Britain dissolve the compromised EDES and arrange for the prewar politicians to join EAM/ELAS. To ensure the success of this move, he suggested that Britain formally declare its support for a popular republic. Peltekis concluded his report with an ominous but prophetic warning that any action short of his proposals would lead to civil war.[11] The Southern Department did not respond. Peltekis's suggestions were similar to the *andarte* proposals at the August conference. Britain had already made its rejection of these proposals quite clear, and the Foreign Office was not sensitive to the developing crisis.

In this period of mounting tensions, the Germans contacted Zervas with an offer of an armistice. Zervas informed Colonel C. E. "Tom" Barnes, the BLO attached to his headquarters. Barnes in turn informed Woodhouse and Cairo. Cairo immediately ordered Zervas to halt any negotiations with the enemy. Barnes and Woodhouse became convinced that Zervas obeyed this order and had no further contact with the Germans. Indeed, the two BLO's became convinced that it was ELAS that had made a pact with the enemy.[12] It was not the end of the affair. In the months that followed this initial contact, Zervas proved to be extremely adept in cunning and intrigue as he exploited his British tie and developed his German connection. In this regard, he confirmed his reputation as a political adventurer.

Early Negotiations and Civil War

The open conflict between EDES and EAM/ELAS broke out on October 9, 1943. Full-scale civil war took place during this time, in contrast to the relatively minor clashes that had begun in the spring of 1943 and ended with the National Bands Agreement of July of that year. A "diplomatic flurry" between Zervas and the *XXII Geb. AK* preceded this new phase of the conflict. On October 5, a civilian delegation from Ioannina, which included the major, Demetrios Vlachlides, and the representative of the International Red Cross, Hans Bickel, went to Zervas's headquarters in Skiadades and asked him to suspend hostilities in order to spare the villagers of Epirus from German reprisals.[13] Zervas replied that only Headquarters Middle East could approve such a request. About the same time another delegation from Arta appeared in the mountains with a similar request. According to Zervas, he again refused this offer, but the German documents reveal another story.

On October 7, 1943, Herr Bickel, the Red Cross representative, reported to General Lanz that Zervas had offered to discuss a suspension of hostilities and had ordered his troops not to fire on German units until October 14. These conditions would hold provided that the Germans followed suit. Bickel explained that Zervas was becoming increasingly concerned about the plight of the Greek population, which suffered from the guerrilla war. According to the Red Cross representative, Zervas had made it clear that he aspired to play a future political role in Greece and that he was anxious to gain widespread public support.[14]

On the day that Bickel reported to Lanz the nature of the delegation's meeting with Zervas, shooting broke out between EDES and ELAS in the area of Goditsa, when units of the ELAS 8th Division moved down from Metsovon. According to an EDES newspaper, ELAS called for a truce, but the newspaper replied that EDES could deal with "red criminals" only when they laid down their arms.[15] At the same time, ELAS attacked EDES in Thessaly.[16] On October 9, EDES handbills declared that ELAS had attacked EDES and was attempting to establish a dictatorship of the proletariat.[17]

On the day hostilities began, a civilian commission from Arta, headed by the bishop of that city, traveled into the Pindus Mountains to call on the resistance, both EAM/ELAS and EDES, to suspend actions against the Germans since the civilian population suffered the reprisals. The usual reprisal was the shooting of hostages at a ratio of ten hostages for each German dead, but the ratio varied depending on the rank of the German. The Germans usually burned the houses of those who fled to the mountains. In Arta, thousands fled to the mountains, and part of the commission's task was to ask them to return home. The commission felt that the refugees would surely die during the coming winter if they remained in the mountains. On meeting an ELAS band of 250 men, they made their plea, but the guerrilla leader suggested that the whole town of Arta had better withdraw to the mountains if it wanted to survive the winter. The *andartes* rejected any armistice.[18]

On October 10, 1943, while the fighting intensified on the slopes of the Pindus Mountains, the Arta commission met Zervas at Voulgarelion and made its proposal. Zervas told the commission that he had given his troops the order not to fire on German troops until October 14. He reportedly told the commission that communists had gained complete domination of EAM/ELAS, with which he had now broken and was engaged in a life-and-death struggle. The civil war became so intense by October 12 that the commission could go no further, and as it learned that Zervas and German officers were meeting to discuss a suspension of hostilities, it returned to Arta.[19]

While the Arta commission carried out its futile mission to halt the resistance attacks, Lieutenant-General Lanz received orders from *HGrE* concerning negotiations with Zervas. *HGrE* told Lanz, who was interested in a local ceasefire, to demand from Zervas what amounted to the *andarte* leader's capitulation to the *Wehrmacht*. The conditions stipulated for any negotiation were: Zervas must surrender all weapons, all German prisoners, all Allied Military Mission liaison officers, and all radio equipment.[20] These absurd conditions reflected how little the Salonica authorities understood the resistance, and how faulty intelligence created in the minds of *HGrE* a far more powerful EDES than actually existed at the time.[21]

The day Lanz received those orders ELAS launched a full-scale attack on EDES forces located on the eastern slopes of the Pindus Mountains, with the goal of either destroying Zervas's forces or of at least reducing them to the territory west of the Arachtos River. EAM/ELAS newspapers and handbills denounced Zervas as a traitor and enemy of Greece. Wall slogans appeared in Athens calling for "death to the traitor Zervas," and EAM/ELAS accused EDES of working with the *Gestapo*, the *Wehrmacht*, and Rallis's security battalions.[22] EDES responded with charges that EAM/ELAS had "murderously" attacked "Free Greece" and had made the first move toward establishing a dictatorship. The EDES publications appealed to "the holy duty" of all Greeks to destroy the "traitorous Eamites and Elasites in order to protect lives, secure religion, and save the honor of Greece."[23]

As the battle intensified, representatives of Zervas contacted Lanz's officers on October 13 and requested a meeting in the village of Aetorrache (12 kilometers southeast of Ioannina).[24] After receiving this information, Lanz immediately requested *HGrE* to postpone a major anti-partisan operation, *"Panther,"* scheduled to begin on the morning of October 14 against *andartes* in eastern Epirus and western Thessaly.[25] *HGrE* agreed to postpone *"Panther"* until October 18 in order to give Lanz an opportunity to work out an agreement.[26] The Germans planned *"Panther"* as a major action designed to clear and to secure the vital supply road connecting Arta-Ioannina-Trikkala by striking the *andartes* in their mountain-based camps. German units moved north and northeast from Ioannina and Arta toward Metsovon as other units moved on the same point west and northwest out of Thessaly. The Joint General Headquarters of the resistance at Pertouli became the center of the German encirclement.[27]

While Zervas's request for a parley postponed the launching

of *"Panther"* from October 14 until the 18th, Aris launched a heavy attack on EDES. On the morning of the 14th, Aris disarmed the Italian *"Pinerolo"* Division, which had gone over to the resistance in September 1943, and transferred its heavy artillery from the eastern to the western slopes of the Pindus Mountains in order to deal EDES a severe blow on October 14-15. According to Woodhouse,[28] Aris was able to move the Italian artillery across the Pindus because he had made a temporary truce with the Germans. Local German commanders did offer truces to ELAS units, but the ELAS GHQ ordered these contacts broken off and reprimanded those who had accepted any of the German proposals. The heavy blow from ELAS came during the lull effected by Zervas's initiative with the Germans. If *"Panther"* had begun on schedule, Aris would never have been able to move his troops, much less heavy artillery across the Pindus. The battles which followed the initiation of *"Panther"* have been described as the "most ferocious battles" that ever took place between the Germans and the resistance.[29]

Zervas failed to appear in Aetorrache on October 16, however. The German representatives, Colonel Dietl and Lieutenant-Colonel Rothfuchs, arrived with Herr Bickel. At 11:00 A.M., a Greek captain and lieutenant-colonel arrived as emissaries from Zervas. The Greek officers informed the others that events had detained Zervas in another area, but that he had commissioned them to schedule another parley for October 21. These two officers then returned in German vehicles to Ioannina to relay the proposal to Lieutenant-General Lanz. *HGrE* refused any further delay of *"Panther"* and interpreted the whole affair as a delaying tactic inspired by British liaison officers. The two Greek officers returned to Zervas with this decision.[30] *HGrE* ordered Operation *"Panther"* to begin on October 17.

The attack caught the resistance by surprise. By October 22, the operation had cleared the Ioannina-Metsovon-Kalambaka-Trikkala road and pushed the *andartes* deep into the Pindus Mountains. ELAS forces caught between EDES on the west and German units on the east and southwest scattered north and south along the Pindus. ELAS moved the Joint General Headquarters from Pertouli to Smokovo, and the AMM moved with Aris and ELAS forces to Karpenision in the south, only to be attacked there in November. The operation cut off ELAS south and north of Metsovon.[31]

A German propaganda barrage, aimed at winning over "nationalists" or, failing that, to intensify the existing hostility among rival *andartes*, accompanied the attack. Leaflets dropped on the area proclaimed that Germany harbored no quarrel with the Greek people, but only fought the Allies and their supporters. The German propaganda claimed that the German army struggled only against communists and not against Greek "nationalists." The Germans defined a "nationalist" as any anticommunist of whatever background from the head of the quisling government to Zervas. To avoid hostilities during the operation, the propaganda handbills called on these nationalists to identify themselves as members of EDES. They appealed to the "patriotic duty" of EDES to join the *Wehrmacht's* struggle against bolshevism.[32]

An EPON newspaper of Karpenision, *Machetes*, reprinted these handbills along with an account of the EDES officers who drove in public view to German military headquarters in Ioannina on October 16 and of the German attack on the *andartes*. EAM/ELAS gave these events widespread publicity throughout Greece in order to back up its charges that EDES was collaborating with the occupation troops to destroy EAM. It called on the EDES rank-and-file to reject their leaders and to join the EAM/ELAS movement to free Greece.[33] This counterpropaganda was successful.[34]

In the midst of the civil war and German attack, EDES and German officers reestablished direct contact and scheduled a parley for October 27. Zervas again failed to appear, and the negotiations collapsed. Contact between the resistance organization and Lanz remained open, however. The apparent readiness to maintain contact and undertake negotiations, supported by the fact that Germany and EDES engaged a common enemy, gave the German authorities in Ioannina continued hopes that some agreement might yet be reached with EDES. These expectations received additional support as Lanz received "reliable" information that Zervas had ordered his *andartes* to cease all action against the occupying troops.[35] The information was correct. Colonel Barnes approved of the suspensions, but he was not aware of the Zervas contacts with Lanz.[36] Weakened by the ELAS and German strikes, EDES needed time to regroup and mend its wounds. Under these circumstances, there is no reason to doubt the ceasefire order, but this is not to say that Zervas gave the order in response to possible cooperation with the *XXII Geb. AK*. The order arose out of the necessity of the situation. It remains possible, nevertheless, that Zervas took advantage of this condition to "leak" the news to Lanz. Whatever may have been the case, the fact remained that EDES halted all action against German forces in late October and during the following weeks and months. On this basis, Lieutenant-General Lanz concluded that his efforts had formed a Balkan "gentlemen's agreement" with Zervas.

Vetrauensmann (*V-Mann*–Intelligence Agent) reports coming from various sources among EDES strengthened Lanz's appraisal of his relation to it. These reports informed the German commander that Zervas planned no further action against his troops, but intended to attack ELAS units located northwest and northeast of Karpenision. This information reopened in the minds of the German authorities in Salonica the possibility of exploiting Zervas. *HGrE* planned a major anti-partisan operation, *"Hubertus,"* in the same area for November 1943. The German authorities no longer considered Zervas and the weakened EDES a threat to their army, but they were very much concerned over the growth of EAM/ELAS. The authorities hoped either to enlist Zervas's direct aid in the attack on Karpenision, or at least to hold him to his neutral position. The commander of operation *"Hubertus"* received authority to negotiate the enlistment of recognized EDES units against EAM/ELAS. Once again, the Germans dropped leaflets calling on EDES members to identify themselves in order to avoid hostilities, but warning that if they resisted, German troops would fire on them. Though no agreements were reached, the propaganda maneuver worked in the interest of the Germans by exacerbating the civil war. As long as the civil war continued, the occupation authorities profited, and they sought to prolong it by any means.[37] Still, the authorities believed cooperation possible, and they would have preferred it to neutrality.

A situation report by *HGrE* referred to Zervas's pacific attitude toward the German authorities, but made clear that no further approaches were made by Zervas during November. These officials believed that Britain created and supported EDES as a counterweight to EAM/ELAS. They concluded that Zervas was trying to conserve his force until an Allied landing would allow him to block any EAM/ELAS *coup* and then take power himself.[38] As EAM/ELAS held the same view, there existed valid evidence for the German conclusions. The

Germans pursued a policy of exposing EDES as an ineffectual block to EAM/ELAS in the hope that "national-minded" Greeks would realize that Germany stood as the only anticommunist force in Greece. Once this realization sank in, serious efforts could be made to destroy the KKE and its satellites, and the Germans could point to their success in the Peloponnese, where the quisling government of Ioannis Rallis, in cooperation with General Schimana, had recruited the Security Battalions from nationalist circles. The Germans and the Rallis government received a psychological boost from the successful Nazi recapture of Lemnos and other Aegean islands from Great Britain. They hoped to win Zervas to the program of the Security Battalions—to make a Mihailović out of him—and they realized that this policy required Zervas to break with the AMM.[39] Support for this policy came from Athens.

On November 6, 1943, a prominent Greek manufacturer and shipowner, who on previous occasions carried out missions for the *GFP* in Salonica, visited the Athens *GFP* to discuss the possibility of turning Zervas into an active supporter of the *Wehrmacht* against EAM/ELAS. The shipowner told the *GFP* that he was no longer interested in wasting his time on small matters of gathering and transmitting intelligence, nor did he seek any monetary reward. He feared the growing power of Greek communism, which he proposed to destroy by creating an efficient national security force. Through his contacts with nationalist leaders he believed that he could put together an organization. He told the *GFP* that Zervas could be persuaded to participate if given assurance of a position in the Ministry of the Interior and command of sufficient police forces. The shipowner then submitted a list of former Greek army officers who would operate these security forces in conjunction with the German authorities. In early December, Woodhouse received documents, mainly letters to Zervas, incriminating the Athenian EDES but acquitting Zervas of participating in this collaboration.[40]

The records of *HGrE* and *F* made no further mention of this proposal, and Zervas either was never contacted or he rejected the offer outright. Within a few months, he denounced the Security Battalions and five members of the Athenians EDES as collaborators.[41] Though Zervas refused active participation with the Germans, he continued to maintain his loose link   with the *XXII Geb. AK.* as it was advantageous in his struggle with EAM/ELAS.

The EDES Counterattack

During the battles of October and November, EDES withdrew from the east side of the Arachtos to a line from Ioannina to Arta, while a smaller group under Dr. Houtas retreated across the Acheloos River to the area northwest of Agrinion. During that period Zervas broke off all action against the Germans in order to rebuild his forces for a counterattack to regain territory lost to ELAS. ELAS, on the other hand, continued its struggle against EDES and the *Wehrmacht*.[42]

By December 18, Zervas was ready to take the offensive against ELAS. Just before his *andartes* took the field, the commander of the *104 Jg. Div.* centered in Agrinion and Arta received a message from an EDES *V-Mann* requesting a meeting to discuss cooperative action against the communists. The Germans were receptive to the request and entered into preliminary negotiations for establishing a time and a meeting place for Colonel Zervas and German representatives. While these early negotiations were underway, Zervas attacked ELAS on December 21 in the area of Amphilochia and Pramanda, which are twenty-five miles northeast of Arta. Zervas successfully pushed ELAS back across the Arachtos and toward the Acheloos. EDES renewed its attack on January 4, 1944, and once again the commander of the *XXII Geb. AK.* received a request for new discussions. Relaying the request to *HGrE* for instructions, Lanz was advised to pursue the negotiations on the condition that Zervas personally appeared.[43] The new attack pushed ELAS across the Acheloos, thereby regaining the territory lost in October. The AMM tried to end the fighting, but ELAS refused until Zervas returned to the west side of the Arachtos. Hostilities continued until January 23, when the EAM central committee gave the order to discuss a truce.[44]

The following day the command of the *XXII Geb. AK.* received *V-Mann* reports that BLO "MacAdam" was negotiating with ELAS leaders Saraphes and Aris to put an end to the war. Subsequent reports indicated that on January 25, 1944, the BLO had contacted Zervas headquarters.[45] The truce was short-lived, however. It ended on January 26, when ELAS under Aris counterattacked and forced EDES back across the Acheloos and to the western side of the Arachtos. By February 1, Zervas faced annihilation. Late that day individuals who identified themselves as *"Zervas-officers"* informed Lanz of

Zervas's situation and of the concentration of ELAS forces in the area of Flamburion (25 kilometers northeast of Ioannina) poised for further attacks. The information alarmed the command of the *XXII Geb. AK.* On account of Zervas's neutrality, the German headquarters did not wish to see EDES weakened or destroyed, and it certainly did not want to see ELAS absorb eastern Epirus, including the Ioannina-Arta road, into its zone of operation. On this basis, Lanz ordered an operation (*"Sperber"*) of battalion strength to begin against ELAS on the morning of February 2.[46]

German units moved against the northern flank of ELAS, striking south from the Metsovon road across to the east bank of the Arachtos and sweeping through Pramanda and Agnanda, where ELAS and EDES had been heavily engaged.[47] The *XXII Geb. AK.* expected EDES to take the offensive the morning that *"Sperber"* began operation.[48] The German operation failed to catch large numbers of ELAS *andartes*, and only met stiff resistance at Agnanda, where it encountered an ELAS band of 200 troops. The severe cold and heavy snowfall hindered the operation on February 7, compelling Lanz to order the German units to return home. On that day, other German units moved north out of Arta.[49] The German thrust against ELAS failed to capture and destroy large segments of the enemy but accomplished its original purpose. After reaching the Arachtos, ELAS had no intention of crossing to the west bank, fearing an encirclement by German troops moving out of Metsovon and Arta.[50] As long as Zervas remained west of the Arachtos, he no longer needed to fear ELAS. Operation *"Sperber"* saved Zervas and blocked ELAS from Epirus. As long as Germans remained in Epirus, ELAS stayed out. Having fallen into a stalemate, both EAM/ELAS and EDES prepared to end the civil war.

Zervas, the Germans, and the Plaka Agreement

On February 4, EAM/ELAS, which on the day before had charged that the Zervas attack had been ordered by the AMM, set down its conditions for peace: (1) EDES and ELAS should occupy the areas held before the renewal of hostilities in December; (2) Zervas must denounce the EDES collaborators; (3) there should be a conference to negotiate the establishment of a unified resistance army and a single government of national unity.[51] The AMM met Zervas on February 6, and it arranged a ceasefire and a meeting at Mirofillo, a village on the Arachtos River which divided EDES and EAM/ELAS territory. The AMM officers, Col. Woodhouse and Major G. K. Wines, arrived there on February 11, followed by Komnenos Pyromaglou and Colonel Petros Nikolopoulos, who represented EDES. The EAM/ELAS representatives were already there, and the Mirofillo conference began on February 15 after the arrival of Kartalis, Colonel Psarros, and other members of the EKKA delegation.[52] Intelligence agents informed the German authorities of the meeting on the very day it convened, although details did not arrive until later. The informants told the authorities that Zervas did not anticipate reaching any permanent agreement and that ELAS was only stalling to gain time to prepare a new attack. Zervas remained determined to hold to his present course regarding the German army, according to the agents' reports. If the need occurred, these reports continued, Zervas would take concerted action against ELAS.[53] Zervas had good reason to believe that there would be no agreement. He and Woodhouse were cooperating to delay and prolong the conference as the best means to prevent a renewal of the civil war.[54] By February 9, Lanz received the names of all the major participants of the conference.

On February 18, Lanz's informers reported that no agreement appeared possible because of EAM/ELAS's excessive demands, and that an attack on EDES was expected on February 21. The attack never materialized even though the talks broke down over EAM/ELAS's proposal for a unified resistance army and a single government of national resistance.[55] Since the proposal offered Zervas command of only one division within the united army, it would leave ELAS the dominant power. According to German information, the EAM/ELAS political and military proposals deadlocked the conference, which ended on February 18. Zervas refused to accept Saraphes as commander-in-chief of the united army, and withdrew his delegation, banking on British support to outlast EAM/ELAS. From these reports, the German authorities properly concluded that the conference had taken place under Allied pressure, but that ideological differences among the resistance made it highly unlikely any unity would come from the meetings.[56]

The substance of the *V-Mann* reports was correct. On orders from Cairo, Woodhouse succeeded in limiting the conference to military issues, and the delegations became deadlocked over the make-up of the joint army and who should command it.[57] Saraphes was not pushed as the commander. EAM/ELAS proposed the merger of the Epirus EDES with the 8th ELAS Division, the 5/42 Regiment of EKKA with the 13th ELAS Division, and the establishment of a five-man General Headquarters represented by one EDES, one EKKA, and three EAM/ELAS members. EAM/ELAS further proposed that the General Headquarters be under the control of a commander-in-chief to be named by the proposed government of national unity. The GHQ would carry on the war against the Germans until the end of the occupation, at which time the commander-in-chief would have the authority to organize a national army. EKKA agreed to the joint army but rejected the GHQ plan, and it proposed that EDES and EKKA have equal voice with EAM/ELAS in running the united army. EDES rejected the joint army but accepted the concept of the different resistance *andartes* under a common commander-in-chief. Under this plan Zervas proposed to command all resistance groups in Epirus and central Greece with an ELAS chief-of-staff. ELAS naturally refused as there were no longer any EDES units in central Greece. All three delegations finally agreed on the Republican General Alexandros Othonaios as commander-in-chief of a united guerrilla army. He was too old to accept, however. No further progress was made on how to unite the different armies or on how to form a coalition government of national liberation.[58]

The conference drifted, and the AMM made no effort to break the stalemate, for as long as the *andartes* talked there was no war. The Mirofillo conference ended on February 22 with no agreement.[59] It reassembled at Plaka on February 27, but failed to achieve a settlement. Then, on February 29, EAM/ELAS made a new offer to maintain the present boundaries among the different *andartes* and to try for cooperation in the future. The offer came as a surprise to EDES and EKKA, as they expected an ELAS attack if the conference failed.[60] The offer became the basis of the Plaka Agreement signed on the bridge of the same name that crossed the Arachtos, the dividing line between EDES and ELAS.

As late as February 27, *V-Mann* reports emphasized to Lanz that no agreement was expected,[61] a feeling common to the participants at that time. The first news of an agreement came from a Cairo radio broadcast of March 3 monitored by

HGrE. The broadcast announced only that the resistance groups had reached an understanding, and they were now to work together against the common enemy with the full support of the Allies.[62] Headquarters Middle East decided not to publish the text of the agreement, and no details were made public.[63] German authorities refused to believe the Cairo broadcast, assuming it to be a propaganda ploy designed to undermine the Zervas-*Wehrmacht* relationship. Not until they received a copy of the Plaka Agreement from an original which which was returned to Zervas on March 6, did the occupation authorities believe an agreement had been concluded.[64] The delay in the German authorities receiving the news of Plaka as compared with the previous intelligence on the conferences was probably due to the reluctance of the *V-Mann* to communicate the bad news, but eventually it was taken to them.

The news of Plaka dealt a hard blow to the hopes of the occupation authorities. They realized that the quisling government of Rallis lacked popular support and existed only by the support of German arms. The Germans pursued the negotiations with Zervas's representatives, hoping to pry him away from the Allies and to use him as a national leader who would rally "nationalist-minded" Greeks in the struggle against bolshevism. The negotiations of October, November, and December 1943 and Zervas's "neutral position" toward them, for whatever reasons, convinced the Germans that Zervas could be useful to them. Their optimism remained guarded, however, as they never forgot Zervas's close ties to the Allies.[65] *HGrE* reminded Lanz that even though communism was the number one internal foe, and EDES only secondarly so, Zervas could again become a major threat if the Allies landed troops on Greece's west coast.[66] Nevertheless, even *HGrE* pursued a policy of weaning Zervas from the Allies to the extent of agreeing with Lanz on operation "*Sperber.*" At first, the agreement at Plaka seemed to indicate the destruction of the hopes that the Germans had in transforming Zervas into a Mihailović, but then evidence began to accumulate indicating that Plaka was not as successful as first believed.

Interrogations and *V-Mann* reports indicated to the authorities that the *andartes* signed at Plaka under intense pressure from the AMM, that deep hatred between EDES and EAM/ELAS continued and was growing deeper, preventing any cooperation between the two major resistance organizations. In the minds of German authorities, the failure of Zervas to move from his "neutrality" to offensive actions confirmed these reports. This impression was further reinforced by news of the renewed struggle by "national bands" in northern Greece against EAM/ELAS. Final confirmation came on March 14. On that day a "special representative" informed the commander of the *XXII Geb. AK.* that Zervas would not give up his attitude toward the *Wehrmacht*, since the victory of EAM/ELAS would mean the destruction of Greece.[67] Since Zervas did not attack any German units in the four months following Plaka, the Germans believed the report to be confirmed.[68] Brigadier K. V. Barker-Benfield, Chief of Operations for Force 133, was convinced that Zervas had an arrangement with the Germans.[69] If Barker-Benfield had access to "Ultra" (the operation that broke the German code) material, he would have known all about Zervas and Lanz. Whatever the sources may have been, the commander of Force 133 decided to test Zervas's loyalty in 1944. He designed a series of anti-German operations for Zervas, but the tests were never carried out. As chief of the AMM inside Greece, Woodhouse considered the missions designed by Barker-Benfield as impossible and suicidal. He told Zervas to ignore them.[70] The order for Zervas to halt his attacks against the Germans came from Colonel Barnes.[71] The order placed Zervas in the advantageous position of being able to hold to the Plaka accords and, at the same time, to preserve his neutrality toward Lanz. The order to halt offensive action against the Germans went to EAM/ELAS, but they disregarded it.

The Reaction of the Athenian EDES

After receiving information of the January and February negotiations to end the civil war, the central committee of EDES in Athens dispatched letters to Zervas warning the mountain leader not to conclude any peace with the communists lest he face expulsion and be declared an outlaw. A letter from the EDES organization in Patras repeated the same message.[72] A third letter came from the commander of the Security Battalions, General Leonidas Dertilis, who was a friend and former colleague of Zervas. (They had commanded the Republican Battalions for General Pangalos in 1926.) [73]

General Dertilis explained to Zervas, without any threats or recriminations, that he would never yield to British pressure for an agreement with EAM/ELAS. He warned Zervas that ELAS sought only to gain time and supplies in order to destroy EDES and that Britain was giving them material aid.[74] He requested Zervas to consider the situation after the Germans withdrew from Greece. In that situation the only way to prevent a communist *coup* would be for EDES to strike EAM/ELAS from one side while the Security Battalions struck from the other.[75]

To individuals like Dertilis who served the quisling government, bolshevism remained the gravest danger to Greece even while the nation lay under German rule. Their greatest concern was always with postwar conditions, and how they could stop communism, which was equated with EAM/ELAS. In April 1944, rumors made the rounds in Athenian government circles that Tavoulares and General Pangalos planned to establish a more effective government to press the campaign against communism.[76] But these remained only rumors, and Rallis continued to head the quisling government.

From Neutrality to Open Hostility

According to the German interpretation of the situation, the maintenance of the Plaka Agreement depended on how long Zervas would be able to resist British pressure to cooperate with EAM/ELAS. Zervas, reported the informants, was observing the Plaka accord only under British pressure.[77] After the guerrilla accord, the Germans continued to receive reports of minor clashes between the two resistance organizations, and they were informed that the EDES rank-and-file disapproved of the agreement and were pressing for a renewal of hostilities. As long as Zervas held to his anticommunist stance, the authorities expected the clashes to go on. Since he continued to hold to his "neutrality," they even remained hopeful that he might yet actively side with the German army. These impressions received encouragement from rumors among EDES circles in Ioannina that the Allies planned to land in Epirus so that Britain could join Germany in the fight against Greek communism,[78] a notion that Hitler was also to entertain in late September 1944.

In the meantime, the Germans contented themselves with the *status quo*. For as long as EDES stayed in Epirus, ELAS remained excluded from the Ioannina-Arta-Agrinion road, and as long as EDES maintained its "neutrality," the task of the *XXII Geb. AK.* to defend western Greece and to keep the road open remained relatively simple. Even more important to the Germans, the continuation of the *status quo* enabled them to concentrate their forces against ELAS. This situation between Zervas and the German army remained unchanged until July 1944. On the other hand, political developments in the mountains and in Cairo changed rapidly.

On March 10, 1944, EAM/ELAS swore in Bakirtzis as the temporary president of the newly created *Politike Epitrope Ethnikes Apeleutherosis* (PEEA—Political Committee of National Liberation).[79] Bakirtzis's desertion of EKKA earned him an immediate repudiation from his former colleagues. On April 20, Alexandros Svolos, professor of constitutional law at the University of Athens, replaced Bakirtzis. During this interim period, on March 31, the republican elements of the Greek armed forces in the Middle East demonstrated in favor of the Greek government-in-exile under Premier Emmanouil Tsouderos joining the PEEA. Forceful measures against these soldiers resulted in a full-scale revolt between April 1 and 23. Tsouderos resigned on the 11th, and he was replaced by Sophocles Venizelos, a politician of republican bent who was unable to resolve the crisis. Admiral Voulgares suppressed the mutiny on April 23, and Venizelos resigned, to be replaced by Georgios Papandreou. The mutiny forced the exiled politicians to recognize the power of the resistance, and a meeting of all the parties concerned was convened in Lebanon on May 17, 1944, to attempt to form a single government of national unity. The Lebanon Conference concluded an agreement on May 20, 1944, but it was not until August 2 that a government of national unity became a reality. In the meantime, ELAS attacked EKKA on the night of April 16-17, dissolving the guerrilla force and murdering its commander, Colonel Psarros. After this action, EDES remained the only organized opposition to EAM/ELAS within occupied Greece.[80]

Until the last week of June 1944, there was no change in the *status quo* between Zervas and the German army. Then on June 29, *HGrE* confirmed that Zervas guerrillas disguised as customs officials had been using the port of Parga to receive munitions and weapons from the Allies. The German authorities regarded this activity as a violation of the "agreement" of early February.[81] On the night of July 5-6, EDES units at-

tacked elements of the *XXII Geb. AK.* on the Ioannina-Igou-
menitsa road and on the Arta-Ioannina road. Both assaults
took place near the coast along roads leading inland. They
occurred while the Germans were conducting a major operation, *"Steinadler,"* against ELAS in northeastern Epirus and
western Macedonia near the villages of Pendalofon, Grevena,
and Vrischohori.[82] The EDES attacks were brief and unsus-
tained, and they failed to relieve the German pressure on
ELAS. In spite of the attacks, the Germans did not plan to
deal with EDES until the completion of *"Steinadler."* The
strikes by EDES ceased within one day, and can be explained by the accidental encounter with German troops as
they moved too close to EDES sources of supply.

Amazed by these attacks, the German authorities refused
to believe that Zervas had ordered them, but accepted reports
that the AMM had taken command of EDES while Zervas was
on an inspection tour and had ordered the attacks in Zervas's
absence. According to the reports, the AMM learned of Zervas's relation to the German army and ordered him seized.[83]
There is no other evidence to corroborate this explanation of
the attacks, and it must be interpreted as the only explanation
the *V-Mann* could contrive under the circumstances. In fact,
Brigadier Barker-Benfield, angered by Zervas's inactivity,
commanded Colonel Barnes to order Zervas to take the offensive against Lanz.[84]

Attempts to Restore the Agreement

The Germans interpreted the attacks as a prelude to an
Allied landing on Greece's western coast, but later they revised
this initial estimate to conclude that the attacks were directed
to securing enlarged areas of the coast around Parga in order
to make it an infiltration point for small Allied units. They
estimated that Zervas had concentrated some 6,000-7,000 troops
at the Parga "bridgehead," as they called it. These estimates
were very exaggerated, as Zervas never had that number of
active guerrillas in his whole force. Having enjoyed EDES's
neutrality for nearly half a year, the German authorities now
overreacted by inflating the danger that Zervas presented as
a hostile force far out of proportion to the actual strength of
EDES.[85] *HGrE* decided that Zervas and his forces, whether
friendly or hostile, presented an acute danger to western

Greece. Following the completion of *"Steinadler,"* *HGrE* planned to strike EDES with operation *"Zeppelin"* to clear up the developing danger. The attack sought to capture Zervas, other officers of EDES and AMM, and to prevent any union between EDES and EAM/ELAS, which was moving into southern Epirus and west central Greece.[86]

Informed of this plan, Lieutenant-General Lanz immediately requested its postponement until he could dispatch a German officer to speak directly to Zervas. Lanz no longer considered his Zervas liaison reliable.[87] He argued that the partisan situation changed daily, and that since ELAS forces had moved into the area between Agrinion and Karpenision, the troops required for *"Zeppelin"* must be directed against the newly arrived ELAS division. Through direct contact with Zervas, he hoped to clear up the situation as to whether or not the armistice remained negotiable.[88] Lanz's argument received reinforcement when the ELAS Division mentioned by him attacked the *104 Jg. Div.* in the Arta-Agrinion area.[89] To meet the threat created by Zervas and the increasing resistance activity all over Greece, *HGrE* requested an additional division from *HGrF*.[90]

During this exchange between Lanz and *HGrE*, operation *"Steinadler"* concluded on July 14 at a heavy toll for ELAS. The Germans counted 455 ELAS men dead, 250-300 wounded, and 951 suspects arrested, including 21 ELAS officers and 7 BLOs.[91] *HGrE* decided to postpone action against Zervas until it could amass what it considered adequate forces for the task. The background for this decision provides an excellent profile of the Greek resistance's motives and goals and the Germans' plan to deal with them.

The German authorities always considered the external enemy, the Allies, as the number one danger to Greece. The resistance movement remained a secondary concern to the end of the occupation. Of the resistance movements, EAM/ELAS presented from the beginning the greatest internal threat. Regarding the conflict between EAM/ELAS and EDES, the German authorities believed the differences to be irreconcilable. Both political organizations concentrated their efforts more against each other than against the occupying power, focusing on their political future in postwar Greece. In this jockeying for position, the political results of the resistance remained in the forefront, while the struggle against the occupying power dropped into the background. In case of a German withdrawal, the army did not expect too much difficulty from the resistance. The Germans expected both EDES and EAM/ELAS to concentrate on moving toward and gaining control of Athens. They expected only individual actions against the *Wehrmacht. HGrE* planned to exploit this situation to its advantage.[92]

Zervas's recent action against the German army and the movement of an ELAS division into the area northeast of Agrinion and east of Mesolongion presented a clear danger of invasion to Greece's west coast. Unable to collect the number of troops required for a successful operation against both EDES and ELAS, the Germans chose a different stratagem. They believed that Zervas's previous neutrality might still be reinstituted, whereas any attack against him would only push him into the arms of the AMM. They rejected action against EDES. Instead, they chose to strike at ELAS, knowing that this course conformed to the interests of Zervas and nationalist circles all over Greece. Then, in any negotiations with either of these two groups, the Germans would possess a strong hand. The attack on ELAS, coupled with pressure on Zervas from nationalist circles in Athens, might make it possible to forge an anticommunist alliance with Zervas. If the stratagem failed, Zervas could be attacked after the close of the operation against ELAS.[93] The German authorities placed a great deal of importance on the Athenian nationalists convincing Zervas to join their scheme. In accordance with this policy, *HGrE* ordered a major operation, *"Kreuzotter,"* against the ELAS forces in central Greece that were headquartered at Karpenision.[94]

Operation "Verrat"

While *"Kreuzotter"* was underway, the Germans attempted to link anti-bolshevik partisans in Macedonia with Zervas. During the discussions between EDES and the German officers, the Germans suggested shifting EDES *andartes* to Macedonia to bolster the nationalists, but to no avail.[95] The AMM "hardened" Zervas's heart in these negotiations.[96] The Germans attempted the same ploy in September with more success.

As this approach failed to win Zervas's support, a new line of communication opened during this period. According to the German records, on August 15, *HGrE* received permission from the *Oberbefehlshalber Suedost* Field Marshal von

Weichs and *Sonderbevollmaechtigter* Neubacher to enter into discussions with "Colonel Tom," presumably Colonel "Tom" Barnes, who was chief of the AMM to Zervas. Two days later on Crete, a Captain "Lodwick," who claimed to be a British officer dispatched from the Middle East Command, turned himself over to German authorities. Captain "Lodwick" claimed to have been sent to arrange transportation of German officers to Cairo to negotiate an end to the war in Greece. He was to remain in Crete as a hostage.[97] The curious incident was a personal fluke, but Barnes was authorized to meet secretly with Lanz and to negotiate the unconditional surrender of the Germans.[98]

The contacts with "Tom" (Barnes) and "Lodwick" convinced *HGrE* that Britain was genuinely interested in negotiations, which might prove useful by gaining time for German forces in Greece. The Salonica authorities even suggested a suitable officer for the mission.[99] In the meantime, *"Kreuzotter"* completed phase I by August 15 as the *4 SS-Pol-Pz-Gren-Division* moved into Greece for deployment against Zervas should the policy of winning an alliance with him fail. Throughout this period, German units avoided all contact with EDES *andartes*.[100] The first elements of the *4 SS-Pol-Pz-Gren-Division* reached Arta by the evening of August 20.

Lanz was angered by Barnes's demand for unconditional surrender, and the initial contacts with "Tom" and Zervas ended on the same day that the *4 SS-Pol-Pz-Gren-Division* was deployed around Arta. Zervas's liaison man reported that the AMM had ordered EDES to cut the Igoumenitsa-Ioannina road. According to the informant, a recent decision by EAM/ELAS to join Papandreou's government-in-exile and to participate in planning a national army forced Zervas to alter his course. Further pressure for action on Zervas came as a result of the agreement between Churchill and Tito on the Yugoslav resistance. Under these new conditions, Zervas could no longer avoid hostilities with the *Wehrmacht*, but the informant continued, Zervas intended to remain in secret contact with German authorities.[101]

The German stratagem failed. Zervas entered into open hostilities against the *Wehrmacht* on August 19, the first attack since the night of July 5-6.[102] The Germans then planned execution of Operation *"Verrat"* to destroy Zervas forces and the Parga "bridgehead" as soon as possible. A strong force consisting of the *4 SS-Pol-Pz-Gren-Division*, the *104 Jg. Div.*, two battalions from the *117 Jg. Div.* located in Tripolis, the *1 Fest. Inf. Btl.* from Cephalonia, and a Security Battalion assembled for *"Verrat."* These units were to sweep north from Arta and south from Ioannina, pushing Zervas's forces west toward the sea and away from the Ioannina-Arta road.[103] The Germans assembled this large force on the basis of their exaggerated evaluation of Zervas's strength, thought to be 26,000 men and enlarged mainly through the infiltration of Greek forces from the Middle East.

The authorities planned a propaganda campaign to coincide with the attack. The propaganda claimed that, under British pressure, Zervas had betrayed his nation and had joined the communists. Britain, the Papandreou government, and Zervas had all betrayed their country to communism. The German press stressed Zervas's previous neutrality and the fact that only after intense British pressure had Zervas given up this position. The Greek press stressed Zervas's opportunism in the face of British pressure and claimed that true "nationalists" did not approve of his "egotistical" maneuvering. Pointing to the example of Mihailović in Serbia, the quisling press stressed the "awakening of the national will" throughout all of southeast Europe and the need to form a united front for the defense against communism. The propaganda barrage concluded by comparing Zervas to Tito as evidence of Britain's support of communism.[104]

Had Zervas been attacked by the collective forces of *"Verrat,"* EDES undoubtedly would have been dissolved. He was saved by the Soviet Union's offensive in Rumania. On August 24, 1944, Rumania dropped out of the war, thereby creating a critical military situation for the Third Reich. On that day *OB Suedost* ordered the *4 SS-Pol-Pz-Gren-Division* north to Skoplje to meet the new crisis, and *HGrE* cancelled operation *"Verrat."* [105] Events in Bulgaria soon paralleled developments in Rumania. Advancing Russian armies to the north threatened to cut off German forces in Greece. The *OKW* ordered *HGrF* to establish a new defense of the economically important central Balkans area and to keep the supply road open to meet any invasion threat. On August 29, 1944, Field Marshal von Weichs ordered *HGrE* to prepare a new defense along a line Corfu-Ioannina-Kalambaka-Olympus. Unable to inflict a military defeat upon Zervas, the German authorities decided to resort to negotiations as a means of making the gradual withdrawal as easy as possible.[106]

The German Withdrawal

On August 28, the German authorities reestablished contact with "Tom" in hope of using the meetings as a cover for the evacuation of southern Epirus, as EDES could make it very difficult for German units withdrawing from Mesolongion and Agrinion along the Arta-Ioannina road.[107] When the German authorities previously contacted Barnes on August 20, he had requested a German capitulation. This request alarmed Zervas, who believed that Greece would fall into the hands of ELAS if the Germans surrendered. "Tom" then explained that he was prepared to accept a counterproposal from the Germans. The negotiations broke off on August 24-26 during plans for "Verrat." They resumed, only to be broken off again when "Tom" learned that the Germans planned to leave Greece.[108] On September 3, the Germans made another offer, which allowed Zervas to move some of his units to the Peloponnese if he would evacuate the coast of Epirus and take a neutral position toward the Wehrmacht. Zervas and "Tom" refused, replying that they would negotiate only a general armistice. Once again the Germans broke off the negotiations. The following day, the OKW forbade any further military talks and ordered all political discussions to be handled by the Auswaertiges Amt.[109] By the middle of September, all attempts to negotiate an EDES evacuation of the western coast failed, and Zervas continued his hostile attitude toward the occupying power.[110]

Paralleling these developments, the Rallis government requested Sonderbevollmaechtigter Neubacher to open negotiations with the Allies in order to work out a plan to prevent a communist coup when the Germans withdrew. HGrE interpreted Rallis's move as a possible means to preserve his government after the German withdrawal, but they remained interested in negotiations as the best means to leave Greece. Hopes for negotiations arose from what the Germans erroneously interpreted as Britain's "positive Haltung" (positive attitude) toward Germany in Greece. This impression was based on Britain's failure to press the Germans with a landing and on Britain's fear of a communist coup. The inaction of Britain encouraged the Germans to believe that the British preferred the Germans to the Russians in Greece. Hitler held on to this notion until September 16, 1944. Then he ordered HGrF to "... kindle and fan strife between Communist and nationalist forces . . ." in an effort to extract the maximum political gain from the coming military withdrawal.[111]

After rejecting direct negotiations as suggested by Rallis, the Germans took up their second line of approach, creating tension and open hostility among the different political organizations in Greece. On September 16, Neubacher, Weichs, and Rallis devised a plan to send the Greek Security Battalions into Macedonia and Thrace in an effort to counter ELAS bands and to organize other nationalist bands.[112] The Rallis government participated in the plan to prevent Bulgarian and EAM/ELAS "communists" from seizing Thrace and eastern Macedonia.[113]

The anticommunist partisans who received support from the Germans consisted of Constantinos Papadopoulos's 2,600 men in Kilkis, a 2,500-man band under Michail Papadopoulos in Kozani, 1,800 men under Kisabajack, 600 men under Tsaous Anton in the Drama area, and a band of 250 men in Thrace under Captain Spiridis.[114] With the help of the Germans, Constantinos Papadopoulos organized his partisans in February 1944 under the name of *Ethnikos Ellenikos Stratos* (EES–Greek National Army). Kisabajack originally joined *Panellenike Apeleutherotike Organosis* (PAO–Panhellenic Liberation Organization), but upon its dissolution in the fall and winter of 1943 from German and ELAS attacks, he formed his own anticommunist band with the support of the Germans.[115] Captain Spiridis's support was of a defensive nature, as he reportedly never took any offensive action against ELAS. The same was apparently true of Tsaous Anton. Anton and Spiridis received support from BLO Captain Miller.[116]

The nationalist partisan bands of the two Papadopouloses and Kisabajack together with the Security Battalions covered the retreat of the German army out of Salonica. As the Germans withdrew, they turned over territory to these bands, who then engaged ELAS. The fighting became particularly heavy in the centers of Trikkala, Kozani, and Ioannitsa, where ELAS temporarily encircled German units, but the anticommunist bands managed successfully to help the Germans clear the main roads.[117] The Germans made a similar and effective use of the Security Battalions, which covered their retreat from the Peloponnese.[118]

On September 22, the Germans moved out of Arta toward Ioannina, harassed by EDES. Two days later, after the Germans withdrew, Zervas occupied Igoumenitsa. Then, on September 24, Zervas representatives proposed to *HGrE* that EDES be allowed to move unhindered toward Athens. Without consulting Neubacher in Belgrade, *HGrE* placed stiff conditions on the proposal: hostilities toward the *Wehrmacht* must halt immediately; EDES must engage in an active struggle against ELAS; Zervas must accept leadership of all national anticommunist forces; and Zervas must break with the Allies.[119] With these impossible terms, *HGrE* hoped to intensify the hostility between EDES and ELAS as the Germans prepared to leave Greece. When Neubacher learned of these conditions, he sent a sharp letter to Loehr, criticizing them as excessive and tending to destroy all threads of communication with Zervas. He requested that in the future Loehr promptly inform his representative in Greece, Franz Hoefinghoff, of all proposals.[120] But none arrived.

On October 2, 1944, *HGrE* received the order to withdraw from Greece. The *XXII Geb. AK.* abandoned Ioannina on October 15, 1944. During this time, a last effort was made to get Zervas to recognize the anticommunist bands in Macedonia as part of EDES. According to German documents, he acknowledged them as such.[121]

Zervas survived the occupation, and he now faced the hostile and overwhelmingly superior force of ELAS. During the conflict of December 1944, ELAS attacked and destroyed EDES as an effective fighting force. On December 29, a British boat carried Zervas and a few survivors from the island of Corfu to safety. Without the presence of the *XXII Geb. AK.* Zervas could not have survived the onslaught of ELAS in 1943. A little more than two and a half years later, however, Zervas, as Minister of Public Order, would settle his accounts with EAM/ELAS.

The Zervas-German Connection

The history of the Zervas-*Wehrmacht* accommodation cannot be dismissed as a tale concocted either by German propaganda or by traitors and miserable characters.[122] It cannot be discounted on the basis that a written agreement has never been discovered, for none ever existed. The explanation that the liaisons, mentioned in the German documents as middlemen, were not in contact with Zervas but with ex-EDES members who had joined the Security Battalions completely misses the point.[123] The contacts made between EDES and the Germans on December 18, 1943, January 4, and February 1, 1944 (the first two occurring just before EDES attacked ELAS, and the third producing operation *"Sperber"* in an effort to save EDES from annihilation), cannot be explained as fortuitous events. The accurate information that the Germans received on the Mirofillo and Plaka conferences indicate that someone close to those meetings kept them well informed.

On the other hand, there is no evidence to support EAM/ELAS's charges of collaboration in October 1943. The documents published by P. K. Enepekides are misleading. By relying on documents written in the summer of 1944,[124] he presents an incomplete picture of the Zervas-German relations. These documents give the impression that an agreement was signed and that Zervas actively worked with the Germans. Throughout the period October 1943 to October 1944, Zervas consistently rejected active collaboration in favor of coexistence. The German records do not sustain Kédros's charges of a German-Rallis-British conspiracy.

Zervas's policy of coexistence, however, enabled the Germans to concentrate on ELAS for at least two major operations, *"Kreuzotter"* and *"Steinadler,"* which angered Brigadier Barker-Benfield.[125] The records of *HGrE XXII Geb. AK. LXXXXI AK* and the *LVXIII AK* contained no evidence of any German-EAM/ELAS accords, and there was no evidence that the Germans purposely let war matériel fall into the hands of EAM/ELAS. Throughout the spring and summer of 1944, no major operation was directed against EDES. Developments in Rumania saved EDES from certain destruction by forcing cancellation of operation *"Verrat."* Any charges that EAM/ELAS failed to engage actively the Germans during the occupation are patently false. Regardless of EAM/ELAS's hostility toward all other resistance organizations, it had no choice but to face the Germans and their anticommunist bands during the summer and fall of 1944.

Zervas's policy of coexistence with the Germans remained both passive and defensive. He remained passive as long as Colonel Barnes allowed him to refrain from offensive action. When it became clear that the Germans would soon be forced to leave the Balkans and that EAM/ELAS had joined Papandreou's government, EDES was forced gradually to give up its policy of coexistence. Still, as the Germans withdrew from Epirus, they informed EDES officers of every step so that

EDES could take over towns as smoothly as possible. The policy of Zervas remained defensive in that he used the German army as a buffer between his forces and ELAS without ever joining the Germans in any concerted action. During this period, he continued to receive full British support in the form of gold sovereigns and matériel. Britain liberally supplied EDES in the hope of transforming it into an effective political and military counterweight to EAM/ELAS.[126]

Zervas's motives were political. In this regard he was no different from EAM/ELAS. Both Lanz and Barker-Benfield agreed on this point. Nevertheless, he failed to pay adequate attention to political realities. He began the resistance as a republican, but then changed to supporting George II when he discovered that Britain backed the monarch's return to Greece. He concentrated all power in his hands and stressed the "cult of personality" at the expense of his organization.[127] He never allowed EDES to develop a stable national policy which could find popular support. EDES remained a regional movement without popular roots. It survived the occupation only as a military force through British support and Zervas's coexistence with the German army. The easy dissolution of EDES by EAM/ELAS in December 1944 made clear the weaknesses of EDES as an effective military force. The Germans failed to make Zervas into a "Mihailović," and Britain's policy of transforming EDES into a counterweight to EAM/ELAS failed. Indeed, Britain's favored treatment of EDES and other pseudo-resistance organizations only infuriated EAM/ELAS and complicated relations between Cairo and EAM/ELAS.

CHAPTER SEVEN

THE RESISTANCE
AND GREEK WARTIME POLITICS

The civil war confirmed Foy Kohler's prediction that Britain's attempt to "sell" the monarchy to the Greeks would fail, and the political problems which dominated 1944 were carried over from 1943 without better resolution. These issues were the question of the return of the King, the formation of a government of national unity, and the unification of the resistance and the Greek armed forces in the Middle East. If 1944 witnessed a replay of the events of 1943, the consequences were decisively different, and they resulted in the defeat of the politics of the resistance and the complete polarization of Greek politics. Each of the four major participants, Britain, the resistance, the Greek exile government, and the reemerging prewar Greek politicians, shared in the responsibility for the failure, but of these four Britain was the crucial and, ultimately, the dominant factor in the situation. While EAM/ELAS made considerable blunders, chiefly the inability to follow a consistent policy of accommodation with Britain, the British prime minister precluded any possible compromise on the issue of the monarchy by his persistent support of the Greek king.

British Policy Between the Civil War
and the Lebanon Conference

The civil war of 1943 renewed the conflict between the Foreign Office and British military authorities over Britain's dual policy of supporting the King and the anti-monarchist resistance. By November, it seemed that London faced a choice of either dropping the monarch and supporting the resistance, or breaking with the guerrillas and continuing full support of the King and his exile government. Mandated to support Allied strategy in Europe by holding down as many German divisions as possible in the Balkans, the military officials remained dissatisfied with Foreign Office support for George II, which conflicted with the military goal of building an effective resistance inside Greece. By attempting to support the King and the resistance, the military were convinced neither goal was well served. If the military objectives of the Allies were to succeed, Brigadier Hollis explained in a memorandum to the Foreign Office, Britain had to work with EAM/ELAS, which was the most effective resistance inside Greece. The Brigadier emphasized, "materials in the hands of the better organized left wing groups produces better results." [1] To achieve their goals and at the same time to neutralize the communist element in the resistance, the Chiefs of Staff recommended a revision of an earlier SOE proposal which proposed to dispatch Plastiras to the mountains of Greece and to establish a regency under Archbishop Damaskinos. [2] The military believed that the Plastiras-Damaskinos scheme, along with a declaration from the King of his acceptance of a plebiscite before returning, was the only viable policy which could achieve their war aims.

Although E. M. Rose (Foreign Office) thought much of Hollis's argument was "so wrongheaded and even fatheaded," he recognized the validity of the Brigadier's point on the monarchy as the source of civil strife, and he accepted the idea of building up a Plastiras-Damaskinos axis to counter the expected EAM/ELAS *coup* at liberation. Ambassador Leeper agreed that the King was the main obstacle to fighting EAM/ELAS, but he was not prepared to accept the Plastiras-Damaskinos scheme without a break with EAM/ELAS, which would be accompanied by a sustained campaign to assist the dissolution of EAM/ELAS while building up Zervas as rapidly as possible. The military officials in Cairo eventually agreed with Leeper in order to get his support for obtaining the King's declaration on the plebiscite. Without a clear statement from the King that he would not return until a plebiscite, which would deprive EAM/ELAS of the claim that Britain planned to return the King with British bayonets, the military in Cairo saw no chance of success for the plan. [3]

Sargent, who was skeptical of the military value of EAM/ELAS and who was not enthusiastic about the suggestions made by Rose and the Middle East Defense Committee (MEDC), remained convinced that the civil war had nothing to do with the political failure of the Cairo conference. Rather, the situation in Greece was the result of "personal rivalries and ambitions" between monarchists and republicans. He did not think that the time was satisfactory for a solution of the constitutional issue, and he requested a review of EAM/ELAS military effectiveness.[4] Churchill went further than Sargent. Not only was it not a time to settle the constitutional issue, but he asked that "ELAS should be starved and struck at by every means in our power."[5] Eden, however, took a cooler view, and in a memorandum to Churchill, he pointed out that while Zervas could become the nucleus of an expanded armed resistance to serve Allied war aims, he thought a regency council of notables under Damaskinos was the only feasible means of saving the monarchy.[6] On November 22, the War Cabinet gave Churchill and Eden the discretionary power to resolve the issue in consultation with the military authorities in the Middle East. The final proposal called for aid to ELAS not to be renewed and for EDES to be incorporated into the Greek army, which would send an officer from the Middle East to join Zervas. The ELAS *andartes* would be invited to join the Greek army on the same basis as EDES. To facilitate success, the King was to declare his acceptance of a regency and his decision not to return before a plebiscite.[7]

This new plan to wean the EAM/ELAS rank and file from the Communist leadership was similar to the policy recommended by Myers and SOE in the spring of 1943, but at that time, and again at the Cairo conference, the Foreign Office had refused the idea of a plebiscite. The problem in November was to gain George II's acceptance of the new policy. The events of the civil war led the King to take a new position on his return. In a letter to Tsouderos on November 8, the monarch agreed to reconsider the timing of his return to Greece at liberation, but he did not go far enough for the Foreign Office, which desired a full commitment to the regency-plebiscite plan. Even Eden and Churchill personally advised the King to agree. On December 13, the King, acting on the inexplicable advice of President Roosevelt, refused. Eden was furious with Roosevelt, but Britain was not prepared to force the King, and the constitutional plan was shelved. In a public statement on December 22, the King revised his position of November 8 to read that he would reconsider the timing of his return at the liberation in consultation with his government, which was a major concession for the obtuse monarch.

In spite of the shelving of the constitutional plan, which had been crucial to the military, Leeper persisted in his aim to destroy EAM/ELAS. Somehow, he won the support of General Henry M. Wilson, the Commander-in-Chief in the Middle East, for ending aid to the resistance and sending all of the guerrillas home.[8] Laskey and his superiors rejected the recommendation on three counts. The Foreign Office was not prepared to jettison the whole war effort in Greece, which the Russians would never accept. Further, as Laskey pointed out, ELAS could not be dissolved on orders from Cairo, and even if by some quirk, they could be disbanded, this dissolution would not resolve the problem of EAM power in Athens.[9] The upshot of the affair was two appeals by Tsouderos in late December and public statements by the British, American, and Soviet governments appealing for unity and an end to the civil war.

After failing to destroy Zervas and suffering a serious loss of popularity for initiating the civil war, EAM/ELAS reacted by indicating to Woodhouse on December 19 that they were prepared to negotiate an end to the conflict. Officials in the Foreign Office and Cairo were prepared to agree, but Churchill, by a secret cipher and unknown to the Foreign Office, ordered Woodhouse not to negotiate and that no "warlike stores" be sent to them.[10]

The decision at Teheran for "Overlord" emphasized the need of the Allies to support Tito and the Greek resistance in order to keep the "Balkan pot boiling" for the Germans, but the Foreign Office, if it could not break with EAM/ELAS, sought to limit this support and to restrict EAM/ELAS influence. The Foreign Office chose to continue the policy of supporting the King and tolerating but not aiding EAM/ELAS. Toward this end, it proposed to restrain the more ruthless members of ELAS and to build an anti-KKE coalition around Damaskinos and the exile government which was to be revived and strengthened by including fresh political moderates from Greece. If a truce could be arranged between the warring resistance groups, the Foreign Office was even prepared to invite EAM representation to join the Tsouderos government.[11] This willingness to accept EAM/ELAS stemmed from a stream of reports from British, American, and Greek sources inside Greece which indicated that the violence of the civil war, bitter economic conditions, and German reprisals had turned the population against EAM/ELAS. In this situation, the Foreign Office no longer feared the resistance, and it became convinced that in any confrontation or *coup* attempt EAM/ELAS could easily be dissolved. Churchill was certain that a mere 5,000 troops would be adequate for the task, but the military, which better understood the attitudes and conditions inside of Greece, predicted that a minimum of 80,000 would be necessary.[12] The British decision to allow EAM/ELAS representatives to join a coalition government was further influenced by the Foreign Office concern that EAM/ELAS might follow the example of Tito and establish a rival government inside Greece. Leeper had reported to London that the only reason EAM/ELAS had not acted in this direction was the refusal of noncommunist politicians to join such a government. The politicians, fearing any association with EAM/ELAS would permanently discredit their political lives, looked to Britain and Tsouderos for support against the resistance.[13]

Political Developments in Greece

In early January, Tsouderos agreed to go along with the British policy except in one important regard. He insisted that any negotiations in Greece be limited to military matters and reconciliation. Then, on January 27, Tsouderos received from Sophoulis, Gonatas, Mylonas, Papandreou, and Petros Rallis a message which endorsed the King's November 8 letter on his return to Greece. Interpreting the letter as an acceptance of a plebiscite, the Greek leaders were willing to work for the formation of a government of national unity by constitutional means.[14] Immediately, Tsouderos contacted the Archbishop, who agreed to make an appeal for reconciliation and to open negotiations with the Athenian politicians on behalf of the Cairo government, which Tsouderos emphasized was and should remain the only Greek government. If EAM/ELAS responded and agreed to an armistice, the Archbishop was to select a committee to discuss the formation of a common national government with EAM/ELAS. While Damaskinos was garnering support for the exile government in Athens, Tsouderos accepted Woodhouse as his representative in any talks with the resistance. The premier insisted on, and won approval for, limiting the negotiations only to military matters and a ceasefire.[15]

Coincidentally, or perhaps because he knew of Tsouderos's contacts with Damaskinos, Siantos telegraphed his terms for a ceasefire to GHQ ME and asked Tsouderos to send two representatives to the mountains to negotiate for a coalition government and a unified armed forces. Siantos's terms for the armistice were that Zervas must denounce the EDES collaborators, accept an in-place ceasefire, and begin discussions for a united guerrilla army.[16] Tsouderos welcomed the ceasefire proposal, but he was not prepared to accept political discussions. Churchill's objections to negotiations with EAM/ELAS were overcome, and a ceasefire was reached on February 4. The representatives of the different organizations met on February 6, 1944, in the village of Mirofillo. Since Tzimas had left the headquarters of ELAS to establish contact with Tito in Yugoslavia, Saraphes and Roussos led the EAM/ELAS delegation to Mirofillo. Kartalis headed the EKKA representatives, which included Psarros and Major Stephanos Doukas, while Pyromaglou and Colonel Petros Nikolopoulos spoke for EDES. Colonel Woodhouse represented both Great Britain and the Greek exile government.

In the fourteen meetings that followed, Woodhouse, with the assistance of Zervas and Kartalis, successfully limited the talks to military affairs. In a bid to achieve its goal of a unified guerrilla army, EAM/ELAS offered Zervas the command for Epirus. The Allied Military Mission (AMM), which had been formed upon the arrival of Major G. K. Wines of the United States, wanted geographical commands, with Zervas having a separate command for Epirus and west-central Greece. Since EAM/ELAS feared this proposal to be part of a plot to use the area as a base of operations against it, it refused to go along.[17] The discussions for a unified army eventually failed, since the resistance leaders could not agree on a suitable commander or on how the forces would be integrated. At one point, EAM/ELAS and EKKA agreed on Bakirtzis as the army's commander-in-chief, but Pyromaglou rejected the candidate, fearing that Bakirtzis would be under EAM/ELAS influence. They finally agreed on the old, respected Venizelist officer, General Alexandros Othonaios, who had presided at the courts-martial of the ministers and officers in 1922 and served as Inspector-General from 1929 to 1935. The differences, however, over the means to amalgamate the guerrilla armies proved insurmountable.

Kartalis proposed the formation of a government of national unity which would include representatives of the three resistance movements, the democratic parties, and the Tsouderos government. To facilitate its creation, he proposed that the resistance leaders form a commission which would negotiate with Cairo and Athens. EDES approved, but the proposal failed in the face of EAM/ELAS insistence that the political committee be formed in Free Greece and that it have full, executive governmental power. Both Pyromaglou and Kartalis opposed this proposal. They wanted a national unity government located outside of Greece and away from the dominating influence of EAM/ELAS.[18] Since the Foreign Office thought it would be difficult to denounce EAM/ELAS if the talks failed, Sargent found it hard to object to the EAM/ELAS proposal.[19] London's dilemma was handily resolved by Zervas, who insisted on a military settlement before pursuing any political discussions. The negotiations then reached an impasse, but Kartalis, cooperating with Woodhouse and pretending to take the side of EAM/ELAS in favoring the need for a political committee in the mountains, succeeded in getting the parties to agree to meet again at Plaka. There, on February 29, the AMM and the three resistance organizations signed an agreement to continue the armistice and maintain the status quo in their respective territories. A vague agreement to cooperate in the future concluded the parleys, but a secret section of the agreement committed EAM/ELAS to cooperate with "Noah's Ark," a military operation to support "Overlord" by harassing the Germans out of Greece.

On the day before the signing of the Plaka Agreement, over three-fourths of the officers of Psarros's regiment dispatched a telegram of support to the King. The initiator of this action was Captain Euthemios Dedouses, who had connections with some military officers associated with the conservative and monarchist *Strateotike Ierarchia* (Military Hierarchy). The action heralded the dissolution of EKKA. Within two weeks of the date of the Dedouses telegram, Bakirtzis defected and joined EAM/ELAS.

After the fruitless negotiations at Mirofillo-Plaka, EAM/ELAS pushed ahead with plans to form a government in Free Greece. In the previous December, EAM/ELAS contacted the traditional politicians and invited them to join in creating a free Greek government.[20] Most of them refused and, like Georgios Papandreou, marked it off as just another communist ploy to advance a dictatorship. Other liberals, republicans, and social democrats took another view and joined EAM/ELAS as a means of moderating the Communist Party influence and achieving the resistance's goals of national self-determination. They agreed to join on the condition that EAM/ELAS end its terror against its rivals.[21] The outstanding examples of these individuals were Professor Alexandros Svolos, a well-known and respected scholar in constitutional law; General Mandakes, who in 1938 had led a Cretan revolt against Metaxas; another professor, Angelos Angelopoulos; the socialist Demetrios Strates; and Bakirtzis.

While the discussions at Mirofillo-Plaka took place, Svolos met with Ioannis Peltekis ("Apollo") in Athens. Svolos stressed that the only way to prevent a communist victory was the formation of a coalition government coupled to a declaration from the King accepting a plebiscite. He warned Peltekis that a military agreement which excluded a political solution was likely to move EAM/ELAS toward unilateral action.[22]

Although Laskey knew that Svolos's wife was a communist feminist, he thought Svolos to be independent and completely honest. Svolos's conversation with Peltekis impressed Laskey, who believed the moderate socialist to have considerable influence over the Greek left, and for these reasons he wanted Tsouderos to include Svolos in the exile government along with Papandreou, Alexandris, and Petros Rallis, as a means of strengthening Tsouderos and keeping EAM/ELAS in check.[23] In less than three weeks, however, Svolos joined EAM/ELAS's *Politike Epitrope Ethnikes Apeleutherosis* (PEEA—Political Committee of National Liberation).

Bakirtzis's reasons for joinning EAM/ELAS were similar to those of Svolos. In a letter to Psarros on October 20, 1943, Bakirtzis indicated that the events since August convinced him that Britain intended to force the King upon Greece at the time of liberation. Only the resistance could stop this policy, but to succeed, the resistance had to remain united. The danger lay in the KKE, which hid its dictatorship behind the democratic front of EAM/ELAS. He recognized that EAM/ELAS was the major resistance force and could not be overcome from the outside. Bakirtzis concluded that only by joining EAM/ELAS could the communists be defeated from the inside, and he recommended this policy to EKKA.[24] No doubt the failure of Mirofillo-Plaka and the telegram from Dedouses acted as the final catalyst for Bakirtzis's defection from EKKA to EAM/ELAS. On March 10, 1943, he was sworn in as the provisional president of the PEEA until Svolos arrived in April from Athens. The efforts of Bakirtzis and Svolos proved futile, as they received little or no support from either London or Cairo. The efforts of Pyromaglou and Kartalis to form a real government of unity failed for the same reasons.

Developments in the Middle East

Instead of seeking a compromise with the resistance, Leeper and Tsouderos devised yet another plan in January 1944 to neutralize it. They proposed to regroup the resistance into fewer and smaller bands which were to be placed at strategic points under the AMM, and on the pretext of reducing German reprisals, they recommended all guerrilla activity be severely reduced. Apparently, General Wilson went along with the plan, but the COS did not. They wanted full suport for EAM/ELAS as the best means to achieve the goals of "Noah's Ark." They requested Wilson to revise his "Noah's Ark" plans to include an expanded and more active campaign against the Germans than originally planned by Cairo. The COS feared that any dampening down of the guerrilla war would be noticed by the Germans, who might then reduce their forces in Greece. The COS did not reject the idea of a reorganization, but insisted on a quick armistice and a short reorganization period in order to avoid signaling to the Germans any slackening of resistance and to avoid producing an embarrassment in regard to the Soviet Union. Reprisals, which had figured prominently in Leeper's thinking, were risks that the COS believed necessary to achieve their military goals.[25]

The Foreign Office readily agreed on the need for a reorganization of the resistance but not on inactivity. Firmly committed to "Overlord," Eden was now prepared to support anyone "who was killing Germans in the next six months even though he be a shocking communist...."[26] In a memorandum to Churchill on February 10, Eden summarized British policy toward Greece. Although he despised EAM/ELAS as "a thoroughly unscrupulous group of communist fanatics, out solely for their own ends...and working for a coup at liberation," Britain had no other resistance to rely upon in Greece. Rather than reducing or breaking EAM/ELAS, Eden argued that Britain should work toward ending the civil war and fully supporting Tsouderos's policy of building a political base around Damaskinos. The Foreign Secretary was not prepared to drop the loyal Zervas and give *full* support to ELAS, however. Eden feared that full support for EAM/ELAS, as advocated by the COS, would mean a continuation of the civil war and thwart any effort for unity. Zervas, in Eden's view, had been too loyal to Britain to be dropped, and complete support for EAM/ELAS would in all probability bring about the downfall of Tsouderos. On February 14, Churchill accepted Eden's argument, which amounted to a continuation of limited support for ELAS as long as the armistice held, but full support for Zervas. The Chiefs of Staff were puzzled by the decision and queried how "Noah's Ark" could be implemented if EAM/ELAS refused to cooperate? They pointed out that Zervas lay across no important strategic point, whereas on the mainland and in the Aegean EAM/ELAS did. The prime minister, however, was unmoved by their rebuttal.[27]

On February 11, 1944, Tsouderos received a message from Damaskinos which shattered his bridge-building policy to the Athenian political world. The Archbishop reported that the old line politicians no longer gave unqualified support to the Tsouderos government; the King's letter of November 8 was apparently too ambiguous as they requested a clear public statement from the monarch that he would not return at liberation. Knowing that the King would refuse, Tsouderos set about more energetically to coopt the Athenians by inviting Papandreou, Alexandris, and Petros Rallis to join the government. Laskey believed that Tsouderos's move fell short of taking the necessary action to ensure the success of a new government which, in Laskey's view, required the inclusion of non-communist representatives of the resistance.[28] Laskey, and later Douglas Howard (Head of the Southern Department) as well, were very much influenced by Svolos, whom they had in mind as a representative of the resistance to join Papandreou and Petros Rallis in the new government. Further, Laskey hoped inclusion of Svolos would help silence strong criticism in parliament of the Foreign Office's support of Greek "reactionaries." [29] Tsouderos did not agree with Laskey, but the Foreign Office was unwilling to force its recommendations upon the Greek premier, who was left to his own counsel in negotiating with the Athenian politicians.

The Plaka agreement of February 29, however, provoked a new urgency in Laskey and the Southern Department as they recognized the imminent danger of EAM/ELAS establishing a mountain government to rival Tsouderos. Once again, Laskey recommended to the King and Greek exile government that resistance representatives be included in any new cabinet in order to prevent EAM/ELAS from seizing the political initiative. On March 5, both Tsouderos and the King again rejected the recommendation. While the King rather naively remarked that the guerrillas were soldiers who ought not concern themselves with politics, Tsouderos feared that EAM/ELAS would make exorbitant demands which he was too weak to resist. Instead, Tsouderos wanted to wait until Damaskinos had completed all efforts to rally the Greek political world to the exile government. Laskey disagreed. He recognized that, if and when ,EAM/ELAS learned that Papandreou and the other politicians were in contact and negotiating with Tsouderos for a new government, the EAM/ELAS leadership would act accordingly and establish some form of government in occupied Greece. Further, if no political opening was made to EAM/ELAS, Laskey argued that EAM/ELAS could justify a renewal of the civil war.

On March 6, Colonel Emmanouil Fradellos returned to Cairo after a three month mission to Greece on behalf of Tsouderos. The colonel had been dispatched to contact Damaskinos about establishing a regency council, and he returned with new disturbing messages for Tsouderos and the King. A memorandum from Damaskinos described the disarray of the Greek political world. The leading personalities continued to oppose the return of the King and remained at odds with EAM/ELAS, which they wanted "depoliticized." Aside from accepting Damaskinos as Regent, they were unable to cooperate among themselves. The message convinced Laskey of the need for the King to accept a plebiscite and a regency, but Churchill immediately rejected this suggestion. Eden, however, ordered the Foreign Offiice to press Tsouderos to counsel the King to accept.[30]

Events quickly overtook the Foreign Office and Tsouderos. As Eden adopted Laskey's recommendations on March 10, EAM/ELAS announced the creation of the PEEA and communicated to Tsouderos a desire to open political discussions, which produced a crisis for Britain and the Greek exile government far more critical than that of the civil war. The PEEA presented London and Cairo with a real if not legal rival. Many republican ministers and officers in the Middle East regarded it as a potential ally against the King. Strong support for the mountain committee came from officers and the rank and file of the Greek armed forces in the Middle East, who enthusiastically hailed the PEEA as truly representative of the popular will and promoted its call for a government of national solidarity.[31] Tsouderos refused to negotiate with PEEA, preferring to ask the Political Committee to join the Damaskinos discussions in Athens. The Southern Department became convinced that if the King did not accept a regency and plebiscite, Tsouderos would be forced to resign, Britain and the Greek exile government would lose control of the Greek armed forces, and EAM would establish a government inside Greece. If all of these events occurred, the Foreign Office believed that it would have a situation worse than existed in Yugoslavia at that time. To persuade the prime minister of the need to act, Eden prepared a memorandum which set out British policy. Eden recommended that Tsouderos ask the King to sign a Constitutional Act appointing Damaskinos as Regent and committing the King not to return to Greece before a plebiscite. There was no necessity to recognize the PEEA, but Eden believed that there was a need to make a constructive offer to the resistance and the PEEA to come to Cairo to discuss administrative and political questions with the King's government and the representatives of Athenian political leaders.[32] While Eden tried to convince Churchill to support the Foreign Office position, the King told Tsouderos on March 13 that he would not sign the Constitutional Act.[33]

If the creation of the PEEA goaded the London and Cairo authorities into action, the news of the Political Committee unleashed the brewing discontent toward the exile government within the Greek armed forces of the Middle East. As early as March 1, Tsouderos warned the King of the need to transfer the First Brigade from Cairo to the Italian front as a means of removing it from the heavy political atmosphere of the Middle East. The discontent among the armed forces was exploited by officers who had been dismissed after the mutiny of 1943. British military authorities expected trouble on March 25, Greek Independence Day, but the day passed without incident.[34] The appeal of PEEA for a government of national unity on March 26 provided the flash point. On the evening of March 31, 1944, a small group of officers delivered to Tsouderos a petition signed by eight officers, forty-eight petty officers, and 269 sailors which demanded that Tsouderos recognize the PEEA and broaden his government. According to Admiral Alexandris, the Commander of the Greek Navy, the lower ranks of Greek seamen were unhappy with the Tsouderos government and its failure to develop any ties to the resistance. Although the PEEA and EAM agitation played a role in the outbreak of the mutiny, the admiral reported that the single most important factor was the refusal of the exile government to cooperate with the guerrillas. Tsouderos concluded that the basic cause of the rebellion was the determination of the army and navy for the King not to return to Greece before a vote of the electorate. If the King had signed the Constitutional Act, Tsouderos was firmly convinced that the unrest could have been aborted. In this conclusion, Tsouderos failed to recognize his own responsibility in the mutiny, which was his refusal to negotiate political issues with EAM/ELAS until it was too late. Alexandris and Tsouderos concurred that the crisis was republican and not communist inspired, and Laskey agreed with them.[35]

After receiving their demands, Tsouderos reported to his cabinet, which supported the premier and recommended that he order the arrest of the officers leading the mutiny. Shortly following this meeting, two Greek colonels, who were personal friends of Tsouderos, called on the premier to impress upon him the seriousness of the demands and to emphasize that he could not successfully resist them. After speaking with the two colonels, Tsouderos concluded that the cabinet's suggestion to arrest the officers had been an intrigue by the Liberals in his cabinet to have him create an explosive incident which would embarrass him and force him from office. In a second meeting in the apartment of Admiral Panagiotes Voulgares on April 3, Sophocles Venizelos (Minister of Marine), Byron Karapanagiotis (Minister of War), and emissaries from republican (Venizelist-Liberal) circles in Athens called on Tsouderos to resign and agreed that Venizelos should succeed him.[36] Venizelos, who apparently was in touch with the rebels, claimed that he had the support of major leaders of the mutiny and that only he as premier could avert bloodshed. Tsouderos turned down the offer but telegraphed the King in London that he was prepared to resign and suggested Venizelos as his successor.[37] Word of the meeting was apparently leaked to the mutineers, and the government's delay in responding to the demands caused the revolt to spread. On April 6, the First Brigade joined in a "sympathy strike" with the mutiny, which the leaders justified by an appeal to "Greek revolutionary law." An attempt to end the "strike" led to a full-scale revolt of the brigade. The only unit that did not join the mutiny was the Sacred Battalion, which had refused to join the 1943 rebellion. At this point, Venizelos claimed that he no longer wanted to be premier, and on April 7, the Tsouderos critics within the cabinet made an unsuccessful bid to name Karapanagiotis head of a new government. As his government and armed forces unraveled, the King stubbornly opposed any political discussions until order was restored. The monarch was saved by the full support of Churchill, who refused to "discard" Britain's ally and head of the "lawfully constituted Greek government" at the "momentary surge of the appetite among ambitious emigré nonentities" and the *"banditti"* of the resistance. The British prime minister ordered the constitutional issue shelved once again until Greece's liberation, and he told the Foreign Office to prepare a statement for Washington blaming the troubles on extremist leftists and communists and omitting any reference to the constitutional issue.[38]

If the King survived the crisis, Tsouderos did not. He resigned on April 13 and was relapced by Venizelos on the following day. Venizelos's short tenure as head of the exile government — he lasted thirteen days in office — tended to verify Churchill's biting remark about ambitious nonentities. The new premier tried unsuccessfully to end the mutiny without resorting to force, but the rebels refused to give up their weapons until a government of national unity was formed.

The delay by Venizelos irritated the British authorities, who insisted on immediate suppression of the mutiny. The British intervention forced the appointment of Admiral Voulgares as chief of the Greek navy to suppress the rebels. After some sharp conflict but little bloodshed, he and the British military broke the mutiny by April 28, 1944. Britain interned 6,397 Greek seamen and soldiers in camps in Eritrea and the Middle East. Eighteen of the rebels received death sentences, which were commuted by the Greek government in October 1944. Another 2,060 were received back into the armed forces, where they finished out the war serving unarmed garrison duty, but 100 "ringleaders" and 1,350 who refused "to take orders" were interned for the duration of the war.[39] The mutiny spelled the ruin of the republican officers. In the reorganization which followed, General Venderes formed one brigade which developed a political reputation for loyalty to the crown and earned a good battle record in Italy by capturing the town of Rimini. This Mountain ("Rimini") Brigade returned to Greece in November 1944 to confront EAM/ELAS in the final crisis of December.

The mutiny failed to achieve any of its political goals and proved a political liability for EAM/ELAS, which was held responsible for the revolt. Still, it did accelerate the process of reorganizing the exile government and convening a general political conference of Greek political leaders in Lebanon. Admiral Sir Andrew Cunningham and General Paget convinced the King of the necessity of the conference, and before his resignation, Tsouderos issued the official invitation to the concerned parties. Venizelos's ineptness forced his resignation in favor of Georgios Papandreou, who became provisional premier and chaired the conference which met in Beirut on May 17.

Prelude to Lebanon

Papandreou began his career as a follower of Eleutherios Venizelos. Between 1923 and 1933, he served in three different cabinet posts and established a solid reputation for advocating progressive legislation. When Venizelos retired from politics in 1935, Papandreou left the Liberal Party and formed his Democratic Socialist Party, under which he was elected to the Chamber that same year. During the crisis of April 1936, he refused to support a motion giving Metaxas a vote of confidence after the general's appointment by the King. In March 1942, his signature was among those of the prominent political personalities who had sent a letter to Cairo calling upon the King not to return before the decision of a plebiscite. In that month, the Italians arrested him for circulating a clandestine journal and imprisoned him for three months. After his release, he worked with Saraphes to organize a resistance band, but he broke with the colonel after Saraphes joined EAM/ELAS.[40] Papandreou's career until 1944 marked him as a republican with a deep commitment to social justice, but he was not at all interested in joining EAM/ELAS. The experience of the occupation turned him into an intense anticommunist. He sent a series of dispatches which served him well to the Anglo-Greek authorities in Cairo in July and December of 1943.

In these communications, Papandreou analyzed the Greek political web and recommended the course Greece should follow during the last years of the war and liberation. The documents reflected the emerging division of Greek politics into an ideological left and right and the growing fear of the traditional political leaders of the resistance and EAM/ELAS. In a memorandum of July, Papandreou neatly divided the world into two simple parts: on the one side stood "Pan-Slavist" communism, which threatened to engulf Greece and Europe; opposed to this danger stood Anglo-Saxon liberalism. Even though he had been sharply critical of Britain's role in Greek affairs before the war, the struggle between these two forces was so great and the stakes so high that he decided Greece had to side with Great Britain. He charged that the KKE controlled EAM/ELAS and used the "popular front" tactic to mask its real aim of establishing a communist dictatorship in Greece. Papandreou proposed to combat the KKE by forming a center for national resistance in Athens and by asking the King not to return before the monarchy's fate could be determined by an election. Once these two goals were achieved, he concluded, the exile government should come to terms with the political leaders in Greece. He expected that the plan would block the resistance and reserve control of postwar politics for the traditional political leaders. The memorandum reached the Foreign Office on September 30, and Laskey minuted that it was "by far the most carefully thought out statement on policy that I have received from any Athens politician." [41]

In two letters of December 10 and 22, which did not arrive in Cairo until February 12, 1944, Papandreou enlarged his arguments against EAM/ELAS by denouncing EAM/ELAS terror and holding it responsible for the civil war. He was convinced that the danger presented by the resistance required the formation of a government of national unity. Interpreting the King's letter of November 8 to mean that the monarch had agreed not to return until the electorate decided the fate of the crown, Papandreou wrote that he no longer saw the King as an obstacle to the formation of a new government supported by all of the noncommunist political leaders. In a telegram to GHQ ME on February 17, he requested Britain to reject the appeal of EAM/ELAS to participate in a coalition govern-

ment. Since Papandreou was convinced that support for EAM/
ELAS was dwindling as a result of the civil war, he considered
it a political blunder to accept them into any new government.
In a statement curiously similar to the King's, he saw no reason
why any guerrilla representatives should be in any government; on the contrary, the *andartes'* only duty was to obey
the Cairo government and abstain from politics.[42]

Papandreou's messages reflected the dilemma of the prewar
political leaders by the end of 1943. Having failed to act in
1941-1942, they found themselves without any moral or political basis of power with which to meet the postwar political
challenge. Ioannis Rallis and Pangalos turned to the Axis as a
means of combating communism and returning to the status
of the pre-1936 political world. Others gravitated toward the
King and Great Britain. This latter move proved easy for the
conservatives, but uncomfortable for the men of the center
and noncommunist left. Papandreou's solution was to delay the
return of the King and use British power to destroy EAM/
ELAS and the politics of the resistance. Tsouderos and Britain
were impressed with his ideas and willingness to cooperate,
and they brought him out of Greece to join the exile government. Papandreou arrived in Cairo on April 15, 1944, at the
height of the government crisis over the mutiny. After meeting
the new arrival, Leeper found him to be the first Greek to arrive from the mainland who was indeed a "leader." Although
Laskey recognized that Papandreou had a very small political
following, he was impressed by Papandreou's intellectual
capacity and the Greek's outspoken criticism of EAM/ELAS.[43]
On April 21, Churchill approved of the new premier. After
breaking the mutiny one week later, the King and the British
forced Venizelos from his office and named Papandreou acting
prime minister. Papandreou's first duty was to chair the all-
party conference scheduled for May 17 in Lebanon.

The intensity of Papandreou's anticommunist attitude was
revealed to Komnenos Pyromaglou, who represented EDES
at the conference. The new premier invited Pyromaglou to a
meeting before the formal opening of the conference. Also
attending the gathering was Constantinos Venderes, who was
associated with RAN and who later reconstructed the Greek
Armed Forces in the Middle East by purging the mutineers
and republicans and replacing them with staunch anticommunists, most of whom were royalists as well.[44] Papandreou
inquired of Pyromaglou if EDES was able to attack and destroy

ELAS. Pyromaglou responded that any such attempt would only lead to a new civil war, and instead, he proposed to balance ELAS by infiltrating an Allied force into Greece. Papandreou did not respond warmly to this suggestion; he told Pyromaglou that he intended to break EAM/ELAS.[45]

As the encounter with Pyromaglou suggested, the Greeks who gathered at the Hotel Bois de Boulogne on the outskirts of Beirut were far from united. The fundamental division between EAM/ELAS and the noncommunist representatives was complicated by fissures within the ranks of each side. Papandreou faced a concerted threat from a group of Liberals led by Venizelos and Demetrios Lambrakis. Lambrakis was an early supporter of Eleutherios Venizelos and an active participant in the expansion of the Greek state against Turkey before the First World War. In 1922 he founded the *Eleutheron Vema* and other publications and became a wealthy and influential power in the Liberal Party. During the occupation, he split with Themistocles Sophoulis over the issue of the King. While Sophoulis collected around him the more moderate Liberals, Lambrakis gathered those who were intensely anti-monarchist. Since leaving the Liberals in 1935, the Lambrakis wing had considered Papandreou a serious rival to their interests—so serious in fact that British authorities reported that Lambrakis had tried unsuccessfully to prevent Papandreou from leaving Greece to join the exile government. The newspaper scion was not a delegate to the conference, but in the eyes of the British he acted as the Liberals' "gray eminence."[46] Between April 1943 and the 1944 mutiny, Lambrakis was represented inside the exile government by Karapanagiotes, and when Venizelos became prime minister, the wealthy newspaper publisher seemingly achieved the political power he had long sought. The fall of Venizelos in so short a time must not have set well with Lambrakis. The other delegates who were associates of Lambrakis were Georgios Exendares, a former editor of a Lambrakis newspaper, and Nikolaos Askoutsis, who had joined the PEEA as a representative of Lambrakis.[47] These Liberals took a more conciliatory view of EAM/ELAS— an attitude which stemmed not from any ideological affinity but from political opportunism.

Aligned with Papandreou in strong opposition to EAM/ELAS were Constantinos Venderes, Philippos Dragoumis, Demetrios Londos, Spyros Theotokis, and Georgios Kartalis. Londos was a republican of the Populist Party, and Theotokis headed the royalist National Populists. Dragoumis was a former collaborator of Kanellopoulos. On May 12, these five individuals called on Leeper and asked for British support of a twofold policy of openly denouncing EAM/ELAS terror and crimes and dissolving the organization in order to build a national army. Leeper avoided a direct answer, and he replied that the conference should decide on their recommendations.[48] Their demands were in tune with Papandreou's strategy to disband the guerrillas and build a "nonpolitical" army from conscripts. Papandreou believed that this goal could be readily achieved once EAM/ELAS joined the government; this would commit them to sharing responsibility for the punishment of the mutineers and would put them in the wrong if they took any action against the national army. He expected Britain to provide him with political support and arms for the new army, which could destroy EAM/ELAS in any confrontation.[49] With the British ambassador on May 13, he outlined his general views, and he discussed his opening speech of the conference in a way which impressed Leeper with Papandreou's blending of idealism and practical common sense. The British ambassador especially liked Papandreou's view of the coming struggle with "Pan-Slavist" communism and his emphatic statement that the large majority of Greeks would welcome the British flag "backed with forces if necessary" to restore law and order. On reading Leeper's report of the meeting, Laskey was also impressed, and he believed that Papandreou "offered the best opportunity to strengthen the Anglo-Greek connection and prevent Greece from passing under Soviet influence."[50] By the time of the conference, Papandreou and senior British officials in the Foreign Office were convinced that EAM/ELAS intended to seize power at liberation and that the only means to prevent it was to use force. Compromise did not appear possible.

EAM/ELAS/PEEA/KKE were represented at Lebanon by Angelos Angelopoulos (PEEA), Alexandros Svolos (PEEA), Nikolaos Askoutsis (PEEA), Demetrios Strates (EAM), Miltiades Porphyrogenis (EAM), Petros Roussos (EAM), and Stephanos Saraphes (ELAS). Roussos and Porphyrogenis were the only KKE members of the delegation. Strates headed the faction of the Socialist Party which joined EAM in 1942. Angelopoulos was a Professor of Jurisprudence at the University of Athens and a former advisor to the Bank of Greece, who joined PEEA as Secretary of Finance in April. Angelopoulos and Svolos lost no time in reporting to Leeper that they joined EAM/ELAS to prevent a Communist monopoly and that they wished to cooperate with the other parties. Their wariness of EAM/ELAS pleased Laskey, who minuted that he thought the conference would be a success.[51]

Kartalis represented EKKA, and Lt. Colonel Stavros Metaxas and his son Captain Alexandros Metaxas (no relation to the late dictator) represented EDES along with Pyromaglou. The moderate Liberals were represented by Constantinos Rendes. Ioannis Sophianopoulos, Alexandros Mylonas, Georgios Sakalis, and Kanellopoulos represented smaller parties. Venderes and Captain Andonios Stathatos represented certain Athenian military circles.

EAM/ELAS hoped to achieve three fundamental goals at the conference: the formation of a coalition government; the creation of a unified military command; and a clearcut resolution from the new government that the monarchy would not return to Greece until advised to do so by a government formed in Greece.[52] The behavior of the *andartes* in April toward EKKA and the mutiny in the Middle East severely weakened EAM/ELAS's position at the conference and provided their opponents with the means to successfully frustrate achievement of its objectives.

Since its second restoration in May-June 1943, EKKA had enlisted over 350 guerrillas under Colonel Psarros in the Parnassos Mountains, but all had not gone well with the organization. After the failure of the Cairo meetings in August 1943, EKKA began to divide. Bakirtzis moved toward EAM/ELAS, as noted earlier, while another faction under the royalist Captain Euthemios Dedouses moved openly toward the King. Then Psarros had to dismiss some EKKA officers who had remained on direct and friendly terms with former colleagues serving in the Security Battalions. Psarros and Kartalis held on to their anticommunist and antimonarchist program. According to Pyromaglou, Dedouses came under the influence of conservative military officers in Athens who were connected with a group known as the *Strateotike Ierarchia* (Military Hierarchy). The Military Hierarchy was associated with General Papagos and other royalist officers, and it served to bring a number of conservative military and political groups under its umbrella of royal support.[53] The Military Hierarchy tried but failed to bring EKKA under its control during the summer and fall of 1943; however, it did wean Dedouses and nearly all of the EKKA's officers to its politics. Contrary to the political ideals and goals of their military commander and their political leader, these officers dispatched a telegram of support to the King on February 28, 1944. In less than two weeks Bakirtzis defected to EAM/ELAS. Between March 10 and April 3, Bakirtzis tried to get EKKA to join the PEEA, but Kartalis refused. Kartalis did not believe the PEEA could serve as a unifying force, and he did not like the role that the KKE played in PEEA. Like Pyromaglou, he preferred a government of national unity which included representatives of the resistance, but located outside of Greece.[54]

The activities of Dedouses gave EAM/ELAS the opportunity to send Psarros an ultimatum to cooperate or face dissolution. On April 13, a British Liaison Officer in Roumeli overheard an ELAS GHQ telephone message ordering ELAS units to move from Agrinion toward the EKKA units, but when the BLO queried ELAS about this information, an ELAS officer professed ignorance. During this time, Rallis was conducting a recruiting campaign in the area for the Security Battalions which was apparently successful among one or two EKKA officers. The alleged provocation toward EAM/ELAS occurred in a clash between the two resistance groups over stores of food and ammunition in the village of Dorida, where an ELAS *andarte* was killed. Psarros promised to restore the plundered supplies and cooperate with ELAS, but he lost control of his subordinates. BLO Hammond met with Saraphes and Despotopoulos on April 18 to discuss the conflict, and the British officer charged EAM/ELAS with deceit, hypocrisy, and fomenting civil war. Saraphes and Despotopoulos admitted to Hammond that Zoulas had been given authority by ELAS only to press an ultimatum upon Psarros over the incident. Hammond did not believe the explanation, but he managed to get Saraphes and Despotopoulos to agree to establish committees which would peacefully settle the issue. Then Aris arrived, and on April 17 ELAS attacked the EKKA guerrillas for being a "royalist" unit and dispersed it.[55] Kapitsonis and a hundred survivors of the ELAS attack fled to Patras. A few of these officers joined the Security Battalions, but the majority were taken into German custody. Under German duress some reluctantly agreed to join the collaborating units.

Psarros was seized and murdered by Zoulas. In a report to Cairo on May 7, Woodhouse telegraphed that Kapitsonis and Dedouses, who hated EAM/ELAS more than the Germans, could not be controlled by Psarros, making EKKA an easy target for EAM/ELAS. At that time, Woodhouse believed that a "show of force [against Psarros] went too far owing to the intervention of Aris acting without orders." [56] Aris's associate, D. Nikephoros, agreed with this judgment.[57] Woodhouse recommended that no action be taken against EAM/ELAS, as any charges would expose the weaknesses of EKKA as a result of the activities of Dedouses, but he planned to have the Allies settle with Aris after the war. When Siantos heard of the murder, he called it a catastrophe, as indeed it was.[58] The dissolution of EKKA guerrillas and the cruel murder weighed heavily on Kartalis, but it did not prevent him from participating in the Lebanon Conference, which he effectively used as an opportunity to expose EAM/ELAS terror and violence.

The Lebanon Conference

In the bitter aftermath of the mutiny and the murder of Psarros, the conference convened on May 17. In his opening remarks Papandreou attacked EAM/ELAS in an "extremely outspoken" speech which charged EAM/ELAS with fomenting civil war and terror and inciting the April mutiny. He warned them that any cooperation was contingent on EAM/ELAS giving up force as a way of achieving their political goals. The Greek prime minister wanted Kartalis to follow with another attack on EAM/ELAS, but Venizelos managed to delay Kartalis's speech for two days. In his two-hour documented catalogue of EAM/ELAS terror, Kartalis stunned the EAM/ELAS representatives who were not prepared to present documented counterarguments. Porphyrogenis was left speechless except for a lame denial that EAM/ELAS was fostering class war. Saraphes's first speech was a defense of his own actions, and he contrasted the BBC and GHQ ME approval of the resistance with the treatment they received at the conference. In a similar vein, Roussos gave a history and defense of EAM/ELAS, and he stated that the KKE wanted a democratic republic. These defensive responses by the EAM/ELAS delegates emphasized the impact that the mutiny and the dissolution of Psarros's guerrillas had on blunting any political gain that EAM/ELAS hoped to win at the conference. On May 20, Svolos tried to raise the issue of the monarchy, but Papandreou ruled him out of order. The subject was dropped, and Papandreou achieved the Anglo-Papandreou goal of having the November 8 letter of the King guide the conference on this issue.[59]

After the critical attacks against EAM/ELAS, Laskey minuted that "If EAM and the Communists now agree to join the Government, this will be tantamount to surrender by them, and there is clearly some danger they may refuse to humiliate themselves in this way. Provided, however, the delegates of the moderate parties maintain a united front, I think that the extreme Left Wing representatives will toe the line."[60] To ensure the solidarity of the moderates and to prevent "intrigues" against the Papandreou government, British authorities, with the approval of the Greek prime minister, arrested Karapanagiotes and his wealthy associate, A. Bodossakis, on charges of inspiring the April mutiny. Venizelos immediately took up their defense, which pressed Papandreou into a difficult position as no evidence was produced to substantiate the charges. Anxious not to offer any opportunity to his critics to compare him to Metaxas, Papandreou wanted the men released. The Foreign Office agreed, but Churchill refused and ordered them exiled far from the Greek government.[61]

The conference ended on May 20 with the signing of the "Charter of Lebanon." The fundamental points of the agreement were (1) the reorganization and restoration of discipline of the Greek armed forces in the Middle East; (2) the unification, at the appropriate moment, of all guerrilla forces under the command of the Greek government; (3) an end to terrorism and a guarantee of political liberty for all Greeks; (4) the dispatch of medical supplies to Greece; (5) the establishment of freedom and order after the liberation to allow the Greek people to freely choose their political and social regime; (6) the severe punishment of traitors and collaborators; (7) the supply of food relief; and (8) the defense of Greece's national rights.[62]

Point Five was not made public and, along with Points Two and Six, proved to be the most troublesome and reflected the basic weakness of the conference. The "Charter" was a compromise document that failed to resolve the outstanding issues. Point Three was aimed against EAM/ELAS, while Point Six was directed against the extreme right. Point Two, which was Papandreou's fundamental means of achieving the final dissolution of ELAS, merely postponed the problem of the military unification of the resistance and the regular Greek armed forces. The issue had not been settled at Mirofillo-Plaka, and it would become one of the basic causes of the December rebellion. Point Five regarding the postwar regime was interpreted differently by the various sides. EAM/ELAS interpreted it as giving the resistance the opportunity to come to power, but the Papandreou government and the King understood that it committed them to no specific policy.[63]

The conference proved to be a great success for Britain and the Papandreou government, but it did not produce a genuine government of national unity. Convinced that EAM/ELAS was committed to seizing power at liberation, Papandreou and Britain did not intend to compromise with EAM/ELAS and the resistance, but planned rather to pursue a policy which would lead to the dissolution of EAM/ELAS. The central issue for them was to select the proper means. On the other side, even though its representatives had signed the charter, the central committees of EAM and the KKE were divided as to whether they should accept the Lebanon conditions. Within the KKE, one faction argued that Lebanon provided them with the opportunity to infiltrate the Greek government, and they were quick to point out that the agreement did not impair the power of ELAS, which remained the only major armed force in Greece. Opposed to the moderates, the militant and revolutionary faction rebutted that too many concessions had been granted to Britain and Papandreou, and they demanded a confrontation with Britain. They pointed out that the power of Great Britain stood behind the Greek government, which did not make Papandreou as weak as the moderates indicated. The militants bolstered their position by pointing to Venderes's rapid rebuilding, out of reactionary elements, of the Greek armed forces in the Middle East. Since the PEEA had received minor posts in the cabinet of the proposed united government, the revolutionaries complained that the KKE was placed in a weak and disadvantageous position. This aggressive faction wanted to reject the Lebanon agreement and to defend its goals by force.[64]

The first EAM/ELAS response to the Charter came after its leaders heard accounts of the proceedings from the BBC. Siantos, Bakirtzis, and Thanases Hadzes telegraphed Svolos their shock at Papandreou's attacks and slander. They asked Svolos to protest directly to Britain, the United States, and the Soviet Union.[65] Then, the EAM/ELAS leadership telegraphed from Greece on May 24 that the Lebanon agreements "contravene and go beyond our written intructions."[66] When Saraphes returned to Mountain Greece on May 29, he met a stinging attack by Siantos and nearly lost his position as Commander-in-Chief of ELAS. The KKE leadership, however, decided that the responsibility lay with the political representatives, and Saraphes kept his command. In response to the Siantos telegrams, Svolos, Porphyrogenis, and Roussos sent the following defense of their actions to Greece on May 31:

> You should take into account that the negotiations have ended and we have signed an agreement on fundamental points. Consequently if you disagree (which astonishes us) tell us so plainly, though you must take into account the difficulty of our personal position and all general developments likely to occur. Otherwise leave us to deal with questions on our initiative and to assume responsibilities with the knowledge of all the facts. . . . Meanwhile, it has been agreed that in the event of your giving an affirmative answer we shall take over five Ministries . . . probably those of Finance, National Economy, Communications, Labor, and Agriculture. Later our policy will be enlarged. The Minister of the Interior will be taken over by Sakalis, who enjoys the general confidence of all including ourselves, and we are insisting that an undersecretary there should be appointed from P.E.E.A. circles. We must repeat we have taken our decisions after studying all factors and are expecting you to agree.[67]

In addition to the hostile political environment which contributed to the EAM/ELAS representatives' readiness to cooperate, the Russian ambassador to the Greek exile government, Nikolai Novikov, told Svolos to accept the agreement and join the new government.[68]

While EAM/ELAS debated their course of action, Papandreou, whom the King and Britain made prime minister, began to build his government. On May 24, the Liberals, who were associated with Lambrakis, and who came to Lebanon to oust Papandreou, joined the government, defeated by Papandreou's skill and recognition that the Greek prime minister had the full confidence of Great Britain. Venizelos became vice-premier, and he was joined in the cabinet by Dragoumis and Lambros Lambrianides. Three days later, Rallis, Sakalis, and

Mylonas entered the government. EAM/ELAS continued to hold out as Siantos refused to accept the arguments of his representatives. In a telegram of June 4, the Communist leader set out the fundamental goal of EAM/ELAS:

> Our object is to establish national unity for [the] sake of the national struggle. To achieve this object and aware of the sentiments of our fighting nation, we finally decided on the necessity of inflexible insistence upon a clear solution of [the] constitutional question based upon our known views.[69]

This old demand provoked a renewed discussion of the constitutional issue among Anglo-Greek officials. The majority of Papandreou's colleagues desired the same settlement as Siantos, and they were unwilling to remain silent and leave EAM/ELAS as the lone champion against the return of the King. Faced with this demand, Papandreou contrived a solution which Eden claimed bordered on the theological. The King, Papandreou proposed to Leeper, should return to Greece at liberation as Commander-in-Chief of the Allied Forces and remain there until the enemy was finally driven out. Then, during the plebiscite, he would go abroad as head of state. Beyond the metaphysical issue of the suggestion, London feared that Papandreou would fall if he accepted any part of the demand, and the Foreign Office rejected the suggestion. No concessions were granted to EAM/ELAS on this vital issue. The Foreign Office position was that the new government should take up the constitutional issue and should resolve it on the basis of the November 8, 1943, letter.[70] On June 8, Papandreou named the remainder of his cabinet, leaving five places for EAM/ELAS to fill later.[71] Without the approval of the King and to strengthen his position against EAM/ELAS, Papandreou, on June 12, publicly announced that the King would not return to Greece before a decision of the electorate.[72] In the mountains of Greece Bakirtzis and other moderates within PEEA and EAM/ELAS pressured Siantos with threats of resignations if Siantos did not approve EAM/ELAS joining the Papandreou government. Tsirimokos explained to Woodhouse that his cooperation with EAM/ELAS was based on expediency, which would end when a government of national unity was formed. Svolos sent out similar signals of dissatisfaction with the PEEA, which he had decided must give way to the Papandreou government.[73]

The Communists within EAM/ELAS, however, refused to compromise, and on June 19, the war of words between EAM/ELAS and Cairo broke out into armed conflict between EDES and EAM/ELAS over supplies. Claiming a recently organized ELAS division near Preveza encroached on EDES territory as defined by the Plaka agreement, Zervas attacked it. EAM/ELAS charged the attack had been inspired by Papandreou, but a local BLO reported that the conflict occurred in an area which had a long history of clashes because the boundaries between the two bands were ambiguous. The BLO concluded that it was impossible to know which side was right, but the Foreign Office was embarrassed by the incident and recommended that Zervas withdraw from the conflict.[74] On June 29 an expanded list of EAM/ELAS demands reached Cairo. After denouncing Papandreou for wanting to destroy EAM/ELAS and fostering the Zervas attack, EAM/ELAS demanded, in addition to the plebiscite, the following: (1) a denunciation of the Security Battalions, (2) an amnesty for those mutineers sentenced to death, (3) an ELAS officer as the Commander-in-Chief of the new armed forces, and (4) the ministries of the Interior, Justice, Education, Labor, Agriculture, and the undersecretary of War. In regard to the last demand, EAM/ELAS charged that Papandreou had violated a commitment to keep the cabinet at fifteen posts. By arbitrarily expanding the number of cabinet posts from fifteen to twenty on June 8, he left EAM/ELAS with only minor offices and a weakened role.[75] In a discussion of the demands with Leeper, Papandreou claimed that he had not spoken of the dissolution of EAM/ELAS but of the replacement of a "class army" with a "national army." On Zervas and the EDES attacks, Papandreou retorted that that was an affair for GHQ ME, not his government. There was no further need to denounce the Security Battalions as they were condemned by the Lebanon agreement. And, as Papandreou carefully pointed out to Leeper, any new public denunciation would be unpopular in Greece. As long as he left five cabinet positions for EAM/ELAS, he saw no reason for not naming more to his cabinet, and therefore he was certain that he had not violated any promise to EAM/ELAS on the total number of cabinet posts.[76] Papandreou concluded that any concession to EAM/ELAS would be a sign of weakness and a capitulation. Rather, he wanted a complete showdown with the resistance and appealed to Britain to support him in denouncing and breaking with EAM/ELAS if necessary. On July 6, he announced his rejection of the demands and stated that negotiations to achieve unity were over[77]. On July 9, a letter from Svolos, Strates, and Roussos, reaffirming the EAM/ELAS demands, charged Papandreou with frustrating the efforts to achieve national unity.[78] Since the British public had become aroused against the proposed executions, Sargent was not anxious to accept Papandreou's proposal for cutting off EAM/ELAS without granting amnesty. Further, aware of Woodhouse's position against breaking with EAM/ELAS, Sargent cautioned that a final decision on the request await discussion with the colonel, who had been invited to London. Churchill and Eden, however, were prepared to support Papandreou even if the decision resulted in a withdrawal of the AMM and cutting of all ties to EAM/ELAS.[79]

The discussions with Woodhouse detoured the decision to sever aid to EAM/ELAS and to launch a propaganda attack to help dissolve it. The goals of Woodhouse's recommendations were the same as those of Papandreou and the Foreign Office, but Woodhouse proposed a far more subtle means of dealing with EAM/ELAS and the Greeks. In this regard, the colonel revealed a far deeper and sophisticated understanding of Greek culture and politics than his fellow officers and officials of the Foreign Offiice.[80] Dissolution of EAM/ELAS and a withdrawal of the AMM, Woodhouse argued, would end all resistance to the Germans and give Greece to EAM/ELAS. Under these conditions, the objectives of "Noah's Ark" would not be achieved, and since it would take fifty-two days to withdraw the 383 Allied Liaison Officers (192 British, 44 American, 26 Greek-Middle East, and 121 Greek-local), the officers' lives could be threatened. Since Britain lacked adequate forces for achieving a quick break and victory over EAM/ELAS, any cutting off of support and denunciation, according to Woodhouse, would only renew the civil war, for which Papandreou and Britain would be held responsible. Further, Woodhouse pointed out that there were a large number of fifth-columnists in EAM/ELAS who would be eliminated in any dissolution under the circumstances existing then in Greece. Woodhouse was convinced that EAM/ELAS was on the way to "self-destruction," and that if they gave "EAM and ELAS a little more rope with which to pull their weight ... in the end they will hang themselves." [81] With a little "influence" at liberation, this natural tendency toward self-destruction would be completed, but he rejected using Zervas or any other bands for this purpose as immoral and impractical. Rather, he recommended the creation of a national army, which, perhaps in a reference to Papandreou's more sanguine view on this possibility, he emphasized could not be "done at the stroke of a pen." While the organization of this army took place, the Allied force, whose nucleus would arrive in Greece before the liberation, would maintain order.[82] Woodhouse thought it best to exploit the discontent against EAM/ELAS, but not by "ramming British policy down Greek throats, since they have a strong national pride and would resent doing something simply because Britain wanted it even if they would otherwise probably choose doing it themselves." [83] The Foreign Office was so impressed with Woodhouse's analyses that they circulated them in the War Cabinet.

When Papandreou met Woodhouse on June 20 he agreed with the essential points of the colonel's recommendations, but the EAM/ELAS demands of June 29 acted to reverse his policy and return to demanding a break. On July 7, Churchill, who needed no pressure to denounce EAM/ELAS, readily marked "good" on the margin of a report on Papandreou's request.[84] Woodhouse convinced the Foreign Office of the need to avoid a rupture and to play for time through sham negotiations. Laskey concluded a break may come, but there was no need for it at that time. Eden agreed and suggested that the King be told it was in Britain's and his interest that there be no break and that the death sentences be commuted. Churchill minuted: "I am afraid I do not like this line," but a visit from Woodhouse made him more agreeable to this decision.[85] Adopting the essential element of Woodhouse's recommendation, Papandreou was told of London's continued support for him and for his insistence that EAM/ELAS honor the Lebanon agreement. If they refused, they would be publicly denounced as being responsible for the failure to establish national unity.

After his discussions with the Prime Minister and the Foreign Office officials, Woodhouse wrote a memorandum to Lord Selbourne, the head of SOE, proposing an important tactic that was not followed during liberation. Woodhouse warned that on no account must a settlement be forced upon EAM/ELAS, and Britain must not take up the cause of those who cry "Down with EAM." Woodhouse pointed out that Britain must not become involved in the scramble for power on liberation as Britain would be acting as an occupying power in a hostile country. British policy, he concluded, would be made much easier by an unequivocal statement on the King's intentions.[86]

Suddenly on July 29, EAM/ELAS dropped all previous demands and Siantos telegraphed Cairo that it was prepared to join the government on the condition that Papandreou resigned. This decision has been attributed to the arrival in Greece of the Soviet mission under Colonel Gregory Popov on July 26. Svolos insisted, however, that this was not the case, but that the decision of EAM/ELAS stemmed from the sustained British support for Papandreou. On July 27, Eden made a strong speech in the Commons rejecting the EAM/ELAS demands as unreasonable, and he charged that if they continued to refuse to join the government, they were responsible for the failure to achieve unity. If EAM/ELAS did not relent and become cooperative, Eden threatened to cut off Allied supplies. Churchill followed Eden with a public statement to the same effect.[87] In the Greek cabinet, the demand provoked a new crisis. According to Tsatsos, after a four-hour session with his cabinet on August 4, Papandreou agreed to resign. The cause was the threat of Venizelos, Rendes, and Mylonas to resign if Papandreou did not accept the EAM/ELAS condition.[88] British support, however, foiled the Liberal attempt to force Papandreou out. Venizelos reversed his position under pressure and reluctantly agreed to call on EAM/ELAS to join the government with Papandreou at its head, but he made his displeasure of the deep British involvement with Greek affairs known to Ambassador MacVeagh.[89] To Leeper, Venizelos complained of Papandreou's "personal government" and refusal to confide in the Greek cabinet. The Foreign Office came to believe that Venizelos and the OSS were involved in some intrigue to remove Papandreou, but the British officials never established any concrete evidence or proof of this conspiracy. In any case, the Foreign Office asked Churchill to make a personal appeal to Roosevelt to instruct American officials to cease obstructing British policy.[90]

While EAM/ELAS attempted to negotiate its single demand, the British War Cabinet on August 8 approved the decision to send a British force to Greece to prevent civil war and to assure the restoration of order, which would enable relief supplies to be distributed and the establishment of a friendly government in Athens. There was some dispute within the British agencies over the size of the force. The Foreign Office thought that 10,000 troops would be sufficient, but the COS disagreed. They concluded that 80,000 troops would be required, and they were convinced that the United States would never agree to that kind of material support for British policy. Expecting British prestige and the use of relief supplies to win over Greek public opinion in the face of the declining popularity of EAM/ELAS, London concluded that 5,000 troops were adequate. British forces were to land at Athens and the key ports as the means to obstruct any EAM/ELAS seizure of power.[91] Acknowledging the distaste among Greeks for the monarch and the smallness of the British force, the members of the War Cabinet pressed to have the King declare unequivocally that he would not return before a plebiscite, but Churchill blocked the move. Eden reluctantly agreed, but he preferred a clear statement from the King and regretted not having obtained it in December 1943.[92] As for the King, he rejected Papandreou's June 12 statement and stood by his November 8 letter. The monarch had no plans to make any other announcements, and he intended to return to Greece before any plebiscite.[93] Later in October, however, the King finally relented under British pressure and agreed not to return until asked by the government.

Having failed to oust Papandreou, and after Churchill's reaffirmation of his support for Papandreou on August 11, Siantos dropped all demands and agreed on August 18 to join the Papandreou government. After consolidating his policy in the War Cabinet and with Russia and the United States, Churchill[94] called Papandreou to a secret meeting in Rome on August 21. At that time, Papandreou insisted that a British force be sent to Greece, but Churchill did not tell the Greek leader of the War Cabinet's decision. Rather, the British prime minister suggested that Papandreou remove his government from the atmosphere of intrigue in Cairo to the clearer air of Italy. Ostensibly, the proposed move was to facilitate plans for the liberation, but in effect proved a perfect means of isolating the Greek government. Papandreou agreed, but upon his return to Cairo he refused to confide the details of his mission to his colleagues, which angered them. Smarting under Venderes's reorganization of the Greek armed forces by purging and reassigning republican officers to unimportant posts, Papandreou's unilateral decision to move the Greek government to Italy prompted the resignation of Venizelos, Rendes, and Mylonas as their final protest against Papandreou's personal rule backed by British power. They were replaced with weaker and lesser known members of the Liberal Party, leaving Papandreou isolated from a major potential source of strength and forcing him to depend on the conservative members of his cabinet who had even less standing than the Liberals.[95]

On September 3, the EAM/ELAS representatives entered the government: Svolos (Finance), Askoutis (Communications), Tsirimokos (Economy), Porphyrogenis (Labor), and Ioannis Zevgos (Agriculture). Angelopoulos became Undersecretary for Finance. The central question that remained was the liberation of Greece and the demobilization of the *andartes*. Representatives of the British government and the resistance organizations met in Caserta to work out these details, and on September 26 signed the Caserta Agreement. Representing Britain were Harold Macmillan, who, as Resident Minister, had been given the responsibility for policy in the Balkans, and Lieutenant General Sir Ronald Scobie, the Allied commander of forces going to Greece. Zervas and Saraphes represented their organizations, while Zevgos stood for EAM and Papandreou for the exile government. The fundamental points of the agreement were that (1) all guerrilla forces in Greece came under the control of the Greek government; (2) the Greek government placed the guerrillas under Scobie as Supreme Allied Commander of Allied Forces; (3) the resistance leaders agreed to forbid any taking of the law into private hands and to condemn as criminal anyone who chose to do so; (4) in Athens the guerrillas agreed to take no actions except under the directives of General Scobie; (5) the Security Battalions were denounced as instruments of the enemy and they would be treated as enemy formations unless they surrendered; (6) the guerrilla organizations agreed to put their rivalries behind them and cooperate; and (7) all parties agreed to recognize Scobie's right to issue operational orders. Despotopoulos prevented the inclusion of the phrase "to restore law and order in Greece" in reference to Scobie's command and mission.[96] A second part of the agreement recognized certain geographical commands. Zervas and ELAS would continue to control their respective territories with three important exceptions. In the area of Attica, ELAS agreed to recognize the command of Colonel Speliotopoulos, an associate of Venderes and one of the phantom "Six Colonels," who would receive his orders directly from Scobie. In the Peloponnese, all forces were placed under a troika, which included an ELAS officer, a Greek army officer, and a BLO. Salonica was placed under the command of a Greek officer to be named by the Papandreou government. The resistance then agreed to harass the Germans out of Greece and to maintain law and order in the liberated areas. The Caserta Agreement was signed by General Wilson, Macmillan, Papandreou, Saraphes, and Zervas.

Although the Caserta Agreement implied the British right to land troops in Greece, there was no formal agreement on this point. Saraphes signed at Caserta, but he insisted that there was no need for British troops to occupy Greece as ELAS had liberated the country. During the December crisis which followed, the Foreign Office discovered this omission and surmised that Papandreou had probably agreed to it before the EAM/ELAS representatives joined the government and that he had acted without consulting his cabinet.[97] Churchill legitimized British intervention on the basis of the Caserta document and the American and Soviet telegrams which approved of his dispatch of troops to Greece.[98]

The December Crisis

The agreement at Caserta did not allay Anglo-Greek concerns that EAM/ELAS would attempt to seize power at liberation. Indeed, exaggerated reports of an ELAS massacre at Pyrgos led Warner and other Foreign Office officials to fear a "bloodbath" in the coming days. Warner requested large-scale intervention to prevent the expected massacre of 60,000 Athenians, yet he knew that there had been no massacres on the liberated Aegean islands or in other towns of the Peloponnese which were being liberated in mid-September as the Germans withdrew. At Kalamata a BLO reported that the town had been taken with light casualties by EAM/ELAS after a one-day battle and that the population was happy with the situation. From the site of the "massacre," Pyrgos, a BLO reported that the situation was less grim than previously rumored but, in his view, bad enough. The source of the massacre story grew from the battle which nearly annihilated a Security Battalion and killed fifty-five civilians in the course of hard fighting.[99] These developments pushed British preparations to land troops and the Papandreou government on Greek soil as quickly as possible to prevent any bold move by EAM/ ELAS. The first elements of Scobie's "Force 140" parachuted into the northwest Peloponnese on September 24 to discover that ELAS had surrounded the port of Patras, trapping the German troops and a Greek Security Battalion.[100] The city was taken and the 1,600 men of the Security Battalion interned. Although the situation remained tense, only the alarmists expected a bloodbath.[101] On October 12, the Germans withdrew from Athens, and the Papandreou government, accompanied by British forces, arrived six days later to a tumultuous welcome by the Athenians.

Throughout the liberation period of September and October, the behavior of ELAS toward the newly arrived Allied forces was orderly .If EAM/ELAS had desired a *coup d'état*, they could have seized Greece during this period, but their actions made it clear that they were not preparing for a violent seizure of power. If EAM/ELAS had been preparing a *coup*, they would neither have participated in "Noah's Ark," which deployed their troops away from Athens, nor would they have signed the Caserta agreement, which made Speliotopoulos commander of all forces in Attica. Further, the Caserta agreement limited ELAS movement by requiring approval of any redeployment from Scobie. On November 9, ELAS requested permission to move a headquarters group to Patras, but Scobie refused. ELAS did not protest.

While the Anglo-Greek authorities aimed to use political and moral pressure backed by the threat of force to break EAM/ELAS at the earliest possible moment, the resistance organization sought to secure its postwar political life through delay, obstruction, and compromise. In a grim and desperate economic and political setting, the collision and explosion in December grew out of the events of November and not from any preplanned conspiracy to seize power. Rather, the December eruption was an attempt by EAM/ELAS to use limited force to gain a political advantage. The maneuver failed because Britain was not willing to recognize EAM/ELAS as a major political force in Greek politics and was waiting for the opportunity to smash ELAS and dissolve EAM.

In two moves to strengthen his position before he returned to Greece, Papandreou, on October 6, asked the King and the British government to accept a regency in a clear, unequivocable public statement. Churchill had already convinced the King to remain out of Greece until conditions were right for his return, but he had assured the monarch that he could return as soon as possible. The British prime minister rejected Papandreou's request, and in a note to Eden wrote:

> This matter turns on the spear-point of a military operation, and nothing must hamper that. I have met all your views about keeping the King of Greece and the Crown Prince in this country for the time being. I certainly had proposed to tell Papandreou that, as soon as he gets established, it is his duty to bring the King back, and that we should certainly use our influence to that end. In fact, I shall lose interest in the Greek situation if Papandreou turns traitor to the King, whose first minister he is.[102]

Churchill advised the King to ignore the regency business. Encouraged by this support, the King demanded that all nominations for ministers from Papandreou should be referred to the crown. The Greek premier complained to Leeper that he did not like this arrangement, but that he was helpless to do other than accept it.[103] The affair clearly demonstrated the limitations of action Papandreou placed upon himself and the Greek Minister-President's complete dependence upon and domination by Britain.

In another maneuver, which has remained shrouded in mystery, the Greek government successfully won approval to cut off funds to SOE's most effective independent agent in Greece, Peltekis ("Apollo"), and to have him brought to Cairo for a court-martial on charges that he had passed gold sovereigns to EAM/ELAS. Peltekis was replaced by Col. Speliotopoulos, who botched his job as "Apollo's" replacement by failing to carry out successful anti-sabotage actions and by using his funds to arm "X" agents.[104] The upshot of the affair was that a brilliant, knowledgeable agent with wide political contacts was removed from Greece at a critical time when good communications among all parties was vital. Coincidentally, Woodhouse was moved from the center of decision-making as well. After the liberation, the Foreign Office tried to post him to Scobie's staff, which rejected the colonel as being too pro-EAM/ELAS! And another informed individual with good contacts to all parties played no role in the events of November and December, at least as far as can be determined from the PRO documents open to research.

The key figures in the drama that unfolded after October 12 on the Anglo-Greek side were Churchill, Scobie, Leeper, and Papandreou, and of these four only Papandreou exhibited any hint of conciliation toward EAM/ELAS. Perhaps the awareness of the enormous consequences of his actions which had developed in Papandreou after his return to Greece made him more cautious than his British associates. To gain support for the Greek government, Leeper met Sophoulis on October 19. The aging Liberal leader approved of British policy in general and accepted the ambassador's criticisms of Venizelos, Karapanagiotes, and Voulgares for their behavior during the mutiny of the past April. Sophoulis was sharply critical of Papandreou, and he offered to hold the Liberals in reserve for an anti-EAM/ELAS coalition should Papandreou fail. Leeper allowed that that was an issue for the Greek government.[105] On October 31, Papandreou declared the resistance over and, on the following day, announced that the EAM civil police would be disbanded on December 1 and the resistance bands on December 10. Following the demobilization, a new National Guard and a new army were to be formed, but disarming the guerrillas proved to be the irresolvable problem which led to the violence of December.

According to KKE documents examined by Iatrides, the KKE in November issued secret directives to its members to cooperate with the Allies and to make a concerted campaign to win the support of the middle classes.[106] A review of the Allied Information Service (AIS) weekly reports on all regions of Greece for October and November produced no evidence that EAM/ELAS was causing any great difficulties for the Anglo-Greek authorities. There was general friendliness and cooperation in Thessaly and Lamia, which was the seat of ELAS GHQ. In Lamia, after honoring the dead of the resistance in a memorial ceremony where British troops participated, the ELAS *andartes* even saluted British officers.[107] According to Allied Headquarters, even the call-up of the new National Guard went well,[108] which confirms the Iatrides documents that, on November 6, the KKE-solicited nominations for the new guard from the ranks of ELAS were submitted to the government.[109] Leeper reported to London that the 2,500 Security Battalion prisoners in a Salonica jail lived in appalling conditions, but there was no ELAS brutality toward them.[110]

From the Peloponnese, the AIS reported conditions calm. There, EAM/ELAS was strong in Kalamata, Tripolis, and

Sparta, but weaker in Patras, where there was great anxiety among a minority of the population. The opposition to EAM/ELAS in Tripolis and Kalamata was characterized as inarticulate.[111]

Since EAM/ELAS controlled all the areas outside of Athens and Zervas controlled Epirus, an ELAS pass was required by Greeks to move about from town to town. The resistance controlled all lines of communication and administration, and taxes in kind were continued. The EAM civil police replaced the former gendarmerie except for Patras. In the controlled areas, People's Courts continued to function and there were executions and camps holding political prisoners, yet the AIS reports reveal no details on these sinister acts. Further, EAM/ELAS claimed to be the sole agent of relief and interfered with the International Red Cross distribution of relief to the benefit of members of EAM/ELAS.[112] Considering the depth of the economic and political collapse—a newspaper in November cost four billion drachmas in Athens—the general impression from the AIS reports is one of relative stability.

Further evidence of EAM/ELAS cooperation is found in Iatrides's examination of EAM/ELAS/KKE publications during this period. Iatrides concluded that there was no propaganda campaign to undermine the British and Papandreou government, or even mild criticism, until November 22 when *Rizospastes* raised, for the first time, the issue of the collaborators by asking why they had not yet been tried.[113] In an interview with the press on November 2, Siantos spoke of KKE cooperation with the government and of a new national army which would contain elements of ELAS, but the EAM/KKE press insisted that ELAS would not disarm before the dissolution of "X," the Sacred Squadron, and the Mountain Brigade. Siantos's claim that the KKE was ready to achieve its goals through political means was confirmed by a number of reports reaching British authorities in November. According to one analysis of EAM/ELAS goals, the guerrillas would keep out of Athens as a body, but carry on underground propaganda and maintain a general state of unrest to hinder the capacity of the government to extend its control over the countryside. Toward this end, EAM/ELAS would foster complaints against the government to hasten its loss of popularity and would use technicalities to delay the disarmament of ELAS. When the government was sufficiently unpopular, EAM/ELAS would demand a new one in its favor.[114]

Another source, which was described as well-tried and with extensive political contacts, reported to British authorities on his conversation with prominent Communist leaders. According to this source, the KKE, which was fully aware of the desperate need for relief and that the Soviet Union could not provide it, feared that any attempt to seize power would result in Britain cutting off relief supplies. Therefore, there would be no seizure of power according to the confidential source.[115] Still another agency of the British authorities reached a similar conclusion as late as the end of November. A 3rd Corps HQ internal security report concluded EAM/ELAS would use procrastination, obstruction, and infiltration of the new government and armed forces to achieve their aims.[116]

The external evidence of these British reports, the EAM/ELAS press, the acceptance of "Noah's Ark" and Caserta, and the KKE documents of Iatrides make it clear that the KKE goal was not revolution but a protracted political struggle aimed at gradually wearing down and exhausting the opposition until the Greeks tired of Papandreou and the British. Then, EAM/ELAS/KKE would get a government more to their liking. Indeed, there is little proof in the PRO documents released to date to indicate that British authorities had any evidence, other than their previously set perceptions, to lead them to expect a violent *coup*. Fully aware of the prospects of a protracted struggle, British officials realized that Papandreou could not survive. And Churchill was certainly not about to engage in any prolonged political conflict.

In an interview with Demetrios Partsalides, the Communist leader insisted the Party had agreed in October not to seize power but to adopt a legal path to power. This decision, he stressed, was unanimous, and he emphatically rejected Eudes's account of a sharp split within the Party on this point. Partsalides claimed that only Zevgos doubted the wisdom of believing Britain would allow the KKE into the political process, but he accepted the Party's line.[117] Well aware that Britain would play the dominant role in Greece in the postwar era, the KKE based its decisions on this fact, according to Partsalides. Their goal was to build a strong political base for support in the postwar elections. The decision to use force, limited force, came after it became clear to the KKE at the end of November that

Papandreou and Britain demanded the disarming and dissolution of ELAS, leaving it without any political advantage and defense against reaction. The KKE asked Popov for advice, but the Russian did not reply. The KKE intention in December was to bring down the Papandreou government and to replace it with one more favorable to EAM/ELAS/KKE. To help achieve its goal, the KKE banked on world opinion, which thought EAM/ELAS had justifiably earned the right to share in political power, and the United States and the Soviet Union to pressure Britain to accede to EAM/ELAS demands.[118] The PRO documents on the December crisis give credence to Partsalides's account, but the strategy failed. The KKE made a fatal mistake by resorting even to limited force. Churchill had diplomatically isolated EAM/ELAS, and he was waiting for the opportunity to strike. When Papandreou's resolution temporarily wavered in the third week of November, Leeper and London put extraordinary pressure on him to stiffen and force the issue of the demobilization of EAM/ELAS.

In contrast to the AIS reports, Leeper's dispatches reflected an extraordinary concern for the need to restore law and order, code words for dissolving ELAS. By November, the British ambassador was convinced that a trial of strength was coming; while, in London, Churchill was becoming impatient with Greek affairs. On November 7, to bolster the Greek government with adequate forces to confront ELAS, Churchill put British troops at Papandreou's disposal and pushed for the quick arrival of the Mountain Brigade, which he hoped would shoot when necessary. The prime minister noted, "I fully expect a clash with E.A.M. and we must not shrink from it, provided the ground is well chosen." [119] On November 9, the day the Mountain Brigade arrived in Athens, Leeper went immediately to Papandreou to remind the Greek premier that he now had the troops to face ELAS and to pressure him to act on the demobilization. In response, Papandreou explained that he had two goals: first to liberate with as little bloodshed as possible, and second to demobilize the resistance without a breach, which he considered the more difficult of the two. Papandreou still hoped to achieve the second goal without civil war Siantos and Zevgos insisted that he delay the demobilization, but when it came, that the Sacred Squadron and the Mountain Brigade also be disarmed. Papandreou assured Leeper that he would not agree to either of these demands.

Rather, the Greek minister-president explained, he was waiting for the appropriate moment to act.[120]

Woodhouse and Partsalides agreed that the return of the Mountain Brigade was the provocation which ignited the December explosion. Woodhouse had advised his government against the brigade's return. Partsalides claimed that the decision to use force against the Greek government came at the Anglo-Greek insistence of disarming ELAS but keeping the Mountain Brigade intact.[121] Immediately after the arrival of the brigade, KKE directives changed their tone and warned of the threat of a rightist coup, insisting that ELAS would not disarm until a new national army was formed.[122] Within a week of the brigade's return, British intelligence sources alerted Leeper of a possible coup, basing their warning on the information that EAM section leaders were told to launch an anti-British propaganda campaign among British troops.[123]

On November 6, the Greek government agreed on General Othonaios as Commander-in-Chief of the new army with Venderes as his Chief of Staff, but little else was achieved on building the new army. In Lamia, Saraphes made it clear to Scobie's liaison that ELAS would not disband unless all units, including the Mountain Brigade, disbanded. Otherwise, Saraphes warned, the process would take a long time. With Leeper's prior approval, Scobie called Saraphes to Athens on November 15 and scolded the guerrilla general for not taking up his position as Deputy Chief of Staff which had been assigned to Saraphes. Saraphes replied that he had not been officially appointed by the Greek government, and since Othonaios had now refused to serve with Venderes, he could not serve under the Chief of Staff. Already upset at receiving ELAS communications signed by Saraphes and Aris, Scobie became angry and denounced Aris as a war criminal. He threatened Saraphes with the strange warning that guerrilla armies could not stand up to modern armies. The British general informed Saraphes that he would disarm any ELAS unit that came to Athens, and if ELAS opposed him by force, Scobie would respond with force. Then Scobie gave Saraphes an ultimatum to cooperate or face the consequences.[124]

On the following day Leeper maintained to Papandreou that the Mountain Brigade must not be demobilized, and at Papandreou's request, the ambassador saw Svolos to ask him to stop demanding from Papandreou the disarming of the Mountain Brigade. Leeper concluded the Communists were testing Britain's resolve, and he believed that Britain must be prepared to use force to prevent the situation from getting worse.[125] In response, the British prime minister ordered General Wilson to prepare a statement declaring Athens a military area, and he informed the general that he had full authority to repress any *coup*. The British officials decided that it would not be in Papandreou's interest to formally request the use of British troops, as this would damage him politically. In what proved to be a simplistic stance, Churchill believed that Scobie could handle any trouble by taking into custody Communist and ELAS leaders like Siantos and Saraphes. He minuted: "If the brains of E.A.M. are dealt with, the body should be useless trouble." [126]

On the same day, Leeper spoke to Svolos, and at the request of Papandreou, Scobie saw Svolos and Zevgos to denounce EAM/ELAS terror and arrests without authority. The EAM ministers insisted that they neither condoned such actions nor considered them legal. When Scobie demanded that they issue orders to the EAM/ELAS/KKE organizations to end the terror and intimidation, the ministers left immediately for Papandreou's home and tendered their resignations, which he rejected. Papandreou then called upon Scobie and Leeper, explaining that he did not want a break with EAM/ELAS on the issue of order. The British officials agreed. Still later the same evening, Svolos went alone to meet with Leeper to explain that the ministers of the Greek government did not take orders from Scobie. If the general had any measures he wanted carried out, Svolos insisted that he send them to the minister president for the cabinet to decide and not to individual ministers. Svolos complained about behavior which Woodhouse had previously warned the Foreign Office to avoid.[127] Scobie's blunder could have provided EAM/ELAS with an embarrassing issue to be used against Papandreou and Britain, but they did not exploit it publicly.

According to PRO materials, the Greek cabinet, in a critical meeting on November 20, worked out a compromise which Leeper and Svolos had informally agreed to on November 18. The proposal called for the government to issue a declaration on the points raised by Scobie, and the KKE would be directed to send out to its members a private endorsement of the measure. The compromise agreement barred demonstrations, forbade the carrying of arms and illegal arrests, and all street paintings (slogans) were to be effaced, beginning with the

British embassy, which was plastered with red hammers and sickles. Papandreou declared that the compromise agreement was adequate and that there was no need to have the KKE issue a special endorsement.[128] The PRO documents refer to a second agreement of the cabinet, which sheds some light on the major controversial issue of whether Papandreou agreed with the EAM/ELAS representatives to demobilize the Mountain Brigade along with the resistance.

Svolos stated that Papandreou agreed on November 22 to disband the Mountain Brigade along with demobilization of the guerrillas, but no other sources have verified the claim.[129] There is no mention of the November 22 meeting or agreement in the currently available PRO materials, but the record of the November 20 conference does make a reference to a Papandreou concession on the Mountain Brigade. Leeper informed London on November 20 that Papandreou had told the British ambassador that the crisis was over and the issue of demobilization resolved by an agreement with the EAM/ELAS representatives which allowed the Sacred Squadron to remain intact and sent the men of the Mountain Brigade on long, extended leaves when the guerrillas disarmed.[130] This concession by Papandreou was the first of a series he made to EAM/ELAS in the next five days during daily, intensive meetings with his ministers of the left.

In another dispatch to London on November 25, Leeper again reported that Papandreou and the "Communists" apparently reached an agreement on demobilization scheduled for December 10, but there is no mention of a November 22 meeting.[131] In the period between the two reports, Papandreou appointed a committee dominated by old Venizelists and members of EAM/ELAS/PEEA to advise the government on selecting men and officers for the new army. The committee members were Othonaios, A. Manetas, Demetrios Katheniotis (Venizelists); Emmanouil Mandakas and P. Sariyiannis (ELAS and PEEA respectively); and Markos Drakos (Albanian campaign). The King did not like these appointments, and he informed the Foreign Office of his displeasure.[132] Papandreou made Sariyiannis Undersecretary of War on November 25.

Although the PRO documents do not provide a clear record of what went on in these discussions between Papandreou and his ministers of the left, Leeper was certainly alarmed by the "agreement," whatever it was, and the meetings. Following the appointment of Sariyiannis, Leeper became convinced that Papandreou was appeasing EAM/ELAS. On two occasions during November 26, he met with Papandreou to tell the Greek minister-president that Britain did not approve of Papandreou's one-sided meetings with the EAM/ELAS ministers. At first, Papandreou assured Leeper that he was making progress, but when Leeper threatened to withhold British support for him if he continued these meetings, Papandreou tendered his resignation. Leeper rejected it, however. He had made his point, and Papandreou then expressed confidence that the issue of building the new army would be resolved shortly, and he assured Leeper and Scobie, who had joined the talks, that the Mountain Brigade would not be disbanded.[133] This British intervention clearly ended the short period of reconciliation between Papandreou and EAM/ELAS. Leeper and Scobie made it clear that EAM/ELAS representatives would have to accept the demobilization of the guerrillas without the retirement of the Mountain Brigade or resign from the government. Papandreou immediately informed them that an ultimatum to that effect would provoke civil war, which he had hoped to avoid. Then he asked for three more days to prepare the National Guard for a confrontation and to try for a compromise before forcing the issue. Leeper and Scobie agreed, and the Foreign Office approved of their intervention.[134] Whatever agreement had been worked out, or was being hammered out between November 20 and 25, was moot after the Scobie-Leeper intervention and threat of withholding British support for Papandreou.

By the third week in November both sides began to prepare for the expected showdown. The KKE on November 22 ordered all members of ELAS who were to join the new National Guard to hand over their weapons to the *andarte* army before taking their posts. EAM/ELAS was continuing to cooperate but, uncertain of the future, was hedging its bets on Papandreou.[135] After failing to get Saraphes and Zervas to agree on disarmament of the guerrillas on November 24, Scobie requested, and received from Churchill, permission and full authority to deal with any direct or indirect obstruction of British policy.[136]

On November 28, Papandreou informed Leeper that the EAM/ELAS ministers agreed to a decree for demobilization and proposed General Plastiras as Commander-in-Chief. Later that day, Leeper learned, the Liberals and Populists believed the document was a victory for EAM/ELAS and refused to support it. He quickly arranged to meet with Sophoulis, and he convinced the Liberal leader to accept the decree, but no sooner had he succeeded with the Liberals than he learned that the Communists wanted to change the text of the decree. The ambassador then reflected that he understood why the King had approved of the Metaxas dictatorship.[137]

In London, an angry but depressed Churchill drafted an acid communication on Papandreou to Eden:

> He really does require some stiffening. When you think of all we have done for him in troops, in operations, in food, in currency, and in cash, one begins to ask oneself the question, "are we getting any good out of this old fool at all" and would it not be better to let them adjust their political difficulties in their own way and without our being involved? If he is not going to put up the slightest resistance to E.A.M. and if no one else appears who will, the usefulness of our remaining in Athens is called in question. . . . Everything is degenerating in the Greek government, and we must make up our minds whether we will assert our will by armed force, or clear out altogether.[138]

The prime minister then asked Eden to inform Papandreou: "As far as I can see from here you seem to be slipping more and more hopelessly into the grip of E.A.M. and E.L.A.S. By pursuing this course you might easily reach the point where His Majesty's Government would not be able to take any more interest in your Administration. My agreement with Marshall Stalin has been faithfully maintained by the Soviets. I hope you will arouse yourself before we have to say goodbye and your country slithers into ruin for another decade." [139] Even the Foreign Office was shocked by these words, and Eden convinced the prime minister to send the message to Leeper rather than to the Greek minister-president.

The draft government decree which created this flurry of activity called for the formation of a national army, but during the period of reorganization, the Sacred Squadron, the Mountain Brigade, one brigade drawn from ELAS, and another proportionate body of EDES would continue to serve. All other units would be disarmed and sent home. Military councils were to be established to select the men for the new National Guard, and the EAM civil police would hand over their duties to the temporary National Guard on December 1 and demobilize on December 17. Demonstrations were free but under some regulation by the Minister of the Interior. The decree agreed to establish special courts to deal with the collaborators. The overall execution of the order was entrusted to Papandreou as Minister of War.

The changes later proposed by EAM/ELAS repudiated the formation of separate units and demanded not only the demobilization of the guerrillas but also of the Sacred Squadron and the Mountain Brigade. EAM/ELAS insisted on keeping their arms, but the police held over from the occupation were to be demobilized and sent home. Nine names were submitted, including that of Pangalos, as traitors who should be tried by December 10. In the original decree, the Minister of the Interior was authorized to prosecute those who carried arms and those committing a breach of the peace. In the new demands, EAM/ELAS accepted the former but asked that the latter be omitted from the text. Finally, they demanded a new authorization which would prohibit organizations and propaganda that favored "Fascism." [140]

Leeper rejected the demands as they would have left the government without any forces to confront ELAS, which would retain its arms. On December 1, Papandreou informed Leeper that he would not yield to the demands and that he would not meet with his cabinet. He had ordered the EAM civil police to turn in their arms on December 1 and ELAS on December 10. If the ministers of the left wanted to resign, he told Leeper, they would have to come to him. [141] Leeper was pleased that Papandreou did not make the decree of November 28 the issue of the break, but made it a breach of faith on the part of the Communists, who refused to let the civil police disarm. In relief, Leeper cabled London: "Personally I am glad that the appeasement period is over. Appeasing the Greek Communists is strangely reminiscent of appeasing Hitler." [142]

In a strongly worded proclamation, Scobie made it clear that Britain would support Papandreou until the Greek government had a lawful army at its command. On December 2, the EAM/ELAS ministers resigned. Sariyiannis, however, did not resign. EAM/ELAS called for an anti-government demonstration on Sunday, December 3, and a general strike for Monday, December 4. During the demonstration, Greek police opened fire and killed twenty-two protesters. The police riot unleashed a general ELAS attack on Greek police stations throughout the city.[143]

The war diary log of British headquarters District 1 for December 3 gives an hour-by-hour account of the incident. Police reporting to the headquarters described unarmed demonstrators moving on to Constitution Square at 11 a.m. There is one report from Pireaus of armed troops moving on the city at 11:30 a.m., but that would have been after the violence or demonstration began at 11 a.m.[144]

After the events of December 3, Sophoulis prepared to pull his Liberals out of the cabinet and form a government which had the support of EAM/ELAS, but Leeper intervened and prevented the fall of Papandreou. Sophoulis agreed to continue supporting Papandreou, but there was general agreement that Papandreou would have to go soon.[145]

The battle which followed was a limited, hastily improvised affair for EAM/ELAS. Troops deployed for "Noah's Ark" were not redeployed in November for a seizure of power, and there was no movement of ELAS toward Athens before December 3. On the night following the violence in Constitution Square, British troops halted and disarmed without resistance 800 ELAS *andartes* moving along the Thebes road to the capital.[146] The decision to launch an attack on the Greek police had been taken so suddenly that many ELAS units in Athens were not provisioned with food.[147] Between December 3 and 12, ELAS did not take offensive actions against British troops, but concentrated on the Greek police, killing 600 of the 3,000 man force. By the end of the first week, ELAS had not fired on British troops unless fired upon.[148]

Further evidence of the limited, hasty nature of the attack lies in the type of ELAS units which took part in the battle. Those ELAS troops captured in the first week of the struggle belonged to no unit previously known to the British to be in Athens, and these were organized on a cell basis rather than brigades, regiments, and divisions. Their equipment was mostly Italian and German light automatic weapons, and the majority of the ELAS fighters were youths, average age 17, drawn from the ranks of the KKE and EPON. They had not participated in the struggle against the Germans. Only a few elements of the 2nd, 3rd, and 13th ELAS divisions were eventually involved in the fighting to some extent, but they were not identified until December 11. Of the 16,900 ELAS troops in Athens on December 29, the British estimated less than a fourth were

mountain troops of the *andartiko*. The British military authorities concluded that the ELAS plan of battle was based on a
January 1944 plan for seizing Athens as the Germans withdrew
by cutting off the city and establishing nests of resistance.
Even ten days after the opening of the struggle, there was no
effort by ELAS to capture strategic airfields or major food
dumps.[149]

EAM feared that the agreement of separate units offered
ELAS no protection since Scobie could order the ELAS units
out of Athens, leaving the Rimini Brigade in control.[150] The
record of the fighting outlined in the previous paragraphs sup-
ports Partsalides's claim that the attack was aimed at Papandreou, but the decision to use limited force against a determined
Churchill was a colossal error. The British Prime Minister was
anxiously waiting for an opportunity to smash EAM/ELAS,
but he lacked the power in Greece to achieve a quick decisive
victory. Regardless, the Anglo-Greek officials had no intention
of letting the KKE play any role in Greek politics.

By December 11, ELAS forces had pressed the British and
Greek troops into the center of Athens between the Acropolis
and Lykabettos, and Field Marshal Harold Alexander described
the situation as grave. While the battle continued, Porphyrogenis met Scobie on December 12 to discuss a settlement, but
as the British general demanded a complete withdrawal and
the disarming of ELAS, there was no agreement. That night,
ELAS escalated the battle by overrunning the 23rd Armoured
Brigade's barracks, but they were driven out after a hard
twelve-hour fight. Three days later, ELAS successfully
launched an attack on the Royal Air Force headquarters at
Kifissia, and by December 19, had captured 500 troops. Still
there was no victory in sight for EAM/ELAS.[151] On December
16, ELAS offered to withdraw from the city if they could
keep their arms; but since he had been reinforced and was
preparing to take the initiative, Scobie rejected the terms.
The direction of the battle was then given to Major General
J. L. I. Hawkesworth, the commander of the 10th Corps in
Italy. If ELAS could not defeat the Allied force, Britain could
not easily dissolve EAM/ELAS. The stalemate led to protracted negotiations which brought Churchill to Athens on
December 24, 1944.

In the early days of the fighting, Harold Macmillan suggested a regency under Damaskinos as a possible means to
resolve the struggle. He recognized that EAM/ELAS's "pat-

riotic" elements, as Macmillan called the non-communists, legitimately feared right wing reaction. The "old left" of Liberals, Venizelists, and Republicans was "violently" anticommunists—according to Macmillan, almost more so than the "old conservatives"—but they opposed the return of the King. Macmillan and Leeper proposed a regency as a means of uniting the "patriotic" elements of EAM/ELAS, the old left, and the conservatives into a solid anti-KKE front. Papandreou and Sophoulis opposed the regency, which they feared would favor a policy of reconciliation to the detriment of an anticommunist state. They insisted that no Communist be allowed to join in any government which followed the termination of the armed conflict.[152] Although the non-communist political personalities were not in general agreement on who should govern and the issue of the crown, they unanimously agreed that Britain should use the insurrection to completely destroy EAM/ELAS and the political goals of this new left.[153] The failure to quickly defeat ELAS caused Churchill, however, to accept the idea of a regency by December 16, but he was not certain that Archbishop Damaskinos, who was suggested as the leading candidate, was the man for the job. The visit to Athens was as much to meet the Archbishop as to convene a conference of EAM/ELAS/KKE and the non-communist political leaders.

The two day conference which followed Churchill's arrival did not settle the conflict. Although all sides willingly accepted the proposed regency under Damaskinos, whom Churchill found very much to his liking after the Archbishop's anticommunist speech on the opening days of the conference, there was little other agreement. The EAM/ELAS/KKE position was similar to that of the Lebanon conference except that their bargaining position was acutely worse, but the KKE leadership failed to realize it. Siantos made demands as if he was coming to the conference as a victor. The non-communist politicians, including the recently arrived Plastiras, used the events of December to denounce the KKE and EAM/ELAS in much the same vein as the anticommunist critics had at Lebanon. Siantos wanted a purge of the collaborators in the police, gendarmerie, and army; 40 to 50 percent of the posts in any new government, including those of the Interior, Justice, Foreign Affairs, and Undersecretary of War; an immediate plebiscite on the monarchy; and a general election in April 1945. Siantos badly misjudged his situation. Neither

Britain nor the Greeks were ready to accept these demands, and the conference ended without resolution.

Rather than renewing their offensive in Athens, ELAS, on December 27, attacked and disbanded Zervas, but this success had no effect on the conflict in Athens. The British forces were not adequate to launch a general offensive throughout Greece, but they were strong enough to hold the city and push ELAS out. By the end of the month, the first ELAS units began to withdraw from the capital. Churchill forced the King to accept the regency, and Damaskinos took office on December 31. On January 4, Plastiras replaced Papandreou as head of the Greek government. If Siantos had misjudged the situation at the December conference, Plastiras was quick to demonstrate that he had forgotten nothing—and learned nothing—while he had been in exile in France. The new premier's aim was not reconciliation, but a rather unrealistic goal of raising an army, paid for by Britain, which would drive ELAS from Athens and crush it throughout Greece. Then he began to name his old cronies to positions of power, and he appointed Gonatas Governor General of Macedonia. Leeper, however, forced Plastiras to withdraw the nomination.[154]

By mid-January, Laskey and the senior officials of the Foreign Office became quite concerned that the defeat of EAM/ELAS would lead to a right wing sweep. After the fighting ended, Laskey and Leeper hoped that the non-communist members of EAM/ELAS could enter the government and serve as a basis of reconciliation, but the Greek political leaders were not about to accept them. Soon, British officials were complaining of police using elements of "X" and EDES to make political arrests under warrants issued by a police magistrate who was a leader of "X."[155]

As diplomatic isolation of EAM/ELAS became clear and neither world opinion nor Stalin would aid them to break Britain's determination to hold Athens, a truce was arranged on January 11, and a political settlement was signed at Varkiza on February 13. Siantos had two fundamental goals at Varkiza, a general amnesty and the recruitment of ELAS into the new army. The general amnesty was the more crucial of these two aims as it would have protected the rank and file from wholesale arrests and political persecution. The opposition refused to accept a general amnesty and insisted on exempting anyone who committed common law crimes (crimes against life and property) which would be subject to prosecution. The position of Siantos was not only weakened by his failure in December, but by the horror of the brutal massacre of hostages by EAM/ELAS. The IRC established that ELAS seized 15,000 hostages during the fighting and released 11,000. The other 4,000 were presumed dead.[156] Some of the victims were prominent collaborators or members of the right, but the great majority were people of the lower classes.[157] British officers found 1,200 of these hostages brutally murdered with knives and axes. There was no apparent political motivation in these crimes, but why so many were executed has never been, nor will ever likely be, explained. British interrogators were told that the hostages were seized as a means of ensuring an amnesty for ELAS at the end of the fighting. British prisoners, on the other hand, tended to be treated fairly by their captors.[158]

The final agreement accepted the modified amnesty which provided the legal means to launch the "white terror" against the rank and file of EAM/ELAS. EAM/ELAS was not allowed to participate in the government, but freedom of the press and association were guaranteed. The government administration and police were to be purged of all collaborators, and the new army was to be open to ELAS members, who would not be punished for their political beliefs. Following the disarming of ELAS, the agreements on the civil service and security forces were ignored, but the arrest of common law criminals was energetically enforced. In spite of releases and convictions, the number of ELAS prisoners continued to grow in 1945. On March 8, there were 12,000. Of these, 8,116 were considered common law offenders, and 2,458 had already been convicted. On the other hand, 1,246 individuals had been charged with collaboration, but the number of convictions was negligible.[159] In spite of 6,204 releases during September and October, the number of incarcerated grew to 18,058 by November 1.[160] A total of 80,000 individuals were eventually arrested. Although the Varkiza agreement called for elections and a plebiscite within a year, the agreement and the insurrection which preceded it marked the defeat not only of the KKE and EAM/ELAS but also of the political program of the resistance.

The Aftermath

The December 1944 disaster emphasized the failure of the

King and the traditional political leaders to assume active leadership in filling the political and moral vacuum left by the debacle of the Metaxas dictatorship and the Axis invasion and occupation. Their *attentisme* left the leadership of the resistance in the hands of a few adventurous republicans and communists. Zervas's political opportunism and weakness wrecked the chances of creating a national republican resistance firmly supported by the Allies. The Greek Communist Party's superior ability at political organization and its willingness to capitalize on the popular aspirations of Greeks under the Axis occupation quickly eliminated the possibility of forming any national resistance which might effectively rival EAM/ELAS. The charge that EAM/ELAS avoided fighting the Axis and concentrated on eliminating its rivals is not true. The German records make it unmistakably clear that EAM/ELAS fought the enemy to a greater extent than did any other resistance force. EAM/ELAS's role in the successful organization of the resistance gave it the right to expect a voice in Greece's postwar politics. The political goals of EAM/ELAS's overwhelmingly non-communist following and of EDES and EKKA were defeated by two things—the insecurity of the KKE, which caused it to vacillate haphazardly between cooperating with its rivals and periodically terrorizing and fomenting civil war against them, and the coalition made up of old-line politicans, the King, and the British, which aimed at the general political negation of the resistance.

The failure of London and of George II to respond to demands for a government of national unity between March and August 1943, and their increasing inflexibility after the Cairo conference, ensured the continued fragmentation and polarization of Greek politics. The KKE assisted this process by its willingness to resort to civil war to attain its ends. The middle ground between the Communists and the traditional political leaders disappeared as the Liberals and the "old left" progressively found themselves displaced by the resistance and coalesced with the "old right" to form a united anticommunist, antiresistance bloc. Although the Communists made up only 10 to 20 percent of the leadership and rank and file of EAM/ELAS, no effort was ever made by Cairo or London to encourage the moderates. Neither Kartalis and Pyromaglou nor Tsirimokos, Svolos, and Bakirtzis ever received constructive support from Britain. The critical moment occurred at the Cairo conference of 1943. Its failure ensured the undoing of the moderate resistance forces. Moreover, the failure at Cairo also meant the failure of Mirofillo-Plaka, Lebanon, and Caserta.

Historically, the strategic geographic location of Greece has encouraged the intervention of the Great Powers in Greek affairs. The experience of Greece during the Second World War once again reaffirmed this rule. The German invasion had been prompted by the strategic necessity to secure Germany's southern flank from possible British attacks during the invasion of Russia. Germany's ruthless occupation policies encouraged the growth of the resistance and intensified the conflict between the resistance and the old-line political parties. The political, strategic, and economic interests of the British in the eastern Mediterranean prompted their active intervention in Greek affairs. If British intervention in December 1944 did prevent a Communist victory, London's opposition to the politics of the resistance and its inflexible support for George II in the three years preceding the insurrection contributed to making the conflict inevitable. The Cold War and the unending series of crises in the Middle East have reemphasized the strategic importance of Greece and have led to the continued intervention of the Great Powers in its affairs. Yet British intervention and penetration of the political system did not stabilize Greek politics.

Frustrated by the Greek scramble for power where every opportunity was seized as a way to profit by the elimination of as many rivals as possible by accusing them of left connections and consolidating their position with the British, British officials in 1945 pursued the mythical goal of an "all party government." On March 5, Leeper and Macmillan requested authorization for a formal agreement with Greece to allow them to become directly involved in the Greek administration of government. Laskey rejected the suggestion as it would give the Soviets an example to follow in central Europe, but Sargent recommended that Leeper follow Lord Cromer's example in Egypt during the 1880's to achieve the desired ends of British policy.[161] The British penetration was complete, but stability remained elusive.

Plastiras proved unsuitable, and he was replaced with Voulgares on April 7. The cavalcade of postwar governments continued, but the administration of government remained in shambles. One year and four governments after the liberation, W. J. Hasler of UNRAA described the complete political collapse. Prices were thirty times their prewar level, but wages only six times higher. The communication and transport systems remained dismantled by the war, and the nation was unable to get roofs over the heads of those left homeless by the war's destruction. Lacking cohesion, the civil service could not function,[162] and Britain lacked the resources to restore the administration and the economy.

In the midst of the instability came the repression of the right. On December 5, 1945, a British Police Mission report concluded that the gendarmerie was not impartial and enforcement of the laws not as energetic against the right as against the former members of EAM/ELAS. Incidents of beatings and murder between left and right continued to increase.[163] Although Woodhouse noted that the KKE often provoked the right, the major responsibility for the disorder and violence lay with the right, which had complete control of authority and power.[164]

Although twenty-four leading collaborators were put on trial, the collaborators were never purged from the state administration and security forces. Rallis died while awaiting trial, and the others received prison terms. The army posthumously promoted Colonel Papadongonas of the Security Battalions to the rank of Major-General, but the government cancelled the promotion on August 22, 1945. In official circles, according to Leeper, membership in the Security Battalions was at worst considered a venal offense.[165] The triumph of the right was completed with the controversial elections of March 1946 and the plebiscite of September 2 that year. The elections placed the conservative Populists under Tsaldaris in power, and the plebiscite returned the monarchy. The King promptly put Generals Speliotopoulos and Venderes, formerly connected with the Military Hierarchy, in charge of the Greek armed forces. In February 1947, Zervas became Minister of Public Order in the reactionary government of Demetrios Maximos. While Speliotopoulos and Venderes made the army the staunchest anticommunist, anti-left, and monarchist institution outside the throne within Greek society, Zervas filled the already packed jails with his former enemies from EAM/ELAS.[166] Meanwhile, Bakirtzis, Saraphes, Mandakas, and thirty of the senior ELAS officers were arrested and exiled to a Greek island. Rather than face island prison, Bakirtzis committed suicide, a symbolic act of the general frustration of the Greek resistance. Saraphes survived to organize a small political leftist party in the 1950's which co-operated with the Communist front party, the United Democratic Left (EDA). The "white terror" which followed the liberation played no small role in forcing many non-communists back "to the mountains."

The insurrection marked the break-up of EAM and end of Siantos's leadership of the KKE. Svolos and Tsirimokos left EAM in March 1945. With the return from Germany of Zachariades in June 1945, the KKE shifted to a more militant, revolutionary policy. Zachariades and Markos Vaphiades would direct the Communist revolution of 1946-1949. Under Zachariades's leadership, the KKE denounced Siantos as a British agent and condemned him for failing to prepare resistance to British intervention in October 1944 and to seize power at that time.[167] Those Communists associated with Siantos's policy were eventually purged from the KKE. In 1956, however, Zachariades was himself purged from the KKE leadership. Yet the EDA coalition of 1956 with other left-of-center parties won 48 percent of the vote, demonstrating the need for a responsible left-of-center party. The failure of the KKE to adhere to a policy of nonviolence in 1943 and 1944 destroyed any chance for the Party developing a wide political base.

The conservative triumph of 1944-1946 was sustained by the renewed civil war which ensued in 1946, and by such outstanding personalities of the 1950's as Papagos and Constantine Karamanlis. Their program, however, remained essentially a defense of the *status quo* and thus, as Professor George Daskalakes pointed out in 1958, prevented the formation of an ideology capable of producing change and progress.[168] The potential for creating this ideology was effectively crushed by the polarization of politics between 1943 and 1944.

NOTES

CHAPTER ONE

[1] Ioannis Metaxas, *To Prosopiko tou Hemerologio* [Diary] (Athens: Ikaros, 1960), Vol. II, p. 456, hereinafter cited as *Hemerologio*. The King expressed his dislike of Greek politicians to Sir Sydney Waterlow, British Minister to Athens, 1933-1939. In Waterlow's view, he and the King had developed a close and candid relationship. See Public Record Office (PRO), Foreign Office (FO) 371/20390 R4920/220/19, Waterlow to FO, May 12, 1936.

[2] Nikiforos P. Diamandouros, "Political Clientalism and Political Modernization in Nineteenth Century Greece," forthcoming, Sage Publications, Inc., p. 24 of typed manuscript.

[3] For an analysis of twentieth century Greek clientage politics, see Keith R. Legg, *Politics in Modern Greece* (Stanford, Calif.: Stanford University Press, 1969), *passim*.

[4] Diamandouros, "Political Clientage," p. 24; John A. Petropulos, *Politics and Statecraft in the Kingdom of Greece 1833-1843* (Princeton: Princeton University Press, 1968), pp. 120-122, 378-385, 501-515; Douglas Dakin, *The Unification of Greece, 1770-1923* (London: Ernest Benn, 1972), pp. 141-142, 180-189, 237-241; and T. Veremis, "The Officer Corps in Greece, 1912-1936," *Byzantine and Modern Greek Studies*, Vol. 2 (1976), 113-135.

[5] The anti-Venizelists supported Constantine, and may be broadly defined as royalists. The Venizelists were later associated with the Republic that was formed in 1923, and until 1933 the terms "royalists" and "antiroyalists" on the one hand, and "republican" and "Venizelists" on the other, were interchangeable. After 1933, the term "Liberal" became more appropriate for Venizelists and "Populist" for supporters of the Crown.

[6] Leften S. Stavrianos, *The Balkans Since 1453* (New York: Holt, Rinehart and Winston, 1958), pp. 607-608, hereinafter cited as *The Balkans*; Bickam Sweet-Escott, *Greece: A Political and Economic Survey, 1939-1953* (London: Royal Institute for International Affairs, 1954), pp. 6-7, hereinafter cited as *Greece*. For details, see Jane Perry Clark Carey and Andrew Galbraith Carey, *The Web of Modern Greek Politics* (New York: Columbia University Press, 1968), pp. 107-110, hereinafter cited as *Modern Greek Politics;* and John Campbell and Philip Sherrard, *Modern Greece* (London: Ernest Benn, 1968), pp. 127-138, 144-154, hereinafter cited as *Modern Greece*.

[7] Constantine Tsoucalas, *The Greek Tragedy* (London: Penguin Books, 1969), p. 42, hereinafter cited as *Greek Tragedy.*

[8] From peasant origins, Kondylis worked his way into the highest ranks of the army to become a great popular hero in the Balkan Wars. He wrote a biography of Alexander the Great, whom he greatly admired, and kept on his office wall a map of the Macedonian's ancient empire. For some time many observers felt that he aspired to be the Mussolini of Greece, but death cut his life short in 1936. He began his political life as a supporter of Venizelos, but he fell out with the statesman over who should control the army. Kondylis played a key role in the return of George II in 1935.

[9] General Pangalos participated in the revolution of 1922 and carried out a *coup* in 1925, ostensibly to save the Republic but in reality to use his power to establish his own dictatorship, whose purpose remained unclear even to Pangalos.

[10] Tsoucalas, *Greek Tragedy*, pp. 46-48.

[11] Royal Institute of International Affairs, *Southeastern Europe: A Political and Economic Survey* (London: Oxford University Press, p. 92, hereinafter cited as *Southeastern Europe;* and Campbell and Sherrard, *Modern Greece,* p. 158.

[12] William Miller, "New Era in Greece," *Foreign Affairs,* Vol. 14 (July 1936), 654-656, hereinafter cited as "New Era in Greece."

[13] The monarchist or anti-Venizelist parties were:

	Votes	*Percent*	*Number of Deputies*
National Radical Union (Kondylis)	253,384	19.89	60
Populist Party (Tsaldaris)	281,597	22.10	72
Free Opinion Party (Metaxas)	50,137	3.94	7
Others	17,822	1.20	4
TOTAL SEATS			143

The republican or Venizelist parties were:

Liberals (Sophoulis)	474,651	37.26	126
Democratic Union (Papandreou)	53,693	4.21	7
Agrarians (Mylonas)	12,333	.97	4
Others	18,119	1.42	4
TOTAL SEATS			141
The Greek Communist Party:	73,411	5.76	15

Source: Georgios Daphnes, *He Ellas metaxy ton thyo Polemon, 1923-1940* [Greece Between The Two Wars, 1923-1940] (Athens: Ikaros, 1955), vol. II, p. 402, hereinafter cited as *He Ellas;* and PRO FO371/20389 R1703/220/19, Waterlow to FO, March 24, 1936.

[14] Daphnes, *He Ellas,* II, pp. 402-403.

[15] *New York Times,* January 30, 1936, p. 9; February 1, 1936, p. 1.

[16] *Ibid.,* February 3, 1936, p. 6.

[17] D. George Kousoulas, *Revolution and Defeat; The Story of the Greek Communist Party* (London: Oxford University Press, 1965), p. 109, hereinafter cited as *Revolution and Defeat.*

[18] PRO FO371/20389 R1345/220/19, Waterlow to FO, February 25, 1936.

[19] PRO FO371/20389 R1345/220/19, Waterlow to FO, March 6, 1936; and PRO FO371/20389 R1703/220/19, Waterlow to FO, March 24, 1936. The claim that General Alexandros Papagos had a plan to establish a directorship at this time is not corroborated by the PRO documents. Cf. Spyros Linardatos, *Pos Ephtasame sten 4e Avgoustou* [How We Arrived at the 4th August] (Athens: Themelio, 1965), p. 178, hereinafter cited as *4e Avgoustou.*

[20] Komnenos Pyromaglou, *Ho Georgios Kartalis kai he Epoxe tou, 1934-1957,* A' Tomos 1934-1944 [George Kartalis and His Times, 1934-1957, Vol. I: 1934-1944] (Athens: Estia, 1965), p. 97, hereinafter cited as *Ho Georgios Kartalis.*

[21] PRO FO371/20390 R4662/220/19, Waterlow to FO, July 20, 1936.

[22] PRO FO371/20389 R228/220/19, Waterlow to FO, January 22, 1936.

[23] Daphnes, *He Ellas,* II, pp. 420-421.

[24] *New York Times,* May 12, 1936, p. 11; May 20, 1936, p. 8; and June 5, 1936, p. 12.

[25] Kousoulas, *Revolution and Defeat,* p. 114; and Daphnes, *He Ellas,* II, pp. 422-426.

[26] PRO FO371/20389 R2897/220/19, Waterlow to FO, May 14, 1936.

[27] PRO FO371/20390 R3310/220/19, Report on Labor Unrest in Salonica, June 2, 1936.

[28] *Ibid.*

[29] Floyd A. Spencer, *War and Postwar Greece: An Analysis Based on Greek Writings* (Washington, D.C.: The Library of Congress, 1952), p. 4; and see Linardatos, *4e Avgoustou,* Part II, Chapter 4.

[30] Kousoulas, *Revolution and Defeat,* p. 120.

[31] Pyromaglou, *Ho Georgios Kartalis,* p. 98.

[32] Daphnes, *He Ellas,* II, pp. 431-432. Daphnes's account is based on an interview with Diakos. Colonel Skelakakis at the time was serving as Minister of Foreign Affairs, and Papademas eventually became Minister of War.

[33] Edward S. Forster, *A Short History of Modern Greece, 1821-1945,* 2nd rev. ed. (London: Methuen & Co. Ltd., 1946), pp. 197-198.

[34] PRO FO371/20389 R44662/220/19, Waterlow to FO, July 20, 1936.

[35] PRO FO371/20390 R4748/220/19, Waterlow to FO, August 8, 1936, and PRO FO371/20390 R4920/220/19, Waterlow to FO, August 12, 1936.

[36] *Ibid.*

[37] This claim is made by Heinz Richter, *Griechenland zwischen Revolution und Konterrevolution, 1936-1946* (Frankfurt am Main: Europaeische Verlagsanstalt, 1973), p. 52, hereinafter cited as *Revolution und Konterrevolution.*

[38] PRO FO371/37231 R4806/220/19, May 6, 1943, Minute by Dixon and Eden. Pierson Dixon was Private Secretary to the Secretary of State Anthony Eden in 1943.

[39] For a recent well-argued statement of this position see Richter, *Revolution und Konterrevolution,* pp. 54-65.

[40] Norman Kogan, "Fascism as a Political System," in S. J. Woolf (ed.), *The Nature of Fascism* (New York: Vintage Books, 1969), pp. 12-16; Juan Linz, "Some Notes Toward a Comparative Study of Fascism in Sociological Historical Perspective," in Walter Laqueur (ed.), *Fascism:*

A Reader's Guide (Berkeley: University of California Press, 1976), pp. 12-13; S. J. Woolf (ed.), *European Fascism* (London: Weidenfeld and Nicolson, 1968), p. 2; John Weiss, *The Fascist Tradition: Right-wing Extremism in Modern Europe* (New York: Harper & Row, 1967), p. 507.

[41] Lucy S. Dawidowicz, *The War Against the Jews, 1933-1945* (New York: Holt, Rinehart, Winston, 1975), p. 393, hereinafter cited as *War Against the Jews.*

[42] Linardatos, *4° Avgoustou*, pp. 23-110.

[43] PRO FO371/20391 R868/349/19, Waterlow to FO, December 29, 1937; and PRO FO371/22370 R992/726/19, Waterlow to FO, January 24, 1938.

[44] U.S. Dept. of State, 868.00/1074, Ambassador MacVeagh to the Secretary of State, February 18, 1939, hereinafter cited as 868.00/1074.

[45] Royal Institute of International Affairs, *Southeastern Europe*, p. 95.

[46] U.S. Dept. of State, 868.00/1074.

[47] Tsoucalas, *Greek Tragedy*, p. 53.

[48] U.S. Dept. of State 869.42/17a, Homer Davis Report of Educational Control in Greece, 1936-1941, February 1, 1942.

[49] Auswaertigen Amt, Staatsekretaer Griechenland, Altenburg to Ribbentrop, May 8, 1941, T120, Roll 157, Frames 127545-46.

[50] PRO FO371/22370 R992/726/19, Waterlow to FO, January 24, 1938; and PRO FO371/21147 R8687/349/19, Summary of a conversation between Metaxas and Captain Anthony Wedgwood Benn, December 29, 1937.

[51] PRO FO371/22370 R1118/726/19, Waterlow to FO, February 5, 1938.

[52] PRO FO371/22371 R2102/726/19, March 17, 1938, Minute by Andrew Ross; FO371/22371 R1118/726/19, Waterlow to FO, February 5, 1938; FO371/22371 R10333/726/19, Waterlow to FO and Minute by Sir Orme Sargent (Deputy Permanent Undersecretary), December 29, 1938.

[53] PRO FO371/22370 R726/726/19, Minute by Ross, January 21, 1938.

[54] PRO FO371/22371 R2102/726/19, Minute by Ross, February 23, 1938; FO371/23769 R556/556/19, Report on Leading Personalities in Greece, January 23, 1939.

[55] Miller, "New Era in Greece," 654-656; Sir Sydney Waterlow, "Decline and Fall of Greek Democracy, 1933-1936," Part I, *Political Quarterly*, Vol. 18 (April-June 1947), 95-106, Part II, Vol. 18 (July-September 1947), 205-219.

[56] See especially C. M. Woodhouse, *Apple of Discord* (London: Hutchinson, 1948), hereinafter cited as *Apple of Discord*; Kousoulas, *Revolution and Defeat*; V. Papadakes, *He Khthesine kai he avriane Ellas* [Greece Yesterday and Tomorrow] (Cairo, 1946); and M. Malenos, *He tetarte Avgoustou, Pos kai diati epevlethe he diktatoria tou I. Metaxa* [The Fourth of August. How and Why the Dictatorship of I. Metaxas was Imposed] (Athens, 1947).

[57] See especially Mario Cervi, *The Hollow Legions: Mussolini's Blunder in Greece 1940-1941* (London: Chatto and Windus, 1972), Chapter 5, hereinafter cited as *Hollow Legions.*

[58] It should be noted that the regime appeared schizoid in dealing with the Axis threat. It was quite willing to risk everything to wage war against Mussolini, but it was hesitant to resist Hitler. See below, Chapter II.

[59] Thomas P. Trombetas, "Consensus and Cleavage: Party Alignment in Greece, 1945-1965," *Parliamentary Affairs*, Vol. 19, No. 3 (1966), 295-296. Trombetas makes this important point, but he devotes only a few paragraphs to the period of Metaxas and the war.

[60] Kousoulas, *Revolution and Defeat*, pp. 121-122. Kousoulas gives the details of Maniadakes's tactics, which included a government-sponsored Greek Communist Party.

CHAPTER TWO

[1] Metaxas, *Hemerologio*, IV, p. 553.

[2] Theodore A. Couloumbis, John A. Petropulos, and Harry J. Psomiades, *Foreign Interference in Greek Politics* (New York: Pella Publishing Co., Inc., 1976), p. 96.

[3] Metaxas, *Hemerologio*, II, pp. 389, 432, and 467; and Harry Cliadakis, "Greece, 1935-1941: The Metaxas Regime and the Diplomatic Background to World War II," Ph. D. dissertation, New York University, 1970, p. 191.

[4] Elisabeth Barker, *British Policy in South-East Europe in the Second World War* (New York: Barnes and Noble, 1976), p. 98, hereinafter cited as *British Policy in South-East Europe*.

[5] PRO FO371/29839 R913/96/19, Palairet to FO, February 9, 1941. Sir Michael Palairet was British Minister to Greece, 1940-1943.

[6] Barker, *British Policy in South-East Europe*, pp. 13-18.

[7] PRO FO371/22372 R5196/189/19, Memorandum by Mr. Hugh Jones, May 19, 1938; and FO371/23777 R886/886/19, Annual Report on Greece, January 31, 1939.

[8] Barker, *British Policy in South-East Europe*, pp. 13-18.

[9] Gerald Weinberg, *Germany and the Soviet Union, 1939-1941* (Leiden: Mouton, 1954), pp. 109-121.

[10] Norman Rich, *Hitler's War Aims*, Vol. I: *Ideology, the Nazi State, and the Course of Expansion* (New York: W. W. Norton, 1973), p. 180.

[11] United States Department of State, *Documents on German Foreign Policy*, Series D (1937-1945), Vol. X, *The War Years*, June 23-August 31, 1940 (Washington, D.C.: U.S. Government Printing Office, 1957), No. 73, pp. 79-83, hereinafter cited as *DGFP*, D, X.

[12] C. A. Macartney and A. W. Palmer, *An Independent Eastern Europe* (London: Macmillan, 1962), p. 426, hereinafter cited as *Eastern Europe*.

[13] *DGFP*, D, X, No. 129, pp. 147-155; No. 343, pp. 481-483; No. 353, pp. 495-498.

[14] Wiskemann, Elizabeth, *Rome-Berlin Axis*, rev. ed. (London: Fontana Library, 1966), pp. 265-266, hereinafter cited as *Rome-Berlin*; Ernst L. Presseisen, "Prelude to 'Barbarossa': Germany and the Balkans, 1940-1941," *Journal of Modern History*, Vol. 32 (December 1960), 360, hereinafter cited as "Prelude to 'Barbarossa.'"

[15] Macartney, *Eastern Europe*, pp. 426-427.

[16] U.S. Department of State, 868.00/1108, Dispatch from MacVeagh

to Secretary of State, April 8, 1940. For an analysis of Metaxas' attempt to steer a neutral course between Great Britain and Germany up to the Italian invasion see Dimitri Kitsikis, "La Grèce entre l'Angleterre et l'Allemagne de 1936 à 1941," *Revue historique*, CCXXXVIII (Juillet-Septembre 1967), 85-116.

[17] F. W. Deakin, *The Brutal Friendship: Mussolini, Hitler, and the Fall of Italian Fascism* (New York: Harper & Row, 1962), p. 13, hereinafter cited as *The Brutal Friendship*.

[18] Wiskemann, *Rome-Berlin*, pp. 267, 273-274.

[19] Ehrengard Schramm-von Thadden, *Griechenland und die Grossmaechte im Zweiten Weltkrieg* (Wiesbaden: Steiner Verlag, 1955), p. 47, hereinafter cited as *Griechenland und die Grossmaechte*. The central point of Schramm-von Thadden's study is that Hitler was prepared to sacrifice Italian interests in favor of avoiding a campaign against Greece, but that Greece rejected his unofficial feelers for German intervention as Nazi attempts to undermine Greek morale. The book was published before the opening of the records of the German Foreign Office for the years 1940-1941, and its interpretation is disputed in this chapter.

[20] *DGFP*, D, X, No. 73, p. 81. See J. R. M. Butler, *Grand Strategy*, Volume II: *September 1939-June 1941* (London: HMSO, 1957), pp. 63-70, hereinafter cited as *Grand Strategy*, II.

[21] Wiskemann, *Rome-Berlin*, p. 268.

[22] *DGFP*, D, X, No. 343, pp. 481-482.

[23] *Ibid.*, No. 320, pp. 453-454; No. 324, pp. 458-460.

[24] Germany. Wehrmacht. Oberkommando. Andreas Hillgruber und Walther Hubatsch (hrgs.), *Kriegstagebuch des Oberkommando der Wehrmacht (Wehrmachtfuehrungsstab), 1940-1945*, (Frankfurt-am-Main: Bernard & Graefe, 1962-1965), Band I: *1940-1941*, August 15, 1940, p. 36, hereinafter cited as *KTB/OKW*, I.

[25] *DGFP*, D, X, No. 333, pp. 471-472.

[26] *Ibid.*, No. 357, pp. 501-502 and No. 367, pp. 512-513.

[27] *Ibid.*, N. 394, pp. 544-545. Ribbentrop did not inform Ciano of this position until September 19. See Wiskemann, *Rome-Berlin*, p. 273.

[28] PRO FO371/24917 R7178/764/19, Palairet to FO, August 19, 1940; *ibid.*, R7225/764/19, FO to Palairet, August 24, 1940; and PRO FO371/24922 R7126/846/19, Palairet to FO, August 17, 1940.

[29] *DGFP*, D, XI, No. 407, pp. 566-567.

[30] Wiskemann, *Rome-Berlin*, p. 270.

[31] Andreas Hillgruber and Ehrengard Schramm-von Thadden believe that Ribbentrop informed Ciano on September 19, 1940, of Hitler's positive reaction to send a mission to Rumania and that Ciano purposely did not inform the Duce. See Andreas Hillgruber, *Hitler, Koenig Carol und Marschall Antonescu: Die deutsch-rumaenischen Beziehungen, 1938-1944* (Wiesbaden: Steiner Verlag, 1954), pp. 99-100, 301, fn. 61; and Schramm-von Thadden, *Griechenland und die Grossmaechte*, pp. 88-90.

[32] *KTB/OKW*, I, October 22, 1940, p. 123.

[33] *Ibid.*, October 24, 1940, p. 125; Franz Halder, *Kriegstagebuch* (Stuttgart: W. Kohlhammer Verlag, 1963), II, p. 148.

[34] *KTB/OKW*, I, October 25, 1940, p. 126.

[35] Wiskemann, *Rome-Berlin*, p. 276.

[36] *KTB/OKW*, I, October 30, 1940, p. 138. Rintelen reported that he did not expect a quick victory since the Italians did not enjoy overwhelm-

ing numerical superiority, but he gave no indications of the collapse that was to befall the Albanian offensive. See Schramm-von Thadden, *Griechenland und die Grossmaechte*, pp. 92-117.

[37] Martin Van Creveld, *Hitler's Strategy, 1940-1941* (London: Cambridge University Press, 1973), pp. 27-49, hereinafter cited as *Hitler's Strategy*.

[38] *Ibid.* See also Andreas Hillgruber, *Hitlers Strategie 1940-1941; Politik und Kriegsfuehrung* (Frankfurt-am-Main: Bernard und Graefe Verlag fuer Wehrwesen, 1965), pp. 178-191, hereinafter cited as *Hitlers Strategie.* Hillgruber emphasizes the improvised character of the "peripheral" strategy, which may explain why the Italian and German cooperation on operational planning did not exist in regard to Greece's role in the "Axis" strategy. Creveld overlooks this improvised character of the strategy and fails to see that only after the failure of the Italian invasion did Hitler begin to press Spain to enter the war and to fully develop the "peripheral" strategy. See Norman Rich, *Hitler's War Aims*, I, p. 171. For a recent analysis of Creveld's thesis see Charles Cruickshank, *Greece, 1940-1941* (London: Davis-Poynter, 1976), pp. 38-39.

[39] Franz Halder, *The Private Journal of Generaloberst Franz Halder 14 August 1939 to 24 September 1942* (Mimeographed English translation in 8 volumes), Volume V: Second Winter, October 31, 1940—February 20, 1941, November 2, 1940, hereinafter cited as *Halder Diary;* and *KTB/OKW*, I, November 3, p. 147.

[40] *KTB/OKW*, I, November 4, 1940, p. 150.

[41] Cervi, *Hollow Legions*, p. 157.

[42] *DGFP*, D, XI, No. 295, pp. 479-480; *Halder Diary*, V, November 5, 1940.

[43] *KTB/OKW*, I, November 9, 1940, pp. 161-162.

[44] U.S. Department of State, *Nazi-Soviet Relations 1939-1941*, ed. by Raymond J. Sontag and James S. Beddie (Washington, D.C.: U.S. Government Printing Office, 1948), pp. 206-207, 230, 231-232, 244-246; Presseisen, "Prelude to 'Barbarossa,' " 362-363.

[45] Germany. Wehrmacht. Oberkommando. *Blitzkrieg to Defeat: Hitler's War Directives 1939-1945*, ed. by Hugh Trevor-Roper (New York: Holt, Rinehart and Winston, 1964), pp. 38-39, hereinafter cited as *Hitler's War Directives.*

[46] *Ibid.*

[47] *KTB/OKW*, I, November 13, 1940, p. 171.

[48] *Halder Diary*, November 13, 1940.

[49] *DGFP*, D, XI, No. 353, p. 606; No. 369, pp. 639-643.

[50] *Grand Strategy*, II, pp. 365-369.

[51] *KTB/OKW*, I, November 22, 1940, p. 185.

[52] *DGFP*, D, XI, No. 388, p. 688.

[53] *DGFP*, D, XI, No. 248 pp. 423-424; No. 287, p. 466; and No. 395, p. 701.

[54] PRO FO371/24921 R9113/764/19, Palairet to FO, December 29, 1940, and a Minute by Edward Warner, Southern Department, December 31, 1940.

[55] *Halder Diary*, V, November 24, 1940.

[56] *KTB/OKW*, I, December 5, 1940, pp. 204-205.

[57] Hillgruber, *Hitlers Strategie*, p. 289, and Charles B. Burdick,

" 'Operation Cyclamen,' Germany, Albania, 1940-1941," *Journal of Central European Affairs*, Vol. 19 (December 1959), 23-25, 30-31.

[58] PRO FO371/24921 R8824/764/19 Hoare (Sir Samuel) to FO, December 5, 1940.

[59] PRO FO371/48266 R6981/4/19, Leeper to Eden, April 18, 1945.

[60] Trevor-Roper (ed.), *Hitler's War Directives*, pp. 46-48.

[61] Schramm-von Thadden, *Griechenland und die Grossmaechte*, pp. 217-218. An *Aufzeichnung* by Admiral Argyropoulos dated July 3, 1952.

[62] *Ibid.*

[63] Cervi, *Hollow Legions*, p. 183.

[64] Schramm-von Thadden, *Griechenland und die Grossmaechte*, p. 218. Hohenberg's *Aufzeichnung* is printed on pp. 218-222.

[65] *Ibid.*, pp. 219-220. In his *Aufzeichnung*, Major Hohenberg claims he obeyed his superiors and avoided further contact with Greeks over this question. The published records of the German Foreign Ministry, however, show that Hohenberg had discussions with Greek politicians and officials as late as March 16, 1941, when he received very important information from Georgios Merkoures. Hohenberg makes no mention of these discussions in his *Aufzeichnung*, but states his foray into diplomacy ended in December 1940. See below, p. 49.

[66] *Ibid.*, p. 152.

[67] *DGFP*, D, XI, No. 540, p. 916.

[68] PRO FO371/24921 R9113/764/19, Palairet to FO, December 29, 1940.

[69] Van Creveld, *Hitler's Strategy*, p. 87.

[70] *Ibid.* For Papagos's views see PRO War Office (WO) 106/3127, Major General T. G. Heywood (Chief of the British Military Mission to Athens) to Wavell, February 7, 1941.

[71] *DGFP*, D, XI, No. 603, p. 1023.

[72] *DGFP*, D, XI, No. 648, pp. 1083-1084.

[73] *Grand Strategy*, II, p. 376.

[74] *DGFP*, D, XI, No. 665, pp. 1114-1116.

[75] E. L. Woodward, *British Foreign Policy in the Second World War* (London: HMSO, 1971), vol. I, p. 520, hereinafter cited as *British Foreign Policy*.

[76] PRO WO106/3127, Heywood to Wavell, February 7, 1941; and PRO FO371/29828 R916/34/19, Greek Minister President (Koryzis) to PM (Churchill), February 8, 1941.

[77] Cervi, *Hollow Legions*, p. 211.

[78] PRO FO371/29839 R913/96/19, Palairet to FO, February 9, 1941.

[79] PRO FO371/29813 R186/9/19, Memorandum by the Bishop of Ioannina, June 16, 1944.

[80] Woodward, *British Foreign Policy*, I, p. 521.

[81] *KTB/OKW*, I, January 29, 1941, p. 285.

[82] *DGFP*, D, XI, No. 738, p. 1236.

[83] *Halder Diary*, V, February 17, 1941.

[84] Anthony Eden, *The Memoirs of Anthony Eden: The Reckoning* (Boston: Houghton Mifflin Co., 1965), p. 232.

[85] *Grand Strategy*, II, p. 441.

[86] PRO PREM 3 206/3, Churchill to Wavell, March 6, 1941.

[87] The controversy over Papagos's failure to withdraw to the Aliakhmon line has been explained by two recent authors who lay the responsi-

bility for the misunderstanding on Eden and the British Military Mission. See M. Van Creveld, "Prelude to Disaster: The British Decision to Aid Greece, 1940-1941," *Journal of Contemporary History*, Vol. 9 (July 1974), 85-86; and Cruikshank, *Greece, 1940-1941*, pp. 179-181.

[88] Barker, *British Policy in South-East Europe*, p. 103.

[89] *Halder Diary*, VI, March 8-10, 1941; *KTB/OKW*, I, March 10, 1941.

[90] *DGFP*, D, XII, No. 155, pp. 279-280. Colonel Petinis was technically correct, as the Australian and New Zealand divisions had not yet moved north into Macedonia.

[91] *Ibid.*, No. 170, pp. 299-300. These discussions are not mentioned in Hohenberg's *Aufzeichnung*.

[92] *Ibid.*, No. 179, pp. 315-316.

[93] Creveld, *Hitler's Strategy*, p. 133.

[94] *DGFP*, D, XII, No. 180, pp. 316-317.

[95] *Ibid.*

[96] *DGFP*, D, XII, No. 191, pp. 331-332.

[97] *KTB/OKW*, I, March 18, 1941, pp. 359-361.

[98] *Ibid.*, March 24, 1941, p. 364.

[99] Field Marshall List's force consisted of six infantry divisions, two motorized divisions, and two Panzer divisions with 1,200 tanks. The German Air Force under General Alexander Loehr consisted of 210 fighters, 400 bombers, and 170 reconnaissance planes. The Italians launched their offensive with twenty-eight divisions and 320 aircraft. Against the Germans, Greece posted six divisions, one motorized, and eighty aircraft plus the British force of two infantry divisions and an armored brigade. Against the Italians, Greece possessed fifteen infantry divisions and two brigades. For the military phases see the official histories I.S.O. Playfair, *The Mediterranean and Middle East*, Vol. I: *Early Success Against Italy* (London: HMSO, 1960), Chapter XX; Gavin Long, *Greece, Crete, Syria, Australia in the War*, Series I, Vol. II (Canberra, 1953), Chs. I-III; William G. McClymont, *To Greece*, Vol. II of the *Official History of New Zealand in World War II* (Wellington, 1959); and Christopher Buckley, *Greece and Crete, 1941* (London: HMSO, 1953) which is a popular history culled from the official accounts; and Anthony Heckstall-Smith, *Greek Tragedy, 1941* (New York: Norton, 1961), a more personal account. The Greek side is presented in Alexandros Papagos, *The Battle of Greece* (Athens: J. M. Scazikis "Alpha" Editions, 1949), and in two works very critical of the general staff's and government's handling of the war: Lieutenant-General Demitrios Katheniotes, *He Kiriotera Stratigike Phasis tou Polemou, 1940-1941* [The Main Phases of the War, 1940-1941] (Athens, 1946). Katheniotes served on a commission appointed to investigate the conduct of the war and wrote a 1,500-page report. After suppression of the report he wrote his own account. Neokosmos Gregoriades, *Ho Pankosmios Polemos, 1939-1945*, Tomos A, *Elleniko-Italo-Germanikos Polemos, 1940-1941* [The World War, 1939-1945, Vol. I: The Greek-Italo-German War, 1940-1941] (Athens, 1945), a leftist account. The German side is presented in George Blau, *The German Campaign in the Balkans, Spring 1941* (Washington, D.C.: U.S. Department of the Army, 1953), a short account based on the records of the German Twelfth Army; Kurt von Tippelskirch, "Der Deutsche Balkanfeldzug, 1941," *Wehrwissenschaftliche Rundschau*, III, Nr. 2 (1955), 49-65; and Alexander Buchner, *Der Deutsche Griechenland Feld-*

zug; Operationen der 12. Armee, 1941, Bd. 14 *Die Wehrmacht im Kampf* (Heidelberg: K. Vowinckel, 1957).

¹⁰⁰ Cervi, *Hollow Legions*, p. 282.

¹⁰¹ PRO FO371/29840 R3895/96/19, Palairet to FO, April 14, 1941.

¹⁰² U.S. Department of State, 868.00/1124, MacVeagh to SS (Ambassador Lincoln MacVeagh to the Secretary of State), June 24, 1941.

¹⁰³ PRO FO371/29840 R4172/96/19, Palairet to FO, April 19, 1941.

¹⁰⁴ *DGFP*, D, XII, No. 409, pp. 946-947. Tsolakoglou made it a point not to surrender to the Italians until after capitulating to the Germans.

¹⁰⁵ U.S. Department of State, 868.00/1124.

CHAPTER THREE

¹ Fuehrer Directive No. 31, June 9, 1941, H. Trevor-Roper (ed.), *Hitler's War Directives*, pp. 74-77. For a general survey of the German administration in Southeast Europe see Norman Rich, *Hitler's War Aims, Vol. II: The Establishment of the New Order* (London: André Deutsch, 1974), Chapter 9.

The charts following p. 55 attempt to clarify this alphabet soup of German agencies.

² *Befh. Saloniki-Aegaeis* included the hinterland of Salonica, Lemnos, Chios, Mytilene, and Skyros. *Befh. Sued-Grld.* contained Athens-Piraeus, Crete, Cythera, Anticythera, and Melos. The *Admiral Aegaeis* dealt with coastal defenses.

³ Fuehrer Directive No. 48, July 26, 1943, Trevor-Roper (ed.), *Hitler's War Directives*, pp. 142-145.

⁴ *HGrE* 65024/2 (*Verschiedenes Berichte. Okdo. H. Gr. E.*, Ia, December 9, 1943-July 30, 1944), *Verwaltungsbericht* September 1943; T-311, Roll 175, Frame 000888.

⁵ *Mil. Befh. Suedost* 75000/5 (*Abwicklung. Mil. Befh. Suedost*, ca. February 13, 1945); T-501, Roll 258. Frames 000479-000482.

⁶ *OKW/731, W. B. Suedost Propaganda-Abt, Lagebericht* April 1942; T-71, Roll 1934, Frames 6506520-6506530.

⁷ *Mil. Befh. Suedost* 75000/5; T-501, Roll 258, Frames 000467-469.

⁸ *Befh. Sued.-Grld.* 40141/3 (*Anlagenband zum KTB* Nov. 20, 1942-Nov. 19, 1943), *Verwaltungsbericht* September 1943; T-501, Roll 252, Frame 000084.

⁹ *Wi/1C1.4* (*OKW/Wi. Stb. Ausl. KTB* September 7, 1943-October 6, 1944), *Vortrag Wi. Stb. Grld.*, February 3, 1944.

¹⁰ Alexander Dallin, *German Rule in Russia* (London: Macmillan & Co., 1957), p. 98.

¹¹ *Persoenlicher Stab RF-SS*, EAP 161-b-12/274b (Miscellaneous Correspondence), Letter from Schimana to Himmler, September 9, 1944; T-175, Roll 75, Frame 2592933.

¹² Council of Foreign Ministers. Annex I: "Statement of Allied Govern-

ments on the German Problem," Memorandum presented by the Greek
Government. (London: Lancaster House, 1947), pp. 82-87.
[13] *Wi/1C1.41 (KTB VO OKW/Wi. Rue. Amt. AOK 12 (IV Wi)*, January 1-December 31, 1942), *Lagebericht W. B. Suedost IV Amt*, March 14,
1942.
[14] *Wi/1C1.42 (Taetigkeitsbericht VO OKW/Wi. Rue. Amt. AOK 12
(IV Wi)*, April 23, 1941-July 31, 1941), *Verordnung ueber Beschlagnahme
in den besetzen griech. Gebieten*, May 15, 1941. See Administrative
Chart II on page 57.
[15] *Wi/1C1.39 (KTB VO OKW/Wi. Rue. Amt. AOK 12 (IV Wi)*, April
26-June 30, 1941) ; May 25, 1941, and June 22, 1941.
[16] *Wi/1C1.40 (KTB VO OKW/Wi. Rue. Amt. AOK 12 (IV Wi)*, July 7-
December 31, 1941), *W. B. Suedost IV Wi to OKW/Wi. Rue. Amt.*, October 9, 1941.
[17] U.S. Department of State, 740.0011/14258, MacVeagh to Secretary
of State, June 16, 1941.
[18] *Wi/1C1.41, Wehrwirtschaftliche Lage im Bereich des W. B. Suedost*, March 14, 1942.
[19] *Wi/1C1.6 [OKW/Fw Amt* December 31, 1943-November 14, 1944
(Folder of the *OKW Feldwirtschaftsamt*)]; *Abschlussbericht ueber die
Erzfoerderung in Griechenland*, September 10, 1944.
[20] *Wi/1C1.9 [OKW/Wi. Rue. Amt.* December 31, 1940-October 31, 1941
(Misc. Reports)]; Memorandum from Greek Minister of Finance Soteris
Gotzamanes to Altenburg, October 10, 1941.
[21] *Wi/1C1.4, Wi. Stb. Grld.*, June 10, 1944.
[22] *Wi/1C1.42*, Letter from *W. B. Suedost* List to Keitel, July 16, 1941.
[23] *Wi/1C1.9*, Altenburg to *OKW*, September 25, 1941.
[24] *Ibid.*, Keitel to Altenburg, October 21, 1941.
[25] *Wi/1C1.31 (KTB WO Athen* June 1943), *Lagebericht* of June 25,
1943, and *Wi//1C1.4, Schnellbriefen Ha Pol* IV b, Nos. 2007/44, September 20, 1944, and 114/44, October 10, 1944.
[26] On November 1, 1943, Neubacher became *Sonderbevollmaechtigter*
for the whole southeast.
[27] *Wi/1C1.27 (KTB WO Athen* October 1, 1942-December 31, 1942),
Entry for October 9, 1942; and *Wi/1C1.30 (KTB WO Athen* March 1942),
Aktennotiz, March 19, 1943.
[28] *Wi/1C1.27, Lagerbericht* for October 1943; and *Wi/1C1.30*, Report
by the *Deutsche Reichsbank*, March 23, 1943.
[29] *Wi/1C1.4*, Report on gold selling by the *Deutsche Reichsbank,
Volkswirtschaftliche Abteilung*, August 8, 1944.
[30] Marshall Lee Miller, *Bulgaria During the Second World War* (Stanford: Stanford University Press, 1975), p. 127.
[31] *Wi/1C1.39*. Entry for June 20, 1941; and *Wi/1C1.10 (OKW Wi. Rue.
Amt.*, Misc. Reports, December 31, 1940-December 31, 1941) ; "*Deutschland und die gegenwaertig Lage in Griechenland*," July 1941.
[32] *Wi/1C1.42, OKW/Wi. Rue. Amt.* to Altenburg, May 15, 1941.
[33] *Wi/1C1.24 (Anlagenband zu KTB WO Athen* August 29-December 31, 1941), *Bremer Baumwoll-Akteingesellschaft* to *OKW/Wi. Rue.
Amt.*, August 11, 1941.
[34] *DGFP*, D, XIII, No. 323, pp. 512-514. Memorandum by Director
of the Economic Policy Department of the Foreign Ministry, Wiehl,
September 15, 1941.

[35] *Wi/1C1.40, W. B. Suedost* to *OKW*, October 9, 1941.

[36] *Wi/1C1.9*, Altenburg to Foreign Minister, September 25, 1941.

[37] *DGFP*, D, XIII, No. 419, pp. 676-678, Memorandum by Minister Eisenlohr of October 24, 1941.

[38] Galeazzo Ciano, *The Ciano Diaries, 1939-1943*, ed. by Hugh Gibson (Garden City, New York: Doubleday, 1946), p. 387.

[39] *Wi/1C1.24*, Altenburg to Foreign Minister, November 3, 1941.

[40] Commission de gestion pour les secours en Grèce sous les auspices du Comité international de la Croix Rouge. *Ravitaillement de la Grèce pendant l'occupation, 1941-1944, et pendant les premiers cinq mois après la libération.* Rapport final (rédigé par Bengt Helger), Athènes, Impr. de la "Société hellénique d'éditions," 1949, p. 33, hereinafter cited as *Ravitaillement de la Grèce*.

[41] *Wi/1C1.40, Wirtschaftslage Griechenland*, November 15, 1941.

[42] *Ravitaillement de la Grèce*, pp. 28-29, 38.

[43] *Ibid.*, 606.

[44] *Auswaertiges Amt, Buero des Staatssekretaers; Griechenland* November 1, 1942-June 30, 1943; Altenburg to Ribbentrop, January 14, 1943; T-120, Roll 166, Frames 81739-81741; hereinafter cited as *Ausw. Amt., Staatssekretaer.*

[45] *Ibid.*, April 1, 1941-April 1, 1942; Altenburg to Ribbentrop, July 14, 1941; T-120, Roll 257, Frame 127662.

[46] U.S. Department of State. *Foreign Relations of the United States, Diplomatic Papers, 1942*, Volume II; *Europe* (Washington, D.C.: U.S. Government Printing Office, 1962), pp. 732-733, Secretary of State Cordell Hull to Ambassador Winant, December 3, 1941, hereinafter cited as *FRUS.*

[47] *Ibid.*, Winant to Secretary of State, January 13, 1942, p. 732.

[48] *Ibid.*, Winant to Secretary of State, January 17, 1942, pp. 734-735.

[49] *Ibid.*, Winant to Secretary of State, February 22, 1942, pp. 739-741.

[50] *Ibid.*, Minister in Sweden (Johnson) to Secretary of State, April 30, 1942, pp. 758-759; June 10, 1942, pp. 761-762; and July 9, 1942, pp. 769-770; and *Mil. Befh. Suedost* 75000/5; T-501, Roll 258, Frame 000490.

[51] *Wi/1C1.30 (WO Athen KTB* May 1943) ; *Lagebericht* May 5, 1943.

[52] Conrad Roediger, "Die Internationale Hilfsaktion fuer die Bevoelkerung Griechenlands im Zweiten Weltkrieg," *Vierteljahrshefte fuer Zeitgeschichte*, XI (1963), 70-71.

[53] *Mil. Befh. Suedost* 75000/5; T-501, Roll 258, Frame 000492.

[54] *Befh. Saloniki-Aegaeis* 15740/1 (*KTB* May 21-July 31, 1941), Entry for June 1, 1941; T-501, Roll 48, Frames 000798-799; and *Befh. Saloniki-Aegaeis* 15740/2 (*Taetigkeitsbericht* August 1-December 31, 1941), *Monatlicher Verwaltungsbericht* September 1941; T-501, Roll 245, Frames 000078-000079.

[55] *Wi/1C1.36, Lagebericht* for May 1941; and *Wi/1C1.27 (KTB WO Athen* October 1-December 31, 1941), Entry for November 1, 1941.

[56] *Wi/1C1.29 (KTB WO Athen* February 1943), Entry for February 1, 1943.

[57] *Befh. Sued-Grld. 40131/1b (Anlagenband zum KTB* November 22, 1942-August 10, 1943), *Bericht am Partisan Taetigkeit* December 2, 1942; T-501, Roll 252, Frames 001109-000110.

[58] *Wi/1C1.29*, Entry for February 25, 1943.

[59] *Wi/1C1.32 (KTB WO Athen* July 1-September 30, 1943), *Lage-*

berichte for June, July, August, and September 1943; *Wi/1C1.33* (*KTB Wi. Stb. Grld.*, October 31-December 31, 1943), *Lageberichte* for October, November and December 1943; and *NOKW*-692.

⁶⁰ *Mil. Befh. Suedost* 75000/5; T-501, Roll 258, Frame 000471, 000591.

⁶¹ Other members of the first quisling government were Lt. Generals Panagiotes Demestichas (Foreign Ministry), Georgios Bakos (National Security), Charalambos Katsimetros (Labor), S. Moutouses (Agriculture), Major General Georgios Vrachnos (Education), Nikolaos Louvares (Communications) and Konstantinos Logothetopoulos (Welfare), *Ausw. Amt., Staatssekretaer Grld.*, Benzler to Ribbentrop April 28, 1941; T-120, Roll 257, Frame 127490.

⁶² *DGFP*, D, XIII, No. 246, p. 394.

⁶³ *Ausw. Amt., Staatssekretaer Grld.*, Altenburg to Ribbentrop May 8, 1941; T-120, Roll 257, Frames 127545-127546.

⁶⁴ *Befh. Saloniki-Aegaeis* 15740/2, *Monatlicher Verwaltungsbericht* September 1941; T-501, Roll 245, Frame 000073; U.S. Department of State OSS (R&A), No. 872, "Report on Greek Quislings and Pro-Axis Organizations," April 26, 1943; and Christos Zalokostas, *To Chroniko tes Sklavias* [The Time of Slavery] (Athens: Estias, n.d.), pp. 34-36, hereinafter cited as *Chroniko tes Sklavias*.

⁶⁵ William Byford-Jones, *The Greek Trilogy* (London: Hutchinson, 1945), p. 117, hereinafter cited as *Greek Trilogy*.

⁶⁶ *Befh. Sued-Grld.* 40131/3b, *Lagebericht* for November 1942; T-501, Roll 252, Frame 000099.

⁶⁷ *Mil. Befh. Suedost* 75000/5; T-501, Roll 258, Frame 000492. In general, the basis of Greek collaborationism was more social and ideological, as in France, than ethnic, as in other Balkan and East European occupied territories. See Stanley Hoffman, "Collaborationism in France during World War II," *The Journal of Modern History*, Vol. 40 (September 1968), 375-395; and John A. Armstrong, "Collaborationism in World War II: The Integral Nationalist Variant in Eastern Europe," *Ibid.*, 396-410.

⁶⁸ Byford-Jones, *Greek Trilogy*, p. 118.

⁶⁹ *Wi/1C1.4*, Rallis Government, August 3, 1943.

⁷⁰ Komnenos Pyromaglou, *"Ta Tagmata Asphaleias"* [The Security Battalions], *Istorike Epitheoresis* [*Historical Review*], VI (Oktombrios-Dekembrios 1964), 530 ff. The article includes a series of Pangalos's letters to Rallis between June 1 and Aug. 1, 1943.

⁷¹ PRO FO371/48278 R14308/4/19, Annual Report on Greek Affairs, 1943, July 27, 1945.

⁷² *Ibid.*

⁷³ Byford-Jones, *Greek Trilogy*, p. 118.

⁷⁴ *Befh. Sued-Grld.* 40131/3b, *Ic* Report of December 11, 1942; T-501, Roll 252, Frame 001034.

⁷⁵ PRO FO371/43687 R7521/9/19, BLO (British Liaison Officer) NW Thessaly to Cairo, May 9, 1944. The BLO identified the Volos group as the *Ethnikos Agrotikos Synthesmos Antikommounistikis Draseos* (EASAD—National Rural Union of Anticommunist Action).

⁷⁶ *Persoenlicher Stab RF-SS*, EAP 161-b-12-274b, *"Auszug aus dem Bericht des HSSPF ueber den Einsatz von Polizeikraeften in Griechenland,"* November 2, 1944; T-175, Roll 75, Frames 2592928-2592930.

[77] *Ibid.*, Himmler to Schimana, November 2, 1944; T-175, Roll 75, Frames 2592926-2592927.

[78] Woodhouse, *Apple of Discord*, pp. 94-96.

[79] See below, Chapter V, pp. 142-143.

[80] *HGrE* 65721/2 (*KTB, Ia,* September 1944), Entries for September 13, 16, 29, and 30; T-311, Roll 182, Frames 000681, 000696, and 000771; and *HGrE* 65036/2 (*Anlagenband zum KTB Ia,* September 1944), Telegram from *LXVIII AK* to *HGrE,* September 15, 1944; T-311, Roll 181, Frame 000748.

[81] Hermann Franz, *Gebirgsjaeger der Polizei* (Bad Nauheim: Podzun, 1963), p. 87.

[82] See below, Chapter VI, pp. 196-197.

[83] *Mil. Befh. Suedost* 75000/2, T-501, Roll 258, Frame 000534.

[84] *OKW/731, W. B. Suedost, Propaganda Abt. Suedost, Lagebericht* for April 1942; T-71, Roll 1034, Frames 6506520-6506525. *OKW/639, HGrE Propaganda Abt., Propaganda Weisungen,* February 3, 1943, and March 4, 1943; T-71, Roll 1006, Frames 2470491-2470502.

[85] *Eleutheron Vema,* February 9, 1943; and *Proia,* January 19, 1944.

[86] Komnenos Pyromaglou, *Ho Doureios Ippos* (Athens, 1958), *passim,* hereinafter cited as *Doureios Ippos* and Pyromaglou, *Ho Georgios Kartalis,* pp. 636-645.

[87] Walter Warlimont, *Inside Hitler's Headquarters* (New York: Frederick Praeger, 1964), p. 282, hereinafter cited as *Inside Hitler's Headquarters.*

[88] *KTB/OKW,* III, pt. i, pp. 121, 209, 265.

[89] *Ibid.,* pp. 747, 767.

[90] *Ibid.,* pp. 9, 261, 767.

[91] *HGrE* 65023 (*Taetigkeitsbericht HGrE aus den Jahren* 1940-1943), *Aktennotiz* March 27, 1942; T-311, Roll 175, Frame 00450; and *HGrE* 65024/2 *Tagesmeldung* May 1-December 31, 1943), List of troop numbers, December 6, 1943; T-311, Roll 175, Frame 000909.

[92] Warlimont, *Inside Hitler's Headquarters,* pp. 317-318, and Deakin, *Brutal Friendship,* pp. 346-357.

[93] *KTB/OKW,* III, pt. ii, p. 1562.

[94] Barker, *British Policy in South-East Europe,* pp. 116-119; and Michael Howard, *The Mediterranean Strategy in the Second World War* (London: Weidenfeld and Nicolson, 1968), Chapter 3. Howard argues that Churchill's interest in a Balkan front grew out of his military strategy for victory rather than a political strategy to block the Russians.

[95] Deakin, *Brutal Friendship,* pp. 352-353.

[96] *Sonderbevollmaechtigter Suedost* 75000/27 (*Bevollmaechtigter des Reiches fuer Griechenland,* May-November 1943), *Sipo* and *SD* to *O. B. Suedost,* May 28, 1943; T-501, Roll 259, Frames 000632-000633.

[97] *HGrE* 65027/1 (*KTB HGrE, Ia,* July 1, 1943-August 31, 1943), Entry for July 26, 1943; T-311, Roll 176, Frames 000046-000048.

[98] *KTB/OKW,* III, pt. ii, pp. 841-842.

[99] *HGrE* 65027/1, *passim;* T-311, Roll 175, Frames 000065-000151.

[100] *KTB/OKW,* III, pt. ii, p. 1562. These units included the following: *Sturm-Division Rhodos, 1 Gebirgdivision, 1 Panzer Division, 104 Jaeg. Division, 117 Jaeg. Division, 11 Fw-Feld-Div., SS-Pol-Pz-Rgts. 1, 2* and *18, Festung-Brigade-Kreta.*

[101] Charles F. Delzell, *Mussolini's Enemies: The Anti-Fascist Resist-*

ance (Princeton, N.J.: Princeton University Press, 1961), pp. 247-248, 253-258, hereinafter cited as *Mussolini's Enemies*.

[102] *HGrE* 65027/2 (*KTB HGrE, Ia,* September 1, 1943-October 31, 1943), Entry for September 8, 1943; T-311, Roll 176, Frame 000166.

[103] *XXII Geb. AK* 46520/2 (*Anlagenband zum KTB, Ia,* August-October 11, 1943), Letter of Gandin to commander of the *Fest.-Rgt 966* of September 11, 1943; T-314, Roll 670, Frame 000390.

[104] *HGrE* 65027/2, Entry for September 14, 1943; T-311, Roll 176, Frame 000105.

[105] *HGrE* 65025 (*Taetigkeitsbericht* May 1-December 31, 1943), Report for September 24, 1943; T-311, Roll 175, Frame 001105.

[106] *HGrE* 65024/2 (Misc. Reports of *HGrE* December 9, 1943-July 30, 1944), *Tagesmeldung* of December 6, 1943; T-311, Roll 175, Frame 000913.

[107] Michael Molho and Joseph Nehama, *In Mémoriam. Hommage aux victimes juives des nazis en Grèce* (Salonique: N. Nicolaides, 1948-1949), Vol. 1, pp. 2-12, 22-28, hereinafter cited as *In Mémoriam*.

[108] Dawidowicz, *War Against the Jews*, p. 343. Dawidowicz cites a figure of 13,000, but Molho and Nehama put it at 4,000.

[109] Gerald Reitlinger, *The Final Solution: The Attempt to Exterminate the Jews of Europe, 1939-1945* (New York: A. S. Barnes, 1961), p. 370, hereinafter cited as *Final Solution*.

[110] Raul Hilberg, *The Destruction of the European Jews* (Chicago: Quadrangle, 1961), p. 442, hereinafter cited as *Destruction of European Jews*.

[111] Molho, *In Mémoriam*, I, p. 35.

[112] Hilberg, *Destruction of European Jews*, p. 443.

[113] Molho, *In Mémoriam*, I, p. 61. Facsimiles of documents relating to the final solution in Greece are published in Molho's *The Destruction of Greek Jewry* (Jerusalem: Yad Yashem, 1965, in Hebrew), between pp. 64-65. There is an Introduction in English to this revised edition of *In Mémoriam*.

[114] Hilberg, *Destruction of European Jews*, pp. 443-448; Molho, *In Mémoriam*, I, pp. 95-100.

[115] *Ibid.*; Reitlinger, *Final Solution*, pp. 375-376.

[116] Reitlinger, *Final Solution*, pp. 374-375.

[117] Hilberg, *Destruction of European Jews*, pp. 449-450.

[118] Molho, *In Mémoriam*, II, pp. 58-59.

[119] PRO 371/43676 R13507/11/19, July 7, 1944, AMM (Allied Military Mission) to Cairo.

[120] Molho, *In Mémoriam*, II, pp. 72-73, 164-166.

[121] Hilberg, *Destruction of European Jews*, p. 453.

[122] Molho, *In Mémoriam*, I, pp. 100-101.

[123] *Ibid.*, II, pp. 39-40, 58-59. Wisliceny and Loehr were tried and executed as war criminals in 1948, Loehr by the Yugoslav government and Wisliceny at Nuremberg. Merten escaped capture until 1959. On January 26, 1959, the Greek parliament passed a bill to halt prosecution of war criminals no longer living in Greece. On March 5, 1959, Merten was arrested in Greece where he was traveling as a tourist. A Greek court sentenced him to twenty-five years in prison after finding him guilty on thirteen of twenty charges. The Karamanlis government, however, released him on November 5, 1959. The West German government rearrested him on his return to Munich, but later released him. See *New*

York Times, January 30, 1959, p. 7; March 6, 1959, p. 14; and November 6, 1959, p. 16; and *Der Spiegel,* No. 40 (1960), p. 34.
¹²⁴ Hilberg, *Destruction of European Jews,* p. 450.

CHAPTER FOUR

¹ U.S. Department of State, 740.0011/13732, Summary Report from Ambassador Lincoln MacVeagh to the Secretary of State, June 28, 1941, hereinafter cited as U.S. Dept. of State, 740.0011/13732.

² Letter to author from E. G. Boxshall, Whitehall, March 21, 1975.

³ *Befh. Saloniki-Aegaeis* 15740/1 (*KTB Befh. Saloniki-Aegaeis,* May 21-July 31, 1942) ; T-501, Roll 48, Frame 000783.

⁴ *Ibid.,* Frame 000788.

⁵ U.S. Dept. of State, 740.0011/13732.

⁶ *Ibid.*

⁷ *Befh. Saloniki-Aegaeis* 15740/1, Entry for July 2, 1941; T-501, Roll 48, Frame 000799.

⁸ *Befh. Saloniki-Aegaeis* 15740/2 (*Taetigkeitsbericht,* August 1-December 31, 1941), *Monatlicher Verwaltungsbericht* for August 1941; T-501, Roll 245, Frames 000061-000062.

⁹ *Wi/1C1.40* (KTB *Wi. Rue. Amt. AOK 12,* July 1-December 31, 1941), Entry for July 5, 1941.

¹⁰ *Befh. Saloniki-Aegaeis* 15740/2, *Monatlicher Verwaltungsbericht,* August 1941; T-501, Roll 245, Frames 000061-000062. *Wi/1C1.24* (*Anlagenband z. KTB Nr. 1 WO Athen,* August 29-December 31, 1941), *Bremer Baumwoll-Aktiengesellschaften* to *OKW/Wi. Rue. Amt.,* August 31, 1941.

¹¹ *Befh. Saloniki-Aegaeis* 15740/2, *Taetigkeitsbericht,* September 15, 1941; T-501, Roll 245, Frame 000029.

¹² *Ibid.,* see Dimitri Kitsikis, "La famine en Grèce (1941-1942). Les conséquences politiques," *Revue d'histoire de la deuxième guerre mondiale,* XIX, No. 74 (Avril 1969), 23-28, hereinafter cited as "La famine en Grèce."

¹³ *Befh. Saloniki-Aegaeis* 15740/2, *Taetigkeitsbericht,* September 15, 1941; T-501, Roll 245, Frame 000028.

¹⁴ *NOKW*-1660 (Daily Reports of the *W. B. Suedost,* July 1-December 31, 1941).

¹⁵ Dominique Eudes, *The Kapetanios: Partisans and Civil War in Greece, 1943-1949* (New York: Monthly Review Press, 1972), pp. 3-4, hereinafter cited as *The Kapetanios;* André Kédros, *La résistance grecque* (Paris: Robert Laffont, 1966), pp. 89-93, hereinafter cited as *La résistance grecque.* Kédros quotes extensively from *Ethnike Antistasi* (Prague), vol. I, p. 81: "Hemerologia tis Antistasis" ["Calendar of the Resistance"]. According to this source, in April 1941 the KKE representatives founded the "Patriotic Front" in Epirus, the "Sacred Battalion" in eastern Macedonia, and the "Friendly Society" in the Peloponnese during June. In Salonica, the source continues, the KKE of Mace-

donia circulated handbills calling on the population to resist the Axis.
[16] See p. 98. Kédros's source claims that three Germans were killed, but
actually only two died. The EDA volumes were published under the direction of Yannis Yannikos, *St'Armata! St'Armata! Istoria tes Ethnikes
Antistasis, 1940-1945* [To Arms! To Arms! The History of the National
Resistance] (Athens: Y. Yannikos, n.d.).

[17] *NOKW*-1660.

[18] *NOKW*-1330 and *NOKW*-1380.

[19] *Befh. Saloniki-Aegaeis* 15740/2, *Taetigkeitsbericht*, October 1941;
T-501, Roll 245, Frames 000036, 000086.

[20] *Befh. Saloniki-Aegaeis* 15740/2, T-501, Roll 245, Frame 000045.
Befh. Saloniki-Aegaeis 27052 (*Taetigkeitsbericht*, January 1-April 30,
1942), *Monatlicher Verwaltungsbericht*, January-April 1942; T-501, Roll
247, Frames 000154, 000161, and 000191. *Befh. Saloniki-Aegaeis* (*Taetigkeitsbericht*, May 1-December 31, 1942), *Monatlicher Verwaltungsbericht*,
May-August 1942; T-501, Roll 247, Frames 000196-000247.

[21] Jozo Tomasevich, *War and Revolution in Yugoslavia, 1941-1945*, vol.
1: *The Chetniks* (Stanford: Stanford University Press, 1975), pp. 121-122,
hereinafter cited as *The Chetniks*.

[22] PRO FO371/29909 R8414/8414/19 Palairet to FO, September 15,
1941; PRO FO371/29842 R10894/96/19 FO to M.I.5 (Cairo), Dec. 30, 1941.

[23] Pyromaglou, *Ho Georgios Kartalis*, p. 140.

[24] PRO FO371/43677 R1861/9/19, Letter from "Military Hierarchy"
to E. Tsouderos, January 24, 1944.

[25] Edmund C. W. Myers, *The Greek Entanglement* (London: Hart-Davis,
1955), p. 103, hereinafter cited as *Greek Entanglement*.

[26] PRO FO371/37206 R10450/4/19, Memorandum by Damaskinos, n.d.;
received by FO October 1, 1943.

[27] PRO FO371/33167 R1362/112/19, FO Memorandum, "The Greek
Constitutional Question, April 1941-February 1942," Feb. 26, 1942.

[28] PRO FO371/33160 R624/40/19, Palairet to FO, March 5, 1942.

[29] PRO FO371/33162 R5766/40/19, FO to Minister of State, Cairo,
September 12, 1942; FO371/33163 R6961/40/19, Warner to FO, Oc-
tober 5, 1942. Edward Warner served in the Foreign Office Southern
Department and was attached to Sir Reginald Leeper's staff. Leeper was
British minister to the Greek government from 1943 to 1945.

[30] PRO FO371/48278 R14308/4/19, Annual Review of Affairs in
Greece, 1943, July 17, 1945.

[31] Zalokostas, *Chroniko tes Sklavias*, pp. 70-73.

[32] PRO FO371/37200 R10452/1/19, Leeper to FO, October 10, 1943.

[33] Stephanos Saraphes, *Greek Resistance Army: The Story of ELAS*
(London: Birch Books, 1951), p. 1, hereinafter cited as *Greek Resistance
Army*; and Stephanos Zotos, *Greece: The Struggle for Freedom* (New
York: T. Y. Crowell, 1967), p. 104.

[34] The following account of the origins of the republican resistance is
based on Komnenos Pyromaglou, *He Ethnike Antistasis* [The National
Resistance] (Athens, 1947), pp. 150-160, hereinafter cited as *He Ethnike
Antistasis*; Pyromaglou, *He Ethnike Antistasis: EAM-ELAS-EDES-
EKKA* (Athens: Ekdoseis "Dodone," 1975), pp. 306-308; and Kédros,
La résistance grecque, pp. 111-114.

[35] C. M. Woodhouse, *The Struggle for Greece, 1940-1945* (London:
Hart-Davis MacGibbon, 1976), p. 29, hereinafter cited as *The Struggle*

for Greece; and Richter, *Revolution und Konterrevolution*, p. 168.

[36] See below Chapter Six.

[37] Quoted from Pyromaglou, *He Ethnike Antistasis*, pp. 165, 167, by L. S. Stavrianos, "The Greek National Liberation Front (EAM): A Study in Resistance Organization and Administration," *The Journal of Modern History*, Vol. 24 (March 1952), 43, hereinafter cited as "The Greek National Liberation Front."

[38] PRO FO371/43674 R224/9/19, Colonel David Talbot-Rice (SOE London) to Armin R. Dew (FO), January 2, 1944; and FO371/33163 R7640/40/19, Warner to Dixon, November 2, 1942.

[39] PRO FO371/43692 R14686/9/19, Wallace to Leeper, August 15, 1944.

[40] PRO FO371/43679 R2850/9/19, Major E. K. Waterhouse to Denis S. Laskey, February 9, 1944. Waterhouse was Second Secretary to Reginald Leeper, and Denis S. Laskey served in the FO's Southern Department.

[41] PRO War Office (WO) Land Forces Greece, Military and Political Reports from the Field, 204/8869, Report on Events in Greece, June 19, 1943-February 1944, March 30, 1944.

[42] PRO FO371/43692 R14686/9/19, Wallace to Leeper, August 15, 1944. The full text is, "Ever since March 1943 when he signed the first agreement with the Middle East, he has been completely loyal and he will do absolutely and exactly as we tell him. He is therefore not only our creation but remains an instrument in our hands."

[43] The following account relies on William P. Chamberlain and I. Iams, "Rise and Fall of the Greek Communist Party," unpublished manuscript (Washington, D.C.: Foreign Service Institute, Dept. of State, 1963), pp. 1-4, hereinafter cited as "Rise & Fall of the Greek CP."

[44] Kousoulas, *Revolution and Defeat*, p. 91; Dimitri Kitsikis, "Le Mouvement communiste en Grèce," *Études Internationales*, 6 (September, 1975), 340-341.

[45] KKE (Esoterikou), *To Kommounistiko Komma Elladas ston Polemo kai sten Antistasi; Episema Keimena*, V, 1940-1945 [The KKE and the War and Resistance, 1940-1945, vol. 5, Official Documents (KKE, Interior)] (Ekdose tou KKE Esoterikou, 1973), p. 11.

[46] *Ibid.*, pp. 23-35.

[47] *Ibid.*, p. 63.

[48] Kédros, *La résistance grecque*, p. 108. These points were popularized throughout Greece in 1942-1944 in the pamphlet written by Demitrios Glenos, "Ti einai kai ti thelei to EAM [What Is EAM and What Does It Want?] (Athens, 1944. Reprinted.)

[49] Demetrios Gatopoulos, *Istoria tes Katoches* (Athens: Ekdotikos Oikos "Melissa," 1966), pp. 232-235, 727. The 1966 single volume is a second edition of the four-volume edition of 1945-1947.

[50] Svetozar Vukmanovic, *How and Why the People's Liberation Struggle in Greece Met With Defeat* (London, 1950), *passim*.

[51] Eudes, *The Kapetanios*. Although documentation is slight, it is clear Eudes's book is based on a number of interviews with exiled Greek communists.

[52] Eudes, *The Kapetanios*, pp. 23-28.

[53] See also Richter, *Revolution und Konterrevolution*, pp. 266-267.

Richter refers to the conservative "Stalinists" in Athens and the progressive "Titoists" in the mountains.

[54] Demetrios Partsalides, Interview, May 17, 1975. Partsalides has been identified with the nationalist and evolutionary wing of the party (right deviationist), who was denounced along with Siantos in 1950. Since 1974, he has been closely associated with the KKE (Interior).

[55] Hagen Fleischer, "Pos Evlepe to KKE ten Antistasi" [How the KKE Viewed the Resistance], *Anti*, May 3, 1975; p. 13; and Hagen Fleischer, "Contacts Between German Occupation Authorities and Major Greek Resistance Organizations: Sound Tactics or Collaboration?" Paper read at the Modern Greek Studies Association meeting, November 10, 1978, p. 13, hereinafter cited as "Contacts."

[56] See below, Chapter Seven.

[57] *HGrE* 65023 (*Taetigkeitsbericht HGrE aus den Jahren 1940-1943*), *Taetigkeitsbericht*, April 24, 1942; T-311, Roll 175, Frame 000120.

[58] *Mil. Befh. Grld.* 40131/3b (*Anlagenband zum KTB*, November 22, 1942-August 10, 1943), *Ic Lagebericht* of November 20, 1942; T-501, Roll 252, Frame 001106.

[59] *Ibid.*

[60] PRO FO371/48274 R12880/4/19, E. C. W. Myers, "Situation in Greece," July 27, 1945. In an article published in 1958 Woodhouse claimed that the armed resistance did not begin until British agents parachuted into Greece and directed the destruction of the Gorgopotamos viaduct. See Woodhouse, "Zur Geschichte der Resistance in Griechenland," *Vierleljahrshefte fuer Zeitgeschichte*, VI (April 1958), p. 144. He has revised this view in his recent book, *The Struggle for Greece*, p. 41.

[61] *Wi/1C1. 27, Lagebericht* of December 30, 1942.

[62] *Mil. Befh. Grld.* 40131/3b, *Befh. Sued-Grld. Verwaltungsbericht*, November-December 1942; T-501, Roll 252, Frame 000911.

[63] *Ibid., Befh. Sued-Grld. Ic Lagebericht*, February 20 and 28, 1943; T-501, Roll 252, Frames 000850, 000827.

[64] *Ibid.*

[65] *Ibid., Befh. Sued-Grld. Ic Lagebericht*, March 9, 1943; T-501, Roll 252, Frame 000765; and PRO 371/37226 R3676/738/19, FO Research Report: Greece, January-March 1943, April 1, 1943.

[66] *Ibid., Befh. Sued-Grld. Ic Lagebericht*, May 4, 1943, T-501, Roll 252, Frames 000704-000705.

[67] See below, Chapter Five, p. 146.

[68] See Chapter III, pp. 72-74.

[69] Brigadier Myers estimated ELAS at 16,000, but Saraphes claimed only 12,000. The Germans estimated ELAS as having 7,000 actives and 24,000 reserves by October 1943. See *LXVIII AK* 44050/3 (*Anlagenband zum KTB, Ia*, August 11, 1943-September 25, 1943), *Lagebeurteilung*, August 15, 1943. *Mil. Befh. Grld.* 40131/3b; T-501, Roll 252, Frames 000310-000311; and *XXII Geb. AK* 46520/8 (*Anlagenband zum KTB, Ic*, August-December 1943), *Lagebericht*, January 9, 1944 (December 1943); T-314, Roll 671, Frame 000791.

[70] This account of EAM/ELAS's organization is drawn from Stavrianos, "Greek National Liberation Front," 44-46.

[71] PRO FO371/37201 R2702/4/19, Colonel J. S. A. Pearson (SOE London) to Dixon, March 23, 1943.

[72] Chief proponents of this interpretation are Komnenos Pyromaglou

and L. S. Stavrianos. This point is pursued further in Chapter VII. The purpose here is to establish the overall strength of the KKE in EAM/ELAS.

[73] *LXVIII AK* 44058/3 (*Anlagenband KTB, Ia*, August 11-September 25, 1943), *Besonderszubeachtende Bandenlage im Peloponnesus*, September 9, 1943.

[74] *XXII Geb. AK* 59644/3 (*Anlagenband zum KTB, Ic*, January 1-June 1, 1944), German translation of captured KKE document (no title); T-314, Roll 673, Frames 000833-000834. Petros Roussos claimed that KKE membership went from 14,000 to 350,000 members during the occupation. See Dimitri Kitsikis, "Greek Communists and the Karamanlis Government," *Problems in Communism*, January-February (1977), p. 45.

[75] Stavrianos, "The Greek National Liberation Front," 44-45.

[76] PRO FO371/37231 R6709/2319/19, "Theros" to E. Tsouderos, March 19, 1943.

[77] PRO FO371/43674 R113/9/19, Waterhouse to Laskey, December 20, 1943.

[78] Kédros, *La résistance grecque*, p. 129. Kédros cites D. N. Demitriou-Nikephoros, *Andartes apo ta Vouna tes Roumelis* [The Guerrillas of the Mountains of Roumeli], 3 vols. (Athens, 1965), to claim that this development in local government began in June 1942. Stavrianos sets it in October 1942.

[79] Stavrianos, "Greek National Liberation Front," 47-48.

[80] PRO FO371/37193 R113/9/19, Waterhouse to Laskey, December 23, 1943; FO371/43680 R3208/9/19, Report by Colonel McMullen, February 19, 1944; and FO371/37201 R13087/4/19, Pearson to Dixon, December 9, 1943. Colonel McMullen traveled throughout the Peloponnese between August 1943 and January 1944.

[81] Woodhouse, *The Apple of Discord*, pp. 146-147.

[82] PRO FO371/48274 R12880/4/19, E. C. W. Myers, "Situation in Greece," July 27, 1945.

CHAPTER FIVE

[1] The government included Tsouderos as Premier, Admiral Sakellariou as Vice-Premier and Commander-in-Chief of the Navy, Theologos Nikoloudes as Minister of Press and Information, Constantinos Maniadakes as Minister of the Interior, Aristides Demetrates as Minister of Labor, General Panos Papagakos as Chief of the Army, General Panos Nikolaides as head of the Air Force, and Spyros Theophanides as Minister of Marine.

[2] PRO FO371/29909 R9987/8414/19, Lampson to FO, November 19, 1941.

[3] Richard Clogg, " 'Pearls From Swine,': the Foreign Office Papers, S.O.E. and the Greek Resistance," in Phyllis Auty and Richard Clogg (eds.), *British Policy Towards Wartime Resistance in Yugoslavia and*

Greece (New York: Barnes & Noble, 1975), p. 169, hereinafter cited as "Pearls From Swine" and *British Policy.*

⁴ PRO FO371/37194 R1871/1/19, Eden to Palairet, March 1, 1943.

⁵ PRO FO371/29909 R9987/8414/19, Lampson to FO, November 19, 1941.

⁶ *Ibid.*, Minute by Eden, December 2, 1941.

⁷ U.S. Department of State, 123 MacVeagh/221; Telegram from MacVeagh to the Secretary of State, June 9, 1941.

⁸ Kitsikis, *"La famine en Grèce* (1941-1942)," 29.

⁹ PRO FO371/33162 R5766/40/19, Draft of FO Letter to Henry Hopkinson (Cairo), n.d., September 1942. Hopkinson was an advisor to Lampson.

¹⁰ Kitsikis, *"La famine en Grèce* (1941-1942)," 19, 29, and 31.

¹¹ PRO FO371/33160 R479/40/19, Hopkinson to FO; Minute by Warner, January 6, 1942.

¹² PRO FO371/33160 R174/40/19, Lampson to FO, January 7, 1942.

¹³ *Ibid.*

¹⁴ PRO FO371/33166 R455/112/19, Memorandum of a Conversation between Dixon and Tsouderos, January 20, 1942.

¹⁵ PRO FO371/33166 R455/112/19, Draft of a Conversation between Lampson and Tsouderos, n.d. January 1942.

¹⁶ PRO FO371/33162 R5766/40/19, Draft of a Letter to Hopkinson, n.d. (September 1942); and PRO FO371/37198 R6491/1/19, Secretary of State to Lord Feather, July 5, 1943.

¹⁷ PRO FO371/33160 R174/40/19, Sargent to Lampson, January 18, 1942.

¹⁸ PRO FO371/37194 R2100/1/19, FO to Minister of State Cairo, March 15, 1943. This document reflected the early antipathy and distrust of the Foreign Office toward SOE. In getting Kanellopoulos out of Greece, the document referred to going through "C" rather than SOE. "C" was the head of MI6 (Military Intelligence, Section 6) or the British Secret Intelligence Service (SIS). Although SIS operated in Greece during the war, nothing is known of their activities, nor is anything likely to be learned about them within the next fifty years. This was the only document the author found in the PRO materials that made a specific reference to SIS.

¹⁹ PRO FO371/33163 R7163/40/19, Notes Prepared for the Secretary of State on Panagiotis Kanellopoulos, October 27, 1942.

²⁰ PRO FO371/33162 R5579/40/19, Minute by Dixon, August 31, 1942; and FO371/33162 R5966/40/19, Tsouderos to Kanellopoulos, September 5, 1942. Kanellopoulos made the request as part of a SOE proposal to smuggle Plastiras into Greece to lead the resistance.

²¹ PRO FO371/33163 R7419/40/19, Record of the Conference of November 3, 1942; and FO371/33173 R8317/150/19, Lampson to FO, December 5, 1942; and FO371/37914 R1799/1/19, Memorandum on Conversation between Dixon and Tsouderos, Feb. 28, 1943.

²² PRO FO371/37221 R2015/356/19, Memorandum of a Conversation between Dixon and Tsouderos, Mar. 4, 1943.

²³ L. S. Stavrianos, "The Mutiny of the Greek Armed Forces, April 1, 1944," *The American Slavic and East European Review*, Vol. 9 (December 1950), 304-305.

²⁴ PRO FO371/37215 R6554/194/19, Report of the British Court of

Inquiry, April 14, 1943; and FO371/48278 R14308/4/19, Political Review of Greek Affairs for 1943, July 17, 1943.

[25] PRO FO371/37216 R6554/194/19, British Court of Inquiry, April 14, 1943.

[26] PRO FO371/37194 R1992/1/19, Minute by Dixon, March 12, 1943.

[27] PRO FO371/37219 R7183/333/19, Leeper to FO, August 2, 1943.

[28] U.S. Department of State, *Foreign Relations of the United States Diplomatic Papers*, 1943, Vol. IV: *Near East and Africa* (Washington, D.C.: U.S. Government Printing Office, 1964), p. 130; Memorandum by Foy Kohler to Secretary of State, March 24, 1943, hereinafter cited as *FRUS, 1943*, IV, Kohler Memorandum.

[29] *FRUS*, 1943, IV, Kohler Memorandum, pp. 126-127.

[30] *Ibid.*

[31] *Ibid.*

[32] PRO FO371/37198 R6583/1/19, Minutes by Laskey, Dixon, and Sargent, July 20, 1943.

[33] Barker, *British Foreign Policy in South-East Europe*, pp. 113-114.

[34] *Ibid.*, pp. 116-117.

[35] *Ibid.*, p. 119.

[36] Quoted in Michael Howard, *The Mediterranean*, vol. 4, *The Grand Strategy* (London: HMSO, 1972), pp. 505, hereinafter cited as *The Mediterranean*.

[37] PRO WO 106/3164, Greek Resistance Post-Mortem, May 20, 1943-February 28, 1944, March 23, 1944. This report was prepared by Military Operations, Section 5C, hereinafter cited as WO 106/3164. See also Brigadier E. C. W. Myers, "The *Andarte* Delegation to Cairo: August 1943," in Auty and Clogg (eds.), *British Policy*, p. 147, hereinafter cited as "*Andarte* Delegation" in *British Policy*.

[38] Clogg, " 'Pearls From Swine,' " in *British Policy*, pp. 170-177; and C. M. Woodhouse, "Early Contacts with the Greek Resistance in 1942," *Balkan Studies*, Vol. 12 (1971), pp. 347-348.

[39] PRO FO371/37201 R2050/4/19, SOE (London) to FO, Report on the Greek Resistance, March 6, 1943.

[40] Later in 1944, in a general report on his mission to Greece, Myers wrote that Zervas had sent another 150 guerrillas in an attack to divert the Italians guarding the bridge. See PRO FO371/48274 R12880/4/19, "Situation in Greece," July 27, 1945.

[41] PRO FO371/37194 R1869/1/19, Greek Intelligence Summary, February 8-14, 1943.

[42] Eudes, *The Kapetanios*, p. 9.

[43] Eudes's *The Kapetanios* is a defense of Aris's position on a full *andartiko* and is a bitter critique of the "Stalinists" of the KKE who betrayed Aris and the *andartiko* for the policy of legitimacy.

[44] PRO FO 371/43675 R751/9/19, Woodhouse to Cairo, August 7, 1944.

[45] Interview with Demetrios Demetriou, April 19, 1975.

[46] PRO FO371/37201 R2050/4/19, SOE (London) to FO, March 6, 1943.

[47] PRO FO371/48278 R14308/4/19, Political Review of Greek Affairs for 1943, July 17, 1945.

[48] PRO FO371/37196 R4209/4/19, SOE Report on the Greek Resistance, May 6, 1943.

[49] PRO FO371/37201 R2050/4/19, SOE (London) to FO, March 6, 1943.

[50] *Ibid.*, and FO371/48278 R14308/4/19, Political Review of Greek Affairs for 1943, July 17, 1943.

[51] PRO FO371/37231 R6709/2319/19, "Theros" to Tsouderos, March 19, 1943; and FO371/37206 R10450/4/19, Memorandum by Archbishop Damaskinos, October 1, 1943.

[52] PRO FO371/37195 R2266/1/19, Copy of Zervas Telegram, March 13, 1943.

[53] PRO FO371/37201 R2232/4/19, Myers to Cairo, March 10, 1943.

[54] Pyromaglou, *Ho Georgios Kartalis*, p. 544.

[55] PRO FO371/37202 R4209/4/19, SOE (London) to FO, May 6, 1943.

[56] *Ibid.*; FO371/37204 R7882/4/19, August 17, 1943, Dilys Powell to Laskey; and FO371/48275 R12880/4/19, "Situation in Greece" (Prepared by Brigadier Myers), July 27, 1945. Unlike the recent accounts by Eudes, Richter, and Kédros, EAM/ELAS did not claim that the BBC lavished praise on Zervas and ignored ELAS. In his retort to Eudes and Kédros, Clogg has overlooked the issue of the term "National Bands." See Clogg, " 'Pearls From Swine,' " in *British Policy*, p. 172. A PRO document dated June 24, 1945, makes it clear that Churchill ordered the BBC not to mention EAM/ELAS in any broadcast reporting on the Greek resistance, but the time period covered by this order is unclear. The order was lifted after April 23, 1944. PRO FO371/48251 R2095/4/19, Memorandum on Greek Affairs for the Prime Minister, June 24, 1945.

[57] PRO FO371/37201 R654/4/19, Minute by Sargent, January 31, 1943.

[58] PRO WO 106/3164.

[59] PRO FO371/37201 R2434/4/19, Ismay to Sargent, March 16, 1943.

[60] PRO FO371/37195 R2432/1/19, CD to Sargent, March 16, 1943. Gubbins adopted CD as his identification in all communications.

[61] PRO WO 106/3164.

[62] PRO FO371/37201 R2702/4/19, Pearson (SOE London) to FO, March 23, 1943; FO371/37202 R4622/4/19, SOE to Leeper, May 12, 1943, Minute by Dixon, May 16, 1943.

[63] PRO FO371/37202 R4460/4/19, Glenconner, Chief of SOE Cairo, to FO, May 17, 1943; FO371/37202 R4209/4/19, SOE (London) to FO, May 6, 1943; and FO371/37202 R4897/4/19, Guerrilla Problems in Greece April 21-May 20, 1943, June 1, 1943.

[64] PRO FO371/33163 R7640/40/19, Warner to Dixon, November 2, 1942; FO371/37202 R4325/4/19, Minute by Dixon, May 16, 1943; and FO371/37202 R4460/4/16, SOE (London) to FO, May 17, 1943.

[65] PRO FO371/37202 R4325/4/19, Minute by Dixon, May 16, 1943.

[66] PRO WO 106/3164.

[67] PRO FO371/37202 R4345/4/19, Minute by Dixon, May 16, 1943.

[68] PRO FO371/37202 R4460/4/19, Glenconner to FO, May 17, 1943.

[69] PRO FO371/37202 R4209/4/19, SOE (London) to FO, May 6, 1943.

[70] *Ibid.*

[71] Interview, April 19, 1975.

[72] Interview with Demetrios Partsalides, May 17, 1975.

[73] Pyromaglou, *Ho Georgios Kartalis*, pp. 144-147.

[74] *Ibid.*

[75] PRO FO371/37202 R4897/4/19, Col. Bickam Sweet-Escott (SOE London), Report on Guerrilla Problems in Greece, April 21-May 20, 1943, to Dixon, June 1, 1943.

[76] PRO FO371/43689 R10083/9/19, Periodical Intelligence Summary No. 24, June 19, 1944.

[77] PRO FO371/48278 R14038/4/19, Political Review of Greek Affairs for 1943, July 27, 1945.

[78] PRO FO371/37204 R213/4/19, Colonel N. G. L. Hammond Telegram, Resistance Organizations-Salonika, July 28, 1943; and FO371/37205 R8725/4/19, SOE Report on Greek Guerrillas to FO, September 17, 1943.

[79] Ibid.

[80] PRO FO371/37206 R10450/4/19, Memorandum by Archbishop Damaskinos, August 5, 1943.

[81] See Chapter Six, p. 174.

[82] PRO FO371/48278 R14038/4/19, Political Review of Greek Affairs for 1943, July 27, 1945. Fleischer has secured evidence that the Bandouvas brothers arranged temporary, local truces with the Germans in 1941-1942, 1943, and 1944. See Fleischer, "Contacts," p. 3.

[83] See Philip P. Argenti, *The Occupation of Chios by the Germans, 1941-1944* (Cambridge: Cambridge University Press, 1966), Chapter VI, pp. 61-78.

[84] *LXVIII AK* 44050/3 (*Anlagenband zum KTB, Ia*, August 11, 1943-September 25, 1943), *Lagebeurteilung* August 15, 1943. *Mil. Befh. Grld.* 40131/3b; T-501, Roll 252, Frames 000310-000311; and *XXII Geb. AK* 46520/8 (*Anlagenband zum KTB, Ic*, August-December 1943), *Lagebericht*, January 9, 1944 (December 1943) ; T-314, Roll 671, Frame 000791. *XXII Geb. AK* 59644/3 (*Anlagenband zum KTB, Ic*, January 1-June 30, 1944), *Geheime Feldpolizei* Interrogation of April 18, 1944; T-314; Roll 673, Frame 000728.

[85] PRO WO 204/8869, May 26, 1944.

[86] Ibid.

[87] Letter to the author from E. G. Boxshall, Whitehall, March 21, 1975.

[88] PRO WO 106/3225, Strategic Position in the Eastern Mediterranean, May 3, 1944.

[89] Letter from E. G. Boxshall, March 21, 1975.

[90] PRO WO 170/7559, War Diary, Athens Military Command, January 1945, "Appreciation of ELAS," February 1, 1945. The Diary gave the following units and their estimated strength:

Division	Location	Strength
1st Division	East Thessaly	4,250
2nd Division	Attica	4,000
3rd Division	Peloponnese	4,000
6th Division	Macedonia	6,000+
8th Division	Northwest Greece	4,000
10th Division	Macedonia	6,000+
11th Division	Macedonia	6,000+
13th Division	Central Greece	3,000
	Other units	4,000
TOTAL ESTIMATED		41,250

[91] PRO WO 106/3225, May 3, 1944.

[92] Stavrianos, "The Greek National Liberation Front," pp. 44-46.

[93] PRO WO 106/3164.

[94] See Woodhouse, *The Struggle for Greece*, p. 104.

[95] *Ibid.*, p. 103.

[96] *Ibid.*, p. 104. Aside from citing SOE sources, Woodhouse does not give any further details on how he arrived at this figure.

[97] Howard, *The Mediterranean*, p. 486.

[98] PRO FO371/43679 R2767/9/19, Leeper to FO, February 20, 1944; and FO371/37202 R4209/4/19, SOE (London) to FO, May 6, 1943.

[99] Eudes, *The Kapetanios*, p. 230.

[100] *Ibid.*

[101] PRO WO 204/8833, Brigadier Barker-Benfield Report on Zervas, December 27, 1944.

[102] Stavrianos, "Greek National Liberation Front," 52.

[103] *Mil. Befh. Grld.* 40131/3b, *Ic Lagebericht*, July 7, 1943, T-501, Roll 252, Frames 000306-000309.

[104] *LXVIII AK* 54961/1 (*Anlagenband z. KTB, Ia*, January 1-June 30, 1944) *Ic Lagebericht*, July 11, 1944.

[105] *Mil. Befh. Suedost* 75000/5; T-501, Roll 258, Frames 000502-000503.

[106] *Mil. Befh. Grld.* 40131/3b, *Ic Lagebericht*, December 11, 1942; T-501, Roll 252, Frame 001042.

[107] PRO FO371/37203 R5573/4/19, Bickam Sweet-Escott (SOE London) to Dixon, June 24, 1943.

[108] PRO FO371/37203 R5909/4/19, Sargent to Leeper, July 16, 1943.

[109] PRO FO371/48278 R14308/4/19, Political Review of Greek Affairs, 1943, July 17, 1945.

[110] Saraphes, *Greek Resistance Army*, p. 96.

[111] *KTB/OKW*, III, pt. i, p. 433.

[112] *Ibid.*

[113] PRO FO371/48275 R12880/4/19, Myers's Report.

[114] Saraphes, *Greek Resistance Army*, pp. 65, 70; and *KTB/OKW* III, pt. i, p. 581.

[115] See Chapter Three, pp. 86-87.

[116] *Mil. Befh. Grld.* 40131/3b, *Ic Lagebericht*, July 7, 1943; T-501, Roll 252, Frames 000310-000314, 000330.

[117] *Ibid.*, Frames 000306-000309.

[118] *NOKW-258*; *DGFP*, D, XIII, No. 344, pp. 541-543.

[119] *NOKW-1494*; and *Mil. Befh. Grld.* 75000/5; T-501, Roll 258, Frames 000602-000607.

[120] Department of the Army. *German Anti-Guerrilla Operations in the Balkans, 1941-1944* (Washington, D.C.; U.S. Government Printing Office, 1954), p. 47, hereinafter cited as *German Anti-Guerrilla Operations*.

[121] *Ibid.*

[122] *LXVIII AK* 44058/5 (*Anlagenband zum KTB, Ia*, November-December 1943), *Gen. Kdo. LXVIII AK.* to *HGrE*, December 23, 1943.

[123] *Ibid.*

[124] *LXVIII AK* 54960/2 (*KTB, Ia*, January 1-June 30, 1944), *Lagebericht* February 6, 1944; and *LXVIII AK* 54960/4 (*Anlagenband zum KTB, Ia*, January 1-June 30, 1944), *Lagebericht*, April 10, 1944.

[125] *NOKW-1803*.

[126] U.S. Department of the Army. *Anti-Guerrilla Warfare* pp. 114-115.

[127] *NOKW*-755; *NOKW*-734; *NOKW*-708; and *NOKW*-647.

[128] *LXVIII AK* 54960/4, 117 *Jg. Div.* orders on reprisals, no date.

[129] *LXVIII AK* 44058/5, 117 *Jg. Div.* to *LXVIII AK*, December 31, 1943.

[130] *LXVIII AK* 54961/2 (*Anlagenband z. Taetigkeitsbericht Ic*, January 1-June 30, 1944), *Lagebericht*, June 3, 1944 (for May).

[131] *LXVIII AK* 44058/8 (*Tagesmeldung Ic* September 16, 1943-December 31, 1943), *passim. LXVIII AK* 54691/2 (*Ic Taetigkeitsbericht* January 1-June 30, 1944), *passim. XXII Geb. AK* 46520/8 (*Anlagenband z. KTB, Ic*, August 1-November 30, 1943); T-314, Roll 671, Frames 000797, 000850, 000881, and 000927. *XXII Geb. AK* 46520/7 (*Anlagenband z. KTB, Ic*, August 24-December 31, 1943); T-314, Roll 671, Frames 000540, 000545. *HGrE* 65721/2 (*KTB Ia*, September 1-30, 1944); T-311, Roll 182, Frames 000670, 000700, and 000755. Greek sources claim a much higher number. Gatopoulos, citing official statistics, lists the following: executed as hostages, 30,000 by the Italians and Germans; 40,000 executed by the Bulgarians; and 50,000 killed in the resistance. See Gatopoulos, *Istoria tes Katoches*, pp. 608-609.

[132] See Chapter Six, p. 170.

[133] *Mil. Befh. Grld.* 75000/5; T-501, Roll 258, Frames 000623-000624. Hermann Neubacher, *Sonderauftrag Suedost* (Goettingen, 1956), pp. 75, 87. At the end of the war, Neubacher was seized and tried as a war criminal by Yugoslavia. He received a twenty-year sentence for his war crimes, but the Yugoslavs released him in 1952. This leniency and his ultimate release was attributed in large measure to his resistance to reprisals. General Loehr did not fare as well. In 1948 the Yugoslav government executed him for having commanded the aircraft that bombed Belgrade without a declaration of war in 1941. Generals Lanz, Felmy, and Speidel were tried at Nuremberg in 1947 and received twelve, fifteen, and twenty-year prison terms respectively. Ninety other German officers who served in Greece were tried by the Greek government for war crimes. Lanz, Felmy, and Speidel were released in the early 1950's.

[134] F. A. Voigt, *Pax Britannica* (London: Constable, 1949), pp. 369-370, and 411; and A. A. Pallis, *Problems of Resistance in Occupied Countries* (London: Greek Office of Information, 1947), *passim*. The latter was written to absolve Greek postwar governments of any political obligations to the resistance.

[135] Woodhouse, *Apple of Discord*, pp. 61 and 139.

[136] PRO FO371/43689 R10469/9/19, Situation in Greece, January-May 1944, May 26, 1944.

[137] PRO FO371/37207 R11645/4/19, Woodhouse Telegram, Nov. 4, 1943.

[138] John O. Iatrides, *Revolt in Athens: The Greek Communist "Second Round," 1944-1945* (Princeton, N.J.: Princeton University Press, 1972), p. 19, hereinafter cited as *Revolt in Athens*.

[139] Woodhouse, *The Struggle for Greece*, pp. 104-107.

[140] Saraphes, *Greek Resistance Army*, pp. 276-277; and Heinz Kuehnrich, *Der Partisanenkrieg in Europa 1939-1945* (Berlin: Dietz Verlag, 1968), p. 530. Kuehnrich, an East German historian, based the sections on EAM/ELAS on exiled-KKE publications. In these accounts, the KKE claimed EAM/ELAS inflicted 37,000 casualties (dead, wounded, and captured) on the Axis. Saraphes claimed a more modest number of 33,000. These figures are very inflated, and they are explained by the

extravagant claims made in individual attacks on the Axis, as in the case of the Tournovo tunnel. EAM/ELAS claimed 500 killed, but the actual number was 92 Italians and 60 Greek hostages. Another example is Saraphes's claims of Germans killed during the heavy fighting in October 1943 which are not substantiated by the German records.

[141] Bickam Sweet-Escott, *Greece*, pp. 25-30.

[142] Winston S. Churchill, *Closing the Ring*, Vol. V of *The Second World War* (New York: Bantam Books, 1962), p. 457, hereinafter cited as *Closing the Ring*.

[143] William Deakin, *The Brutal Friendship* (New York: Harper & Row, 1962), pp. 95-96.

[144] *Ibid.* Deakin quoted from a minute recorded by Hitler's adjutant Paul Schmidt on December 18, 1942, "[Hitler] stressed again the utmost importance of the pacification of these regions in face of an eventual British front in the Balkans. Every measure must be taken to prevent the outbreak of fire in our rear in case an Anglo-Saxon landing takes place. For otherwise all the heroic courage of the Axis troops in Crete and the Peloponnese (in 1941) would have been in vain; for apart from the above-mentioned railway line, no other route was available. If this was lost the Balkans were finished for the Axis. The recent blowing up of a bridge had shown how disagreeable for supplies such a disruption of traffic could be . . . The enemy must therefore be prevented from continuing with their partisan war against Axis communications, otherwise a catastrophic situation would arise."

[145] *HGrE* 65023 (*Taetigkeitsbericht HGrE aus den Jahren* 1940-1943), *Taetigkeitsbericht*, May 1, 1943; T-311, Roll 175, Frames 000382, 000583.

[146] See Chapter Three, fn. 91.

[147] PRO WO 106/3164.

[148] *KTB/OKW*, III, pt. ii, pp. 539, 779-780, 1252.

[149] PRO WO 106/3164.

[150] No single summary of German casualties, or of reprisals, exists in the records of *HGrE* or of other German agencies available to the author. Weekly, biweekly, and monthly summaries begin only with January 1944 in the War Diaries of *HGrE*. These figures were compiled from various *Taetigkeitsberichte, Tagesmeldungen, Lageberichte,* and war diaries of various units in Greece. See *HGrE* 65025 (*Tagesmeldung*, May 1-December 31, 1944); T-311, Roll 175, Frames 001277, 001290, 001310, 001350, 001391, 001441, 001456, 001458, and 001462. *HGrE* 65027/4 (*KTB, Ia*, January 1-February 29, 1944); T-311, Roll 177, Frames 000572, 000634, and 000655. *HGrE* 65027/5 (*KTB, Ia*, March 1-April 30, 1944); T-311, Roll 176, Frame 000681. *HGrE* 65028/3 (*Anlagenband z. KTB, Ia*, July 1-31, 1944); T-311, Roll 177, Frame 000975. *HGrE* 65721/1 (*KTB, Ia*, July 1-August 31, 1944); T-311, Roll 182, Frames 000405, 000438, 000464, 000521, 000548, 000569. *HGrE* 65721/2 (*KTB, Ia*, September 1-30, 1944); T-311, Roll 182, Frames 000675, 000700, and 000746. And *HGrE* 65721/3 (*KTB, Ia*, October 1-31, 1944); T-311, Roll 183, Frames 000017 and 000484.

[151] PRO FO371/43688 R9330/9/19, Diary of ELAS Activity Against the Enemy, October 1943-April 1944, Talbot-Rice to FO, June 8, 1944; and PRO FO371/43688 R9772/9/19, SOE Game Book-Greece-May 1944. The "Game Book" recorded twenty-six actions: 16 for ELAS, 9 for the AMM (8 of which were supported by ELAS), and 1 for EDES.

[152] See fn. 150.

[153] *Ibid.* The records reporting German losses also reported resistance casualties. Brigadier Myers defended guerrilla warfare for its morale-raising contribution to victory in spite of enemy reprisals. See Myers, *Greek Entanglement*, p. 213. Aris's retort on this question, according to Myers, was that those who died in reprisals and suffered from the movement would never add up to those who died of starvation in Athens during the winter of 1941-1942. See Myers, *Greek Entanglement*, p. 169.

[154] Komnenos Pyromaglou, *"La résistance grecque et les Alliés,"* in *Second International Conference of Resistance Movements* (Milan, 1961), p. 310.

[155] Pyromaglou, *Ho Georgios Kartalis*, p. 206; Saraphes, *Greek Resistance Army*, p. 97; and Myers, *Greek Entanglement*, p. 226.

[156] Gatopoulos, *Istoria tes Katoches*, pp. 708-710.

[157] PRO FO371/37203 R5845/1/19, Warner to Dixon, June 27, 1943.

[158] United States, Office of Strategic Services (OSS), 41871, July 30, 1943.

[159] Myers, *Greek Entanglement*, p. 214.

[160] *Ibid.*, pp. 215 and 221.

[161] PRO FO371/37203 R6555/4/19, Minute on Wallace, July 14, 1943.

[162] Auty and Clogg (eds.), *British Policy*, pp. 147-208.

[163] PRO FO371/37199 R8314/1/19, Leeper to Sargent (Personal Letter), August 25, 1943. This letter sharply contradicts Pyromaglou's published accounts, which claim he sided with the other resistance delegates on the issue of the monarchy. See Pyromaglou, *Ho Georgios Kartalis*, pp. 190-192.

[164] PRO FO371/37198 R7514/1/19, Leeper to Sargent, August 11, 1943; and FO371/37204 R7884/4/19, Leeper to FO, August 13, 1943.

[165] *Ibid.*

[166] PRO FO371/37201 R48/4/19, FO to Leeper, August 16, 1943.

[167] Myers, *"Andarte* Delegation," in *British Policy*, p. 151.

[168] After the resistance leaders had been returned to Greece, the Foreign Office succeeded in forcing the removal of Lord Glenconner from SOE Cairo, preventing the return of Myers to Greece, and dismissing Brigadier C. M. Keble as head of operations for Force 133. In London, Sir Charles Hambro, the executive head of SOE, was another casualty of the conference. General Gubbins was sent to Cairo to reorganize SOE and place it under the direct military command of Wilson. See Clogg, " 'Pearls From Swine,' " in *British Policy*, pp. 266-268.

[169] Shortly before leaving Greece, Wallace sent a series of sharply critical reports on EAM/ELAS through SOE to Leeper, but a shortage of cipher experts delayed their arrival to Leeper. Leeper and Wallace believed that SOE had deliberately delayed these messages, but they were in error. See *ibid.*, p. 189.

[170] For the details of the SOE-FO conflict see *ibid.*, pp. 173-193.

[171] PRO FO371/37198 R7950/1/19, Leeper to FO, August 27, 1943.

[172] *Ibid.* Churchill to War Cabinet, August 30, 1943; FO371/37199 R8263/1/19, Minute by Laskey, September 8, 1943.

[173] PRO FO371/37199 R8382/1/19, Minute by Laskey, September 4, 1943; and R8484/1/19, Minute by Laskey, September 8, 1943.

[174] PRO FO371/37198 R7546/1/19, Warner to Dixon, August 6, 1943.

[175] Pyromaglou, *Doureios Ippos*, pp. 199-200.

[176] *Ibid.,* p. 177.

[177] Pyromaglou, *Ho Georgios Kartalis,* p. 200. Pyromaglou quotes approvingly from Pipineles's biography of George II to make this point. See Panagiotes Pipineles, *Georgios B* [George II] (Athens, 1951), p. 157.

CHAPTER SIX

[1] PRO FO371/37205 R9253/4/19, Woodhouse to SOE (Cairo), September 15, 1943.

[2] PRO FO371/37208 R11673/4/19, Woodhouse Report, October 17, 1943.

[3] PRO FO371/37205 R9853/4/19, SOE Weekly Intelligence Report No. 60, September 16, 1943.

[4] PRO FO371/37205 R9817/4/19, Woodhouse to SOE (Cairo), September 29, 1943.

[5] PRO FO371/37207 R12222/4/19, Periodical Intelligence Summary No. 5, Nov. 10, 1943.

[6] PRO FO371/37200 R10453/1/19, ELAS to Wilson, October 9, 1943.

[7] PRO WO 106/3164 Greek Resistance Post-Mortem, May 20, 1943-February 28, 1944, dated March 23, 1944.

[8] PRO FO371/372006 R10450/4/19, Leeper to FO, October 9, 1943; Minute by Laskey, November 8, 1943; and Jeanne Tsatsos, *The Sword's Fierce Edge: A Journal of the Occupation of Greece, 1941-1944* (Nashville, Tenn.: Vanderbilt University Press, 1965), pp. 74-76. For a discussion of the regency proposal see below Chapter Seven, *passim.*
The PRO records do not make clear which agency Macaskie represented in Greece. He was not under the command of the BMM, but he may have been an agent of MI9 (Military Intelligence, Escape), since Leeper's report of October 9 mentions Macaskie's work in this area. Macaskie, who was twice captured by the Germans and twice escaped, arrived in Cairo in early October 1943, but returned to Greece and lived with Damaskinos until the liberation. See Henry Maule, *Scobie, Hero of Greece* (London: Arthur Barker, 1975), pp. 63-64, hereinafter cited as *Scobie.*

[9] PRO FO371/37206 R10450/4/19, Leeper to FO, October 9, 1943; and FO371/37206 R10938/4/19, Political Intelligence Summary No. 2, October 20, 1943 (prepared by Major E. K. Waterhouse for Leeper); and FO371/37207 R12222/4/19, Periodical Intelligence Summary No. 5, November 10, 1943 (prepared by Waterhouse for Leeper).

[10] PRO FO371/43676 R1046/9/19, Laskey Minute, January 21, 1944.

[11] PRO FO371/37206 R10239/4/19, "Apollo" to SOE (Cairo), October 6, 1943.

[12] PRO FO371/43688 R9898/9/19, Col. C. E. Barnes, Report on Observations in Greece, July 1943-April 1944, hereinafter cited as Barnes Report.

[13] U.S. Military Tribunal, V, Case No. 7 (Hostage); U.S. vs. Wilhelm

List *et al*, Series 2, Book 18, Zervas Affidavit, Greek Document No. 5, pp. 6-7, hereinafter cited as U.S. vs. List *et al*.

[14] *XXII Geb. AK* 46520/1 (*KTB XXII Geb.* AK, *Ia*, August 24-December 31, 1943); T-314, Roll 670, Frame 000103; and *XXII Geb. AK* 46520/7 (*Anlagenband zum KTB XXII Geb. AK., Ic*, August 24-December 31, 1944); T-314, Roll 670, Frames 000327-000328.

[15] *Peristrofe*, October 8, 1943. Copy in *XXII Geb. AK* 46520/7; T-314, Roll 670, Frames 000484-000485.

[16] Woodhouse, *Apple of Discord*, p. 167.

[17] *XXII Geb. AK* 46520/7, EDES *Flugblaetter*; T-314, Roll 671, Frame 000316.

[18] *XXII Geb. AK* 46520/7, *Bericht ueber die Aussprache mit die Kommission von Arta*, October 21, 1943; T-314, Roll 671, Frame 000313.

[19] *Ibid.*

[20] *Ibid.*, *HGrE* to *XXII Geb. AK.*, October 10, 1943; T-314, Roll 671, Frame 000323. With the arrival of OSS agents in Greece during the fall of 1943, the BMM became the AMM. Woodhouse remained chief of the Mission.

[21] *Ibid. HGrE* believed that EDES possessed 20,000 rifles, 400 light machine guns, 100 heavy machine guns, 100 mortars, and 20 cannons, and that the AMM with Zervas consisted of 300 men. Zervas definitely did not possess the cannons, and the AMM never reached that size until the summer of 1944. After the anti-partisan operations of October and November, the Germans revised their estimate of EDES strength to about 3,500 active guerrillas, which was closer to the truth. See *XXII Geb. AK* 46520/8 (*Anlagenband zum KTB XXII Geb. AK., Ic*, August 24-December 31, 1943), *Ic Bericht*, December 1, 1943; T-314, Roll 671, Frames 000813-000816.

[22] *XXII Geb. AK* 46520/7, EAM *Flugblaetter*, October 12, 1943; T-314, Roll 671, Frame 000482.

[23] *Ibid.*, EDES *Flugblaetter*, October 12, 1943; T-314, Roll 671, Frame 000483.

[24] *Ibid., 1. Geb. Div.* to *XXII Geb. AK.* October 13, 1943; T-314, Roll 671, Frame 000169. *XXII Geb. AK* 46520/1 (*KTB XXII Geb. AK, Ia*, August 24-December 31, 1943), *XXII Geb. AK* to *HGrE*, October 13, 1943; T-314, Roll 670, Frame 000109.

[25] Operation *"Panther"* was one of a series of major actions planned in September 1943 in accordance with Fuehrer Directive No. 48, July 26, 1943, which included orders for anti-partisan operations as part of an overall effort to bolster the defense of Southeast Europe. Other operations in Greece were *"Tiger," "Puma," "Hubertus," "Adler," "Seepferd,"* and *"Leopard."*

[26] *HGrE* 65027/2 (*KTB, OB Suedost, Ia*, September 1-October 31, 1943), Entry for October 13, 1943; T-311, Roll 176, Frame 000311. *HGrE* 65024/1 (*Aktennotizen der Chefsbesprechung des Ia*, April 13-December 31, 1943); T-311, Roll 175, Frame 000750.

[27] *HGrE* 65027/2 (*KTB, HGrE, Ia*, September 1-October 31, 1943), Entry for September 25, 1943; T-311, Roll 176, Frame 000249.

[28] Woodhouse, *Apple of Discord*, p. 167.

[29] Fleischer, "Contacts," p. 13; and Woodhouse, *Apple of Discord*, p. 78.

[80] *HGrE* 65034/2 (No Title), *HGrE* to *HGrF*, October 21, 1943; T-311, Roll 179, Frame 000841.

[31] Saraphes, *Greek Resistance Army*, p. 126.

[32] *XXII Geb*. *AK* 46520/7, *Machetes*, October 19, 1943; T-314, Roll 671, Frame 000450.

[33] *Ibid.*, T-314, Roll 671, Frames 000450-000451.

[34] Some sources estimate that Zervas lost 1,500 active *andartes* between October and November 1943. Most of these left because of German and ELAS military successes, but the political effect of EAM/ELAS charges must not be overlooked. See Woodhouse, *Apple of Discord*, p. 79; Saraphes, *Greek Resistance Army*, p. 127; and Chamberlain and Iams, "Rise and Fall of Greek CP," p. 125.

[35] *XXII Geb*. *AK* 46520/8 (*Anlagenband zum KTB XXII Geb. AK*, *Ic*, August 1-November 30, 1943), *Ic Lagebericht*, October 22, 1943; T-314, Roll 671, Frames 000904-000905. *Ibid.*, *Ic Lagebericht*, November 26, 1943; T-314, Roll 671, Frames 000849-000850.

[36] PRO FO371/43688 R9898/9/19, Barnes Report.

[37] *LXVIII AK* 44508/4 (*Anlagenband zum KTB, LXVIII AK. Ia*, September 1-November 30, 1943), *SS-Pol-Pz-Gren-Rgt. 2 "Feindlage,"* November 4, 1943. The document states: "Nach V-Meldung ist zu erwarten dass Zervas in naechster Zeit aus dem Raume NO Karpenision gegen die Kommunisten ziehen wird. Ein Zusammentreffen mit deutscher Truppe erscheint daher nicht ausgeschlossen. Durch Flugblattabwurf ist Zervas bekannt gegeben worden, dass seine Einheiten sich der deutschen Truppen als nationale Partisanen erkanntlich muessten. In anderen Falle wird auf sie geschossen. Ein moegliches Zusammengehen mit *erkannten* Zervas-Banden im Kampf gegen die Kommunisten *bleibt den Gruppenfuehren ueberlassen*. Verbindungsaufnahmen durch die Btl. ist dem Rgt. sofort zu melden."

[38] *XXII Geb*. *AK* 46520/8, *Ic Lagebericht*, November 26, 1943; T-314, Roll 671, Frames 000899-000900. "Die Zervas-Leute versichern immer wieder, ihr Kampf richte sich nicht gegen die Deutschen, sondern nur gegen die Kommunisten, eine Aussage die durchaus geeignet ist, unter dem Deckmantel der nationalen Sache den Kampf gegen den deutschen Okkupater zu verschleiern. Es besteht der strenge Befehl, zunaechst noch jedem Kampf gegen die deutsche Truppe zu vermeiden, es sei denn, die Zervas-banden werden von ihr angegriffen.

"Im Falle einer englischen Landung im griechischen Raum sei es daher auch die erste Aufgabe die Zervas-Bewegung, den Kommunismus weiter zu bekampfen und zu verhueten, dass dieser, da er dann nicht mehr von den Deutschen in Sach gehalten werde, die Macht ergreife."

[39] *HGrE* 65032 (*Anlagenbuch zum KTB HGrE, Ic*, July 1, 1943-January 31, 1944), *Ic Lagebericht* for November 1943; T-411, Roll 178, Frames 000378-000383. The report concludes: "Ob eine Zusammenarbeit mit Zervas moeglich sein wird haengt vor allem von dessen bisher noch nicht bestaetigten Bruch mit der All. Militaermission ab. Seine Bekaempfung duerfte bei gleichzeitiger Werbung nationaler Freiwilliger zum Kampf gegen dem Kommunismus gegenwaertig nicht zweckmaessig sein, in Anbetracht seines gegenueber der deutschen Besatzung passierven Verhaltens duerfte es zunaechst ausreichend sein ihn weiter durch die ELAS bekaempfen zu lassen."

[40] PRO FO371/37210 R13509/4/19, Woodhouse Telegram to SOE (Cairo), December 17, 1943.

[41] On February 15, 1944, at Mirofillo, Zervas denounced General Gonatas, Colonels Papageorgiou and Papathanasopoulos, Tavoulares, and Voulpiotis. Gonatas favored the establishment of the Security Battalions, but was arrested along with Papageorgiou on May 17, 1944, by the Athenian *Sipo*. Tavoulares became Minister of the Interior in the Rallis government, and Voulpiotis directed Radio Athens. See *NOKW*-1804; Saraphes, *Greek Resistance Army*, p. 157; and Woodhouse, *Apple of Discord*, pp. 116-117.

[42] *XXII Geb. AK* 46520/8, *104 Jg. Div. Ic Lagebericht* for December 1943; T-314, Roll 671, Frame 000806: "Die Kommunisten setzen in den von ihnen beherrschten Gebieten Gewahltsherrschaft fort. Die verstaerkte propagandastische Aktivitaet haelt an. Der Kampf, nicht nur gegen die Nationalen, sondern auch gegen die Besatzungmacht ist in letzter Zeit haeufiger ausgesprachen worden."

[43] *IIGrE* 65027/4 (*KTB zum HGrE, Ia*, January 1-December 31, 1944), Entry for January 4, 1944; T-311, Roll 176, Frame 000531.

[44] Saraphes, *Greek Resistance Army*, pp. 146-149.

[45] *XXII Geb. AK* 59644/2 (*Anlagenband zum KTB XXII Geb. AK, Ia*, January 1-June 30, 1944), *XXII Geb. AK to HGrE*, January 26, 1944; T-314, Roll 673, Frames 000522-000524. The account of the negotiations that resulted in the Plaka Agreement of February 29, 1944, are accurate and correspond to the accounts of Woodhouse, Saraphes, and Komnenos Pyromaglou. On most occasions, the German authorities in Ioannina received their information within 24-48 hours after the meetings in the mountains. They received a signed copy of the Plaka Agreement one week after it was signed. The accuracy of these reports given by agents identified as "*Zervas-Leute*" attests to the fact that they were close to high authorities in EDES. See below, pp. 183-186, 206-207.

[46] *Ibid., XXII Geb. AK to HGrE*, February 1, 1944; Roll 673, Frame 000484. Two documents written in August and September 1944 give more details of the February 1 meeting:

"Lage Westgriechenland.–Zervas

"Das XXII Geb. AK schloss Anfang Febr. 44 mit Zervas dem Fuehrer einer nationalen Bandengruppe in NW-Griechenland ein uebereinkommen, demzufolge die beiden Teile sich verpflichteten, sich gegenseitig jeder Kampfhandlung zu enthalten. Zervas verpflichte sich einen 5 km breiten Kuestenstreifen bei Parga von Zervas-Truppen freizuhalten. Bis Juni 1944 hilft Zervas die getroffene Vereinbarung."

See *HGrE* 65721/1 (*KTB HGrE, Ia*, July 1-August 31, 1944), Summary Report of August 8, 1944; T-311, Roll 182, Frame 000526.

A second summary report of September 9, 1944:

"Das OkdoHGrE hat daher, solange Zervas an seinem friedlichen verhalten gegen uns und seiner Gegnerschaft gegen EAM festhaelt, ein Interesse daran, A.) dass Zervas in diesem Raum verbleibt, damit eigene Sicherungskraefte an der Strasse Jannina—Arta eigenspart werden, B.) dass Zervas das GenKdo 22 Geb. AK staendig ueber seine absichten, ueber die Verteilung seiner Kraefte und ueber die ihm bekannte Feindlage unterrichtet, C.) dass von Fall zu Fall gemeinsame aktionen im Kuesternfernen Gebiet zur Bekampfung und Vernichtung von EAM-Banden vereinbart werden."

See *HGrF* 66142 (*Anlagenband Ic AO*, *HGrE*, February 10-November 4, 1944), *HGrE* to *HGrF*, September 9, 1944; T-311, Roll 286, Frames 000034-000035.

[47] *XXII Geb. AK* 59644/2, *XXII Geb. AK* to *HGrE*, February 1, 1944; T-314, Roll 673, Frame 000484.

[48] *XXII Geb. AK* 59643/1 (*KTB XXII Geb. AK, Ia*, January 1-June 30, 1944), Entry for February 1, 1944; T-314, Roll 671, Frames 000991-000993. The entry states:

"Das Gen. Kdo. beabsichtigt von der Arachtosbruecke Badsa aus mit einem verst. Btl. in die Nordflanke der am Arachtos mit den Z-anhaengern im Kampf stehenden Kommunisten zu stossen."

The operation began at 1200 hours on February 2. By the morning of February 3, it reached the Badsa bridge and moved on to Pramanda. Then on February 5, it moved east and south from Pramanda reaching Agnanda on February 7.

[49] *Ibid.*, entries for February 3-7, 1944; T-314, Roll 671, Frames 001001-001007.

[50] Saraphes wrote that it was the movement of German troops out of Metsovon south toward Pramanda on February 3, 1944, and the movement of troops north out of Arta, which halted the ELAS advance. If ELAS had crossed the Arachtos, he continued, the Germans would have hit ELAS from the rear. See Saraphes, *Greek Resistance Army*, pp. 151-152.

[51] *Ibid.*, p. 149.

[52] Woodhouse, *Apple of Discord*, p. 177; Saraphes, *Greek Resistance Army*, p. 153; and Pyromaglou, *Ho Georgios Kartalis*, pp. 239-241. EAM was represented by Elias Tsirimokos and Miltiades Porphyrogenis, and ELAS by Saraphes and Petros Roussos. Porphyrogenis and Roussos were members of the KKE. Major Wines represented OSS.

[53] A report from the *XXII Geb. AK* to *HGrE* of February 15, 1944, reads: "Zervas teilt mit:

1) Nachricht ueber das Ergebnis der Verhandlung Zervas-Elas bisher nicht eingegangen. Voraussichtlich erst am 15.2.44 Nachmittags. 2) Zervas glaubt nicht, dass Vereinbarung zu Stande kommt, da Elas schaerfer Forderungen stellt als frueher und nur Zeit gewinnen will, um neuen Angriff vorzubereiten. Neugruppierung von Elas-Kraeften auf O Arachtosufer im Gange, Angriffe in etwa drei Tagen zu erwarten. 3) Zervas entschlossen, bisherigen Kurs uns gegenueber beizubehalten, glaubt sich halten zu koennen, wenn beiderseitige Aktion gegen Elas auf einander abgestimmt werden."

See *HGrE* 65031/1 ("*Sammelmappe Zervas*," February 24-October 20, 1944); T-311, Roll 284, Frame 000124.

⁵⁴ PRO FO371/43680 R3102/9/19, Colonel Hammond to GHQ ME, February 10, 1944.

⁵⁵ *Ibid., XXII Geb. AK* to *HGrE*, February 18, 1944; T-311, Roll 284, Frame 000133.

⁵⁶ *Ibid., HGrE* to *HGrF*, February 20, 1944; T-311, Roll 284, Frame 000135.

⁵⁷ PRO FO371/43681 R3442/9/19, Leeper to FO, March 1, 1944.

⁵⁸ Saraphes, *Greek Resistance Army*, pp. 158-159, 163. See below pp. 206-207.

⁵⁹ Pyromaglou, *Ho Georgios Kartalis*, p. 270.

⁶⁰ Woodhouse, *Apple of Discord*, p. 179; Pyromaglou, *Ho Georgios Kartalis*, pp. 239-242; and Saraphes, *Greek Resistance Army*, p. 165.

⁶¹ *HGrE* 65031/1, *XXII Geb. AK* to *HGrE*, February 27, 1944; T-311, Roll 284, Frame 000148.

⁶² *HGrE* 65031/1, *XXII Geb. AK* to *HGrE*, March 6, 1944; T-311, Roll 284, Frame 000152.

⁶³ *The New York Times*, March 6, 1944, p. 4.

⁶⁴ *HGrE* 65031/1, *XXII Geb. AK* to *HGrE*, March 6, 1944; T-311, Roll 284, Frame 000152.

⁶⁵ *XXII Geb. AK* 46520/8, *Ic Lagebericht*, January 9, 1944; T-314, Roll 671, Frames 000832-000833.

⁶⁶ *HGrE* 65027/4 (*KTB, Ia, HGrE*, January 1-December 31, 1944), *HGrE* to *XXII Geb. AK*, Entry for March 10, 1944; T-311, Roll 176, Frame 000567.

⁶⁷ *HGrE* 65031/1, *Abwehrtrupp 376* report from Ioannina to *HGrE*, March 14, 1944; T-311, Roll 284, Frame 000128.

⁶⁸ *HGrE* 65721/1 (*KTB HGrE, Ia*, July 1-August 31, 1944), Entry for August 8, 1944; T-311, Roll 182, Frame 000526. See Komnenos Pyromaglou, Letter to *To Vema*, June 29, 1963, reprinted P. K. Enepekides, *He Ellenike Antistasis, 1941-1944* (Athens: "Estia," 1964), pp. 235-236, hereinafter cited as *He Ellenike Antistasis*.

⁶⁹ PRO WO 204/8333, Report on Arms Supplied to Zervas (prepared by Barker-Benfield), December 27, 1944.

⁷⁰ Woodhouse Interview, March 7, 1975.

⁷¹ PRO FO371/43688 R9898/9/19, Barnes Report.

⁷² *HGrE* 65031/1, Report on four letters intercepted by *V-Mann* on February 24, 1944; T-311, Roll 284, Frame 000154.

⁷³ Eleuthère Dzélépy, *Le drama de la résistance grecque* (Paris: Editions Raisons d'être, 1946), p. 50; Kousoulas, *Revolution and Defeat*, p. 46.

⁷⁴ Dertilis remained oblivious to Allied policy toward EAM/ELAS in November and December 1943, when it withheld supplies as a means of forcing the *andartes* to end their disputes.

⁷⁵ *HGrE* 65031/1, February 24, 1944; T-311, Roll 284, Frame 000154.

⁷⁶ *LXVII AK* 54961/1 (*Taetigkeitsbericht Ic LXVIII AK*), *Ic Lagebericht*, April 10, 1944.

⁷⁷ *XXII Geb. AK* 59644/3 (*Anlagenband zum KTB, Ic*, January 1-June 30, 1944), *GFP* Interrogation of April 18, 1944; T-314, Roll 673, Frame 000730.

⁷⁸ *Ibid.*, *GFP* Interrogation of April 25, 1944; T-314, Roll 675, Frame 000732.

⁷⁹ The following paragraphs on Greek politics are intended only to

serve as background information and are sketched in the briefest outline. Chapter Seven examines this problem in greater detail.

[80] Kousoulas, *Revolution and Defeat*, pp. 179-180; Leften S. Stavrianos, "The Mutiny of the Greek Armed Forces, April, 1944," 302-311; Pyromaglou, *Ho Georgios Kartalis*, pp. 320-330, 335-338.

[81] *HGrE* 65031/1, *HGrE* to *XXII Geb. AK*, June 29, 1944; T-311, Roll 284, Frame 000068.

[82] *Ibid., XXII Geb. AK* to *HGrE*, July 6, 1944; T-311, Roll 284, Frame 000119.

[83] *HGrE* 65036/1 (*Anlagenbuch KTB HGrE, Ia*, July 1-July 31, 1944), *HGrE* to *HGrF*, July 8, 1944; T-311, Roll 181, Frame 000360.

[84] PRO WO 204/8333, Barker-Benfield Report, December 27, 1944.

[85] Pyromaglou states that the strength of EDES never surpassed that of 7,000 and reached its high point in the summer of 1943. See Komnenos Pyromaglou, Letter of June 29, 1963, to *To Vema* reprinted in Enepekides, *He Ellenike Antistasis*, p. 237.

[86] *HGrE* 65036/1, *HGrE* to *HGrF*, July 8, 1944; T-311, Roll 181, Frames 000359-000360. *Ibid., Ic Abendsmeldung*, July 7, 1944; T-311, Roll 284, Frame 000112. The ELAS units were taking up new positions to harass the German units according to the Allied operation "Animals."

[87] *HGrE* 65031/1, Lanz to *HGrE*, July 13, 1944; T-311, Roll 284, Frame 000104.

[88] *Ibid., XXII Geb. AK* to *HGrE*, July 14-15, 1944; T-311, Roll 284, Frames 000104-000105.

[89] *HGrE* 65036/1, *Tagesmeldung* for July 16, 1944; T-311, Roll 181, Frame 000150.

[90] *HGrE* 65031/1, *HGrE* to *HGrF*, July 16, 1944; T-311, Roll 284, Frame 000302.

[91] *HGrE* 65036/1, final report on *"Steinadler,"* July 15, 1944; T-311, Roll 181, Frame 000156. Captured equipment included 48 heavy machine guns, 82 light machine guns, 519 rifles, 376,000 rounds of ammunition, and 2,000 rounds of artillery.

[92] *HGrF* 75319/2a (*Kriegsakten OB Suedost HGrF, Ia*, January 17-September 30, 1944), *Ic Stellungnahme*, July 27, 1944; T-311, Roll 285, Frame 000560.

[93] *Ibid.*

[94] *HGrE* 65031/3 (*Anlagenbuch Unternehmung "Kreuzotter,"* July 14-August 30, 1944), *HGrE* to *OB Suedost*, July 27, 1944; T-311, Roll 178, Frames 000278-000279. *"Kreuzotter"* called for units of battalion strength to move from Agrinion, Lamia, and Amphissa and converge through an encircling maneuver on Karpenision.

[95] *HGrE* 65721/1 (*KTB HGrE*, July 1-August 31, 1944), Entry for August 13, 1944; T-311, Roll 182, Frame 000544.

[96] Woodhouse, *Apple of Discord*, p. 95.

[97] *HGrE* 65033/1 (*Anlagenband zum KTB HGrE, Ic*, August 1944), *Ob Suedost* to *HGrE*, August 14, 1944; T-311, Roll 178, Frame 000565; and *HGrE* 65721/1, Entry for August 17, 1944; T-311, Roll 182, Frame 000555.

[98] PRO FO371/43692 R14538/9/19, Leeper to FO, August 28, 1944.

[99] See fn. 97.

[100] *HGrE* 65721/1, Entries for August 19-20, 1944; T-311, Roll 182, Frames 000452-000569.

[101] *Ibid.*

[102] *Ibid.*

[103] *HGrE* 65031/1, *OB Suedost* to *HGrE*, August 20, 1944; T-311, Roll 284, Frames 000088-000089.

[104] *HGrF* 75139/2a, *HGrE* to *OB Suedost*, August 23, August 25, and August 29, 1944; T-311, Roll 286, Frames 000564-000565, 000568.

[105] *HGrE* 65721/1, Entries for August 20 and August 24, 1944; T-311, Roll 182, Frames 000567-000560, 000580.

[106] *Ibid.*, Entry for August 29, 1944; T-311, Roll 182, Frame 000599.

[107] *HGrE* 65030 (*Anlagenbuch z. KTB HGrE, Ia*, August 20-September 1, 1944), *HGrE* to *XXII Geb. AK*, August 31, 1944; T-311, Roll 178, Frame 000031.

[108] *HGrE* 64271 (*KTB HGrE, Ia*, September 1-30, 1944), Entries for September 3-4, 1944; T-311, Roll 182, Frames 000629-000631.

[109] *Ibid.; HGrE* 65031/1, *OB Suedost* to *HGrE*, September 4, 1944; T-311, Roll 284, Frame 000011; and *HGrF* 66142 (*Anlagenband KTB, Ic,* February 1-November 4, 1944), Letter from Weichs to Loehr, September 5, 1944; T-311, Roll 286, Frame 000021.

[110] *HGrE* 75139/2a, *Ic Lagebericht*, September 17, 1944; T-311, Roll 286, Frame 000749.

[111] *HGrE* 65030 (*Anlagenband HGrE, Ia*, August 20-September 1, 1944), *HGrE* to *OB Suedost*, September 2, 1944; T-311, Roll 178, Frame 000053. Warlimont, *Inside Hitler's Headquarters*, p. 471.

[112] *HGrE* 65031/1, Neubacher to Weichs, September 16, 1944, and Weichs to *HGrE*, September 16, 1944; T-311, Roll 284, Frames 000045-000046.

[113] Athanasios Chrisohou, Letter to *To Vema*, July 3, 1963, reprinted in Enepekides, *He Ellenike Antistasis*, pp. 245-248. Chrisohou was Governor General of Macedonia for the Rallis government.

[114] *LXXXXI AK* 65959/2 (*Anlagenband zum KTB, Ia, LXXXXI*, October 1-31, 1944, *Ic Lagebericht*, October 1-15, 1944; and *HGrE* 65721/3, Entry for October 4, 1944; T-311, Roll 183, Frame 000760.

[115] General Argiropoulos, Letter to *To Vema*, June 14, 1963, reprinted in Enepekides, *He Ellenike Antistasis*, pp. 240-244. To the deep regret of many who participated in the resistance, EES is officially recognized by the National Resistance Organizations.

[116] *Ibid.*, Woodhouse, *Apple of Discord*, pp. 94-96; Saraphes, *Greek Resistance Army*, pp. 260-263.

[117] *LXXXXI AK* 65959/2, *Ic Lagebericht*, November 6, 1944. Saraphes claimed that EDES Captain Asterios Mikhalakis, a close associate of Colonel "Tom" Barnes, drew up the plan of cooperation between the Germans and the anticommunist partisans of Macedonia. Captain Mikhalakis did serve as the mediator between Lanz and Colonel "Tom" in August and September 1944. See *HGrE* 65031/1, Letter from Mikhalakis to "Tom," September 11, 1944; T-311, Roll 284, Frame 000010. In his book, Saraphes produced a document allegedly signed by Captain Strack of "the German Aegean Command" and Mikhalakis on September 25, 1944, which outlined the plan of turning Macedonia over to the anticommunist *andartes*. There is no record of this agreement in the files of *HGrE*, but the *Ic Lagebericht* of November 6, 1944, of the *LXXXXI AK* gives credit to the substance of Saraphes's document. Saraphes also claimed that Lieutenant-General Scobie asked ELAS to recognize these

nationalist bands as EDES units. ELAS refused, and after some discussion with British officers, attacked and disbanded them in November 1944. See Saraphes, *Greek Resistance Army,* pp. 257-258.

[118] See Chapter Three, pp. 82-83.

[119] *HGrE* 65031/, *HGrE* to *OB Suedost,* September 24, 1944; T-311, Roll 284, Frame 000031.

[120] *Ibid., OB Suedost* to *HGrE,* September 26, 1944; T-311, Roll 284, Frame 000029.

[121] *LXXXXI AK,* 65959/2, *Ic Lagebericht,* October 16-31, 1944.

[122] Stelios Houtas, Letter to *To Vema,* June 26, 1963, in Enepekides, *He Ellenike Antistasis,* pp. 231-235.

[123] Komnenos Pyromaglou, Letter to *To Vema,* June 29, 1963, in Enepekides, *He Ellenike Antistasis,* pp. 235-236.

[124] Enepekides, *He Ellenike Antistasis,* pp. 12-13, 194-195. Since Enepekides does not use the classification system adopted by Britain and America when they began to catalogue the captured German documents at the end of the war, it is difficult to trace many of the documents found in his book. There is no problem as long as he cites the heading of his documents, but often he merely cites the German unit involved and the date with no further identification. The basic document to prove Zervas's collaboration with the Germans is *HGrE* 65034/3, which includes an *Aktennotiz* dated July 8, 1944. It is a summary of the German interpretation of their agreement with Zervas concluded in early February.

[125] PRO WO 204/8833, Barker-Benfield Report, December 27, 1944.

[126] *Ibid.* Between January 1 and December 27, 1944, Zervas received the following supplies:

Arms	5,000	small arms (mostly machine guns)
	140	3-inch mortars
	7,500,000	rounds of small arms ammunition
	16,000	mortar rounds
	6,000	radio sets
Money	168,000	gold sovereigns
Food	296.5	tons
Clothing	53,400	items

[127] Pyromaglou, *He Ethnike Antistasis,* p. 167.

CHAPTER SEVEN

[1] PRO FO371/37206 R10177/4/19, Hollis to E. M. Rose, October 14, 1943.

[2] PRO FO371/37208 R1221/4/19, Middle East Defence Committee (MEDC) to FO and COS, October 12, 1943.

[3] *Ibid.* FO371/37206 R10295/4/19, Leeper to FO, October 16, 1943; FO371/37208 R11753/4/19, Letter from Leeper to Sargent, November 2, 1943; and R11908/4/19, Leeper to FO, November 18, 1943.

⁴ PRO FO371/37206 R10894/4/19, Sargent to Halifax, October 30, 1943.

⁵ PRO FO371/37208 R11058/4/19, Minute by Churchill, November 3, 1943.

⁶ PRO FO371/37208 R11453/4/19, Eden to P.M., November 19, 1943.

⁷ PRO CAB 65/40 W.M.(43) 160, Minutes, November 22, 1943.

⁸ PRO FO 371/37209 R1342/4/19, Minute by Laskey, December 20, 1943.

⁹ Ibid.

¹⁰ PRO FO371/37210 R13635/4/19, Minute by Laskey, December 28, 1943.

¹¹ PRO FO371/37210 R13883/4/19, Sargent to Leeper, January 6, 1944.

¹² PRO FO371/43674 R227/9/19, Minute by Laskey, January 12, 1944; FO371/43675 R936/9/19, Leeper to FO, January 16, 1944; and Office of Strategic Services (OSS) 56200, Memorandum by Captain McCulloch, January 26, 1944.

¹³ PRO FO371/43677 R1642/9/19, Leeper to FO, January 22, 1944.

¹⁴ PRO FO371/43676 R1202/9/19, Tsouderos to Woodhouse, January 18, 1944; and R1440/9/19, Leeper to FO, January 27, 1944.

¹⁵ FO371/43676 R1563/9/19, Leeper to FO, January 30, 1944.

¹⁶ PRO FO371/43676 R1440/9/19, Leeper to FO, January 27, 1944; and R1454/9/19, Leeper to FO, January 28, 1944.

¹⁷ Saraphes, Greek Resistance Army, p. 153.

¹⁸ Pyromaglou, Ho Georgios Kartalis, p. 246; PRO FO371/43697 R2697/9/19, Woodhouse tel., February 17, 1944.

¹⁹ PRO FO371/43679 R2706/9/19, Sargent to Leeper, February 23, 1944.

²⁰ Georgios Papandreou, He Apeleutherosis tes Ellados (Athens; Ekdoseis "Alpha" I. Skazike, n.d.), p. 17, hereinafter cited as Papandreou, He Apeleutherosis.

²¹ Kousoulas, Revolution and Defeat, p. 180.

²² PRO FO371/43679 R2697/9/19, Memorandum of Svolos-"Apollo" Conversation, February 14, 1944.

²³ PRO FO371/43680 R2997/9/19, Minute by Laskey, February 25, 1944.

²⁴ Pyromaglou, Ho Georgios Kartalis, pp. 219-220.

²⁵ PRO FO371/24677 R1687/9/19, War Cabinet to GHQ ME, February 2, 1944.

²⁶ PRO FO371/43676 R1484/9/19, COS Paper on "Noah's Ark," January 24, 1944; Minutes by Eden and Sargent, January 29, 1944.

²⁷ PRO FO371/43678 R1940/9/19, Eden to P.M., February 10, 1944; Minute by Churchill, February 14, 1944; and FO371/43679 R2553/9/19, COS Conference, February 18, 1944.

²⁸ PRO FO371/43678 R2276/9/19, Leeper to FO, February 11, 1944; Laskey to Leeper, February 14, 1944.

²⁹ PRO FO371/43680 R2997/9/19, Minute by Laskey, February 25, 1944.

³⁰ PRO FO371/43681 R3810/9/19, Leeper to FO, March 9, 1944; Minute by Laskey, March 10, 1944; Minute by P.M., March 10, 1944.

³¹ Stavrianos, "Mutiny of the Greek Armed Forces," 307; and Harold

Macmillan, *The Blast of War, 1939-1945* (London: Macmillan, 1967), p. 571, hereinafter cited as *Blast of War*.

[32] PRO FO371/43682 R3988/9/19, Leeper to FO, March 14, 1944; Memorandum from Eden to P.M., March 15, 1944; and FO to Leeper, March 17, 1944.

[33] Woodward, *British Foreign Policy*, III, p. 407.

[34] Iatrides, *Revolt in Athens*, pp. 47-48.

[35] PRO FO371/43714 R7081/273/30, Laskey Memorandum, April 28, 1944; FO371/43728 R5501/745/19, Leeper to FO, April 6, 1944; and R5317/745/19, Leeper to FO, April 3, 1944.

[36] OSS 80514, "Greek Revolutionary Movement and Mutiny in the Middle East, April, 1944," MacVeagh to Sec. of State, June 13, 1944. The basic source of the ambassador's report was Tsouderos.

[37] Iatrides, *Revolt in Athens*, pp. 54-55.

[38] PRO FO371/43728 R5667/745/19, P.M. to Leeper, April 9, 1944; FO371/43728 R5692/745/19, P.M. to Leeper, April 8, 1944; and FO371/43729 R5972/745/19, P.M. to FO, April 11, 1944.

[39] PRO FO371/43714 R7081/273/30, Wilson to War Office, July 19, 1944.

[40] Kédros, *La résistance grecque*, pp. 413-414.

[41] PRO FO371/37200 R9388/1/19, September 30, 1943.

[42] The memorandum of July 1943 was published in Papandreou, *He Apeleutherosis*, pp. 13-15; reprinted in George Papandreou, *The Third War* (Athens, "Hellas," 1948), pp. 15-26. PRO FO371/43678 R2263/9/19, Leeper to FO, February 12, 1944; and FO371/43679 R2562/9/19, Leeper to FO, February 17, 1944.

[43] PRO FO371/43685 R6101/9/19, Leeper to FO, April 16, 1944; FO371/43679 R2562/9/19, Minute by Laskey, February 17, 1944; and FO371/43730 R7288/745/19, Minute by Laskey, May 9, 1944.

[44] William H. McNeill, *The Greek Dilemma: War and Aftermath* (Philadelphia: J. B. Lippincott, 1947), pp. 129-130, hereinafter cited as *Greek Dilemma*.

[45] Iatrides, *Revolt in Athens*, pp. 64-65.

[46] PRO FO371/43732 R9776/745/19, List of Delegates to the Lebanon Conference, n.d.

[47] *Ibid.*

[48] PRO FO371/43731 R7607/745/19, Leeper to FO, May 13, 1944.

[49] PRO FO371/43731 R7608/745/19, Leeper to FO, May 13, 1944.

[50] PRO FO371/43731 R7608/745/19, Leeper to FO, May 13, 1944; Minute by Laskey, May 17, 1944.

[51] *Ibid.*

[52] OSS 75732, Research and Analysis Report on EAM at Lebanon, June 1, 1944.

[53] Pyromaglou, *Ho Georgios Kartalis*, p. 561. Two prominent members and officers who would play important roles in postwar affairs were Generals Speliotopoulos and Venderes. Political leadership for the Military Hierarchy came from conservatives Spyros Theotokis and Spyros Markezines. Markezines played a key role in the formation of Papagos's Greek Rally in 1950. See Carey and Carey, *Modern Greek Politics*, p. 154.

[54] Pyromaglou, *Ho Georgios Kartalis*, pp. 313-314; and Fleischer, "Contacts," p. 2.

[55] PRO FO371/43686 R6692/9/19, Cairo Telegram 3441, April 13, 1944, Cairo Telegram 3442, April 14, 1944, and Cairo Telegram 3468, April 18, 1944.

[56] PRO FO371/43675 R751/9/19, Woodhouse to Cairo, May 7, 1944.

[57] Interview, May 17, 1975.

[58] Kousoulas, *Revolution and Defeat*, p. 186; and Pyromaglou, *Ho Georgios Kartalis*, p. 326.

[59] PRO FO371/43731 R7823/745/19, Leeper to FO, May 14, 1944; R7895/745/19, Minute by Laskey, May 20, 1944; R7969/745/19, Leeper to FO, May 20, 1944; and R7970/745/19, Leeper to FO, May 20, 1944.

[60] PRO FO371/43731 R7895/745/19, Minute by Laskey, May 20, 1944.

[61] PRO FO371/43731 R8299/745/19, Minute by Laskey, May 20, 1944; and R8331/745/19, FO to Leeper, May 28, 1944.

[62] Papandreou, *He Apeleutherosis*, 59-66.

[63] McNeill, *Greek Dilemma*, pp. 140-141.

[64] Kousoulas, *Revolution and Defeat*, p. 190; and Eudes, *The Kapetanios*, pp. 141-144.

[65] PRO FO371/43731 R8104/745/19, May 23, 1944.

[66] PRO FO371/43731 R8186/745/19, Bakirtzis, Siantos, and Hadzes to Svolos, May 24, 1944.

[67] PRO FO371/43782 R8636/745/19, Leeper to FO, June 1, 1944. Georgios Sakalis was a former Venizelist who had reformed seamen's pensions in 1906. He refused to cooperate with Plastiras and in 1932 joined Kaphandaris's Progressive Party, which he represented at Lebanon.

[68] PRO FO371/43693 R15286/9/19, Brigadier Barker-Benfield Memorandum, September 28, 1944. Svolos passed this information on to Brigadier Barker-Benfield who was on an SOE mission to Greece during August 1944.

[69] PRO FO371/43732 R8789/745/19, Leeper to FO, June 4, 1944.

[70] PRO FO371/43746 R8886/1402/19, Leeper to FO, June 6, 1944; Minute by Eden, June 8, 1944; and R9408/1402/19, Leeper to FO, June 14, 1944.

[71] The government on June 8 included Venizelos as Vice-Premier (Liberal); Constantinos Rendes (Liberal), Minister without portfolio; Themistocles Tsatsos (Liberal), Justice; Gerasimos Vaseliades (Liberal), Undersecretary of the Navy; Lambros Lambrianides (Social Democrat), Political Office of the Prime Minister; Georgios Sakalis (Progressive) Interior; Alexandros Mylonas (Agrarian Democrat), Navy; P. Kanellopoulos (National Unity), Finance; S. Theotokis (National Populist), Relief; Charalambos Zgouritsas (Social Democrat), Undersecretary of Foreign Affairs; P. Dragoumis (Independent), Foreign Affairs; Petros Rallis (Populist), Air Force; Demetrios Londos (Populist), Social Welfare; and Kartalis (EKKA), Press.

[72] Iatrides, *Revolt in Athens*, p. 68.

[73] PRO FO371/43688 R9537/9/19, Woodhouse telegram, June 5, 1944.

[74] PRO FO371/43676 R1012/9/19, Leeper to FO, June 27, 1944.

[75] PRO WO 106/3225, Copy of Memorandum from Leeper to FO, July 9, 1944.

[76] PRO FO371/43689 R10466/9/19, Leeper to FO, July 4, 1944.

[77] PRO FO371/43689 R10506/9/19, Minute by Sargent, July 6, 1944.

[78] Iatrides, *Revolt in Athens*, pp. 296-303. Iatrides has published a full text of the letter.

[79] PRO FO371/43689 R10506/9/19, Minute by Sargent, July 6, 1944, and Eden to P.M., July 7, 1944.

[80] The senior officials of the Foreign Office were quite frustrated by the situation in Greece by the summer of 1944, but few exhibited the scorn and cynicism of David Wallace, the Foreign Officer sent back into Greece in July and August 1944. In a long report covering his travels in Epirus before he was killed by a German attack, Wallace telegraphed:

> In spite of much kindness and hospitality I can see no reason to modify my view of Greeks as formed in the Middle East. I am convinced they are a fundamentally hopeless and useless people with no future or prospect of settling down to any form of sensible life within any measurable time. Our effort in Greece, in men and money, has not only been out of all proportion to the results we have achieved against the Germans but also to the value of the Greek people, who are not capable of being saved from themselves nor for themselves ... This is the unanimous opinion of all British liaison officers who have long been in the country.

He added:

> Unfortunately Greece's geographical position makes her of vital importance to our strategic interests in the eastern Mediterranean.

Laskey minuted his approval of Wallace's observations. See PRO FO371/43692 R14686/9/19, Wallace to Leeper, August 15, 1944. Another case was that of BLO Major W. S. Jordan who reported on April 22, 1944:

> I found it important to take the trouble to make living standard conditions as comfortable and pleasant as possible. Tablecloths, curtains, and serviettes were made from parachutes, cutlery and crockery procured, and I insisted on food being cooked as nearly possible according to British standards. Some took the view we should live as the Greeks live. I consider such a view pernicious. Greek living conditions and hygienic standards are revolting. I consider my attitude good for our morale and for British prestige. Frequently when setting up an HQ in a new village I had to build a lavatory—the first the village had ever seen.

See PRO FO371/43686 R7187/9/19, April 22, 1944.

[81] PRO FO371/43686 R7387/9/19, Woodhouse to GHQ ME, May 3, 1944.

[82] PRO FO371/R4186/9/19, Woodhouse tel., April 22, 1944; and FO371/43688 R9811/9/19, Leeper to FO, June 21, 1944.

[83] Ibid.

[84] PRO FO371/43689 R10506/9/19, Eden to P.M., July 7, 1944.

[85] PRO FO371/43689 R10612/9/19, Minute by Laskey, July 8, 1944; Eden to P.M., July 8, 1944; and FO371/43715 R12977/273/19, P.M. to Eden, July 15, 1944.

[86] PRO FO371/43715 R12781/273/19, Woodhouse Memorandum, July 25, 1944; Minute by G. L. McDermott, August 22, 1944.

[87] Iatrides, *Revolt in Athens*, pp. 101-102.

[88] PRO FO371/43733 R12153/745/19, Leeper to FO, August 4, 1944; and FO371/43734 R12437/745/19, Leeper to FO, August 10, 1944.

[89] Iatrides, *Revolt in Athens*, p. 102.

[90] PRO FO371/43733 R12371/745/19, Leeper to FO, August 9, 1944.

[91] PRO FO371/43715 R12457/273/19, Foreign Office Notes for Cabinet Paper, August 8, 1944.

[92] PRO FO371/43746 R/13199/1402/19, Minute to Eden, August 27, 1944.

[93] PRO FO371/43746 R13756/1402/19, Leeper to FO, August 31, 1944.

[94] Churchill cabled FDR on August 17 of his conviction that EAM/ELAS would attempt to seize power and that only British forces could prevent it, and on August 26 Roosevelt replied that he had no objection to Churchill's preparations. Although the Stalin-Churchill agreement on the Balkans was not finalized until October, there had been a tacit agreement to divide Rumania and Greece between the two powers since May 5, 1944. There was nothing in Russian behavior to indicate that the Soviets were not abiding by the May understanding, and Moscow approved of the dispatch of British forces to Greece on September 23. See PRO FO371/43693 R15193/9/19, Soviet Memorandum to FO, September 23, 1944.

[95] Iatrides, *Revolt in Athens*, pp. 111-112; and PRO FO371/43691 R13843/9/19, Leeper to FO, September 3, 1944. Iatrides has published a letter from Rendes to Zervas which explained their reasons for resigning.

[96] Iatrides, *Revolt in Athens*, p. 115.

[97] PRO PREM/3 212/12, Dixon to J.H. Peck, December 15, 1944.

[98] PRO CAB 66/59 W.P. (44) 743, December 19, 1944.

[99] PRO FO371/432692 R14436/9/19, Warner to FO, September 12, 1944; and *Ibid*, BLO telegram 1521, September 12, 1944.

[100] Henry Maule, *Scobie*, p. 60.

[101] PRO FO371/43736 R20177/9/19, Allied Information Service (AIS) Weekly Report, November 7, 1944.

[102] PRO FO371/43717 R16400/273/19, P.M. to Eden, October 6, 1944.

[103] PRO FO371/43717 R16474/273/19, Leeper to FO, October 13, 1944.

[104] PRO FO371/43693 R16288/9/19, David Talbot-Rice to Laskey, October 8, 1944. Peltekis was exonerated by his trial, and in 1945 Britain awarded him the Distinguished Service Order. At the time of the affair, Col. David Talbot-Rice was incensed at the efforts of Warner and Waterhouse to destroy the reputation and effectiveness of a loyal and able agent, and he eventually won from the Foreign Office an admission of error on their part in the affair. The records of the trial, which should reveal a lot about internal Greek politics, are not available to researchers.

[105] PRO FO371/43717 R18019/273/19, Leeper to FO, October 20, 1944.

[106] Iatrides, *Revolt in Athens*, pp. 149-150. These documents were captured by British authorities during the December conflict.

[107] PRO FO371/43736 R19953/9/19, A.I.S. Weekly Report: Thessaly, No. 1, November 9, 1944.

[108] PRO FO371/43736 R20091/9/19, AFHQ to FO, December 2, 1944.

[109] Iatrides, *Revolt in Athens*, p. 156.

[110] PRO FO371/43736 R20162/9/19, Leeper to FO, November 26, 1944.

[111] PRO FO371/43736 R20177/9/19, A.I.S. Weekly Report, November 7, 1944.

[112] *Ibid.*

[113] Iatrides, *Revolt in Athens*, pp. 166-167.

[114] PRO FO371/43736 R20177/9/19, Situation in Greece–November 1944 by Major W. F. Reid, November 16, 1944.

[115] PRO WO 204/8858, Greece: Communist Party, October 31, 1944.

[116] PRO WO 170/251, War Diary 3rd Corps, General Staff Branch November-December, Fortnightly Internal Situation Summary (Mimeographed copy, n.d.).

[117] Interview, April 30, 1975.

[118] *Ibid.*

[119] PRO FO371/43695 R17752/9/19, Leeper to FO, November 2, 1944; and R17961/9/19, Minute by Churchill, November 7, 1944.

[120] PRO FO371/43695 R18257/9/19, Leeper to FO, November 9, 1944.

[121] Interview, April 30, 1975.

[122] Iatrides, *Revolt in Athens*, pp. 157-158.

[123] PRO FO371/43695 R18600/9/19, Leeper to FO, November 15, 1944.

[124] PRO FO371/43695 R18644/9/19, Leeper to FO, November 16, 1944.

[125] PRO FO371/43695 R18645/9/19, Leeper to FO, November 16, 1944.

[126] PRO FO371/43695 R18655/9/19, Churchill to Wilson, November 15, 1944; and FO to the Resident Minister's Office Central Mediterranean, Caserta, from the Prime Minister, November 19, 1944.

[127] PRO FO371/43695 R18677/9/19, Leeper to FO, November 17, 1944.

[128] PRO FO371/43695 R18677/9/19, Leeper to FO, November 18, 1944; and FO371/43696 R18941/9/19, Leeper to FO, November 20, 1944.

[129] The controversy surrounding the November 22 meeting is typical of the problems encountered in writing on this period of Greek history. EAM sources document the meeting, but it is not recognized by EAM's opponents. See National Liberation Front, *EAM White Book, March 1944-March 1945* (New York: Greek American Council, 1945), Doc. 28. This edition is a translation of the original published five months earlier in Trikkala by EAM. Another account of the meeting is given in Svolos's article, which he wrote for the Socialist newspaper *Mache* (Combat) on December 5, 1944. Svolos, a leading non-communist member of EAM, headed the EAM ministers who negotiated with Papandreou on the question of demobilization of the guerrillas. A long excerpt from the article is reprinted by Stavrianos on page 249 of "Immediate Origins." There is no reference to the November 22 meeting in the British White Paper, which was issued during the crisis. See Great Britain, Foreign Office, Documents Regarding the Situation in Greece, January 1945 (London: H.M.S.O., 1945). The accounts by Churchill, Eden, Macmillan, Papandreou, and Kousoulas begin with the November 28 meeting and ignore November 22. *Cf.* Churchill, *Triumph and Tragedy*, Chapters 18-19; and Macmillan, *Blast of War*, Chapters XXI-XXII. Iatrides implies a modified acceptance of Svolos, but Woodhouse argues strongly against it. See Iatrides, *Revolt in Athens*, pp. 169-173; and Woodhouse, *The Struggle for Greece*, pp. 117-118.

[130] PRO FO371/43696 R18941/9/19, Leeper to FO, November 20, 1944.

[131] PRO FO371/43735 R19286/745/19, Leeper to FO, November 25, 1944.

[132] PRO PREM/3 212/10, Memorandum by the King of the Hellenes, November 27, 1944.

[133] PRO FO371/43735 R19341/745/19, Leeper to FO, November 26, 1944; and R19306/745/19, Leeper to FO, November 26, 1944.

[134] Ibid.

[135] Iatrides, Revolt in Athens, pp. 169-170.

[136] PRO CAB 59 W.P. (44) 686, Scobie Telegram, November 25, 1944.

[137] PRO FO371/43696 R19559/9/19, Leeper to FO, November 28, 1944; and R19560/9/19, Leeper to FO, November 28, 1944.

[138] PRO FO371/43697 R19672/9/19, Churchill to Eden, November 28, 1944.

[139] Ibid.

[140] PRO FO371/43736 R19718/9/19, Leeper to FO (Copy of Original Draft Decree on Demobilization), November 30, 1944.

[141] PRO FO371/43693 R9766/9/19, Leeper to FO, December 1, 1944.

[142] PRO FO371/43696 R19802/9/19, Leeper to FO, December 1, 1944.

[143] The controversy over who was responsible for the outbreak of violence continues. The debate centers over whether the demonstrators were armed or unarmed, and who fired the first shot. At least one account charges that a Communist *agent provocateur* disguised as a Greek policeman fired into the crowd with a submachine gun in order to blame the police and government for causing the violence and to justify the EAM/ELAS cause. The majority of the eyewitness accounts, however, report that the demonstrators were unarmed and that the police fired not blanks but real bullets into the crowd. *Cf.* Kousoulas, Revolution and Defeat, p. 207; Stavrianos, "Immediate Origins," 250-251; and Byford-Jones, Greek Trilogy, pp. 138-140.

[144] See PRO WO 170/4049, War Diary HQ 1 District, December 3, 1944. The PRO documents have not produced any new evidence which resolves either the issue of who fired the first shot or the charge that communists conspired to provoke the police attack. The best account remains Iatrides, Revolt in Athens, pp. 181-193.

[145] PRO FO371/48279 R15585/4/19, Political Review of Greek Affairs for 1944, September 5, 1945.

[146] Ibid.

[147] PRO WO 170/581, War Diary of the 23rd Armoured Brigade, December 6, 1944.

[148] PRO WO 204/8837, Main HQ to HQ 3 Corps, December 8, 1944.

[149] PRO WO 170/4048, War Diary HQ Military Commander Athens, December 17-December 31, 1944, Intelligence Summary, December 14, 1944; and FO371/43739 R26412/745/19, Leeper to FO, December 10, 1944.

[150] Interview with D. Partsalides, April 30, 1975.

[151] PRO FO371/48279 R15585/4/19, Political Review of Greek Affairs for 1944, September 5, 1945.

[152] PRO PREM/3 212/12, Leeper to FO, December 15, 1944.

[153] Macmillan, Blast of War, p. 612. In 1948 the leading Athenian daily, Kathemerine, attacked Papandreou for allowing the KKE (EAM/ELAS) to take cabinet posts in the Greek government after Lebanon. The editorial used the 1948 Czech *coup* to reemphasize the folly of compromising with the communists. In his reply, Papandreou justified his policy as part of a plan to give Britain the legal right to land troops in Greece and to use force against EAM/ELAS. Papandreou objected to the editor's

reference to the December insurrection as "a gift from heaven," that is, a blunder that gave Britain and the Greek government the opportunity to smash EAM/ELAS. Papandreou indicated that December was not a fortuitous or divine act, but that his policy brought about December. He claimed that his policy placed EAM/ELAS on the horns of a dilemma; they had to accept disarmament peacefully or attempt an insurrection, which could occur only under conditions favorable to the government. See Papandreou, *The Third War*, pp. 30-38.

[154] PRO FO371/48245 R579/4/19, Minute by Laskey, January 9, 1945.

[155] PRO FO371/44249 R1325/4/19, Leeper to FO, January 17, 1945; and R1373/4/19, Leeper to FO, January 18, 1945.

[156] PRO FO371/48266 R6820/4/19, Leeper to FO, April 5, 1945.

[157] PRO FO371/48256 R4036/4/19, Leeper to FO, March 15, 1945.

[158] PRO FO371/48268 R7928/4/19, Hepple to Dixon, January 9, 1945; and FO371/48256 R3218/4/19, Minute by Howard, February 22, 1945.

[159] PRO FO371/48279 R15198/4/19, Leeper to FO, September 7, 1945; and FO371/48281 R16303/4/19, September 24, 1945.

[160] PRO FO371/48286 R19943/4/19, Leeper to FO, November 26, 1945.

[161] PRO FO371/48259 R4385/4/19, Athens to FO, March 5, 1945, Minutes by Laskey and Sargent.

[162] PRO FO371/48285 R19684/4/19, Notes on Visit to Greece, October-November, November 14, 1945.

[163] PRO FO371/48372 R21325, British Police Mission Report, December 5, 1945.

[164] PRO FO371/48279 R14973/4/19, Report on the Situation in the Peloponnese, August 11, 1945.

[165] PRO FO371/48263 R5857/4/19, Leeper to Eden, March 29, 1945.

[166] Frank Smothers, William H. McNeill, and Elizabeth McNeill, *Report on the Greeks* (New York: The Twentieth Century Fund, 1948), pp. 28-30.

[167] Kousoulas, *Revolution and Defeat*, p. 197. Zachariades's charge is repeated in Zizis Zografos, "Some Lessons of the Civil War in Greece," *World Marxist Review*, VII (November 1964), 43-50.

[168] Thomas P. Trombetas, "Consensus and Cleavage: Party Alignment in Greece, 1945-1965," *Parliamentary Affairs*, XIX, No. 3 (1966), 305.

GLOSSARY AND ABBREVIATIONS

Abendsmeldung		Evening report
Abschlussbericht		Final report
Abwehr		Central Intelligence of the German Army
Abwicklung		Final report
Allied Military Mission	AMM	
Andartes		Greek for guerrillas
Anlagenband		Appendix to War Diary
Apeleutherotike Stratiotike Organosis	ASO	Military Liberation Organization
Armeekorps	A.K. (AK.)	Army Corps
Armeeoberkommando	AOK	Headquarters of an Army
Banden		Partisans or guerrillas
Befehlshaber Saloniki-Aegaeis	Befh. Saloniki-Aegaeis	Commander Salonica-Aegean
Befehlshaber Sued-griechenland	Befh. Sued-Grld.	Commander Southern Greece
Bevollmaechtigter		Plenipotentiary
British Liaison Officer	BLO	
British Military Mission	BMM	
Chiefs of Staff	COS	
Documents on German Foreign Policy	DGFP	
Ethniko Apeleutherotiko Metopo	EAM	National Liberation Front
Ethniki Drasis	ED	National Action
Ethnikos Democratikos Ellenikos Synthesmos	EDES	National Republican Greek League
Ergatiko Ethniko Apeleutherotiko Metopo	EEAM	Workers National Liberation Front
Ethnikos Ellenikos Stratos	EES	National Greek Army; an independent collaboration unit
Ethnike Enosis Ellados	EEE	National Union of Greece; a fascist party
Ethnike Kai Koinonike Apeleutherosis	EKKA	National and Social Liberation

301

Ellenikos Laikos Apeleutherotikos Stratos	ELAS	Popular Greek Liberation Army; guerrilla arm of EAM
Ethnike Organosis Ellenon Andarton	EOEA	National League of Greek Guerrillas; part of EDES
Ethnike Sosialistike Politike Organosis	ESPO	National Socialist Political Organization; Greek Nazi party
Foreign Office	FO	
Foreign Relations of the United States	FRUS	
Freiwilliger	Freiw.	Indigenous collaborator (military)
Freiwilligen-Verbaende	Freiw.-Verb.	Volunteer formations; Greek Security Battalions
Gebirgs-Division (Gebirgsdivision)	Geb. Div.	Mountain Division
Geheime Feldpolizei	GFP	Secret Field Police (army)
General Headquarters Middle East	GHQ ME	
Generalkommando	Gen. Kdo. (GenKdo)	Army Corps Headquarters
Heeresgruppe	HGr	Army Group
Heeresgruppe E	HGrE	Army Group E
Hilfswilliger	Hiwis	Indigenous volunteer (labor)
Hoeherer SS-und Polizeifuehrer	HSSPF	Higher SS and Police Leader
Ia		Staff officer for operations in the German Army
Ic		Staff officer for counter-intelligence in the German Army
International Red Cross	IRC	
IV Wi		Staff section for economics in the German Army
Jagdkommando		Small, mobile anti-partisan unit
Jaeger-Division (Jaegerdivision)	Jg. Div.	Light Infantry Division
Joint General Headquarters (Greek Andartes)	JGHQ	

Kommounistikon	KKE	Greek Communist Party
Komma Ellados		
Kriegstagebuch	KTB	War Diary
Kriegstagebuch HGrE	KTB/HGrE	War Diary of
		Army Group E
Kriegstagebuch	KTB/OKW	War Diary of
Oberkommando		the Armed Forces
der Wehrmacht		High Command
Lagebericht		Situation Report
Luftwaffenfeld-	Lw-Feld-	Infantry division made
Division	Div.	up of Air Force
		personnel
LXVIII Armeekorps	LXVIII A. K.	68th Army Corps
	(AK.)	
Militaerbefehlshaber	Mil. Befh.	Military Commander
		(rear areas)
Militaerbefehlshaber	Mil. Befh.	Military Commander
Griechenland	Grld.	Greece
Militaerbefehlshaber	Mil. Befh.	Military Commander
Suedost	Suedost	Southeast
Nuremberg-	NOKW	Nuremberg documents
Oberkommando		pertaining to
der Wehrmacht		the Armed Forces
Oberbefehlshaber	O.B.	Armed Forces Theater
		Commander
Office of Strategic	OSS	
Services		
Organosis Politikes	OPLA	Organization of Political
Laikes Amynas		Popular Security
Panellenios Apeleutherotike	PAO	Pan-Hellenic
Organosis		Liberation Organization
Politike Epitrope	PEEA	Political Committee for
Ethnikes		National Liberation
Apeleutherosis		
Public Record Office	PRO	
Roumeli-Avlon-Nisi	RAN	Roumeli-Valona-Islands
Sammelmappe		Portfolio
Sicherheitsdienst	SD	SS security and
		intelligence service
Sicherheitspolizei	Sipo	Security police
Special Operations	SOE	
Executive		
Sonderbevollmaechtigter		Special Plenipotentiary
SS-Polizei-Panzer-	SS-Pol-Pz-Gr-	SS Police Motorized
Grenadier-Regiment	Rgt.	Infantry Regiment

Taetigkeitsbericht		Activity report
Tagesmeldung		Daily report
Vertrauensmann	V-Mann	Intelligence agent, informer
Verwaltungsbericht		Administration report
War Office	WO	
Wehrmachtsbefehlshaber	W.B.	Armed Forces Commander; highest ranking military officer in a rear area under civilian control
Wehrwirtschaftsoffizier	WO	Economic Officer of the German Army
Wirtschaftsstab Griechenland	Wi Stb Grld	Economic staff Greece
Wi/1C1.		OKW/Wi Rue Amt records for Greece
Wirtschafts-und Ruestung Amt	Wi Rue Amt	Economic Armament Office of the OKW
XXII Gebirgsarmeekorps	XXII Geb. A.K. (AK.)	22nd Mountain Army Corps
Yperaspistai Boreiou Ellados	YBE	Defenders of Northern Greece

BIBLIOGRAPHY

A. PRIMARY SOURCES

1. Unpublished Materials

NATIONAL ARCHIVES
Washington, D.C.

U.S. Department of State, Decimal File 740.0011 (1940-1941).
_____, Decimal File 868.00 (1936-1944)
_____, Decimal File 869.42 (1942).
World War Two Records Division, Nurenberg Trials Collection, Series NOKW (Photostatic copies of documents relating to the *Oberkommando der Wehrmacht*).
_____. Office of Strategic Services (OSS).
872, 75732, 80514, 92056, and 107604

NATIONAL ARCHIVES
World War Two Records Center, Alexandria, Va.

Records of the German Army Field Commands:
Army Corps (LXVIII Armeekorps).

LXVIII 37616/2, "Anlagen zum Kriegstagebuch Nr. 2 Gen.Kdo. LXVIII. A.K., Ia," Feb.-July 1943.
LXVIII AK 37616/3, "Taetigkeitsbericht Gen.Kdo. LXVIII.A.K., Ic," Mar.-June 1943.
LXVIII AK 44058/1, "Kriegstagebuch Nr. 3 Gen.Kdo. LXVIII.A.K., Ia," July-Dec. 1943.
LXVIII AK 44058/2, "Anlagen zum Kriegstagebuch Gen.Kdo. LXVIII. A.K., Ia," July-Aug. 1943.
LXVIII AK 44058/4, "Anlagenband 3 zum Kriegstagebuch Nr. 3 Gen. Kdo. LXVIII.A.K., Ia," Sept.-Oct. 1943.
LXVIII AK 44058/5, "Anlagenband 4 zum Kriegstagebuch Nr. 3 Gen. Kdo. LXVIII. A.K., Ia," Nov.-Dec. 1943.
LXVIII AK 44058/6, "Anlagenband 5 zum Kriegstagebuch Nr. 3 Gen. Kdo. LXVIII.A.K., Ia," July-Dec. 1943.
LXVIII AK 44058/8, "Anlagenband zum Taetigkeitsbericht Gen.Kdo. LXVIII.A.K., Ic," Sept.-Dec. 1943.

LXVIII AK 44058/9, "Kriegstagebuch Nr. 3 LXVIII/Abt. Qu.," July-Dec. 1943.
LXVIII AK 44058/10, "Anlagenband 1 zum Kriegstagebuch Nr. 3 Gen. Kdo. LXVIII/Abt. Qu.," July-Dec. 1943.
LXVIII AK 54960/1, "Kriegstagebuch Nr. 4 Gen.Kdo. LXVIII.A.K., Ia," Jan.-June 1944.
LXVIII AK 54960/2, "Anlagenband 1 zum Kriegstagebuch Nr. 4 Gen. Kdo. LXVIII.A.K., Ia," Oct. 1943-Feb. 1944.
LXVIII AK 54960/3, "Anlagenband 2 zum Kriegstagebuch Nr. 4 Gen. Kdo. LXVIII.A.K., Ia," Mar.-Apr. 1944.
LXVIII AK 54960/4, "Anlagenband 3 zum Kriegstagebuch Nr. 4 Gen. Kdo. LXVIII.A.K., Ia," Jan.-June 1944.
LXVIII AK 54960/6, "Anlagenband zum Kriegstagebuch Nr. 4 Gen. Kdo. LXVIII.A.K., Ia," Jan.-June 1944.
LXVIII AK 54961/1, "Taetigkeitsbericht Gen.Kdo. LXVIII.A.K., Ic," Jan.-June 1944.
LXVIII AK 54961/2, "Anlagenband zum Taetigkeitsbericht Gen.Kdo. LXVIII.A.K., Ic," Jan.-June 1944.
LXVIII AK 54962/1, "Kriegstagebuch Nr. 4 LXVIII/Abt. Qu.," Jan.-June 1944.
LXXXXI AK 65959/2, "Anlagenband Ia," Oct. 1944.

Record Groups 1016 and 1026, German Armed Forces High Command, Economic and Armament Office, (OKW/Wi Rue Amt), "Greece File":

Wi/1C1.1 OKW/Wirtschafts-und Ruestungsamt (Misc. Economic Documents), Mar. 10-Sept. 11, 1942.
Wi/1C1.2 OKW/Wirtschafts-und Ruestungsamt (Misc. Economic Documents), Dec. 31, 1942-Apr. 30, 1943.
Wi/1C1.3 OKW/Wirtschafts-und Ruestungsamt (Misc. Economic Documents), Sept. 1939-June 1941.
Wi/1C1.4 OKW/ Wirtschaftsstab Ausland (Misc. Economic Documents), Sept. 7, 1943-Oct. 6, 1944.
Wi/1C1.5 Wirtschaftsstab Griechenland (Misc. Economic Documents), Nov. 1943.
Wi/1C1.6 OKW/FW Amt (Misc. Economic Documents), Dec. 31, 1943-Nov. 14, 1944.
Wi/1C1.7 OKW/Wirtschafts-und Ruestungsamt (Folder on oil situation in Greece), Nov. 30, 1939-Feb. 28, 1942.
Wi/1C1.8 OKW/Wirtschafts-und Ruestungsamt (Folder containing mostly Taetigkeitsberichte), Nov. 27, 1941-Jan. 15, 1942.
Wi/1C1.9 OKW/Wirtschafts-und Ruestungsamt (Misc. Economic Documents), Dec. 31, 1940-Oct. 1, 1941.
Wi/1C1.10 OKW/Wirtschafts-und Ruestungsamt (Misc. Economic Documents), Dec. 1, 1940-Dec. 31, 1941.
Wi/1C1.11 OKW/Wirtschafts-und Ruestungsamt (Misc. Economic Documents), Jan. 1-Nov. 30, 1941.
Wi/1C1.12 OKW/FW Amt (Mostly Feldwirtschaftsamt reports on ore production), May-June 1944.
Wi/1C1.13 OKW/FW Amt (Tables on ore production for Greece and Southeast Europe), May-Dec. 1944.

Wi/1C1.14 OKW/FW Amt (No title), Oct. 1944.

Wi/1C1.15, "Kriesgtagebuch Wirtschaftsoffizier Saloniki," Apr. 9, 1941-Nov. 30, 1941.

Wi/1C1.16, "Kriegstagebuch Wirtschaftsoffizier Saloniki v. Oct. 1, 1941-Sept. 30, 1942, mit Anlagen."

Wi/1C1.17, "Kriegstagebuch Wirtschaftsoffizier Saloniki v. Oct. 1, 1942-Dec. 31, 1942, mit Anlagen."

Wi/1C1.18, "Kriegstagebuch Wirtschaftsoffizier Saloniki v. Jan. 1-Mar. 1943, mit Anlagen."

Wi/1C1.19, "Kriegstagebuch Wirtschaftsoffizier Saloniki v. Apr. 1-June 30, 1943"

Wi/1C1.20, "Kriegstagebuch Wirtschaftsoffizier Saloniki v. July 1-Sept. 30, 1943, mit Anlagen."

Wi/1C1.21, "Lagebericht Wirtschaftsoffizier Saloniki Jan. 1-Dec. 31, 1942."

Wi/1C1.22, "Lagebericht Wirtschaftsoffizier Saloniki Jan. 1-Oct. 31, 1943."

Wi/1C1.23, "Kriegstagebuch Nr. 1 Wirtschaftsoffizier Athen v. Aug. 29-Dec. 31, 1941."

Wi/1C1.24, "Anlagenband 1 zum Kriegstagebuch Nr. 1 Wirtschaftsoffizier Athen v. Aug. 29-Dec. 31, 1941."

Wi/1C1.25, "Kriegstagebuch Nr. 1 Wirtschaftsoffizier Athen v. Jan. 1-Sept. 30, 1942."

Wi/1C1.26, "Anlageband zum Kriegstagebuch Wirtschaftsoffizier Athen Nr. 2 v. Jan. 1-Sept. 30, 1942."

Wi/1C1.27, "Kriegstagebuch Nr. 2 Wirtschaftsoffizier Athen v. Oct. 1-Dec. 31, 1942, mit Anlagen."

Wi/1C1.28, "Kriegstagebuch Wirtschaftsoffizier Athen, Jan. 1943, mit Anlagen."

Wi/1C1.29, "Kriegstagebuch Wirtschaftsoffizier Athen, Feb. 1943, mit Anlagen."

Wi/1C1.30, "Kriegstagebuch Wirtschaftsoffizier Athen, Mar. 1943, mit Anlagen."

Wi/1C1.31, "Kriegstagebuch Wirtschaftsoffizier Athen v. Apr. 1-June 30, 1943, mit Anlagen."

Wi/1C1.32, "Kriegstagebuch Wirtschaftsstab/Kdo v. July 1-Sept. 30, 1943, mit Anlagen."

Wi/1C1.33, "Kriegstagebuch Wirtschaftsstab Griechenland v. Oct. 1-Dec. 31, 1943, mit Anlagen."

Wi/1C1.34, "Kriegstagebuch Wirtschaftsstab Griechenland v. Jan. 1-March 31, 1944, mit Anlagen."

Wi/1C1.35, "Kriegstagebuch Wirtschaftsstab Griechenland v. Apr. 1-June 30, 1944, mit Anlagen."

Wi/1C1.36, "Wirtschaftsoffizier Athen Lagebericht Nov. 1, 1941-July 31, 1942."

Wi/1C1.37, "Wirtschafsoffizier Athen Lagebericht Aug. 1-Dec. 31, 1942."

Wi/1C1.38, "Wirtschaftsoffizier Athen Lagebericht Jan. 1-Dec. 31, 1943."

Wi/1C1.39, "KTB VO OKW/Wi Rue Amt AOK 12 (IV Wi), Apr. 26-June 1941, mit Anlagen."

Wi/1C1.40, "KTB VO OKW/Wi Rue Amt AOK 12 (IV Wi), July 7-Dec. 31, 1941, mit Anlagen."

Wi/1C1.41, "KTB VO OKW/Wi Rue Amt AOK 12 (IV Wi), Jan. 1-Dec. 31, 1942."

Wi/1C1.42, "Taetigkeitsbericht VO OKW/Wi Rue Amt AOK 12 (IV Wi), Apr. 1941, mit Anlagen."

Wi/1C1.43, "Lagebericht Wirtschaftskommando Saloniki, July 10-Dec. 31, 1941."

Wi/1C1.44-45, (Two folders containing misc. economic documents on Greek economy, July 1938-July 1942).

2. Microfilmed Documents

NATIONAL ARCHIVES
World War Two Records Division, Washington, D.C.

Microcopy T-77, Records of Headquarters, German Armed Forces High Command (Oberkommando der Wehrmacht/OKW):

OKW/WSFt OKW/639, "Geheim Akten Propaganda Angelegenheiten," Feb. 1942. Roll 1006, Frames 247088-2470512.

OKW/WPr OKW/731, "W.B. Suedost, 'Prop-Abt.' Lage-und Taetigkeits-bericht," Mar.-May 1942. Roll 1034, Frames 6506446-6506609.

OKW/WPr OKW/734, "W.B. Suedost, 'Prop.-Abt.' Lage-und Taetigkeits-bericht," Mar. 1943. Roll 1035, Frames 6507609-6507652.

OKW/WPr OKW/744, "W.B. Suedost, 'Prop.-Abt.' Lage-und Taetigkeits-bericht," June-Oct. 1942. Roll 983, Frames 4472726-4472988.

Microcopy T-120, Records of the German Foreign Ministry (Auswaertiges Amt):

Auswaertiges Amt, Buero des Staatssekretaers; Griechenland, April 1, 1941-Mar. 31, 1942. Roll 157, Frames 127417-127810.

Auswaertiges Amt, Buero des Staatssekretaers; Griechenland, Apr. 1, 1942-Oct. 31, 1942. Roll 166, Frames 81263-81826.

Auswaertiges Amt, Buero des Staatssekretaers; Griechenland, Nov. 1, 1942-June 30, 1943. Roll 166, Frames 81627-82009.

Microcopy T-175, Records of the Reich Leader of the SS and Chief of the German Police (Reichsfuehrer SS und Chef der Deutschen Polizei):

Persoenlicher Stab der RF-SS, EAP 161-b-12/28 (Misc. Correspondence); Roll 117, Frames 2642387-2642395.

Persoenlicher Stab RF-SS, EAP 161-b-12/274b (Misc. Correspondence, Roll 75, Frames 2592925-2592935.

Microcopy T-311, Records of German Field Commands: Army Groups E and F (Heeresgruppe E and Heeresgruppe F):

HGrE 65023, "Taetigkeitsbericht aus den Jahren 1940-1943 H. Gr. E./OB Suedost," Roll 175, Frames 000001-000465.

HGrE 65024/1, "Aktennotizen der Chefsbersprechung des Ia Chef Generalstabes d. H. Gr. E," Apr. 13, 1942-Dec. 31, 1943. Roll 175, Frames 000466-000852.

HGrE 65024/2, "Verschiedenes Berichte OKdo. H. Gr. E., Ia," Dec. 9, 1943-July 30, 1944. Roll 175, Frames 000853-000999.

HGrE 65025, "Tagesmeldungen H. Gr. E., Ia," May 1-Dec. 31, 1943 Roll 175, Frames 001000-001469.

HGrE 65027/1, "Kriegstagebuch des H. Gr. E./OB Suedost," July 1-Aug. 31, 1943. Roll 176, Frames 000001-000140.

HGrE 65027/2, "Kriegstagebuch H. Gr. E./OB Suedost-Ia/01," Sept. 1-Oct. 31, 1943. Roll 176, Frames 000141-000373.

HGrE 65027/3, "Kriegstagebuch H. Gr. E./OB Suedost Ia," Nov. 1-Dec. 31, 1943. Roll 176, Frames 000372-000519.

HGrE 65027/4, "Kriegstagebuch des H. Gr. E., Ia Suedost," Jan. 1-Dec. 31, 1944. Roll 176, Frames 000520-000680.

HGrE 65027/5, "Kriegstagebuch H. Gr. E., Ia Suedost," Mar. 1-Apr. 30, 1944. Roll 176, Frames 000681-000911.

HGrE 65027/6, "Kriegstagebuch H. Gr. E., Ia Suedost," May 1-June 30, 1944. Roll 177, Frames 000001-000270.

HGrE 65028/1, "Anlagen des Verteiler H. Gr. E," 1943-1944. Roll 177, Frames 000271-000343.

HGrE 65028/2, "Schriftsachen, O Kdo H. Gr. E., Ia," Aug. 1944. Roll 177, Frames 000344-000691.

HGrE 65028/3, "Anlagenbuch O Kdo H. Gr. E., Ia," July 1944. Roll 177, Frames 000692-0001095.

HGrE 65029, "Anlagen des Besprechungen mit Kom. Gen. H. Gr. E., Ia," May 1944. Roll 177, Frames 001096-001418.

HGrE 65030, "Anlagenbuch H. Gr. E., Ia," Aug. 20-Sept. 1, 1944. Roll 178, Frames 000001-000126.

HGrE 65031/1, "Sammelmappe Zervas," Feb. 24-Oct. 2, 1944. Roll 284, Frames 000001-000156.

HGrE 65031/3, "Anlagenbuch Unternehmung Kreutzotter," July 14-Aug. 30, 1944. Roll 178, Frames 000233-000334.

HGrE 65032, "Anlagenbuch Ic," July 1943-Jan. 1944. Roll 178, Frames 000335-000474.

HGrE 65033/1, "Anlagenbuch zum KTB Okdo H. Gr. E., Ia, Ic, August 1944. Roll 178. Frames 000475-001026.

HGrE 65033/2, "Anlagenband zum Kriegstagebuch Okdo. H. Gr. E., Ia, Ic," Sept. 1944. Roll 179, Frames 000001-000438.

HGrE 65033/3, "Misc Correspondence and Operations Bulletins (No German Title)," Jan. 20, 1943-Feb. 12, 1944. Roll 179, Frames 000439-000567.

HGrE 65034/2, "Misc. Correspondence and Bulletins (No German Title)," 1943. Roll 179, Frames 000727-001424.

HGrE 65034/3, "Anlagenband des Okdo. H. Gr. E., Ia," Apr. 21-Sept. 2, 1944. Roll 180, Frames 000001-000317.

HGrE 65035/1, "Tagebuch O. Kdo/H. Gr. E., Ia," Mar. 11-June 30, 1944. Roll 180, Frames 000318-000787.

HGrE 65035/2, "Kriegstagebuch Okdo. H. Gr. E., Ia," July 1-Sept. 30, 1944. Roll 180, Frames 000788-001460.

HGrE 65036/1, "Anlagenbuch zum Kriegstagebuch d. Okdo. H. Gr. E., Ia," July 1944. Roll 181, Frames 000062-000641.

HGrE 65036/2, "Anlagenband zum Kriegstagebuch Okdo. H. Gr. E., Ia," Sept. 1944. Roll 181, Frames 000641-001230.
HGrE 65721/1, "Kriesgtagebuch des Okdo. H. Gr. E., Ia," July 1-Aug. 31, 1944. Roll 182, Frames 000358-000614.
HGrE 65721/2, "Kriegstagebuch des Okdo. H. Gr. E., Ia," Sept. 1944. Roll 182, Frames 000615-001305.
HGrE 65036/3, "Anlagenband H. Gr. E.-1-3-Ia," Feb. 13-Aug. 30, 1944. Roll 182, Frames 000001-000357.
HGrE 65721/3, "Kriegstagebuch des Okdo. H. Gr. E., Ia," Oct. 1944. Roll 183, Frames 000001-000120.
HGrE 65721/11, "Anlagenband des Okdo. H. Gr. E., Ia," Sept. 15-Dec. 16, 1944. Roll 185, Frames 000301-000391.
HGrE 65721/7, "Anlagenband des Okdo. H. Gr. E., Ia," Nov. 1-Dec. 22, 1944. Roll 184, Frames 000001-000731.
HGrE 65722, "Kriegstagebuchdurchslaege Okdo. H. Gr. E., Ia," Oct. 1-Dec. 31, 1944. Roll 185, Frames 000435-000802.
HGrE 65723, "Anlagenband des Okdo. H. Gr. E., Ia," May-Dec. 1944. Roll 185, Frames 000802-001137.
HGrF 66142, "Anlagenband Ic/AO/Okdo. H. Gr. F.-Chefsachen," Feb. 10-Nov. 4, 1944. Roll 286, Frames 000001-000075.
HGrF 66144, "Heeres Gruppe F/Ia/Ic Lagebeurteilungen aus dem Bereich der unterstellten Kdo-Behoerden," June 15-Sept. 17, 1944. Roll 286, Frames 000077-000167.
HGrF 75139/2a, "Kriegsakten OB Suedost/H. Gr. F./Ic/AO," Jan. 17-Sept. 30, 1944. Roll 286, Frames 000168-000762.

Microcopy T-314, Records of German Field Commands:
Army Corps (XXII Gebirgsarmeekorps):

XXII Gebirgsarmeekorps 46520/1, "Kriegstagebuch Gen.Kdo. XXII Geb. A.K., Ia," Aug. 24-Dec. 31, 1943. Roll 670, Frames 000001-000205.
XXII Geb. AK 46520/2, "Anlagen zum Kriegstagebuch Gen.Kdo. XXII Geb. A.K., Ia," Aug. 8-Oct. 11, 1943. Roll 674, Frames 000205-000673.
XXII Geb. AK 46520/3, "Anlagen zum Kriegstagebuch Gen.Kdo. XXII Geb. A.K., Ia," Oct. 11-Nov. 18, 1943. Roll 670, Frames 000674-000967.
XXII Geb. AK 46520/4, "Anlagen zum Kriegstagebuch Gen.Kdo. XXII Geb. A.K., Ia," Nov. 18-Dec. 18, 1943. Roll 670, Frames 000968-001175.
XXII Geb. AK 46520/6, "Taetigkeitsbericht der Abt. Ic., Gen.Kdo. XXII Geb. A.K.," Sept.-Dec. 1943. Roll 670, Frame 001176.
XXII Geb. AK 46520/7, "Anlagen zum Kriegstagebuch, Ic, XXII Geb. A.K.," Aug. 24-Dec. 31, 1943. Roll 671, Frames 000001-000788.
XXII Geb. AK 46520/8, "Anlagen zum Kriegstagebuch XXII Geb. A.K., Ic," Aug.-Nov. 1943. Roll 671, Frames 000789-000948.
XXII Geb. AK 59643/1, "Kriegstagebuch Gen.Kdo. XXII. Geb. A.K., Ia," Jan. 1-June 30, 1944. Roll 671, Frames 000951-001266.
XXII Geb. AK 59643/2, "Anlagen zum Kriegstagebuch Gen.Kdo. XXII Geb. A.K., Ia," Dec. 31, 1943-Mar. 3, 1944. Roll 671, Frames 00127-001597.
XXII Geb. AK 59643/3, "Anlagen zum Kriegstagebuch Gen.Kdo. XXII Geb. A.K., Ia," Mar. 4-Apr. 4, 1944. Roll 672, Frames 000001-000254.

XXII Geb. A.K., 59643/5, "Anlagen zum Kriegstagebuch Gen.Kdo. XXII Geb. A.K., Ia," May 20-June 30, 1944. Roll 672, Frames 000457-000763.

XXII Geb. AK 59643/8, "Anlagen zum Kriegstagebuch Gen.Kdo. XXII Geb. A.K., Ia," May 1-June 30, 1944. Roll 673, Frames 000001-000030.

XXII Geb. AK 59644/1, "Taetigkeitsbericht der Abt. Ic d. Gen.Kdo. XXII Geb. A.K.," Jan. 1-June 30, 1944. Roll 673, Frames 000031-000042.

XXII Geb. AK 59644/2, "Anlagen zum Kriegstagebuch Gen.Kdo. XXII Geb. A.K., Ic," Roll 673, Frames 000043-000592.

XXII Geb. AK 59644/3, "Anlagen zum Kriegstagebuch XXII Geb. A.K., Ic," Jan. 1-June 30, 1944. Roll 673, Frames 000593-001053.

XXII Geb. AK 59643/4, "Anlagen zum Kriegstagebuch Gen.Kdo. XXII Geb. A.K., Ia," Apr. 5-May 20, 1944. Roll 672, Frames 000255-000456.

Microcopy T-501, Records of German Field Commands:
Rear Areas, Occupied Territories, and Others:

Armeegruppe Suedgriechenland 35042/1, "Kriegstagebuch Nr. 1 des Deutschen Generalstabes beim ital. AOK 11 bezw. Armeegruppe Suedgriechenland/Ia," July 19-Oct. 4, 1943. Roll 330, Frames 000942-001060.

Armeegruppe Suedgriechenland 35042/2, "Anlagen 1 zum Kriegstagebuch Nr. 1 der Armeegruppe Suedgriechenland/Ia," Aug.-Oct. 1943. Roll 330, Frames 001061-001245.

Armeegruppe Suedgriechenland 35042/3, "Anlagen Band 2 zum Kriegstagebuch. Deutscher General stab beim ital. AOK 11," Aug. 20-Sept. 9, 1943. Roll 331, Frames 000001-000187.

Armeegruppe Suedgriechenland 35042/4, "Anlagen Band 1 zum Kriegstagebuch. Deutscher General stab beim ital. AOK 11," Aug. 28-Sept. 9, 1943. Roll 331, Frames 000313-000415.

Armeegruppe Suedgriechenland 35042/5, "Anlagen Band 2 zum Kriegstagebuch. Deutscher Generalstab beim ital. AOK 11," Aug. 28-Sept. 9, 1943, and Armeegruppe Suedgriechenland, Sept. 9-Oct. 10, 1943. Roll 331, Frames 000416-000451.

Befehlshaber Saloniki-Aegaeis 15740/1, "Kriegstagebuch Befh. Saloniki-Aegaeis," May 21-July 31, 1941. Roll 48, Frames 000758-000880.

Befehlshaber Saloniki-Aegaeis 15740/2, "Taetigkeitsbericht des Befh. Saloniki-Aegaeis," Aug. 1-Dec. 31, 1941. Roll 245, Frames 000016-000110.

Befehlshaber Saloniki-Aegaeis 27052, "Taetigkeitsberichte des Befh. Saloniki-Aegaeis," Jan. 1-Dec. 31, 1942. Roll. 247, Frames 000142-000287.

Befehlshaber Saloniki-Aegaeis 41551, "Taetigkeitsbericht des Saloniki-Aegaeis," Jan. 1-June 30, 1943. Roll 252, Frames 001116-001158.

Befehlshaber Saloniki-Aegaeis 75000/22, "Besondere Anordnungen," Apr.-Aug. 1943. Roll 259, Frames 000403-000533.

Befehlshaber Saloniki-Aegaeis 85526/3, [Misc. documents of Mil. Befh. Suedost including a Monatlicher Verwaltungsbericht for December 1941 by the Befh. Saloniki-Aegaeis]. Roll 267, Frames 000027-000057.

Befehlshaber Sued-Griechenland 16492/1, "Kriegstagebuch Nr. 1 des

Stabes. Befehlshaber Sued-Griechenland," Oct. 1, 1941-Jan. 9, 1942. Roll 246, Frames 000835-000874.

Befehlshaber Sued-Griechenland 16492/2, "Anlagen zum Kriegstagebuch Nr. 1 des Befh Sued-Grld.," Sept. 30, 1941-Jan. 15, 1942. Roll 246, Frames 000875-001055.

Befehleshaber Sued-Griechenland 27752/1-27752/13, "Kriegstagebucher Befh. Sued-Grld./Qu.," June 14-Dec. 31, 1942. Roll 247, Frames 000288-000479.

Befehlshaber Sued-Griechenland 27753/1, "Kriegstagebuch Nr. 2 Stab. d. Befh. Sued-Grld.," Jan. 1-Nov. 22, 1942. Roll 247, Frames 000480-000635.

Befehlshaber Sued-Griechenland 40131/1, "Kriegstagebuch Nr. 3 d. Stabes. Sued-Grld.," Nov. 22, 1942-Nov. 20, 1943. Roll 251, Frames 001011-001123.

Befehlshaber Sued-Griechenland 40131/2, "Anlagenband Nr. 1 zum Kriegstagebuch Nr. 3 Befh. Sued-Grld./Ia," Mar. 24, 1943. Roll 251, Frames 001123-001183.

Militaerbefehlshaber Griechenland 40131/3, "Anlagenband 2 zum Kriegstagebuch Nr. 3, Mil. Befh. Grld., Ia," Nov. 20, 1942-Nov. 19, 1943. Roll 252, Frames 000001-000267.

Militaerbefehlshaber Griechenland 40131/3b, "Anlagen zum Kriegstagebuch, Befh. Grld.," Nov. 22, 1942-Aug. 10, 1943. Roll 252, Frames 000268-001115.

Militaerbefehlshaber Griechenland 58004/1, "Kriegstagebuch Nr. 5, Mil. Befh. Grld.," Apr. 27-Aug. 31, 1944. Roll 254, Frames 000981-001056.

Militaerbefehlshaber Griechenland 58004/2, "Kriegstagebuch Nr. 4, Mil. Befh. Grld.," Nov. 21, 1943-Apr. 26, 1944. Roll 255, Frames 000001-000091.

Militaerbefehlshaber Griechenland 58004/3, "Anlagen zum Kriegstagebuch Nr. 5, Mil. Befh. Grld., Ia," Apr. 27-Sept. 1, 1944. Roll 255, Frames 000092-000398.

Militaerbefehlshaber Griechenland 58004/4, "Anlagen zum Kriegstagebuch Nr. 4, Mil. Befh. Grld., Ia," Nov. 21, 1943-Apr. 27, 1944. Roll 255, Frames 000399-000743.

Militaerbefehlshaber Griechenland 58005/1-58005/7, "Kriegstagebuecher, Mil. Befh. Grld./Qu.," Jan.-July, 1944. Roll 255, Frames 000744-000795.

Militaerbefehlshaber Suedost 75000/5, "Abwicklung. Mil. Befh. Suedost," ca. Feb. 13, 1945. Roll 258, Frames 000459-000826.

Oberbefehlshaber Suedost/Ic 75000/27, "Misc. documents including reports from the German Embassy in Athens and the Bevollmaechtigter des Reiches fuer Griechenland, May-Nov. 1943." Roll 259, Frames 000628-000646.

Sonderbevollmaechtigter Suedost/Athen 75000/28, "Teuerungszuschlaege," 1942-1944. Roll 259, Frames 000647-000813.

PUBLIC RECORD OFFICE
London

Foreign Office. General Correspondence 371 (FO 371).

Year	Folders/Volumes
1936	20389–20391
1937	21147-21150
1938	22355-22371
1939	23769-23779
1940	24902, 24908, 24910, 24917, 24921, 24922, 24924-24925
1941	29813-29821, 29827-29844, 29847, 29856-29858, 29879-29880, 29884, 29888, 29909-29910, 29914
1942	33157-33158, 33160, 33162-33164, 33166-33169, 33171-33173, 33175-33177, 33193, 33197-33198, 33204, 33206, 33212
1943	37193-37210, 37214-37216, 37220, 37222, 37231-37235, 37240-37241
1944	43674-43705, 43714-43717, 43728-43739, 43746-43747, 43751, 43772, 43778, 43783
1945	48244-48289, 48364-48372

Prime Minister's Office Papers (PREM 3)
211/ 5–211/ 7   September-November 1943
212/10–212/14   November 1944-January 1945

War Cabinet   (CAB)
  CAB 65/40 W.M. (43) 160
  CAB 66/59 W.P. (44) 686 and 743

War Office   (WO)
  WO 106 Director of Military Operations and Intelligence, 1940-1944
    3127, 3164, 3169, 3225
  WO 170 War Diaries, 3 Corps (Force 140) August 1944-March 1945
    239, 242, 243, 244, 250-259, 581, 4014, 4018, 4048, 4049,
    7559, 7560, 7530, 7532, 7535
  WO 201 Military Headquarters, Middle East Forces, 1940-1944
    18, 50, 51, 52
  WO 204 Military Headquarters Papers, Allied Forces HQ, Land
    Forces Greece 8833, 8837, 8858, 8869

3. Published Materials

Germany. Auswaertiges Amt, 1939/41, Nr. 7, *Dokumente zum Konflict
  mit Jugoslawien und Griechenland.* Berlin, 1941.
Germany. Wehrmacht. Oberkommando. *Blitzkrieg to Defeat: Hitler's
  War Directives, 1939-1945.* Ed. by Hugh Trevor-Roper. New York:
  Holt, Rinehart and Winston, 1964.
Germany. Wehrmacht. Oberkommando. *Kriegstagebuch des Oberkom-
  mando der Wehrmacht (Wehrmachtfuehrungsstab), 1940-1945.*

4 Bde. Gefuehrt von Helmuth Greiner und Percy Ernst Schramm. Hrsg. von Percy Ernst Schramm, Hans Adolf Jacobsen, Andreas Hillgruber, und Walther Hubatsch. Frankfurt-am-Main: Bernard & Graefe, 1961-1966.

Glenos, Demetrios. *Ti Eivai kai ti Thelei to EAM* [What is and What does EAM Want?]. Athens, reprint of 1944 edition.

Great Britain. Foreign Office. *Documents Regarding the Situation in Greece, January 1945.* London: H. Majesty's Stationery Office, 1945.

International Military Tribunal. *Trial of the Major War Criminals before the International Military Tribunal, Nuremberg. 14 November, 1945-1 October, 1946.* 42 vols. Nuremberg, 1947-1949.

Kommounistiko Komma Elladas. *To Kommounistiko Komma Elladas ston Polemo kai sten Antistase. Episema Keimena,* tomos pemptos, 1940-1945. [The Greek Communist Party in the War and the Resistance. Official Texts, vol. 5, 1940-1945.] Published by the Greek Communist Party of the Interior, 1973.

National Liberation Front (EAM), *EAM White Book, May, 1944-March, 1945.* New York: Greek American Council, 1945.

United States, Department of State, *Documents on German Foreign Policy, 1918-1945.* Series D (1937-1945):

Vol. X, *The War Years,* June 23-August 31, 1940. Washington, D.C.: U.S. Government Printing Office, 1961.

Vol. XI, *The War Years,* September 1, 1940-January 31, 1941. Washington, D.C.: U.S. Government Printing Office, 1961.

Vol.. XII, *The War Years,* February 1, 1941-June 22, 1941. Washington, D.C.: U.S. Government Printing Office, 1962.

Vol. XIII, *The War Years,* June 23, 1941-December 11, 1941. Washington, D.C.: U.S. Government Printing Office, 1964.

United States, Department of State, *Foreign Relations of the United States, Diplomatic Papers, 1942,* Vol. II: *Europe.* Washington, D.C., U.S. Government Printing Office, 1962.

_____, *1943,* Vol. IV: *Near East and Africa.* Washington, D.C., U.S. Government Printing Office, 1964.

_____, *1944,* Vol. IV: *Near East and Africa.* Washington, D.C., U.S. Government Printing Office, 1965.

_____, Sontag, Raymond J. and James S. Beddie (eds.), *Nazi-Soviet Relations, 1939-1941.* Washington, D.C.: U.S. Government Printing Office, 1948.

United States, Department of State, Nuremberg Military Tribunals. *Trial of War Criminals Before the Nuremberg Military Tribunals Under Control Council Law No. 10.* Case 7. Vol. IX "Hostage Case." Washington, D.C.: U.S. Government Printing Office, 1953.

4. Diaries and Memoirs

Byford-Jones, William, *The Greek Trilogy.* London: Hutchinson, 1945.

Capell, Richard, *Simiomata: A Greek Note Book 1944-1945.* London: MacDonald & Co., 1946.

Chandler, Geoffrey, *The Divided Land: An Anglo-Greek Tragedy.* London: Macmillan, 1959.

Churchill, Winston Spencer, *The Second World War,* 6 vols. [Boston,

Houghton Mifflin, 1948-1953] New York: Bantam Paperback Edition, 1962.
Vol. I: *The Gathering Storm* (1948/1962).
Vol. II: *Their Finest Hour* (1949/1962).
Vol. III: *The Grand Alliance* (1950/1962).
Vol. IV: *The Hinge of Fate* (1950/1962).
Vol. V: *Closing the Ring* (1951/1962).
Vol. VI: *Triumph and Tragedy* (1953/1962).
Ciano, Galeazzo, *The Ciano Diaries, 1939-1943*. Edited by Hugh Gibson. Garden City, New York: Doubleday, 1946.

Crisp, Robert, *The Gods Were Neutral*. New York: Norton, 1961.
Demetriou-Nikephoros, D.N., *Andartes apo ta Vouna tes Roumele* [The Guerrillas of the Mountains of Roumeli] 3 vols. Athens, 1965.
Eden, Sir Anthony, *The Reckoning: The Memoirs of Anthony Eden*, Earl of Avon. Boston: Houghton Mifflin, 1965.
Fielding, Ian, *Hide and Seek: The Story of a Wartime Agent*. London: Seecker and Warburg, 1954.
Franz, Hermann, *Gebirgsjaeger der Polizei*. Bad Nauheim: Podzun, 1963.
Halder, Generaloberst Franz, *Kriegstagebuch: Taegliche Aufzeichnungen des Chef des Generalstabes des Heeres, 1939-1942*. Bde. 3. Bearbeit von Hans-Adolf Jacobsen. Stuttgart: W. Kohlhammer Verlag, 1962-1964.
Halder, Franz, *The Private Journal of Generaloberst Franz Halder 14 August 1939 to 24 September 1942* (Mimeographed English translation in 8 volumes).
Hampe, Roland, *Die Rettung Athens im Oktober 1944*. Wiesbaden: Steiner Verlag, 1955.
Hamson, Denys, *We Fell Among Greeks*. London: Jonathan Cape, 1948.
Houtas, Stelios, *He Ethnike Antistasis ton Ellenon* [The National Resistance of the Greeks]. Athens, 1961.
Jecchinis, Chris, *Beyond Olympus: The Thrilling Story of the "Trainbusters" in Nazi Occupied Greece*. London: George Harap and Co., 1961.
Lanz, Hubert, "Partisan Warfare in the Balkans," Unpublished Manuscript MS-P-055a; Koenigsten EUCOM Historical Division, 1950.
Leeper, Sir Reginald, *When Greek Meets Greek*. London: Chatto and Windus, 1950.
Mackenzie, Compton, *Wind of Freedom: The Story of the Invasion of Greece by the Axis Powers, 1940-1941*. London: Chatto and Windus, 1943.
Macmillan, Harold, *The Blast of War, 1939-1945*. New York: Macmillan & Co., 1967.
Metaxas, Ioannis P., *To Prosopiko Hemerologio* [Diary], 4 vols. Athens: Ikaros, 1951-1964.
McNeill, William H., *The Greek Dilemma: War and Aftermath*. Philadelphia: J. B. Lippincott, 1947.
Myers, E. C. W., *The Greek Entanglement*. London: Hart-Davis, 1955.
Neubacher, Hermann, *Sonderauftrag Suedost, 1940-1945*. Goettingen, 1956.

Papagos, Alexander, *The Battle of Greece, 1940-1941*. Athens: J. M. Scazikis "Alpha" Editions, 1949.
_____, *Thyo Chronia* [Two Years]. New York: Anatolia Press, 1946.
Papandreou, George, *He Apeleutherosis tes Ellados* [The Liberation of Greece]. Athens: Ellenike Ekthotike Etairia, 1945.
Pipineles, Panagiotes, *Giorgios B* [George II]. Athens, 1951.
Pyromaglou, Komnenos, *He Ethnike Antistasis* [The National Resistance]. Athens, 1947.
Saraphes, Stephanos, *Greek Resistance Army: The Story of ELAS*. London: Birch Books, 1951.
_____, *Ho ELAS* [The ELAS]. Athens: Ta Nea Biblia, 1946.
Sweet-Escott, Bickam, *Baker Street Irregular*. London: Methuen, 1965.
Tsatsou, Jeanne, *The Sword's Fierce Edge; A Journal of the Occupation of Greece, 1941-1944*. Nashville, Tenn.: Vanderbilt University Press, 1969.
Tsouderos, Emmanouil, *Ellenikes Anomalies ste Mese Anatole* [Greek Anomalies in the Middle East]. Athens: Aetos A. E., 1945.
Voigt, Fritz August, *The Greek Sedition*. London: Hollis & Carter, 1949.
_____, *Pax Britannica*. London: Constable, 1949.
Warlimont, Walter, *Inside Hitler's Headquarters*. New York: Frederick Praeger, 1964.
Woodhouse, Christopher Montague, *Apple of Discord: A Survey of Recent Greek Politics in Their International Setting*. London: Hutchinson, 1948.
Wilson, Henry Maitland, *Eight Years Overseas*. London: Hutchinson, 1950.
Zalokostas, Christos, *To Chroniko tes Sklavias* [The Time of Slavery]. Athens: "Estias," n.d.
Zotos, Stephanos, *Greece: The Struggle for Freedom*. New York: T. Y. Crowell, 1967.

B. SECONDARY SOURCES

1. Books

Argenti, Philip P., *The Occupation of Chios by the Germans, 1941-1944*. Cambridge: Cambridge University Press, 1966.
Armstrong, John, ed., *Soviet Partisans in World War Two*. Madison, Winconsin: University of Wisconsin Press, 1966.
Auty, Phyllis and Richard Clogg, eds., *British Policy Toward Wartime Resistance in Yugoslavia and Greece*. New York: Barnes & Noble, 1975.
Barker, Elisabeth. *British Policy in South-East Europe in the Second World War*. New York: Barnes & Noble, 1976.
Blau, George, *The German Campaign in the Balkans, Spring 1941*. Washington, D.C.: U.S. Department of the Army, 1953.
Buchner, Alexander, *Der Deutsche Griechenland Feldzug: Operationen der 12. Armee, 1941, Bd. 14 Die Wehrmacht im Kampf*. Heidelberg: K. Vowinckel, 1957.

Buckley, Christopher, *Greece and Crete, 1941*. London: H. Majesty's Stationery Office, 1953.

Butler, James Ramsay Montagu, ed., The Grand Strategy, H. Majesty's Stationery Office, 1956-:
Vol. II: *September 1939-June 1941*, by J. R. M. Butler (London: H. M. S. O., 1957).
Vol. III: *July 1941-August 1942*, by J. M. A. Gwyer (London: H. M. S. O., 1964).
Vol.. IV: 1943. *The Mediterranean*, by Michael Howard (London: H. M. S. O., 1972).
Vol. V: *August 1943-September 1944*, by John Ehrmann (London: H. M. S. O., 1956).
Vol. VI: *October 1944-August 1945*, by John Ehrmann (London: H. M. S. O., 1956).

Campbell, John and Philip Sherrard, *Modern Greece*. London: Ernest Benn, Ltd., 1968.

Carey, Jane Perry Clark and Andrew Galbraith Carey, *The Web of Modern Greek Politics*. New York: Columbia University Press, 1968.

Cervi, Mario, *The Hollow Legions: Mussolini's Blunder in Greece, 1940-1941*. London: Chatto & Windus, 1972.

Chamberlain, William C. and John Iams, "The Rise and Fall of the Greek Communist Party," Unpublished manuscript [typewritten]. Washington, D.C.: Foreign Service Institute, Department of State, 1963.

Cliadakis, Harry, "Greece, 1935-1941: The Metaxas Regime and the Diplomatic Background to World War II," Ph.D. dissertation, New York University, 1970.

Commission de gestion pour les secours en Grèce sous les auspices du Comité international de la Croix Rouge. *Ravitaillement de la Grèce pendant l'occupation, 1941-1944*. Report final [rédige par Bengt Helger]. Athènes: Impr. de la "Société hellénique d'éditions," 1949.

Comstock, John M., *History of the Greek Revolution*. London: William Reed & Co., 1829.

Condit, D. M., *Case Study in Guerrilla War: Greece During World War II*. Washington, D.C.: Special Operations Research of American University, 1961.

Conference on Britain and European Resistance, 1939-1945. Oxford, 1962. Proceedings. Oxford: St. Antony's College, 1964.

Council of Foreign Ministers. Annex I: "Statement of Allied Governments on the German Problem," Memorandum presented by the Greek Government. London: Lancaster House, 1947.

Couloumbis, Theodore A., *Greek Political Reaction to American and NATO Influences*. New Haven: Yale University Press, 1966.

_____, John A. Petropulos, and Harry J. Psomiades, *Foreign Interference in Greek Politics: An Historical Perspective*. New York: Pella Publishing Co., Inc., 1976.

Creveld, Martin van, *Hitler's Strategy 1940-1941: The Balkan Clue*. London: Cambridge University Press, 1973.

Cruickshank, Charles, *Greece 1940-1941*. London: Davis-Poynter, 1976.

Dakin, Douglas, *The Unification of Greece, 1770-1923*. London: Ernest Benn, 1972.

Dallin, Alexander, *German Rule in Russia*. London: Macmillan & Co., 1957.

Daphnes, Georgios, *He Ellas metaxy ton thyo Polemon, 1923-1940* [Greece Between the Two Wars, 1923-1940]. Athens: Ikaros, 1955.

Dawidowicz, Lucy S., *The War Against the Jews, 1933-1945.* New York: Holt, Rinehart, Winston, 1975.

Deakin, F. W., *The Brutal Friendship: Mussolini, Hitler, and the Fall of Italian Fascism.* New York: Harper & Row, 1962.

Delivanis, Demetrios and William Cleveland, *Greek Monetary Developments, 1939-1949,* Social Science Series No. 6. Bloomington, Indiana: University of Indiana Press, 1949.

Department of the Army. *German Anti-Guerrilla Operations in the Balkans, 1941-1944.* Washington, D.C.: U.S. Government Printing Office, 1954.

Dzélépy, Eleuthère Nicolas, *Le drama de la résistance grècque.* Paris: Editions Raisons d'etre, 1946.

Enepekides, Polychrone K., *He Ellenike Antistasis 1941-1944; Opos Apokalyptetai apo ta Mystika Archeia tes Vermacht eis ten Ellada* [The Greek Resistance, 1941-1944; Based on the Secret Archives of the Wehrmacht in Greece]. Athens: Estia, 1964.

Eudes, Dominique, *The Kapetanios: Partisans and Civil War in Greece, 1943-1946.* New York and London: Monthly Review Press, 1972.

Foot, M. R. D., *Resistance: European Resistance to Nazism, 1940-1945.* London: Eyre Methuen, 1976.

Fabry, Philipp W., *Balkan-Wirren, 1940-1941: Diplomatische und militaerische Vorbereitung des deutschen Donauuberganges.* Darmstadt: Wehr und Wissen Verlagsgesellschaft mbH, 1966.

Forster, Edward S., *A Short History of Modern Greece, 1821-1945.* 2nd rev. ed. London: Methuen & Co., 1946.

Gatopoulos, Demetrios, *He Istoria tes Katoches.* 4 vols. in 1. Athens: Ekdotikos Oikos "Melissa," 1966.

Great Britain, Foreign Office. *Greece: Basic Handbook.* London: H. Majesty's Stationery Office, 1943.

Greece Since the Second World War: On the Occasion of the Twentieth Anniversary of the Truman Doctrine. Symposium 10-12 April 1967, University of Wisconsin. *Balkan Studies,* VIII, No. 2 (1967). Salonica: Institute for Balkan Studies, 1967.

Greece. Office National Hellénique des Criminels de Guerre. *Les atrocités des quatre envahisseurs de la Grèce: Allemands, Italiens, Bulgares, Albanais.* Athènes, 1946.

Greece. Office of Information. *He Enantion tes Ellados Epivoule* [The Plot Against Greece]. Athens: Ministry of Press and Information, 1947.

Gregoriades, Neokosmos, *Ho Pankosmios Polemos, 1939-1945,* A Tomos, *Elleniko-Italo-Germanikos Polemos, 1940-1941* [The World War, 1939-1945, vol. I: The Greek-Italian-German War, 1940-1941]. Athens: 1945.

Halle, Louis J., *The Cold War As History.* New York: Harper & Row, 1967.

Heckstall-Smith, Anthony, *Greek Tragedy, 1941.* New York: Norton, 1961.

Herzog, Robert, *Grundzuege der deutschen Besatzungsverwaltung den ost- und suedosteuropaeischen Laendern waehrend des 2. Weltkrieges.* (Studies des Instituts fuer Besatzungsfragen in Tuebingen zu den deutschen Besetzungen im 2. Weltkrieg, No. 4) Tuebingen: Institut fuer Besatzungsfragen, 1955.

Heurtley, W. A., H. C. Darby, C. W. Crawley, and C. M. Woodhouse, *A Short History of Greece From Earliest Times to 1965*. Cambridge: Cambridge University Press, 1965.

Hilberg, Raul, *The Destruction of the European Jews*. Chicago: Quadrangle, 1961.

Hillgruber, Andreas, *Hitler, Koenig Carol und Marschall Antonescu: Die deutsch — rumaenischen Beziehungen, 1938-1944*. (Veroeffentlichungen des Instituts fuer Europaeische Geschichte, Mainz, No. 5). Wiesbaden: Steiner Verlag, 1954.

_____, *Hitlers Strategie: Politik und Kriegfuehrung, 1940-1941*. Frankfurt-am-Main: Bernard & Graefe Verlag fuer Wehrwesen, 1965.

Horowitz, David, ed., *Containment and Revolution*. Boston: Beacon Press, 1967

Howard, Michael, *The Mediterranean Strategy in the Second World War*. London: Weidenfeld and Nicolson, 1968.

Iatrides, John O., *Revolt in Athens: The Greek Communist "Second Round," 1944-1945*. Princeton, N.J.: Princeton University Press, 1972.

International Conference on the History of Resistance Movements. Second, Milan, 1961. *European Resistance Movements, 1939-1945*. New York: Macmillan & Co., 1964.

International Conference of the History of Resistance Movements. Third, Prague, 1963. *L'occupazione nazista in Europa*, a cura di Enzo Collotti. Rome: Editori Riuniti, 1964.

Katheniotes, Demetrios, *He Kiriotera Stratigike Phases tou Polemou, 1940-1941* [The Main Phases of the War, 1940-1941]. Athens, 1946.

Kédros, André, *La résistance grecque, 1940-1944*. Paris: Robert Laffont, 1966.

Kofos, Evangelos, *Nationalism and Communism in Macedonia*. Salonica: Institute for Balkan Studies, 1964.

Kousoulas, D. George, *Revolution and Defeat: The Story of the Greek Communist Party*. London: Oxford University Press, 1965.

Kuehnrich, Heinz, *Der Partisanenkrieg in Europa 1939-1945*. East Berlin: Dietz-Verlag, 1968.

Laqueur, Walter, ed. *Fascism: A Reader's Guide*. Berkeley, Calif.: University of California Press, 1976.

Legg, Keith R. *Politics in Modern Greece* Stanford, Calif.: Stanford University Press, 1969.

Linardatos, Spyros, *Pos Ephatasame sten 4ᵉ Augoustou* [How We Arrived at the 4th of August]. Athens: Themelio, 1965.

Long, Gavin, *Greece, Crete, Syria*. Canberra: Aus. War Memo., 1953. Vol. II of *Australia in the War*, Series I.

Loverdo, Costa de, *La Grèce au combat, de l'attaque italienne à la chute de la Grète (1940-1941)*. Paris: Calmann-Lévy, 1966.

_____, *Les maquis rouges des Balkans, 1941-1945*. Paris: Stock, 1967.

Lukacs, John, *The Great Powers and Eastern Europe*. New York: American Book Co., 1953.

Macartney, C. A. and A. W. Palmer, *An Independent Eastern Europe.* London: Macmillan & Co., 1962.

McClymont, William G., *To Greece.* Vol. II of *The Official History of New Zealand in World War II.* Wellington, 1959.

Manuelides, Dimitri, "Communist Tactics in Greece," M. A. Thesis, University of Virginia, 1952.

Medlicott, William N., *The Economic Blockade,* 2 vols. London: H. Majesty's Stationery Office, 1952. *History of the Second World War. United Kingdom Civil Series.*

Michel, Henri, *La seconde guerre mondiale,* vol. I: *Les succès de l'Axe (1939-1943),* vol. XXI of *Peuples et Civilisations.* Paris: Presses Universitaires de France, 1968.

Miller, Marshall Lee, *Bulgaria During the Second World War.* Stanford, California: Stanford University Press, 1975.

Molho, Michael and Joseph Nehama, *The Destruction of Greek Jewry.* Jerusalem: Yad Yashem, 1965, in Hebrew.

_____, *In Mémorian. Hommage aux victimes juives des nazis en Grèce,* 2 vols. in 1. Salonique: N. Nicholaids, 1948-1949.

Myridakes, M., *Agones tes Phyles, He Ethnike Antistasis, EDES, EOEA, 1941-1944* [The National Resistance, EDES, EOEA, 1941-1944]. Athens: 1948.

Nadel, George (ed.), *Studies in the Philosophy of History.* New York: Harper & Row, 1965.

Noel-Baker, Francis, *Greece: The Whole Story.* London: Hutchinson, 1946.

O'Ballance, Edgar, *The Greek Civil War.* London: Faber and Faber, 1966.

Orlow, Dietrich, *The Nazis in the Balkans: A Case Study of Totalitarian Politics.* Pittsburgh: University of Pittsburgh Press, 1968.

Pallis, A. A., *Problems of the Resistance in Occupied Countries.* London: Greek Office of Information, 1947.

Papadakes, Basileos P., *Diplomatike historia tou Ellenikou Polemou, 1940-1945* [Diplomatic History of Greece, 1940-1945]. Athens, 1956.

Papakonstantinou, Theodoris, *He Anatomia tes Epanastaseos* [The Anatomy of Revolution]. Athens, 1952.

Papandreou, George, *The Third War.* Athens: "Hellas," 1948.

Petropulos, John, *Politics and Statecraft in the Kingdom of Greece, 1833-1843.* Princeton: Princeton University Press, 1968.

Playfair, Ian S. O., *The Mediterranean and Middle East,* 4 vols. London: H. Majesty's Stationery Office, 1960-. Vol. XIV of *History of The Second World War. United Kingdom Military Series,* ed. J. R. M. Butler.

Pyromaglou, Komnenos, *Ho Doureios Ippos: He Ethnike kai Politiki Krisis kata ten Katoche* [The Trojan Horse; the National and Political Crisis Following the Occupation]. Athens, 1958.

_____, *Ho Giorgios Kartalis kai he Epoche tou 1934-1957,* A' Tomos 1934-1944 [George Kartalis and His Times, 1934-1957, vol. I: 1934-1944]. Athens: Estia, 1965.

_____, *He Ethnike Antistasis, EAM-ELAS-EDES-EKKA.* [The National Resistance, EAM-ELAS-EDES-EKKA]. Athens: "Dodone," 1975.

Reitlinger, Gerald, *The Final Solution: The Attempt to Exterminate the Jews of Europe, 1939-1945.* New York: A. S. Barnes, 1961.

Rich, Norman, *Hitler's War Aims,* 2 vols. New York: W. W. Norton, 1973.

Richter, Heinz, *Griechenland zwischen Revolution und Konterrevolution (1936-1946).* Frankfurt am Main: Europaische Verlangsanstalt, 1973.

Ristic, Dragisa N., *Yugoslavia's Revolution of 1941.* Philadelphia: University of Pennsylvania Press, 1966.

Royal Institute of International Affairs, *Southeastern Europe: A Political and Economic Survey.* London: Oxford University Press, 1938.

Schmidt-Richberg, Erich, *Der Endkampf auf dem Balkan. Die operation der Heeresgruppe E von Griechenland bis zu den Alpes, Bd. V Die Wehrmacht im Kampf.* Heidelberg: K. Vowinckel, 1955.

Schramm-von Thadden, Ehregard, *Griechenland und die Grossmaechte im Zweiten Weltkrieg.* (Veroeffentlichungen des Instituts fuer Europaeische Geschichte, Mainz, No. 9). Wiesbaden: Steiner Verlag, 1955.

Seton-Watson, Hugh, *The East European Revolution.* New York: Frederick A. Praeger, 1955.

_____, *Eastern Europe Between the Wars, 1918-1941,* Third edition. Camden, Conn.: Archon Books, 1962.

Smothers, Frank, William H. McNeill, and Elizabeth McNeill, *Report on the Greeks.* New York: Twentieth Century Fund, 1948.

Spencer, Floyd A., *War and Postwar Greece: An Analysis based on Greek Writings.* Washington, D.C.: The Library of Congress, 1952.

Sophocles, Sophocles, *A History of Greece.* Salonica: Institute for Balkan Studies, 1961.

Stavrianos, Leften S., *The Balkan Federation,* Second ed. Camden, Conn.: Archon Books, 1964.

_____, *The Balkans Since 1453.* New York: Holt, Rinehart and Winston, 1958.

_____, *Greece: American Dilemma and Opportunity.* Chicago: Henry Regnery, 1952.

Stewart, I. McD., *The Struggle for Crete, 20 May-1 June 1941.* London: Oxford University Press, 1966.

Svoronos, Nicholas, *Histoire de la Grèce moderne.* Paris: Presses universitaires de France, 1953.

Sweet-Escott, Bickam, *Greece: A Political and Economic Survey, 1939-1953.* London: Royal Institute for International Affairs, 1954.

Tomasevich, Jozo, *War and Revolution in Yugoslavia, 1941-1945,* vol. 1: *The Chetniks.* Stanford, California: Stanford University Press, 1975.

Tsoucalas, Constantine, *The Greek Tragedy.* London: Penguin Books, 1969

Vukmanovic, Svetozar, *How and Why the People's Liberation Struggle in Greece Met with Defeat.* London, 1950.

Weinberg, Gerald L., *Germany and the Soviet Union, 1939-1941.* Leiden: Mouton, 1954.

Weiss, John, *The Fascist Tradition: Right Wing Extremism in Modern Europe.* New York: Harper and Row, 1967.

Wiskemann, Elizabeth, *The Rome-Berlin Axis*, Rev. ed. London: Fontana Library, 1966.

Wolff, Robert Lee, *The Balkans in our Time*. Cambridge, Mass.: Harvard University Press, 1956.

Woodward, Sir Llewellyn, *British Foreign Policy in the Second World War*. 3 vols. London: Her Majesty's Stationery Office, 1971.

Woodward, E. Llewellyn, *British Foreign Policy in the Second World War*. London: H. Majesty's Stationery Office, 1962.

Woodhouse, Christopher Montague, *The Story of Modern Greece*. London: Faber and Faber, 1968.

Woodhouse, Christopher Montague, *The Struggle for Greece, 1941-1949*. London: Hart-Davis MacGibbon, 1976.

Woolf, S. J., ed. *The Nature of Fascism*. New York: Vintage Books, 1969.

_____, ed. *European Fascism*. London: Weidenfeld and Nicolson, 1968.

Wright, Gordon, *The Ordeal of Total War, 1939-1945*. New York: Harper & Row, 1968, in *Rise of Modern Europe* ed. by William Langer.

Xydis, Stephen G., *Greece and the Great Powers, 1944-1947*. Salonica: Institute for Balkan Studies, 1963.

Yannikos, Yannis, *St'Armata! St'Armata! Istoria tes Ethnikes Antistasis* [To Arms! To Arms! The History of the National Resistance]. Athens: Y. Yannikos, 1964.

2. Articles

Armstrong, John A., "Collaborationism in World War II: The Integral Nationalist Variant in Eastern Europe," *Journal of Modern History*, vol. 40 (December 1968), 396-410.

Bariety, Jacques, "Quelques sources recentes pour l'histoire de la seconde guerre mondiale," *Revue historique*, CCXXXVII (Jan.-Mars 1966), 63-98.

Batovski, H., "Pour une alliance balkanique en 1941," *Revue d'histoire de la deuxième guerre mondiale*, XIX, No. 74 (Avril 1969), 1-16.

Burdick, Charles, "L'Axe Berlin-Rome et la campagne italo-grècque," *Revue historique de l'armée*, No. 3 (1960), 71-84.

_____, " 'Operation Cyclamen,' Germany and Albania, 1940-1941," *Journal of Central European Affairs*, Vol. 19 (December 1959), 23-31.

Chandler, Geoffrey, "The Unnecessary War: The Greek Civil War of 1946-1949," *History Today*, Vol. 8 (Oct. 1958), 715-724.

Creveld, Martin van., "Prelude to Disaster: The British Decision to Aid Greece, 1940-1941," *Journal of Contemporary History*, Vol. 9 (July 1974), 65-92.

Diamandouros, Nikiforos P., "Political Clientalism and Political Modernization in Nineteenth Century Greece," forthcoming Sage Publications, Inc.

Eckstein, Harry, "On the Etiology of Internal Wars," *History and Theory*, Vol. 4, No. 2 (1965), 133-165.

Fleischer, Hagen, "Contacts Between German Occupation Authorities and Major Greek Resistance Organizations: Sound Tactics or Collaboration?" Paper read at the Modern Greek Studies Association meeting, November 10, 1978.

Fleischer, Hagen, "Pos Evlepe to KKE ten Antistase" [How the KKE Viewed the Resistance], *Anti*, May 3, 1975, pp. 11-16.

Hoffmann, Stanley, "Collaborationism in France During World War II," *Journal of Modern History*, Vol. 40 (December 1968), 375-395.

Kitsikis, Dimitri, "The Greek Communists and the Karamanlis Government," *Problems in Communism*, January-February (1977), 42-56.

_____, "La famine en Grèce (1941-1942). Les conséquences politiques," *Revue d'histoire de la deuxième guerre mondiale*, XIX, No. 74 (Avril 1969), 17-42.

_____, "La Grèce entre l'Angleterre et l'Allemagne de 1936 à 1941," *Revue historique*, CCXXXVIII (Jul.-Sept. 1967), 85-116.

McNeill, William H., "The Outbreak of Fighting in Athens, December, 1944," *The American Slavic and East European Review*, Vol. 8 (December 1949), 252-261.

Miller, William, "New Era in Greece," *Foreign Affairs*, Vol. 14 (July 1936), 654-661.

Presseisen, Ernst L., "Prelude to 'Barbarossa': Germany and the Balkans, 1940-1941," *Journal of Modern History*, Vol. 32 (December 1960), 359-370.

Pyromaglou, Komnenos "Ta Tagmata Asphaleias" [The Security Battalions] *Istorike Epitheoresis* [*Historical Review*], Vol. 6 (Oct.-Dec. 1964), 530-545.

Roediger, Conrad, "Die Internationale Hilfsaktion fuer die Bevoelkerung Griechenlands im Zweiten Weltkrieg," *Vierteljahrshefte fuer Zeitgeschichte*, XI (Jan. 1963), 49-71.

Roehricht, Edgar, "Der Balkanfeldzug 1941," *Wehrwissenschaftliche Rundschau*, XII, Nr. 4 (1964), 214-225.

Stavrianos, L. S., "The Greek National Liberation Front (EAM): A Study in Resistance Organization," *Journal of Modern History*, Vol. 24 (March 1952), 42-55.

_____, "The Immediate Origins of the Battle of Athens," *The American Slavic and East European Review*, Vol. 8 (December 1949), 239-251.

_____, "The Mutiny of the Greek Armed Forces, April, 1944," *The American Slavic and East European Review*, Vol. 9 (December 1950), 302-336.

Stavrianos, L. S. and E. P. Panagopoulos, "Present Day Greece," *Journal of Modern History*, Vol. 20 (June 1948), 149-158.

Svolopoulos, Constantine, "Greece: Achievements and Possibilities," *Journal of Contemporary History*, Vol. 4: "The New History" (New York: Harper & Row, 1967), 236-252.

Tippelskirch, Kurt von, "Deutsche Balkanfeldzug 1941," *Wehrwissenschaftliche Rundschau*, III, Nr. 2 (1955), 49-65.

Treue, Wilhelm, "Das Dritte Reich und die Westmaechte auf dem Balkans," *Vierteljahrshefte fuer Zeitgeschichte*, I (Jan. 1953), 45-64.

Trombetas, Thomas, "Consensus and Cleavage: Party Alignment in Greece, 1945-1965," *Parliamentary Affairs*, Vol. 19, No. 3 (1966), 295-311.

Venier, B., "Les opérations grècs-italiennes du 28 Octobre 1940 au 20

Avril 1941," *Revue d'histoire de la deuxième guerre mondiale*, X, No. 38 (Avril 1960), 15-36.

Vogel, G., "Mussolinis Ueberfall auf Griechenland im Oktober 1940," *Europa-Archiv* (1950), 3389-3398.

Veremis, T., "The Officer Corps in Greece, 1912-1936," *Byzantine and Modern Greek Studies*, Vol. 2 (1976), 113-135.

Waterlow, Sir Sydney, "Decline and Fall of Greek Democracy, 1933-1936," Part I: *Political Quarterly*, Vol. 18 (April-June 1947), 95-106; and Part II: Vol. 18 (July-Sept. 1947), 205-219.

Wheeler, Marcus, "Greece: Grapes of Wrath," *World Today*, Vol. 23 (Jan.-Dec. 1967), 231-239.

Woodhouse, C. M., "Early Contacts with the Greek Resistance in 1942," *Balkan Studies*, Vol. 12 (1971), 347-363.

_____, "Zur Geschichte der Resistance in Griechenland," *Vierteljahrshefte fuer Zeitgeschichte*, VI (Apr. 1958), 138-150.

Zografos, Zizis, "Some Lessons of the Civil War in Greece," *World Marxist Review*, Vol. 7, No. 11 (November 1964), 43-50.

3. Newspapers

Eleuthere Ellada
Evrytanikon Vema
New York Times
Rizospastes

C. OTHER

1. Interviews

C. M. Woodhouse, March 7, 1975
Demetrios Partsalides, May 17, 1975
Demetriou Demetriou ("Nikephoros"), April 19, 1975.

2. Communications

E. G. Boxshall, March 21, 1975.

INDEX

A

AAA (Agon-Anorthosis-Anechartesia), 134
"Achse," Operation (German), 85-90
"Acqui" Division (Italian), 89-100
AKE (Agrotiko Komma Ellados), 109, 110
Albania, 29, 33, 34, 38, 40, 42, 45, 47, 48, 50-51, 165
Alexander, Field Marshal Sir Harold, 247
Alexandris, Admiral, 208, 210, 213
Alfieri, Dino, 42
Altenburg, Guenther, 58, 60, 62, 64-65, 69-70, 72, 78
AMM (Allied Military Mission, 1943-1945), 159, 177, 181;—and Mirofillo-Plaka negotiations, 182-187, 206-207; 190, 192, 228. See also BMM (British Military Mission).
Andorka, Rudolf, 42-43
Angelopoulos, Angelos, 208, 219-220, 232
Anglo-Greek Committee, 102, 103
"Animals," Operation (Allied), 150-151, 160, 161-162
Anti-*andarte* operations (German), 86, 153-159, 177-183, 190-194
Anticommunism, 27, 72, 80, 83-85, 159, 169, 172, 174, 179, 181, 182, 188, 190, 194, 215-219, 248-249, 251
Anti-semitism, 24, 92. See also Jews.
Anti-Venizelists, 13, 15, 21, 24, 27, 126, 256 fn. 13. See also Royalists.
Anton, Tsaous, 196
Antonescu, General Jon, 32, 36
Antonopoulos, Colonel Michael, 174
Apokoritis, Colonel, 46
Argyropoulos, Admiral Perikles, 42-45
Aris, see Velouchiotis
Asimakes, Demetrios, 118
Askoutsis, Nikolaos, 218-219, 232
ASO (Apeleutherotike Stratiotike Organosis), 128, 130
Asopos viaduct, 152
Austria, 68

B

Badoglio, Marshal Pietro, 36, 38, 88-89
Barkitzis, Colonel Euripides, 103, 127, 140;—leaves EKKA for EAM/ELAS, 189, 208-209, 211, 221; 206, 220, 224, 226, 251, 253

H

Hadjistaris, Colonel, 128
Hadzes, Thanases, 224
Halder, Colonel General Franz von, 36, 37, 42
Hambro, Sir Charles, 135, 282 fn. 168
Hammond, Colonel N. G. L., 142, 221
"Harling" Operation (British), 114, 132
Hasler, W. J. 252-253
Hawkesworth, General J. L. T., 247
Himmler, Heinrich, 59, 83
Hitler, Adolf, 26;—strategy in Southeast Europe, 29-31, 39-42, 45-48, 51, 55, 195-196;—and Italian attack on Greece, 34-37;—and famine in Greece, 70; 83;—and operation "Achse," 85-90; 161, 188, 245, 281 fn. 144
Hoefinghoff, Franz, 197
Hohenberg, Major Clemm von, 44, 49, 50, 262, fn. 65
Hollis, Brigadier, 202
Hopkinson, Henry, 125-127
Houtas, Stelios, 106, 182
Howard, Douglas, 210
Howard, Michael, 148, 268 fn. 94
"Hubertus," Operation (German), 180
Hull, Cordell, 130
Hungary, 31-33, 69
"Husky," Operation, 131, 136

I

Iatrides, John O., 160, 236-238, 297 fn. 129
Ioannides, Ioannis, 112
IRC (International Red Cross), 60, 66, 70-71, 75-76, 84, 237, 250
Italian attack on Greece, 33-44
Italy, 27, 31, 32, 33, 36, 40, 41, 58, 74, 87, 90, 131, 150

J

Jews, 90-94
JGHQ (Joint General Headquarters—*Andartes*), 151, 171, 177, 178
Jodl, General Alfred, 37, 52, 86
Jordan, Major W. S., 295 fn. 80

K

Kacdas, Pericles, 79
Kalomiris, Ioannis, 109
Kanellopoulos, Panagiotes, 102, 103, 104;—as Minister of War, 127-129; 219-220, 275 fn. 18, 294 fn. 71